orld Press P

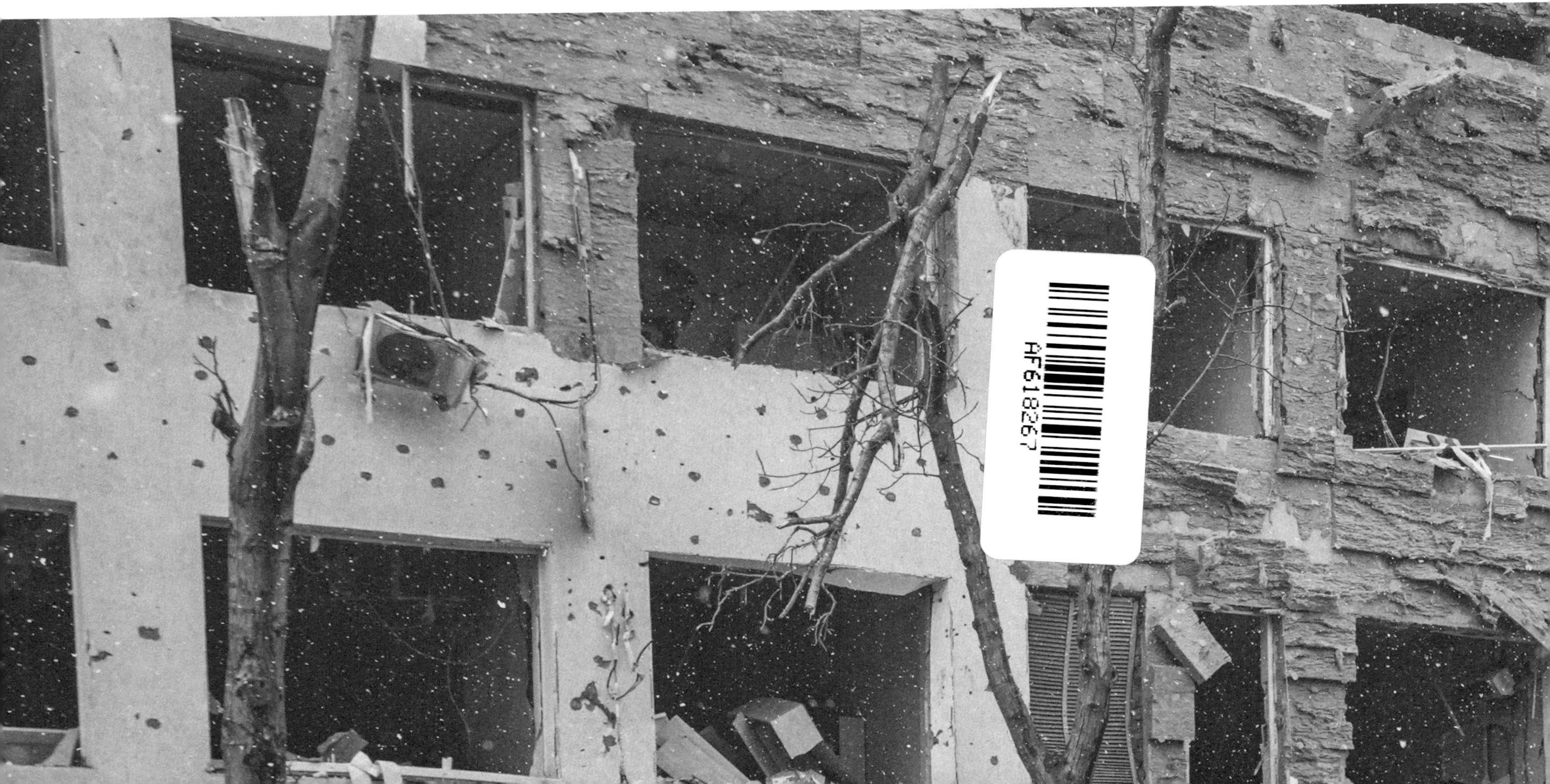

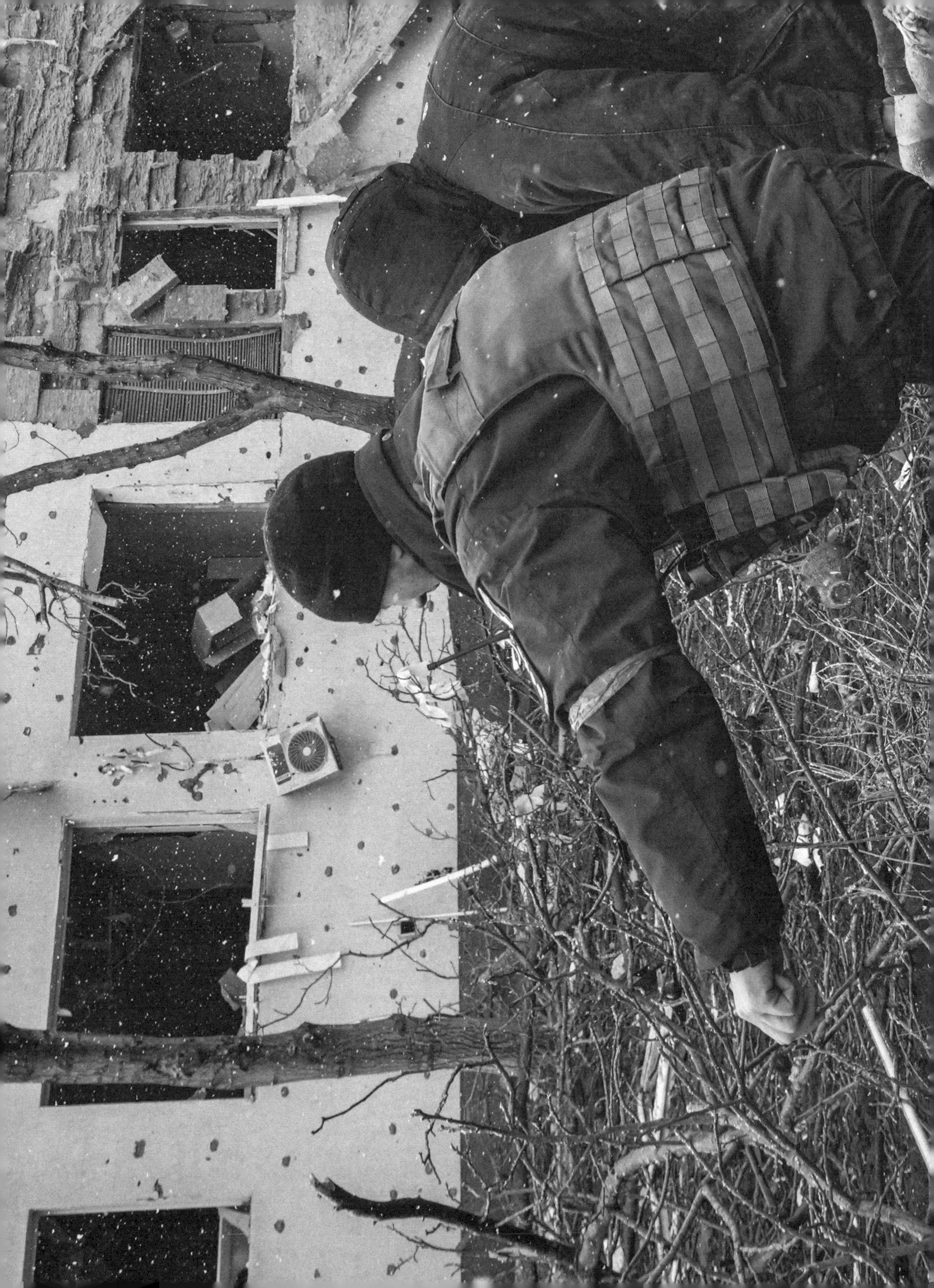

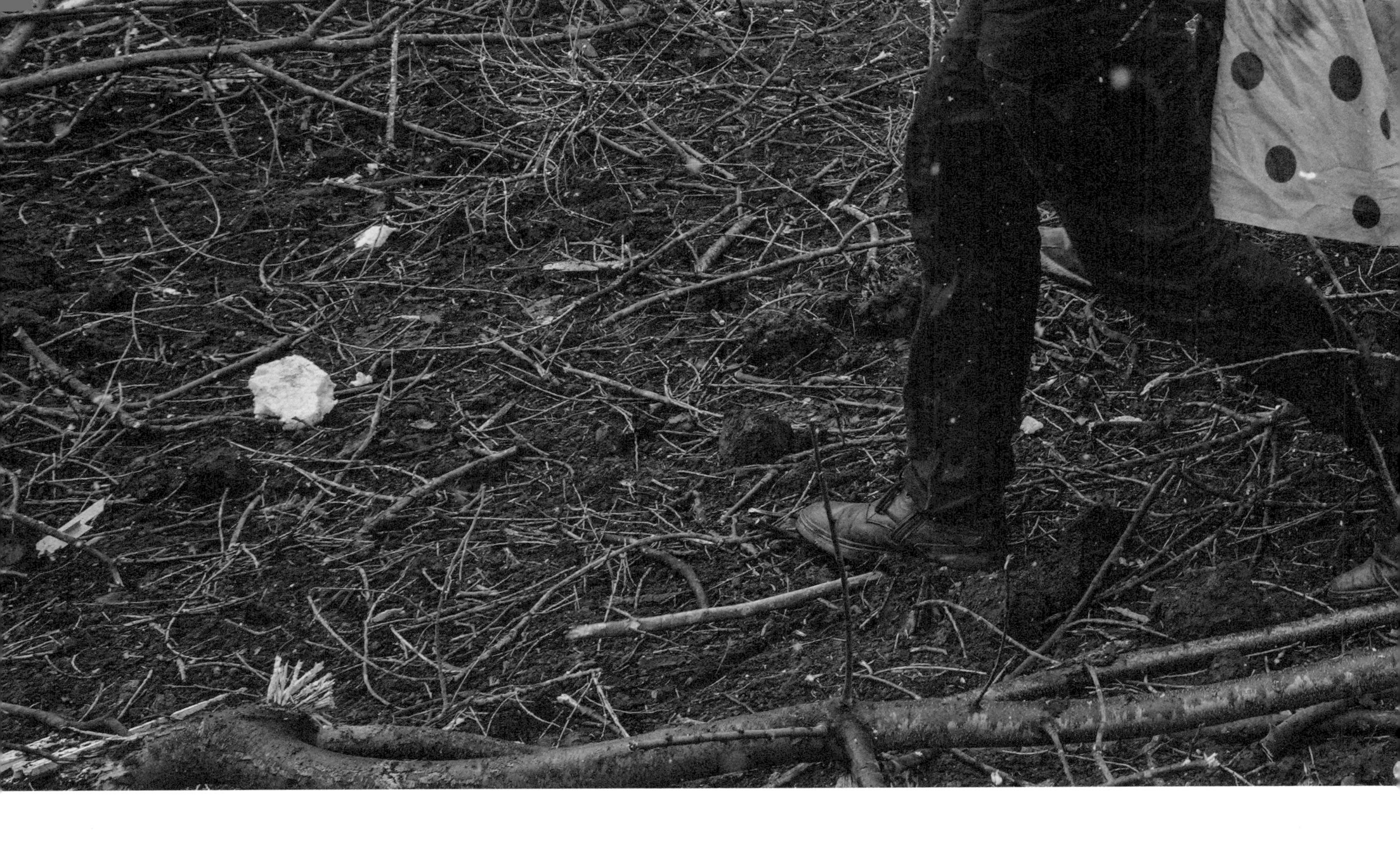

# ne Siege of N

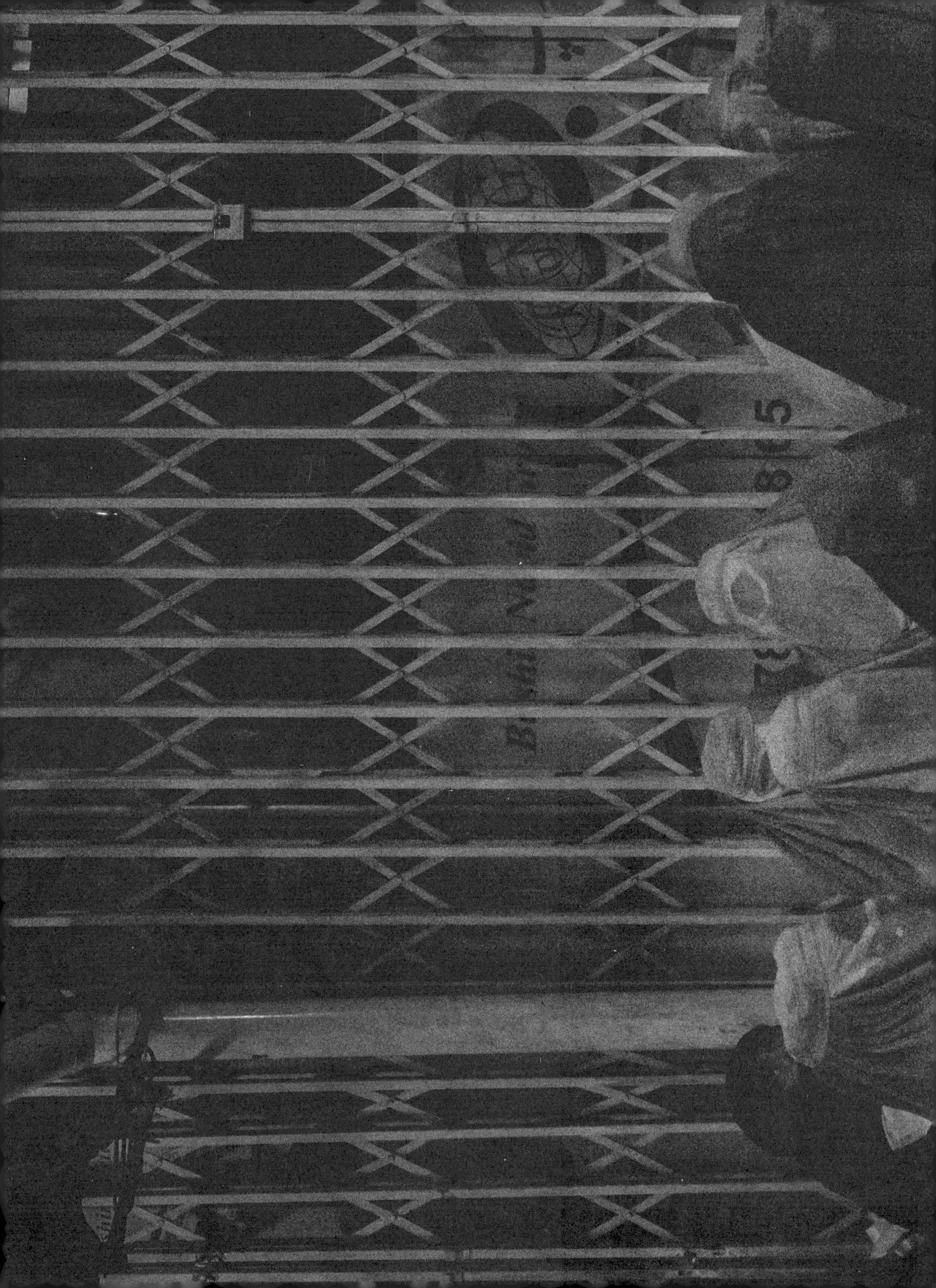

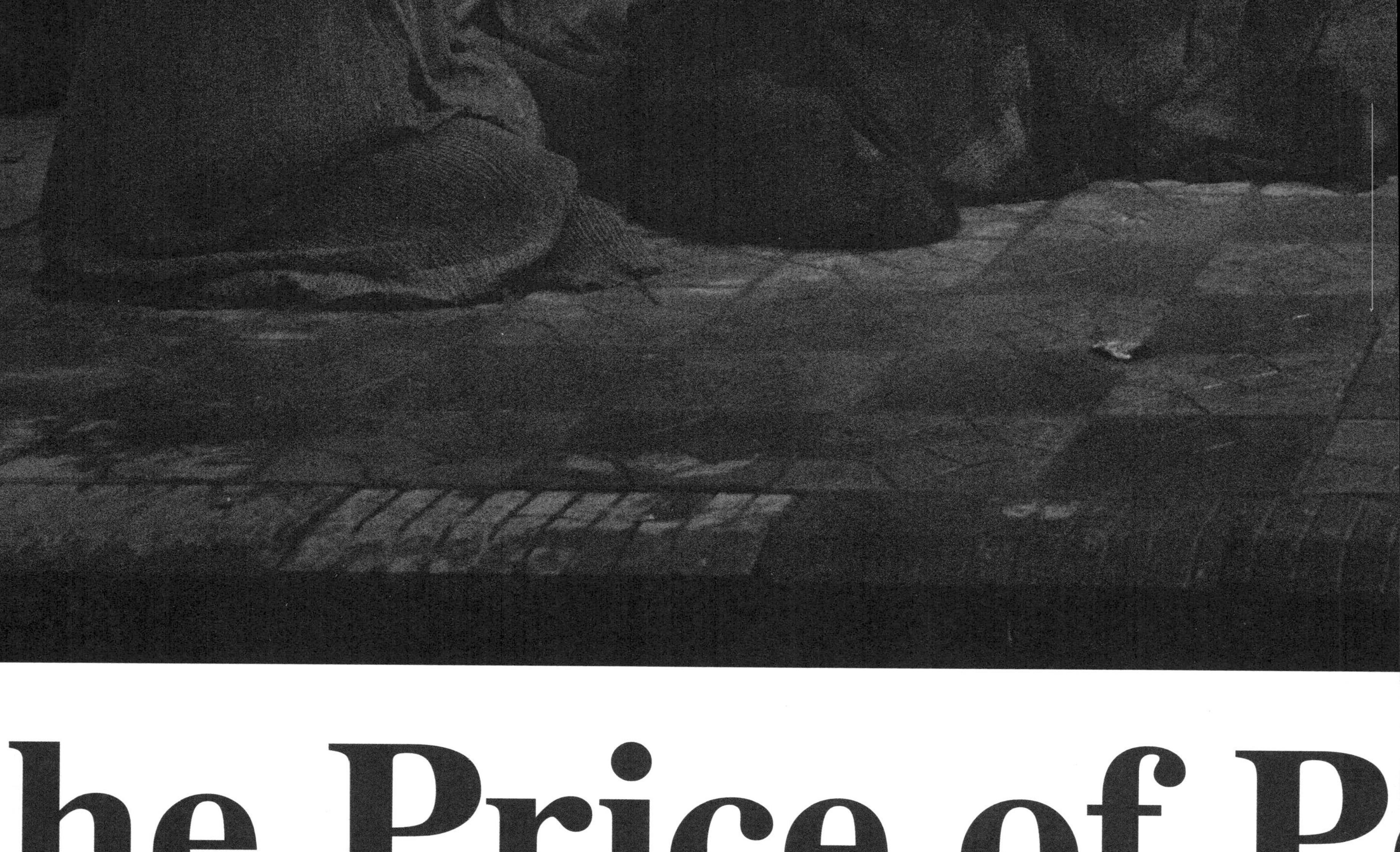

# he Price of P

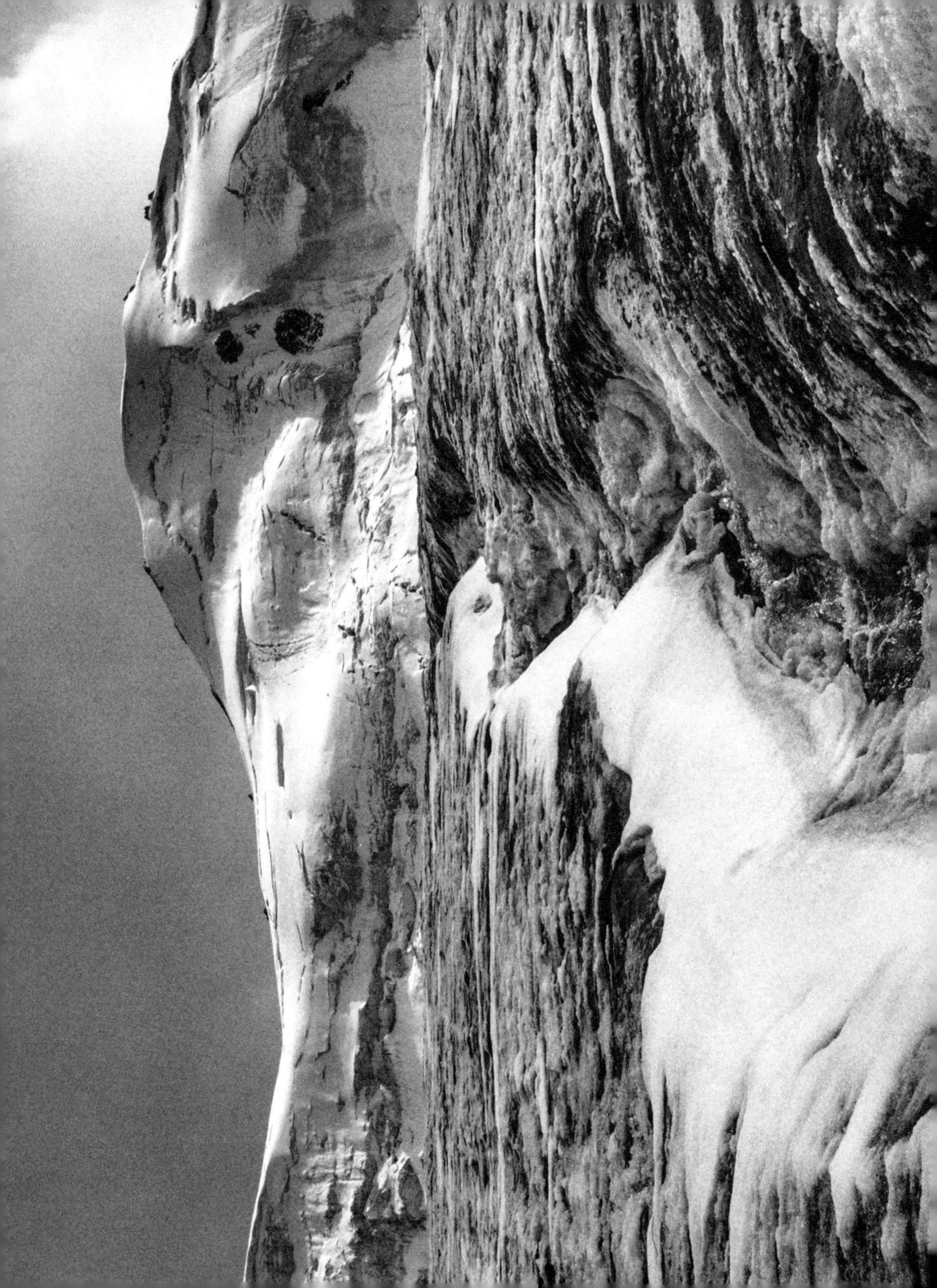

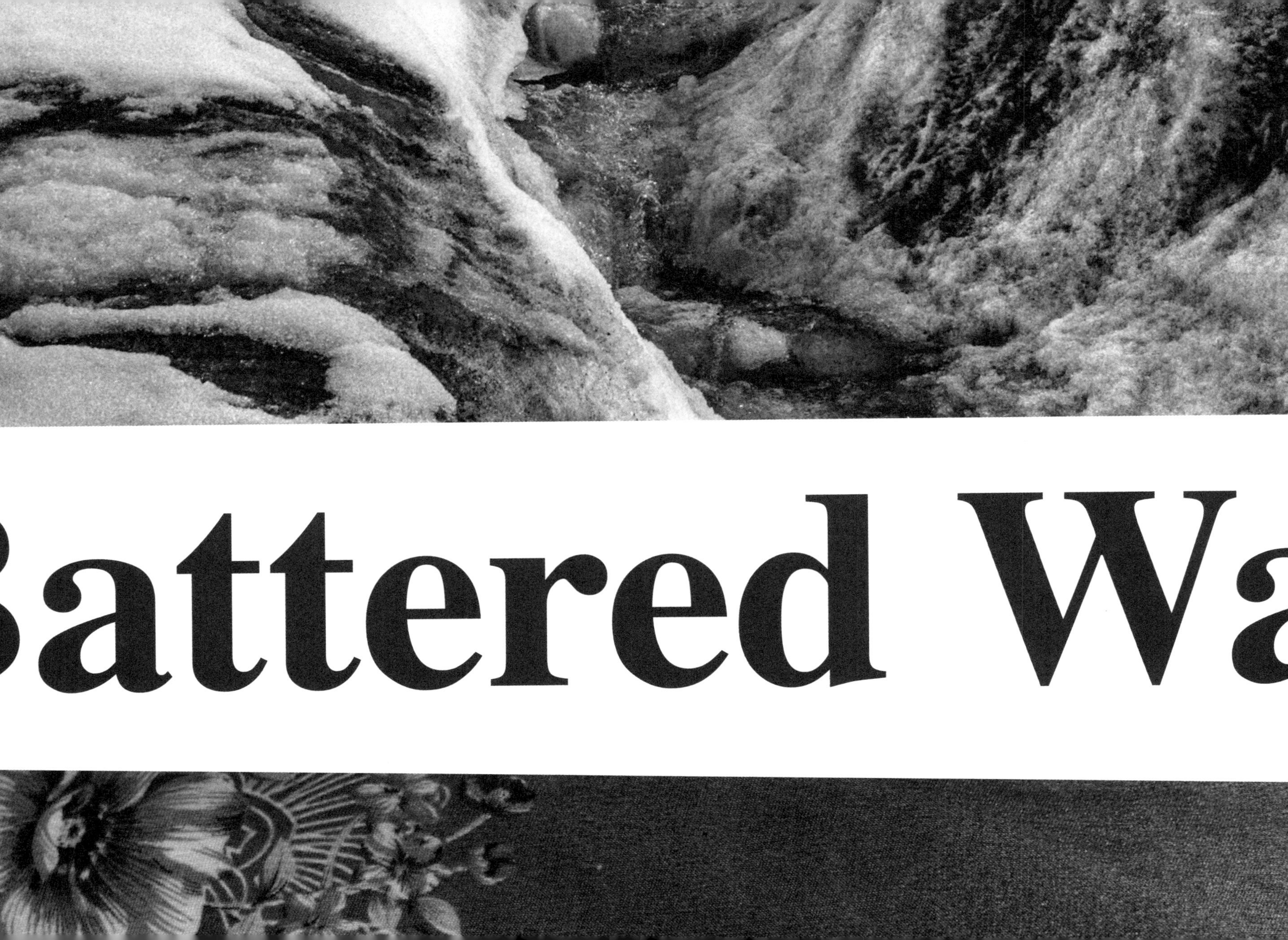
attered Wa

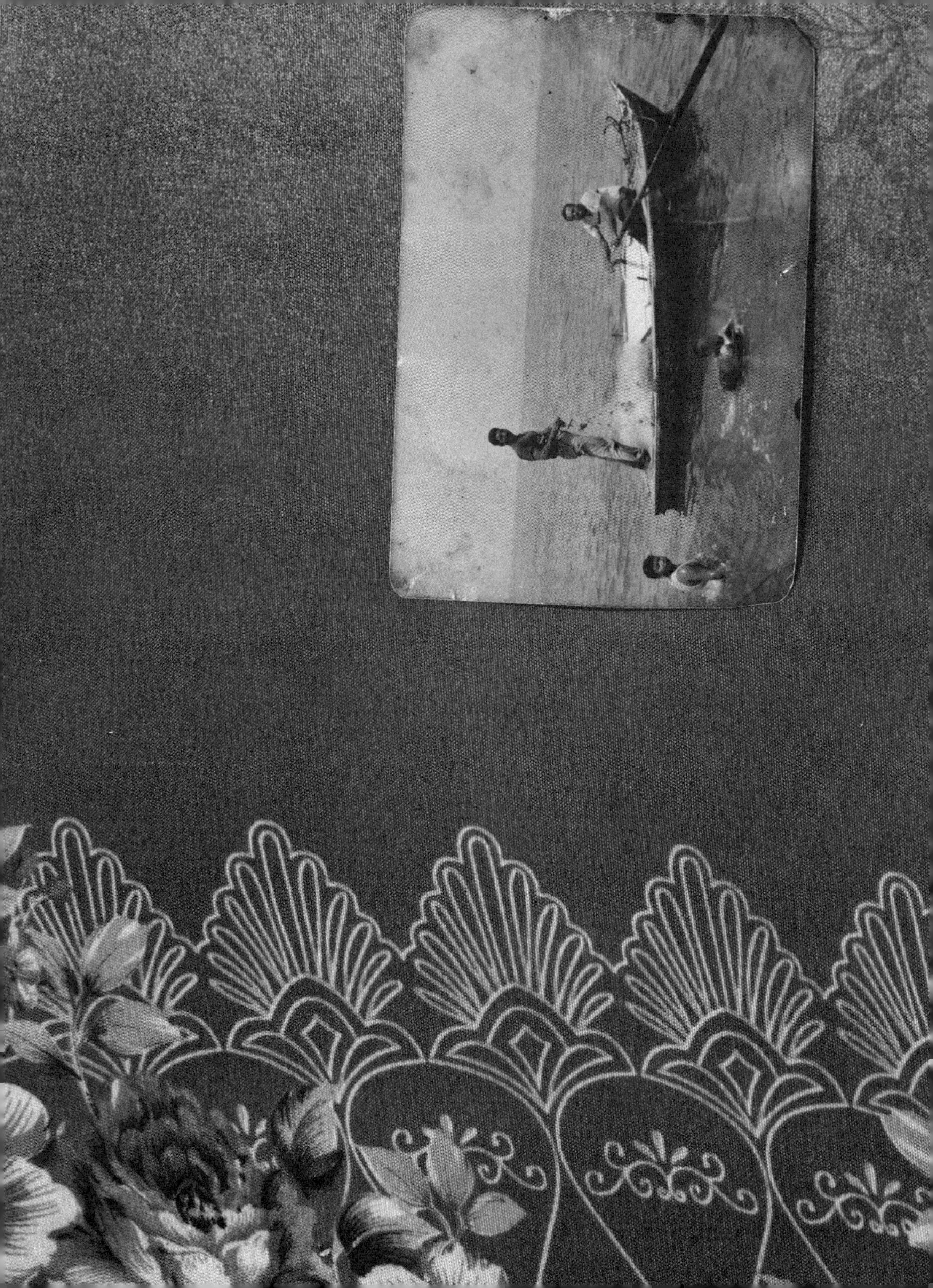

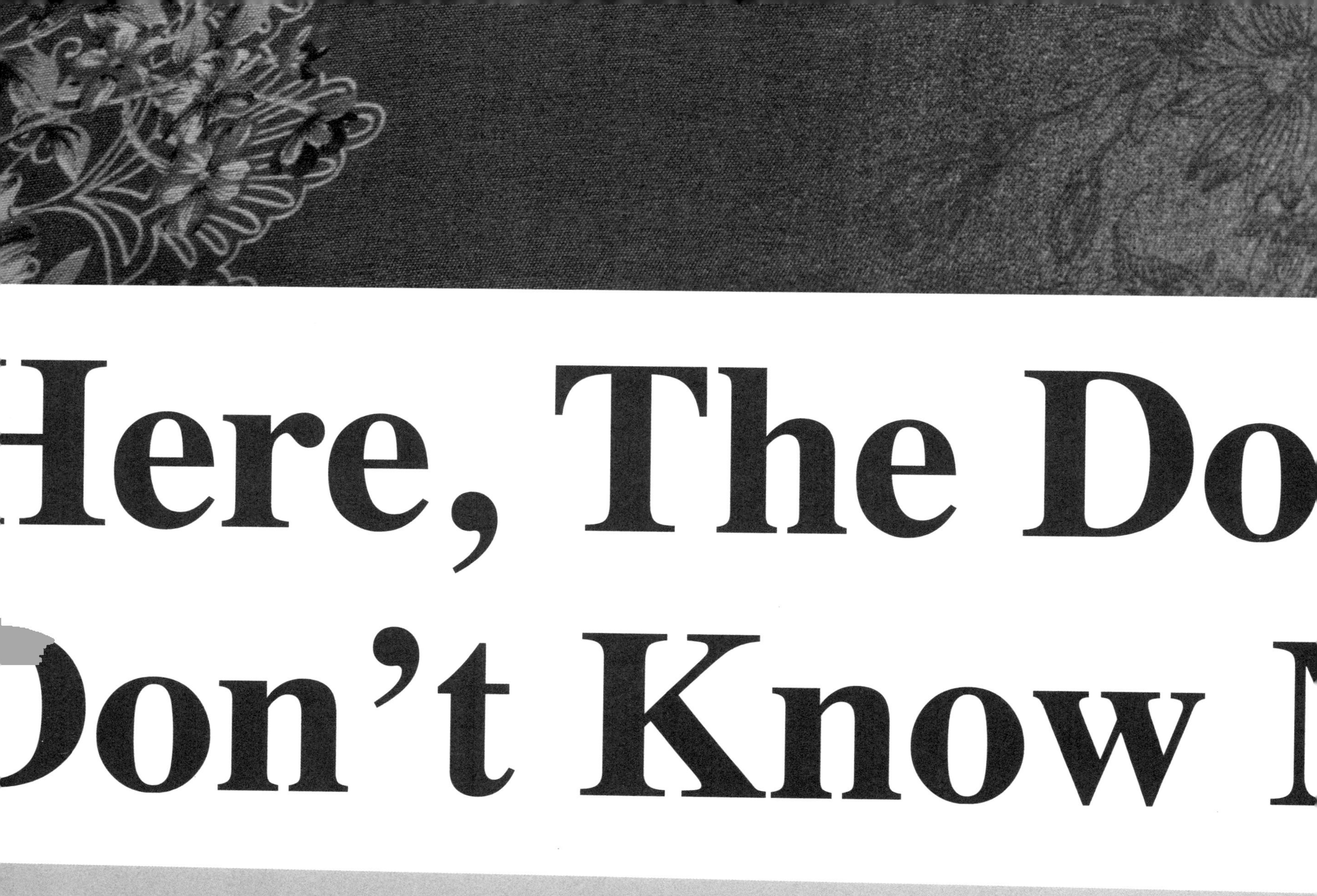

Here, The Do
Don’t Know

The World Press Photo Yearbook is a book built with photos. These well-crafted and moving images represent the best photojournalism and documentary photography of the previous year, often pushing the boundaries of the medium itself.

But in the end, those photographs are a means to an end; they are windows. Through them we are allowed a glimpse into realities that we otherwise might have missed, making us aware of injustices and conflicts we might otherwise have stayed oblivious to.

The fact that these realities are often neglected and ignored by mainstream media and politicians only proves that we need to do a bit more, flip the script as it were, create a new angle and perspective. This book tries to achieve this in a simple way: we haven't flipped the script, we flipped the book. Not to be different, but to de-automatize our reading routines. Stealing time from the reader, giving them less opportunity to "look away" and indeed giving the stories more prominence.

Sybren Kuiper

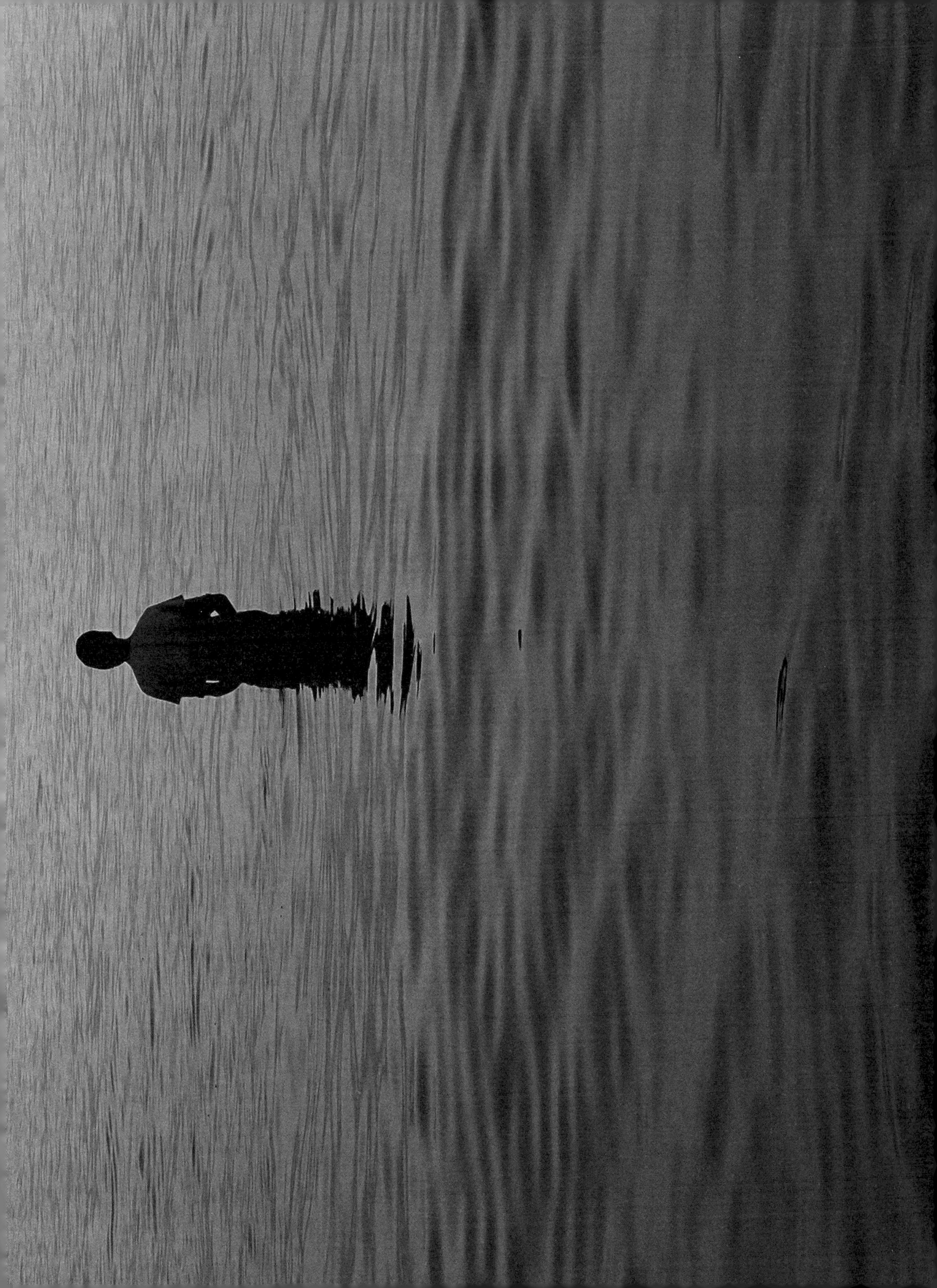

# WORLD PRESS PHOTO 2023

## REGIONAL WINNERS



## REGIONAL WINNERS



## REGIONAL WINNERS



## GLOBAL WINNERS

## Africa

## Asia

## Europe

## North & Central America

## South America

## Southeast Asia & Oceania

The sequence in which the regions appear in this book follows alphabetical order in English

The 2023 World Press Photo Contest works with six regions worldwide – Africa, Asia, Europe, North and Central America, South America, and Southeast Asia and Oceania. Entries are judged and awarded in the region in which the photographs and stories are made, rather than according to the nationality of the photographer.

Each region has four format-based categories: Singles, Stories, Long-Term Projects, and Open Format. These categories encompass entries that document news moments, events, and aftermaths, as well as social, political, and environmental issues or solutions.

**Singles**
Single frame photographs shot in 2022. All winning singles are eligible for the World Press Photo of the Year award.

**Stories**
Stories containing four to ten single frame photographs, shot in either 2021 or 2022, with at least four photographs from 2022. All winning stories are eligible for the World Press Photo Story of the Year award.

**Long-Term Projects**
Projects on a single theme containing between 24 and 30 single frame photographs, shot over at least three different years, with a minimum of six photographs shot in 2022. All winning projects are eligible for the World Press Photo Long-Term Project award.

**Open Format**
Projects using a range and/or mixture of formats such as polyptychs; multiple exposure images; photographic collages; interactive documentaries; short documentary videos. The main visual content of the project must be still photography, and the project must have been produced or first published in 2022.
All winning projects are eligible for the World Press Photo Open Format award.

**Honorable Mentions**
In addition to the regional and global winners, the jury may choose to draw attention to an entry that deserves special recognition by awarding it an Honorable Mention. Honorable Mentions are reserved for entries that witness or report on significant news moments, events and/or their aftermaths from the contest year (2022).

# Taking Responsibility

Joumana El Zein Khoury
Executive Director, World Press Photo Foundation

"*Spannend*" is a Dutch word that describes a feeling of expectation and excitement, but without knowing if the outcome will be positive or negative. *Spannend* is the general feeling at the World Press Photo Foundation when, in February each year, the judging of thousands of images takes place.

Each year we review entry rules, implement outreach campaigns for photographers all over the world, com-

The 2023 jury was no exception. The way in which every image is dissected and discussed, placing it in its local, regional, and global context, is a unique experience.

In 2023, we discussed with jury members the importance of not only putting the focus on images and stories from the different regions of the world – the core of our new strategy – but also on showcasing the most important events that shaped 2022.

themselves and the photographers to, and most importantly the respect they showed every single photograph through the time they took to discuss it, shows that there is still hope in humanity; a hope that I had started losing after having lived with the thousands of images for the past three months.

One outcome of all our discussions was an immediately visible change. The cover of the 2023 Yearbook is pose juries, plan the process to the last detail, organize forensic expert checks, and much more. We are in charge of every single step, until it comes to the selection of the winners. At this point the process is transferred to the juries. And it is precisely the letting go of the most essential part – the selection of the winners – that makes the whole process so *spannend*. We fully trust and value the knowledge, expertise and ethics of the jury members, and it is they who must take on the huge responsibility of deciding what the most important images of 2022 have been. The results of their decisions will not only be shared with billions of people around the world, but will be a benchmark for future generations who will want to know what 2022 looked like.

It is very special to witness the time, dedication and seriousness that the jury members place in their judging. In 2022 alone, 59 journalists died while exercising their profession – the highest number since 2018.[1] We thus were very aware that our responsibility lay with ensuring that the stories and images that they died for or risked their lives for were shared with as many people as possible through World Press Photo's communication channels and exhibitions.

As you will see, the 2023 winners cover a mix of very diverse topics from football and migration, to war and alpaca farming. But 2022 was a gruesome year, filled with horrendous killings, sacrifices from people that should never be faced with the need for such sacrifices, protests from every single region, and environmental disasters. If I were to sum up the 2023 jury process in one word, it would be "emotional". The tears the jury members shed, the nightmares they had, the debates they led, the ethics they held the first that doesn't showcase the World Press Photo of the Year. This is a conscious stance to show our respect towards the victims and our rage against the inhuman loss of lives. With that decision, the choice of the cover picture became obvious. This image says it all: it defies you to look at a young woman of our times, to look at the danger that she is putting herself in to make this photo, but more importantly to understand that she will stop at nothing to get justice for what she deserves and believes her right to be. This cover is not only a testimony against the violence still directed at women in 2022, but more importantly to the incredible courage that they have shown in Iran and around the world. It is a testament to strength.

[1] The number of journalists and media workers killed in 2022, according to Reporters Without Borders: rsf.org/en/barometer

# Africa

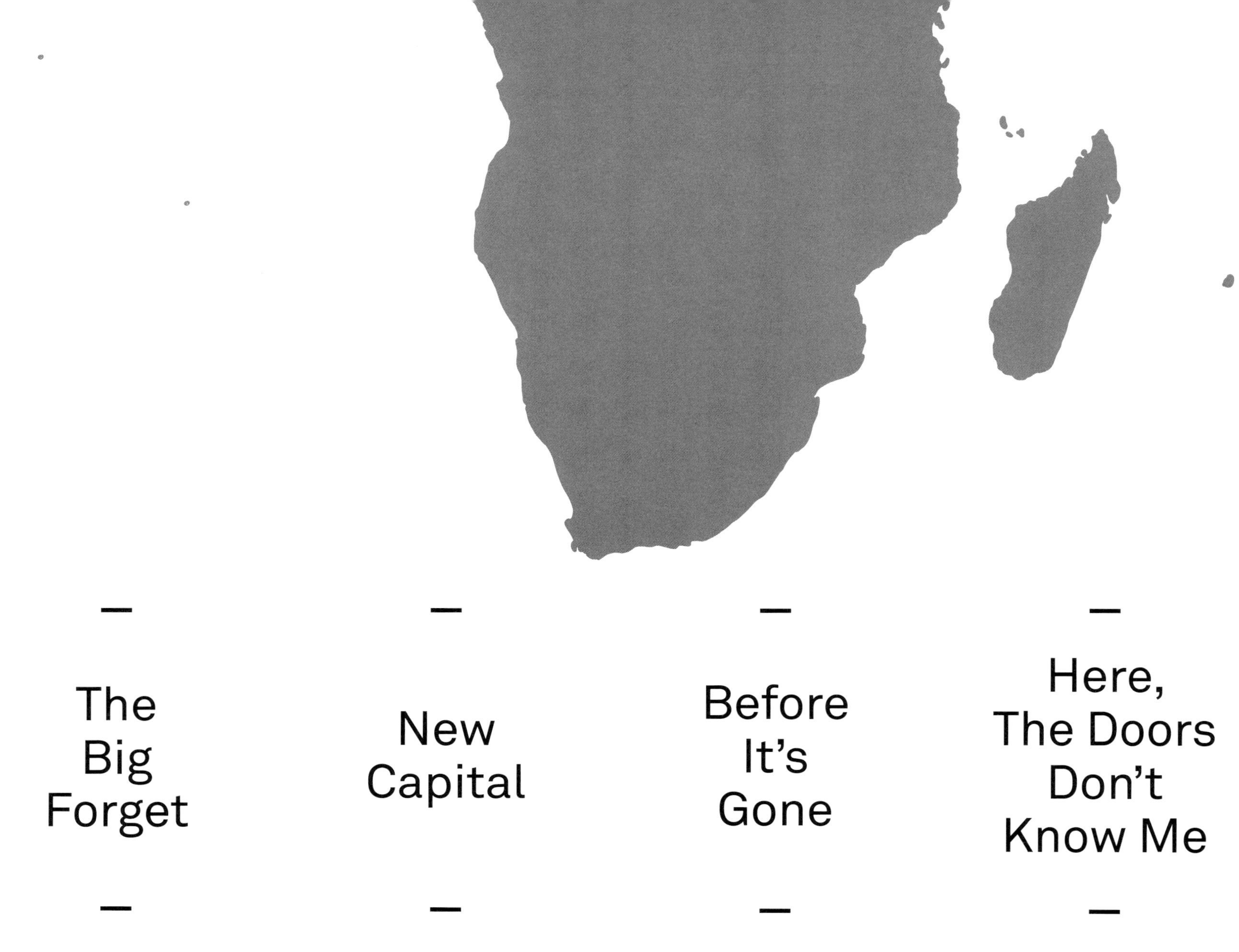

The Big Forget

New Capital

Before It’s Gone

Here, The Doors Don’t Know Me

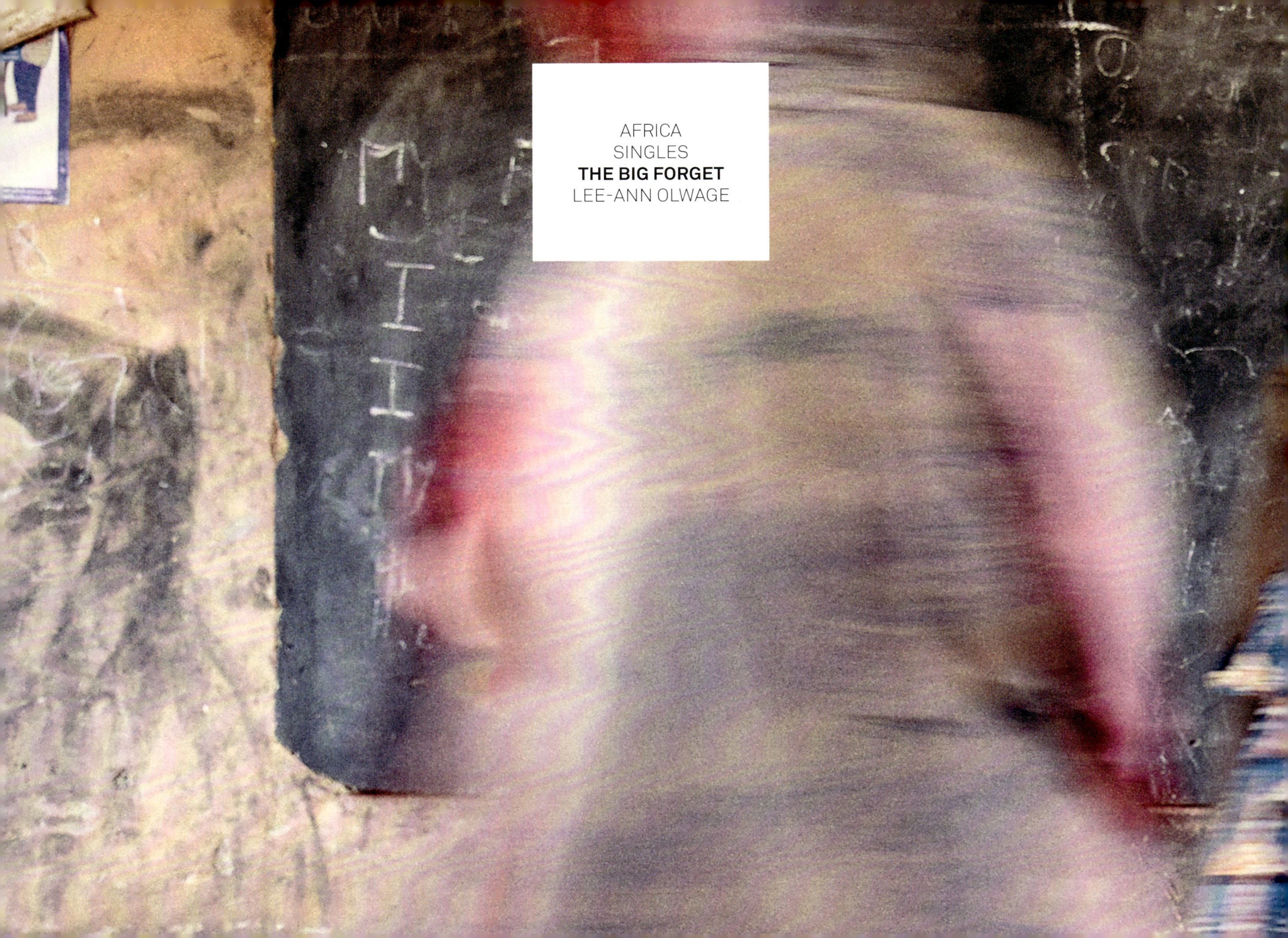

AFRICA
SINGLES
**THE BIG FORGET**
LEE-ANN OLWAGE

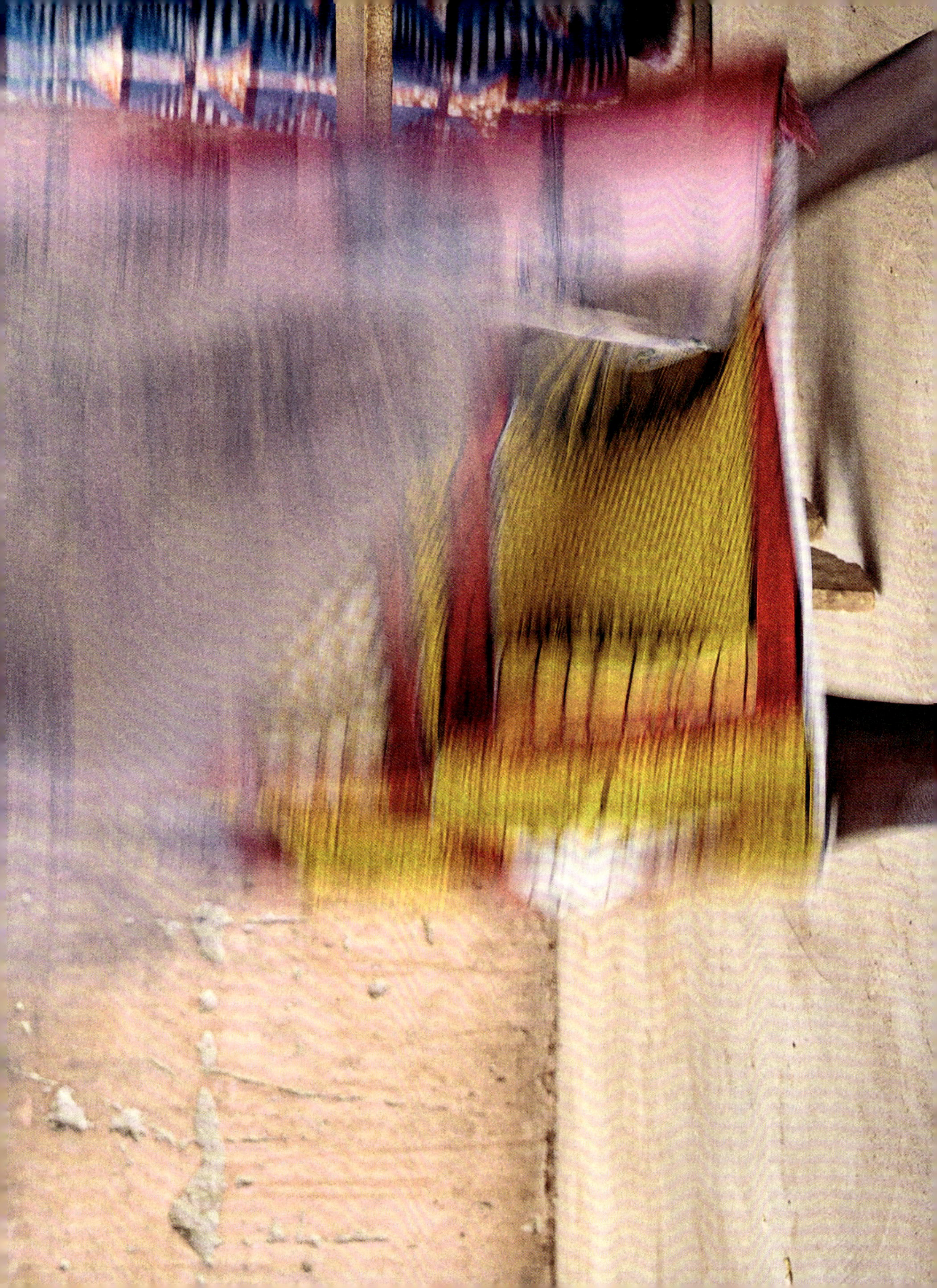

# The Big Forget

Sugri Zenabu, a *mangazia* (female community leader) of the Gambaga “witch camp”, sits encircled by residents in Gambaga, Ghana, on 27 October 2022. Zenabu shows some signs of confusion and memory loss associated with dementia. As life expectancy rises, dementia is increasingly becoming a public health and socio-cultural issue in Ghana and across Africa. Lack of public awareness of behavior associated with the condition means that women displaying symptoms are sometimes perceived as witches. In Ghana, they may be sent away to live in so-called “witch camps”. Lee-Ann Olwage’s personal project attempts to bring attention to often overlooked stories about dementia from the African continent.

Published in *Der Spiegel* and supported by the Bob & Diane Fund.

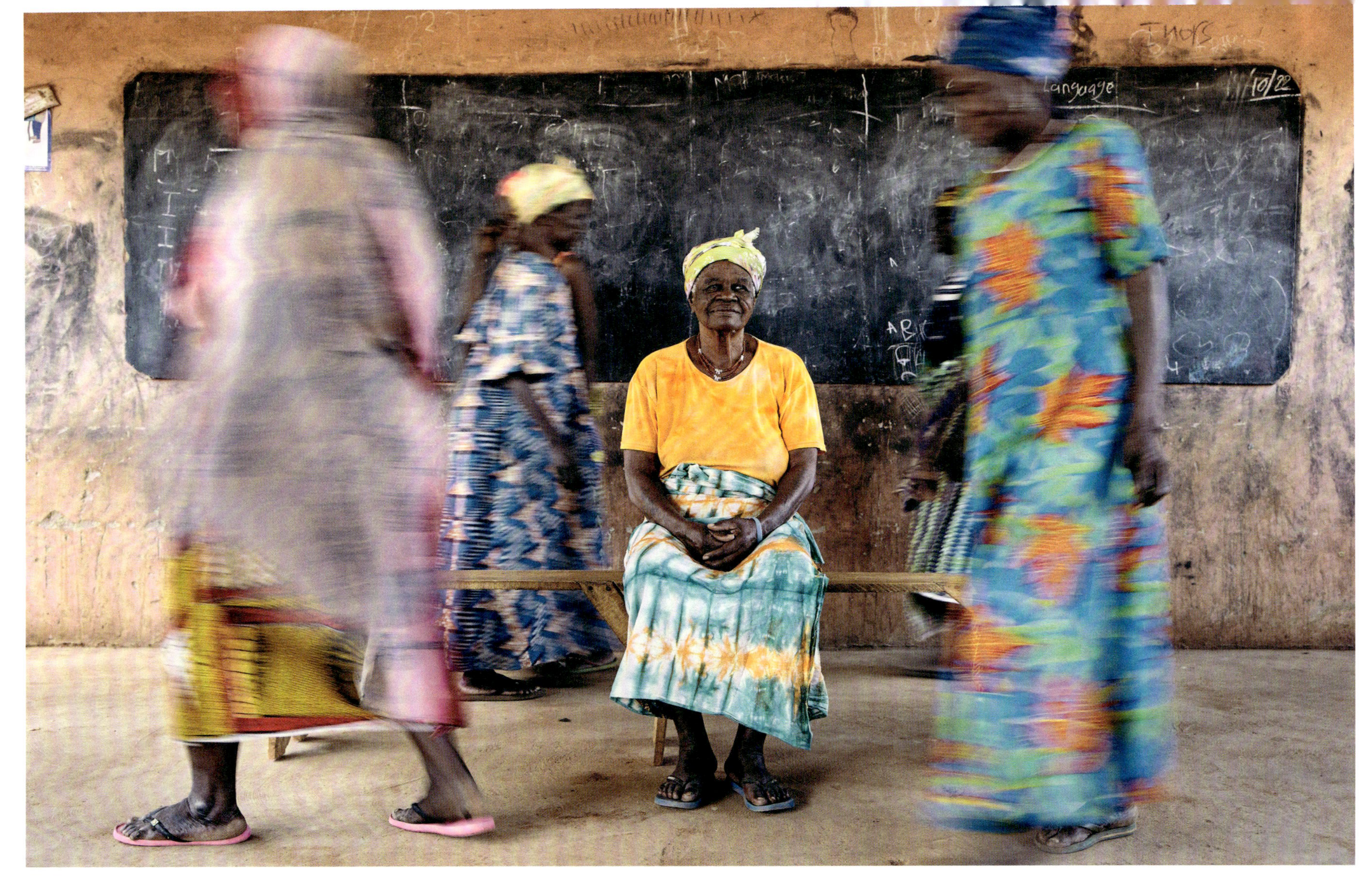
Language
10/22

AFRICA
STORIES
**NEW CAPITAL**
NICK HANNES

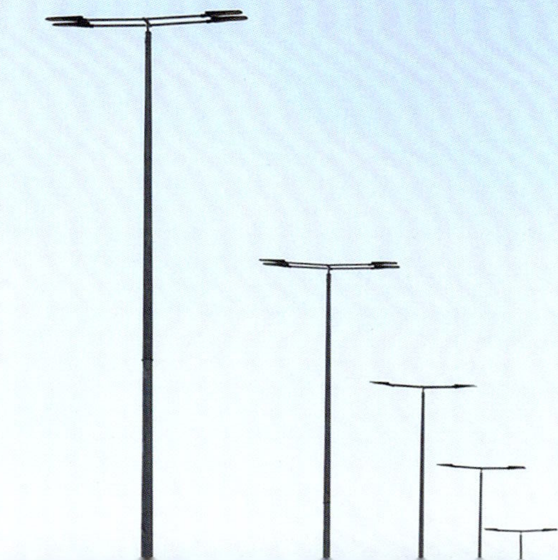

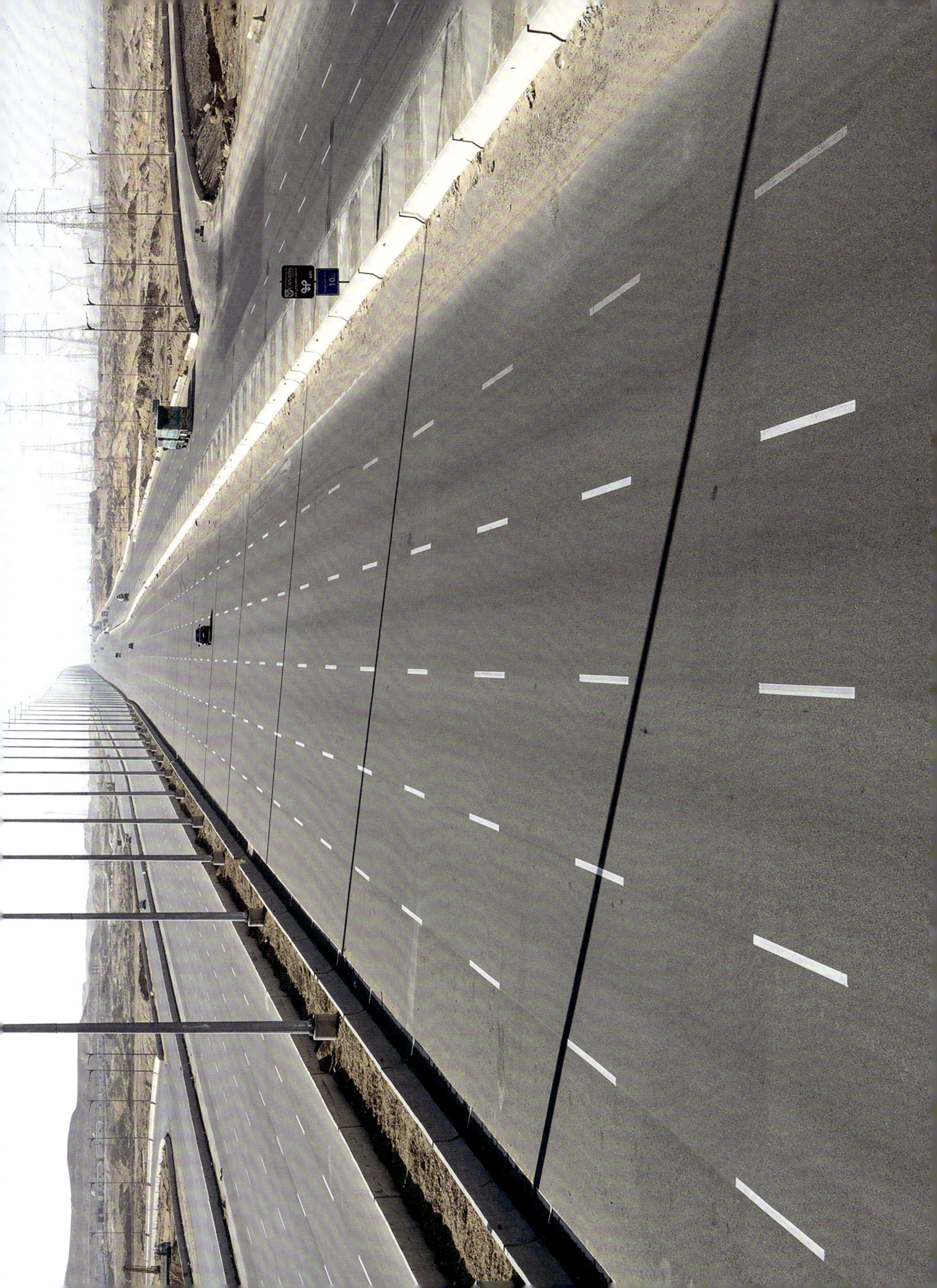

# New Capital

In 2015, the Egyptian government began constructing a New Administrative Capital (NAC) in the desert east of Cairo to accommodate ministries, top companies, and relieve chronic congestion and pollution in the city. Modeled on Dubai, this new urban environment will house 6.5 million people. Critics of the project argue that the NAC caters to the privileged minority and serves President Abdel Fattah el-Sissi's efforts to consolidate power and establish a legacy. These images constitute part of a larger project on new capitals that addresses notions of labor, neoliberal urban development, and inequality.

Nick Hannes is a member of Panos Pictures.

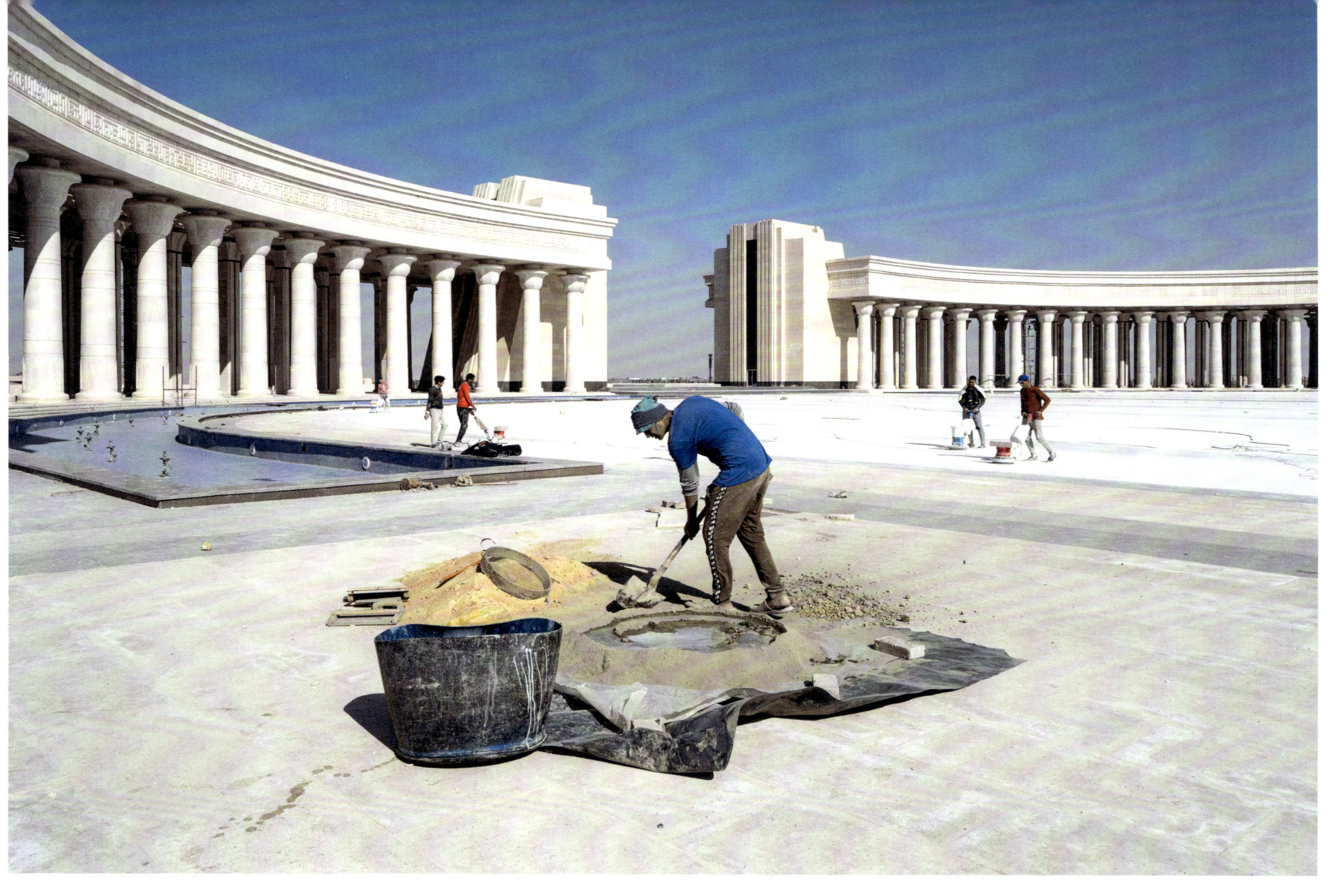

Workers fill joints between paving stones at the Arc de Triomphe in Egypt's New Administrative Capital (NAC), under construction near Cairo, on 13 January 2022. Some workers earn as little as US$200 a month building a city where a two-bedroom apartment will cost around US$50,000.

Welders work near the future Central Business District of Egypt's NAC, on 17 January 2022.
The Iconic Tower (center) will be Africa's tallest building, at 394 meters high.

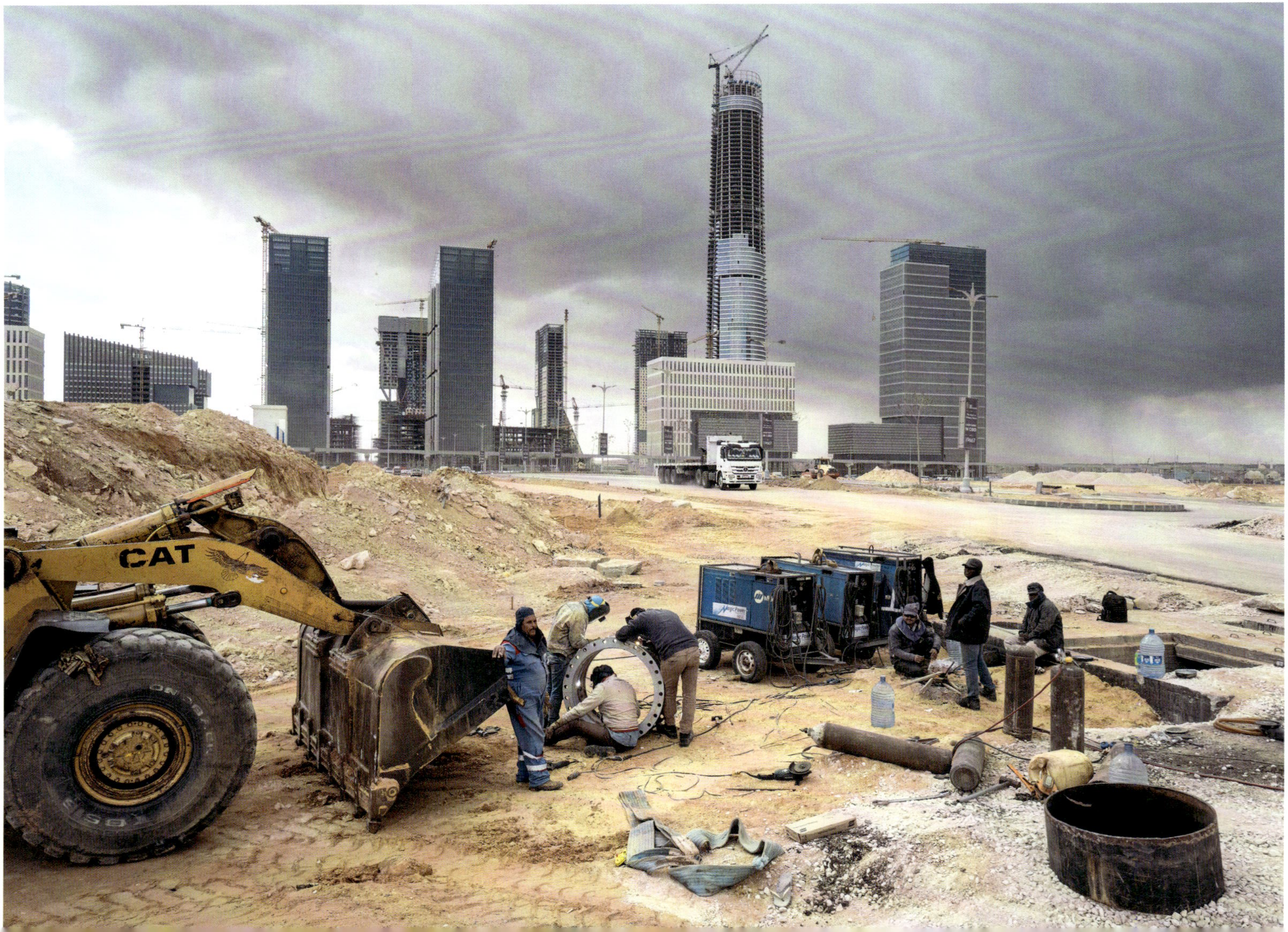

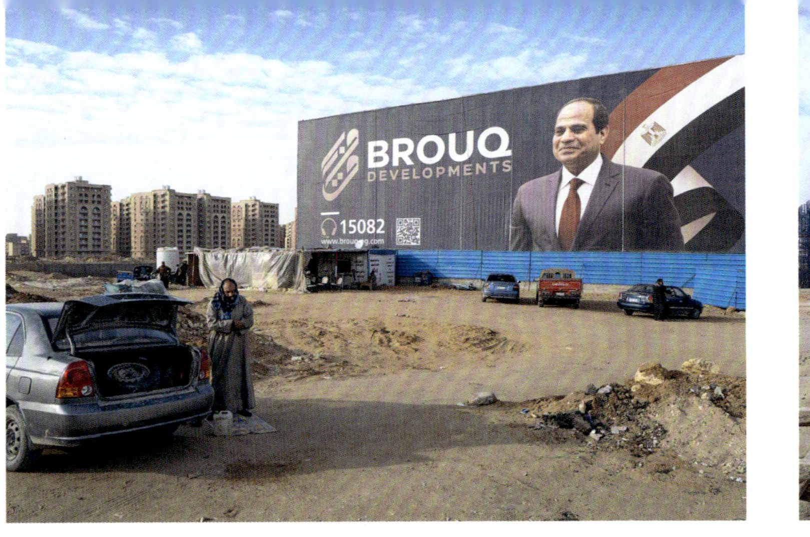


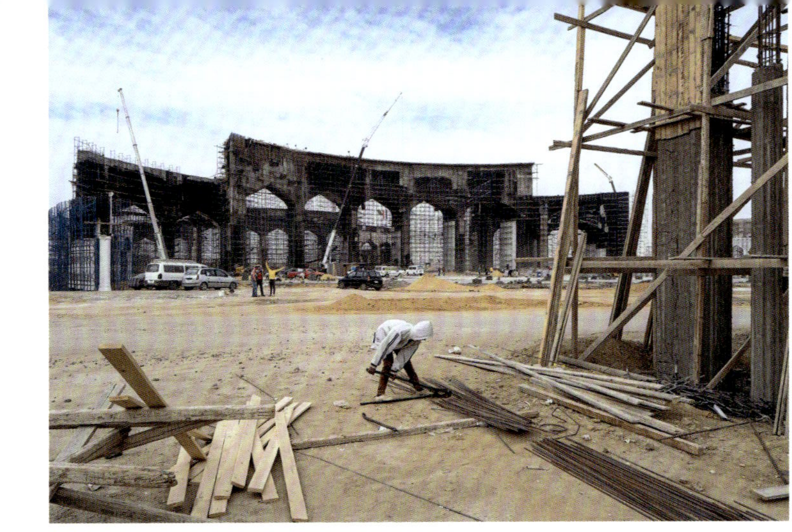

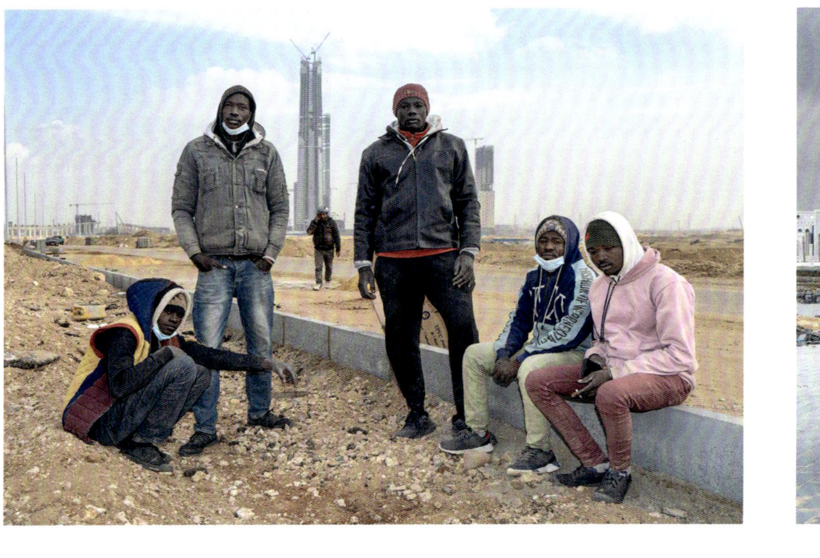

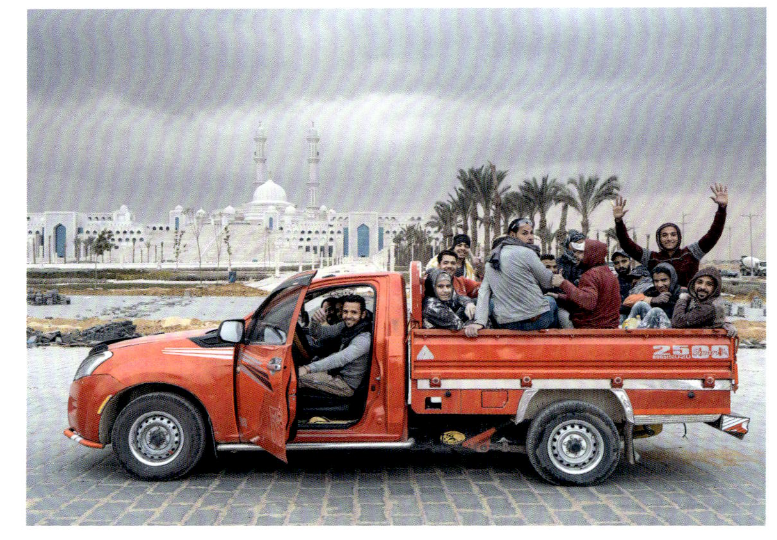

A man prays near a billboard depicting Egyptian president Abdel Fattah el-Sissi, in the NAC, on 12 January 2022.

Mahfouz Abib, John Madesto, Angelo Saimon, Abdel Baset Omar, and Mosab Abdel Wahab (left to right), workers from South Sudan, pose in front of the Iconic Tower rising in Egypt's NAC on 16 January 2022.

Workers construct one of the giant entrance gates to Egypt's NAC on 16 January 2022.

Workers on their way home pass the newly built Misr Mosque on 16 January 2022. The mosque will be one of the largest in the world, with a capacity to accommodate more than 100,000 worshippers.

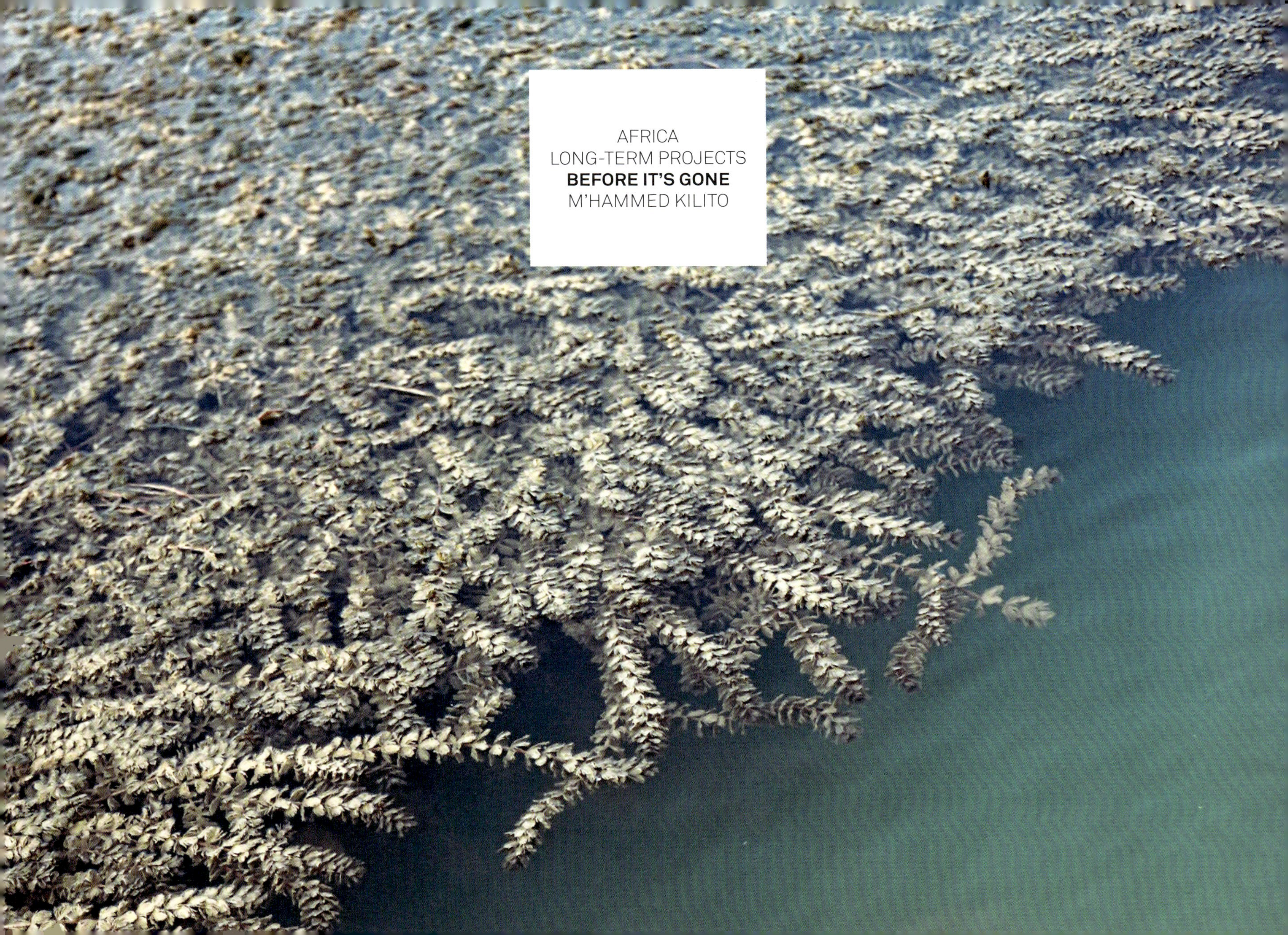

AFRICA
LONG-TERM PROJECTS
**BEFORE IT'S GONE**
M'HAMMED KILITO

# Before It’s Gone

Oases depend on a delicate balance of three elements – abundant water supply, good quality soil, and date palms – to function as islands of biodiversity and barriers against desertification. In Morocco, destructive human activity and global heating are currently disrupting this ecosystem. Roughly two-thirds of Morocco’s oasis habitat has disappeared in the past century due to such factors as steadily rising temperatures, fires, and water scarcity. Oasis degradation in turn impacts inhabitants, causing decreased agricultural production, poverty, and displacement. The jury appreciated the project for its subtle study of a vanishing environment.

Supported by VII Mentor Program and Visura.

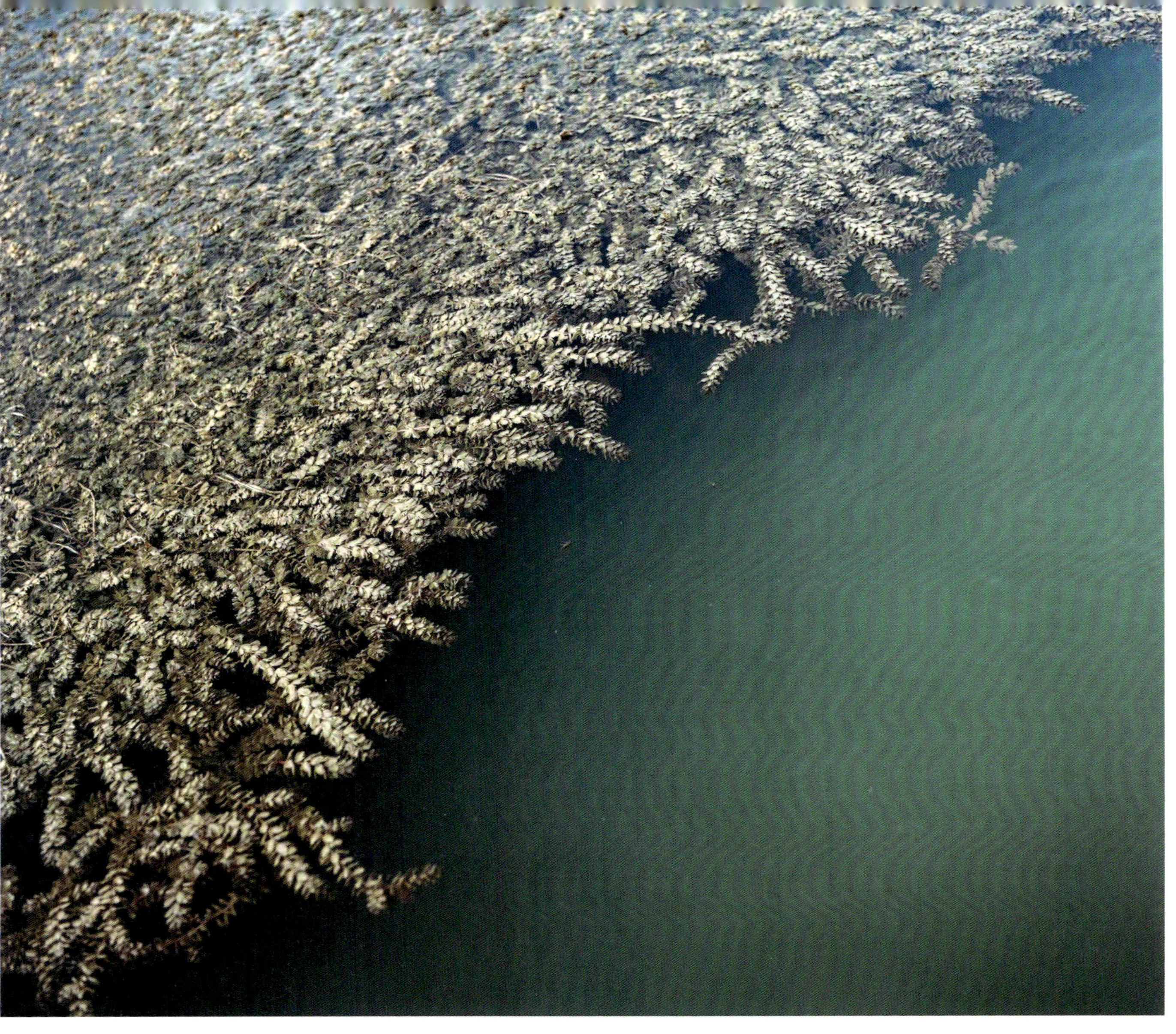

The only water source in Tighmert Oasis, Morocco, photographed on 12 March 2021.
The level of the water table has dropped drastically in Tighmert oasis over the last five years.

Mohammed Elfakhar, a potter, collects wood at the Skoura Oasis, Morocco, on 24 April 2022. He does this every Sunday, when he fires the pottery he has made during the week in a kiln.

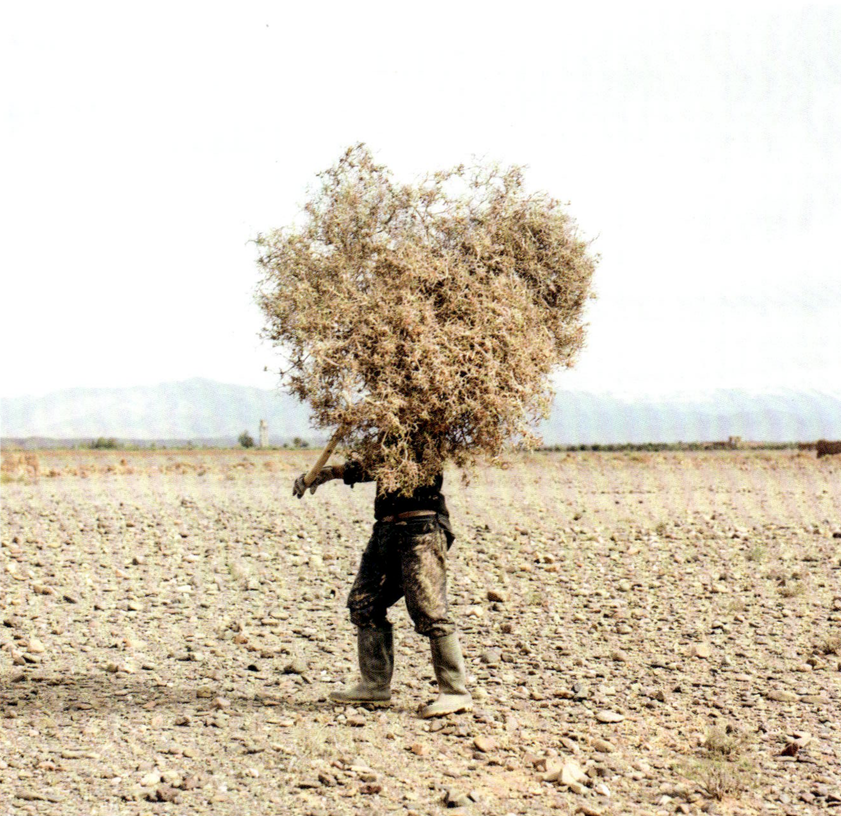

The carcass of a dromedary that died of thirst after being lost in the desert lies near the Tighmert Oasis, on 23 March 2019.

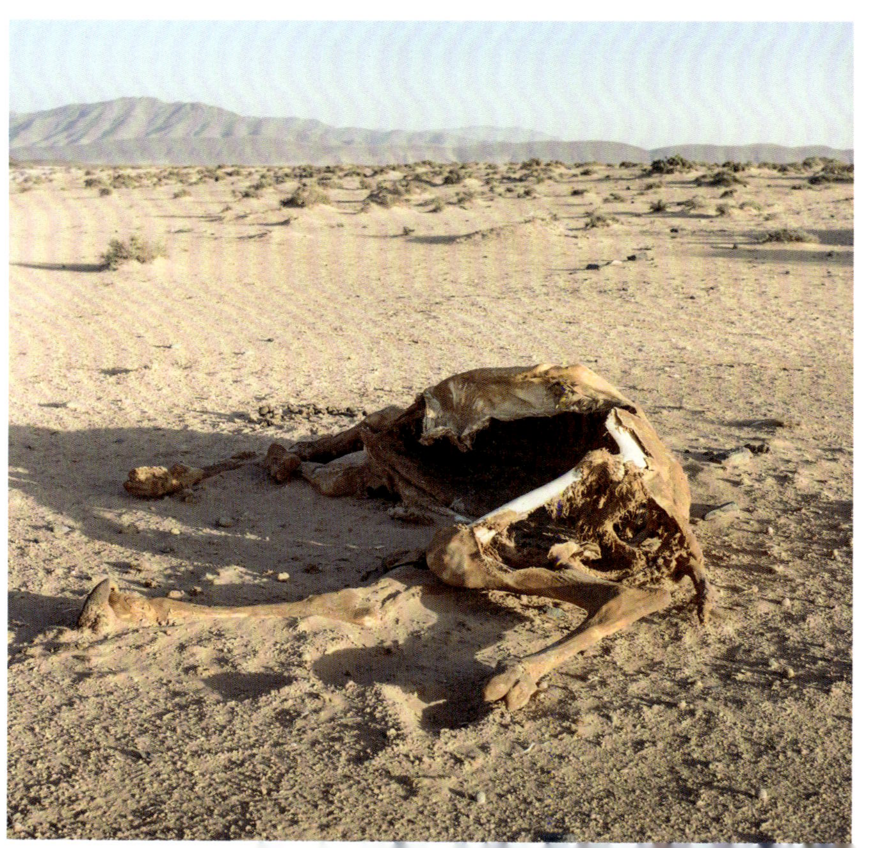

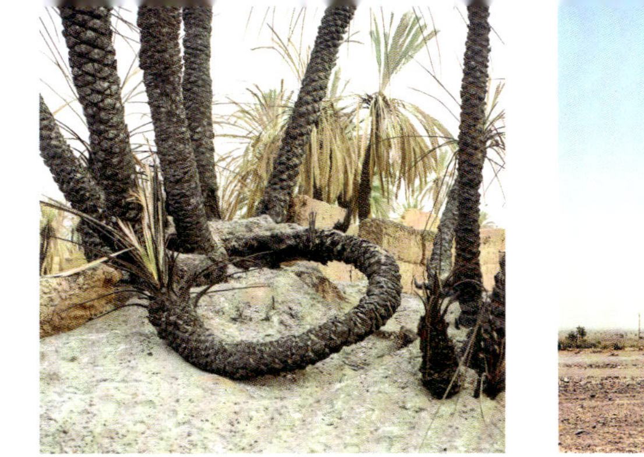

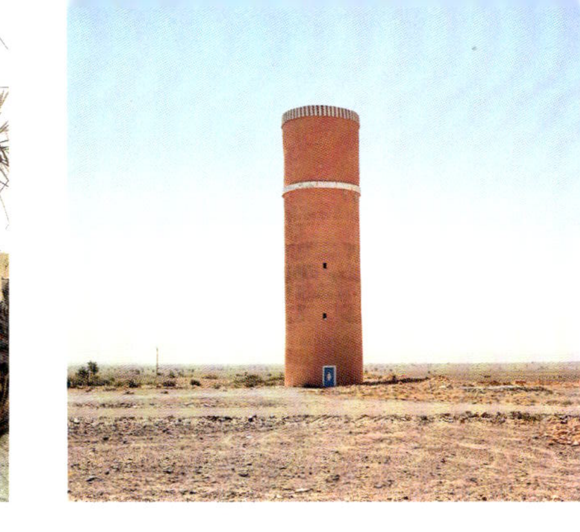

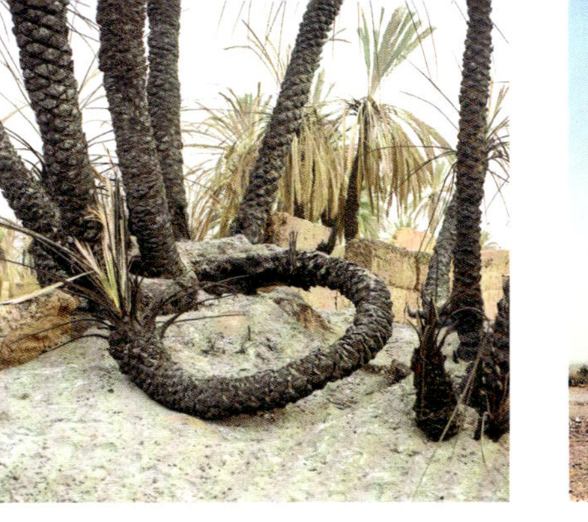

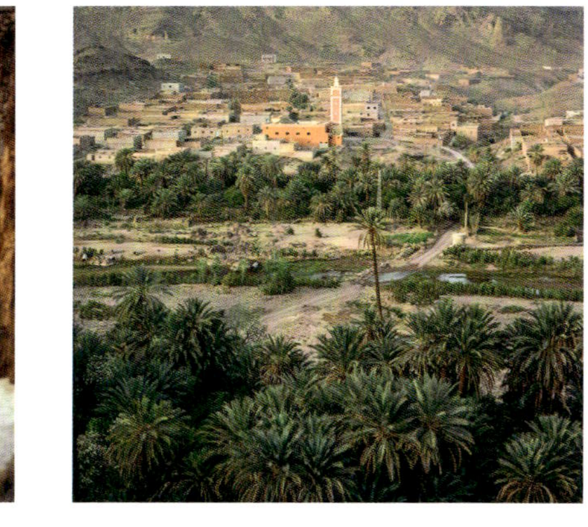

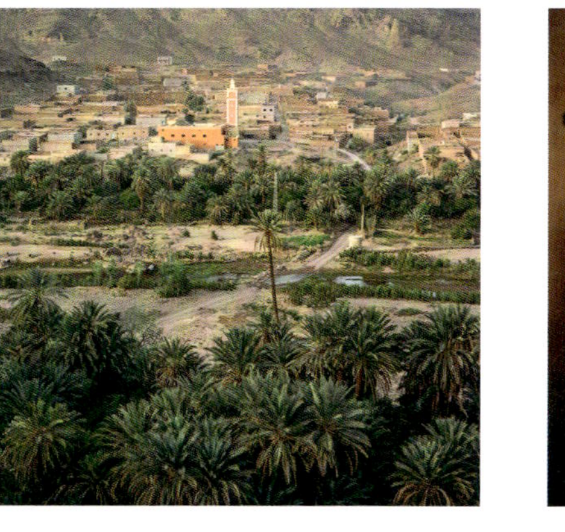

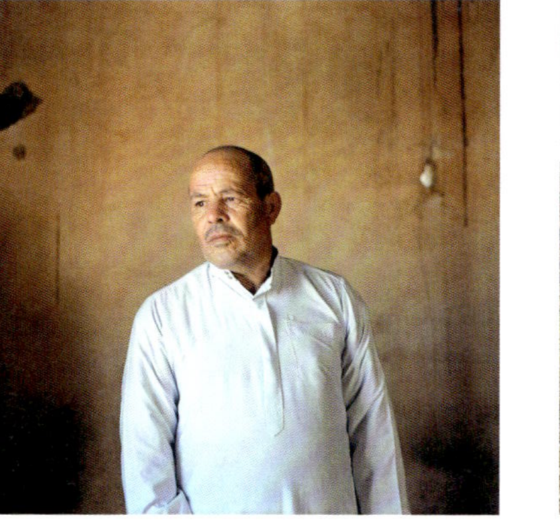

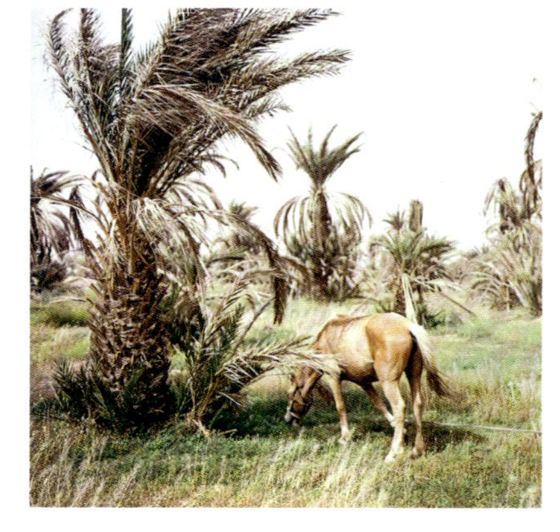

Vegetation parched by heat and water stress in the Tighmert Oasis poses a fire threat, on 18 September 2020. A few weeks earlier, fire had destroyed houses, hundreds of date palms and vegetable gardens, and killed around 400 cattle.

Farmer Hamdani's sheep enter a fold in Zagora, beside the Oued Draa river in eastern Morocco, on 11 May 2022.

A water tower in Zagora, pictured on 6 May 2022. Associations of families often build and finance these towers to benefit from a more stable water supply.

The Fint Oasis, near Ouarzazate in southern Morocco, pictured on 10 March 2022, is home to around 1,500 people.

Allocations of water are transferred to users via stone dividers and earthen canals, at Figuig Oasis, on 6 February 2021.

Mohammed (pictured on 6 April 2020) says that wells dug upstream of the underground springs serving the Ifrane Middle Atlas Oasis are reducing available water levels.

Pots from the Tighmert Oasis are on display at the Kasbah Caravanserail Museum, which is dedicated to oasis domestic culture, on 8 May 2022.

A horse grazes at M'hamid El Ghizlan Oasis, on 12 April 2022. The oasis is home to around 7,500 people.

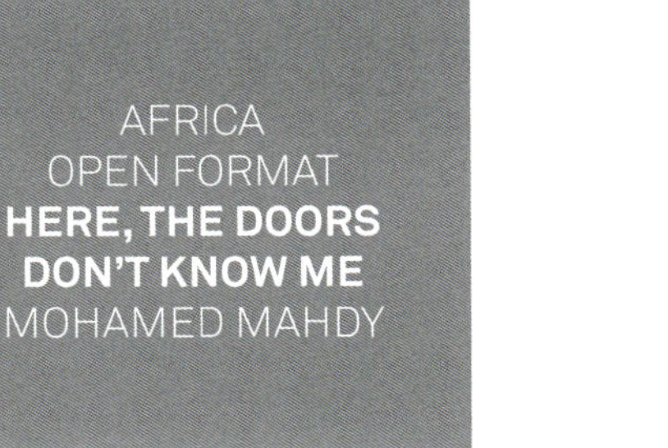
AFRICA
OPEN FORMAT
HERE, THE DOORS
DON'T KNOW ME
MOHAMED MAHDY

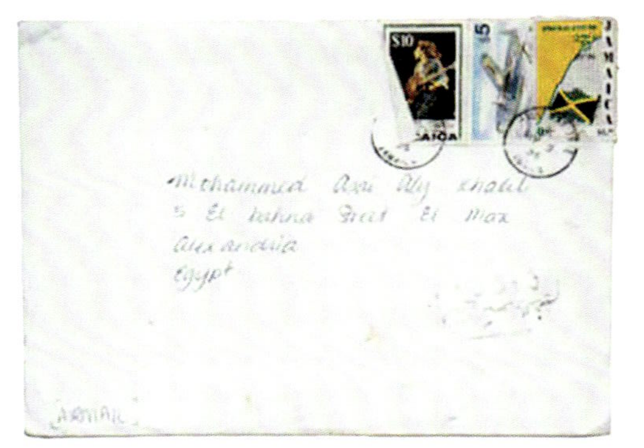
JAMAICA
Alexandria
Egypt

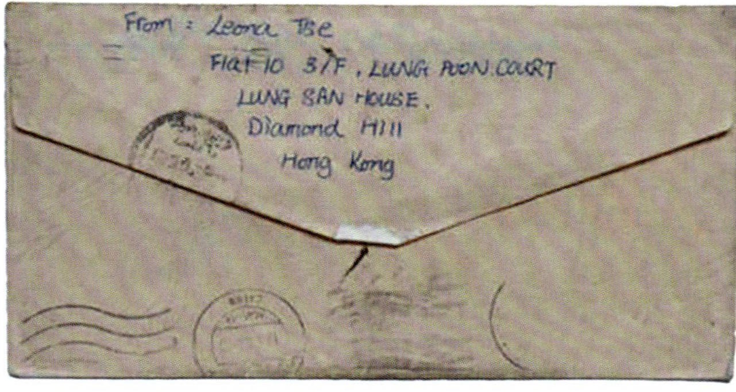
From : Leona Tse
Flat 10 3/F, LUNG POON COURT
LUNG SAN HOUSE.
Diamond Hill
Hong Kong

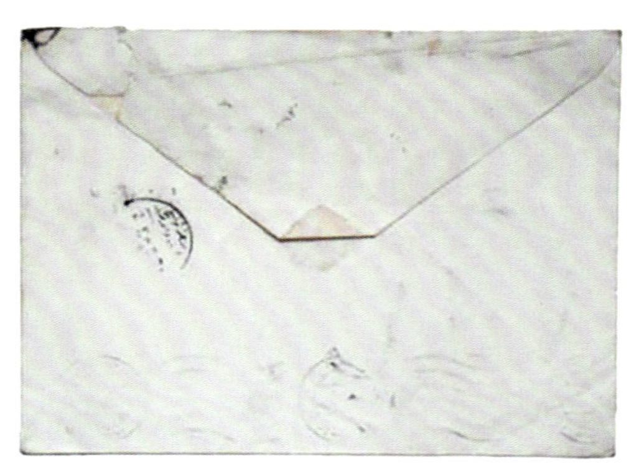

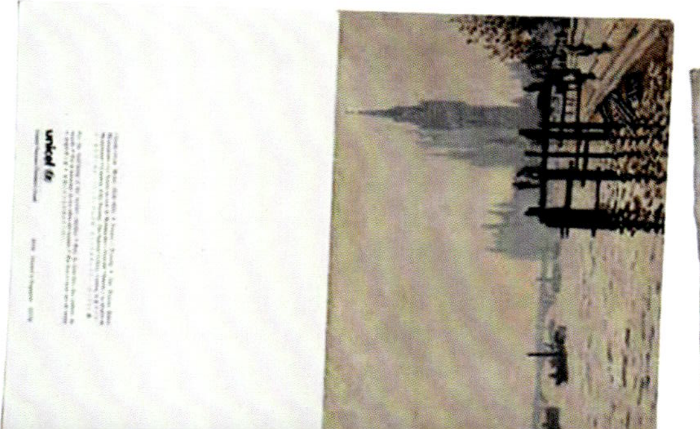

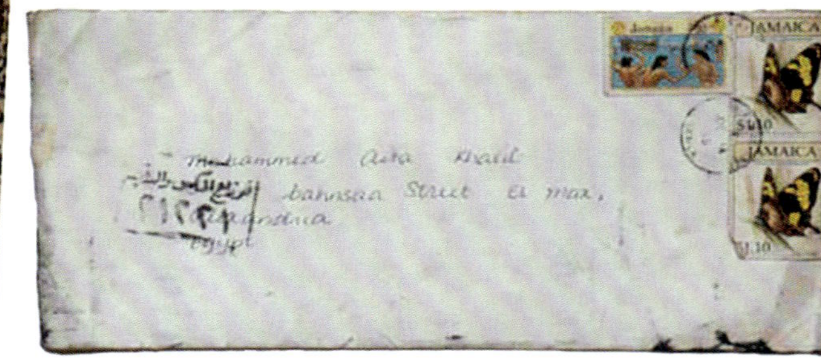
JAMAICA
JAMAICA
Egypt

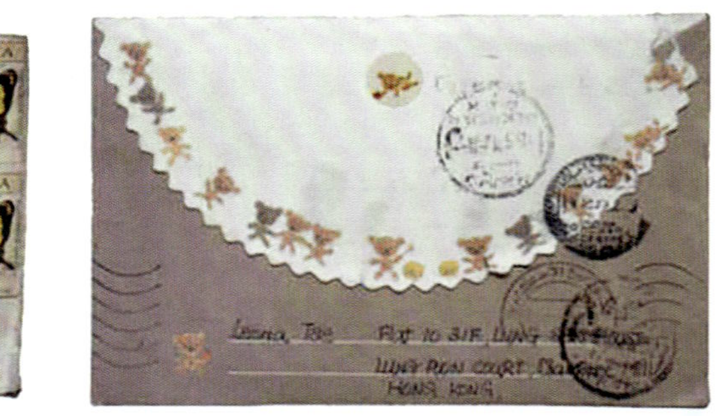
Leona Tse
Hong Kong

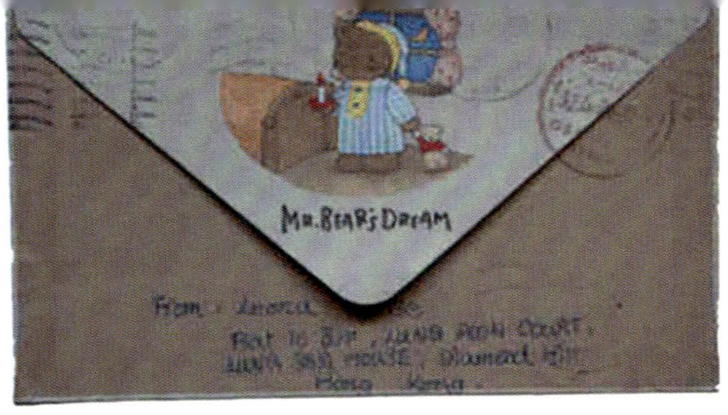
MR. BEAR'S DREAM

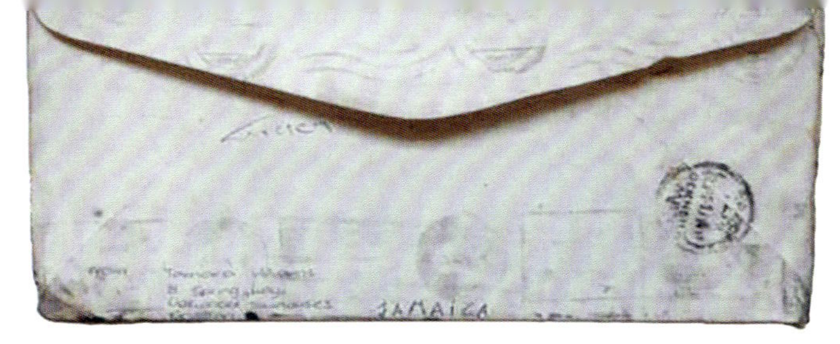
JAMAICA

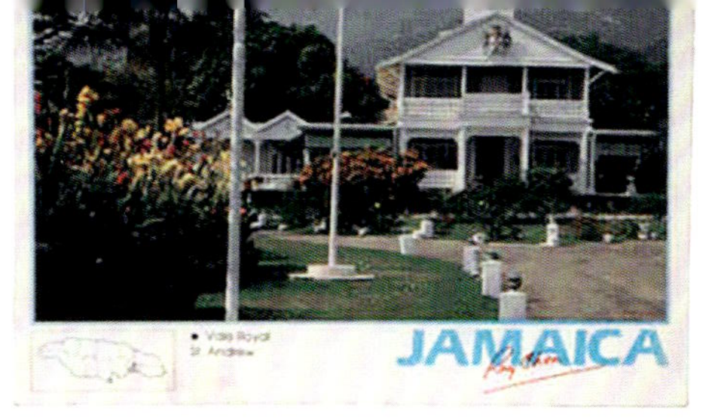
JAMAICA

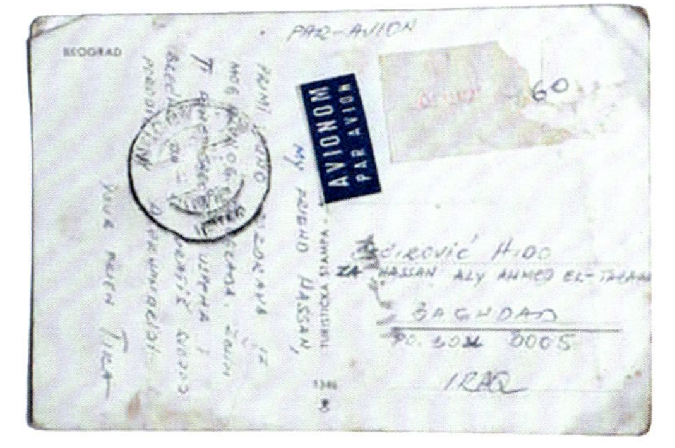
PAR-AVION
AVIONOM
PAR AVION
MY FRIEND HASSAN,
BAGHDAD
IRAQ
YOUR FRIEN TIKA

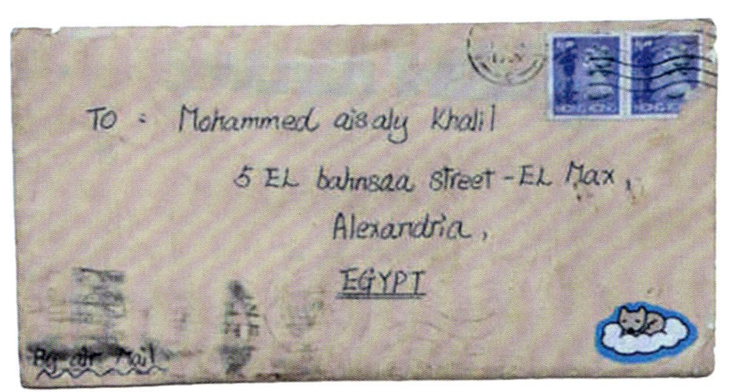
TO : Mohammed ais aly Khalil
5 EL bahnsaa street - EL Max,
Alexandria,
EGYPT
By air Mail

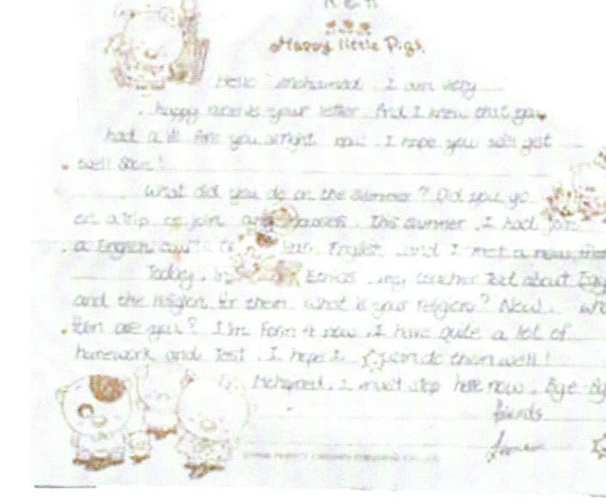
Happy little Pigs

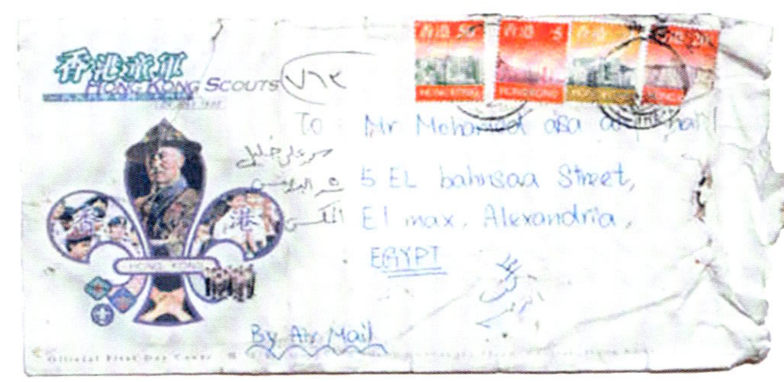
香港童軍
HONG KONG SCOUTS
5 EL bahnsaa Street,
El max, Alexandria,
EGYPT
By Air Mail

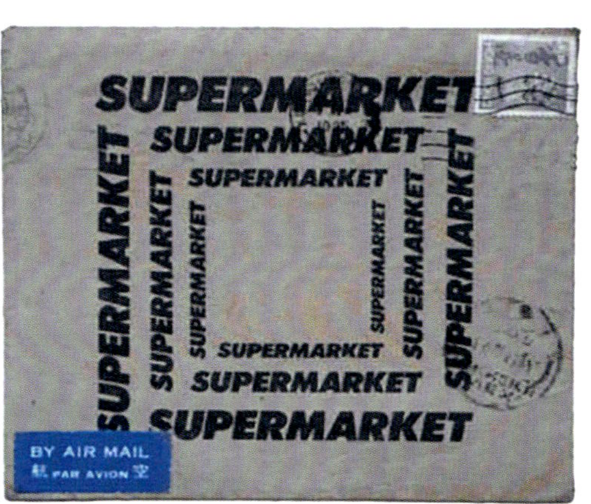
SUPERMARKET
BY AIR MAIL
PAR AVION

Scan the QR code to experience the website.

# Here, the Doors Don’t Know Me

This web-based project explores the effects of rising seas on the local community in Al Max, a fishing village situated along the Mahmoudiyah canal in Alexandria, Egypt. For generations, its residents have lived and worked on the canal that leads to the Mediterranean Sea. In 2020, the Egyptian government began evicting and relocating them to housing several kilometers away from the canals, not only demolishing homes, but also endangering the collective memories and local culture embedded in Al Max. The stories featured here speak to the precarity of people everywhere striving for recognition amid global economic and environmental upheaval. People of the Al Max community speak of love letters or last words found in bottles that would wash up on their shores. For this project, Mohamed Mahdy encouraged residents to write their own letters, building an archive of private memories for future generations. Utilizing found imagery and the artist’s own photography, Mahdy’s project presents an elegy to a communal way of life on the cusp of disappearing.

"I challenge you if you sit on her shores once and do not return to her again. [...] Once you fall under her spell, you are able to feel it, and there are no words that can describe its beauty."
*Fouaad Freha, resident of Al Max.*

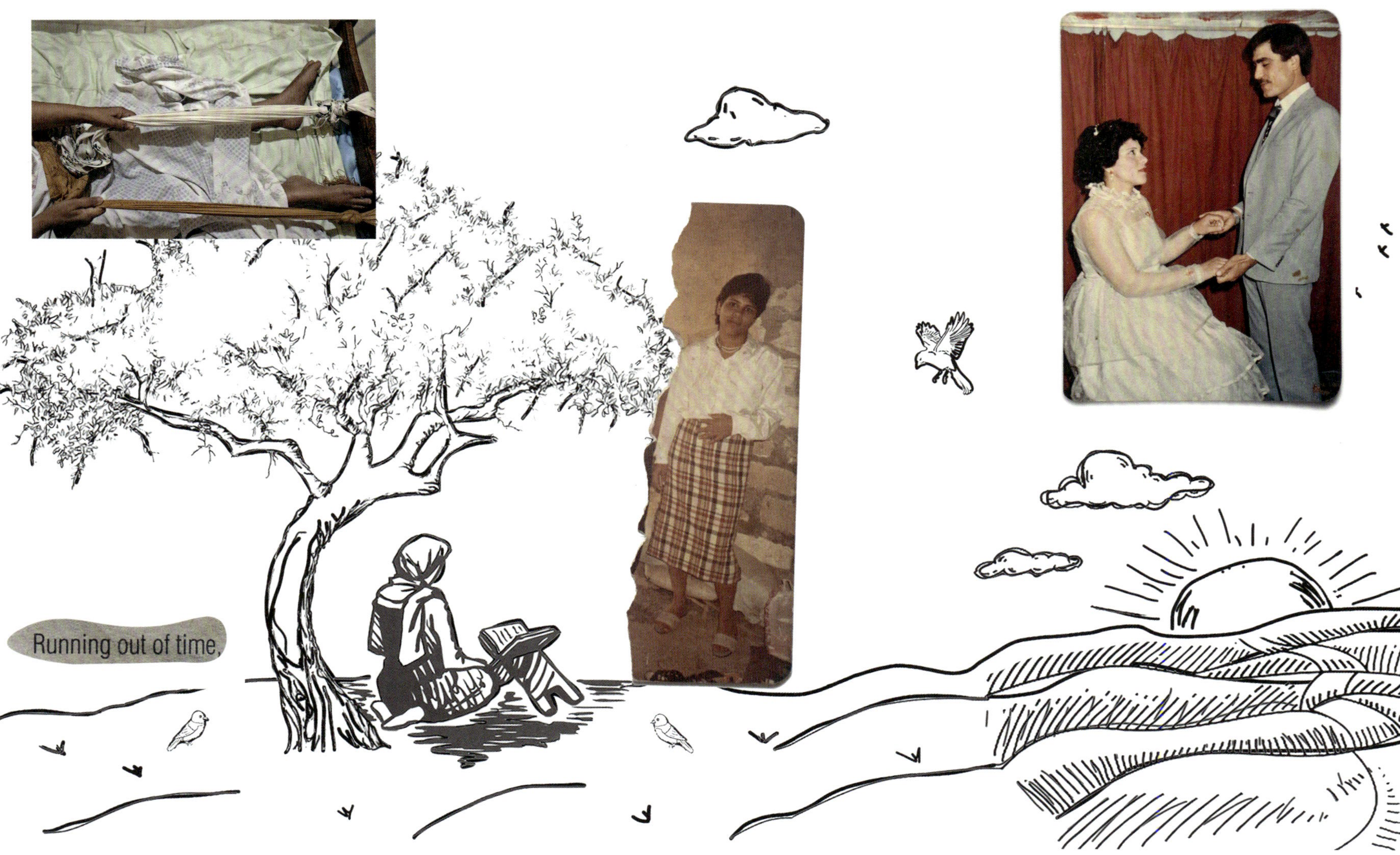
Running out of time.

* رسالة من شاطئ اليود إلى الضفاف البعيدة *

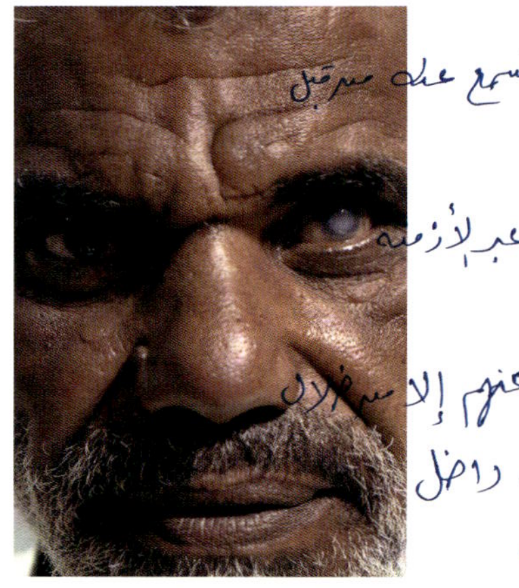

ما يجب أن تعرفه عن شاطئ اليود ربما لم تسمع عنه من قبل
عن مكان يحتل المركز الأول في العالم باليود،
حلم وانتهى بحقيقة وسيظل الشعر المنشود عبر الأزمنة
لشط ورمل المكس بالإسكندرية،
عشت وعاشت أجيال هنا لن تسمع عنهم إلا من خلال
الشهيق والزفير باليود الذي يتوغل داخل
وجدانك وفؤادك لترى سحر الخيال
ويتاخم روح الساكنة فيه
ليفتح البحر رئتيه ليتنفس الهواء الممتد على امتداد القارات
الممزوج بإلهام الشعراء، والملون بانتظار العاجزين
عن لقاء أحبابهم، والمشتاقين إلى أمسيات
الذين يبيتون على أمل بزوغ الفجر حتى
يحققوا ما يصبو إليه الخلق من أحلام
حلم وعشقها المكس
يا حبيبي إلى الأبد

V٦٢

香港童軍 HONG KONG SCOUTS
28 JULY 1998

To: Mr Mohamed aisa al-...
محمد علي خليل
5 EL bahnsaa Street,
شارع البهنسا
El max, Alexandria,
المكس
EGYPT

By Air Mail

Official First Day Cover

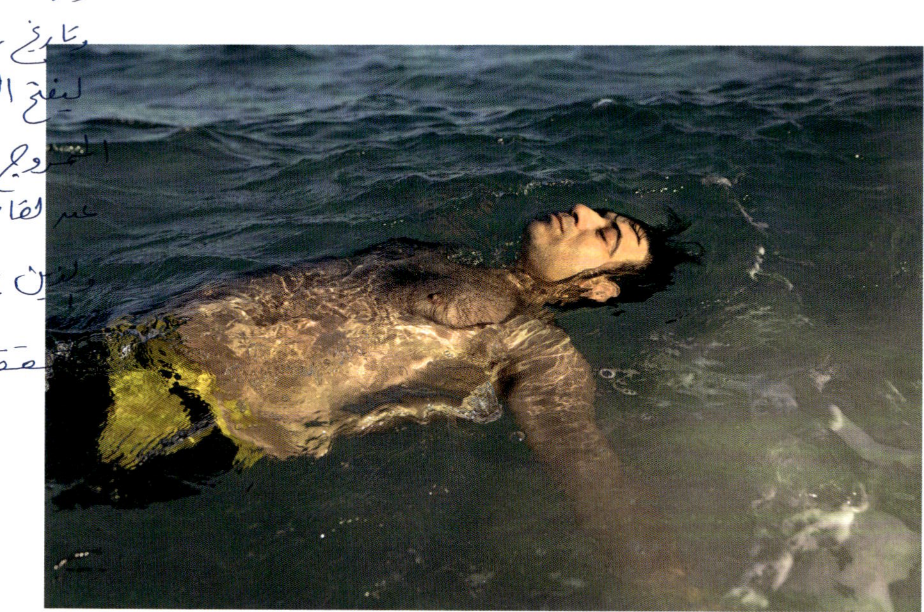

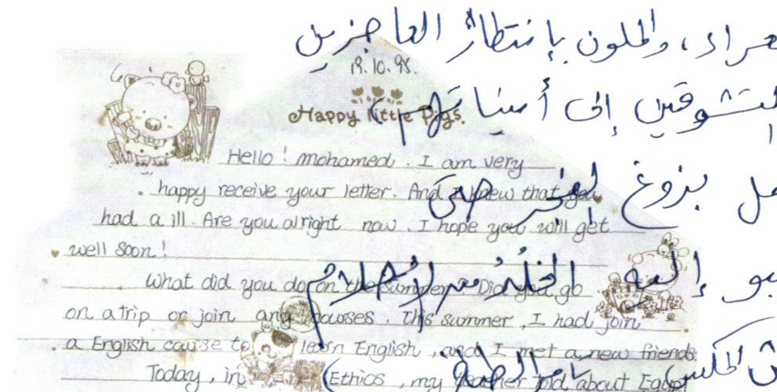

19.10.98.

Happy Little Days

Hello! mohamed. I am very happy receive your letter. And I knew that you had a ill. Are you alright now. I hope you will get well soon!

What did you do on the summer? Did you go on a trip or join any courses. This summer, I had join a English course to learn English, and I met a new friends. Today, in Ethics, my teacher told about Egypt and the religion for them. What's your religion? Now, what form are you? I'm Form 4 now, I have quite a lot of homework and Test. I hope I can do them well!

Mohamed, I must stop here now, Bye-Bye friends

Leone

©1994 PERFECT CHILDREN PUBLISHING CO., LTD

39

AFRICA

## HONORABLE MENTIONS

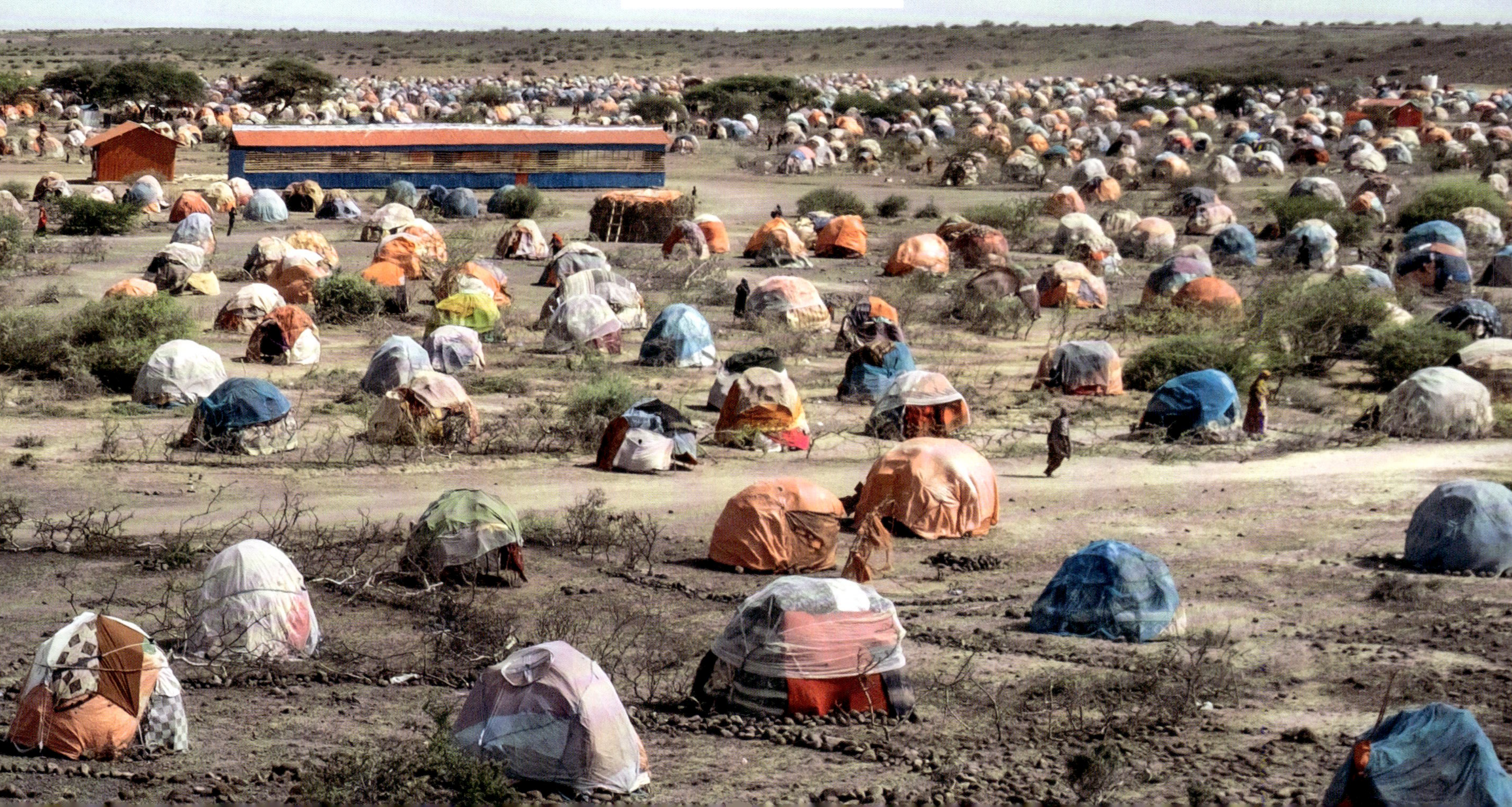

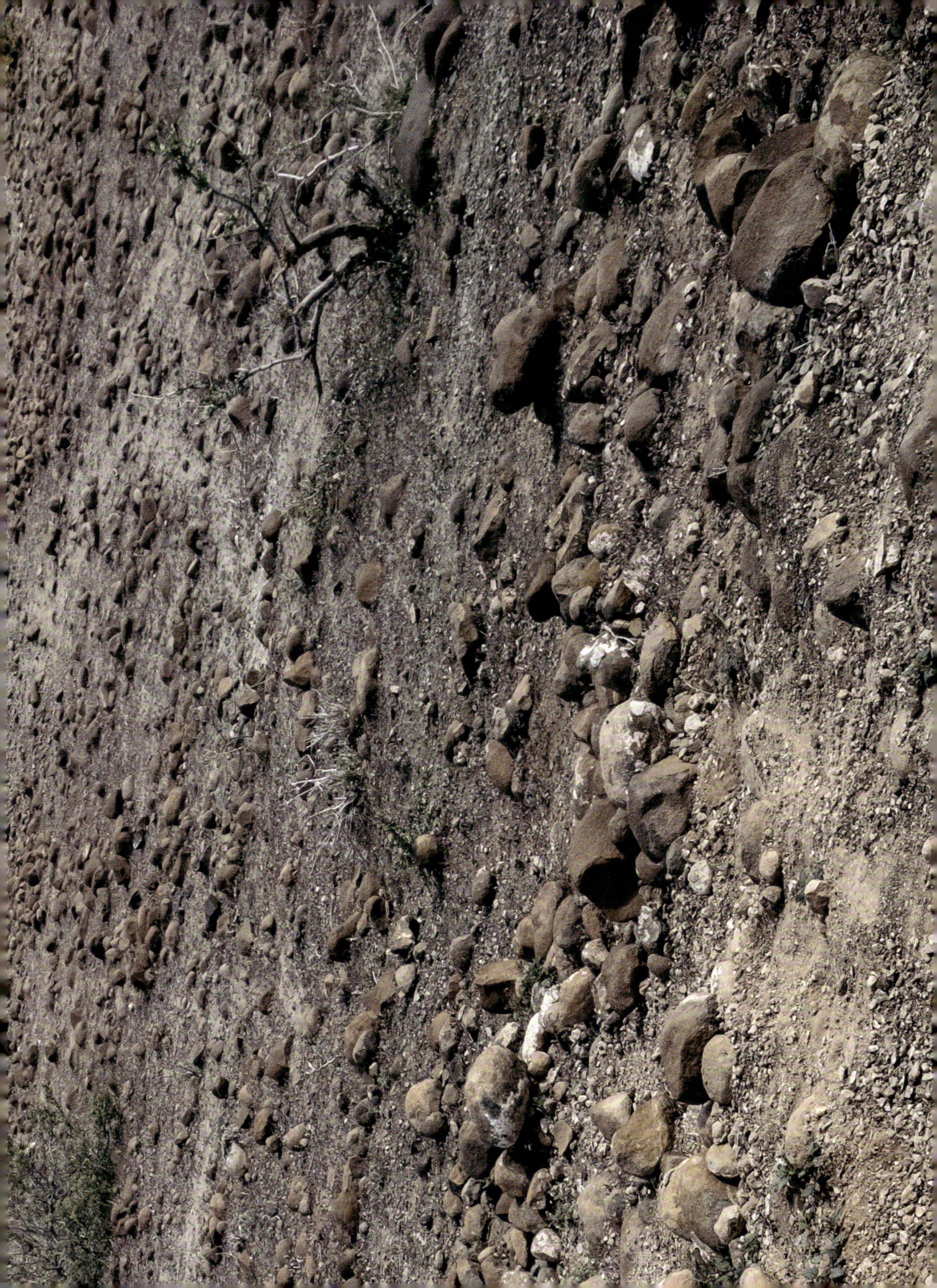

# The Nomad's Final Journey

—

Nomadic peoples of Ethiopia and Somalia depend on their livestock, and migrate across their territory to pasture their animals. In recent years, water scarcity has threatened these livestock. Exacerbated by the climate crisis, droughts have devastated the region, which according to the World Food Programme now endanger the food security of over 26 million people. With many families forced to seek aid in climate refugee camps, social structures are weakening, precipitating violence against women and a host of mental health crises. As droughts persist annually, women, who are often responsible for finding water, bear an enormous share of the physical and mental toll exacted by the ongoing crisis.

Jonathan Fontaine
France, 1984

–

Jonathan Fontaine is a freelance documentary photographer whose work focuses on social and humanitarian consequences of globalization, climate change, deforestation and the many ecological crises that affect the lives of communities around the world. He is a member of Hans Lucas.

–

Instagram: @jonathanfontaine

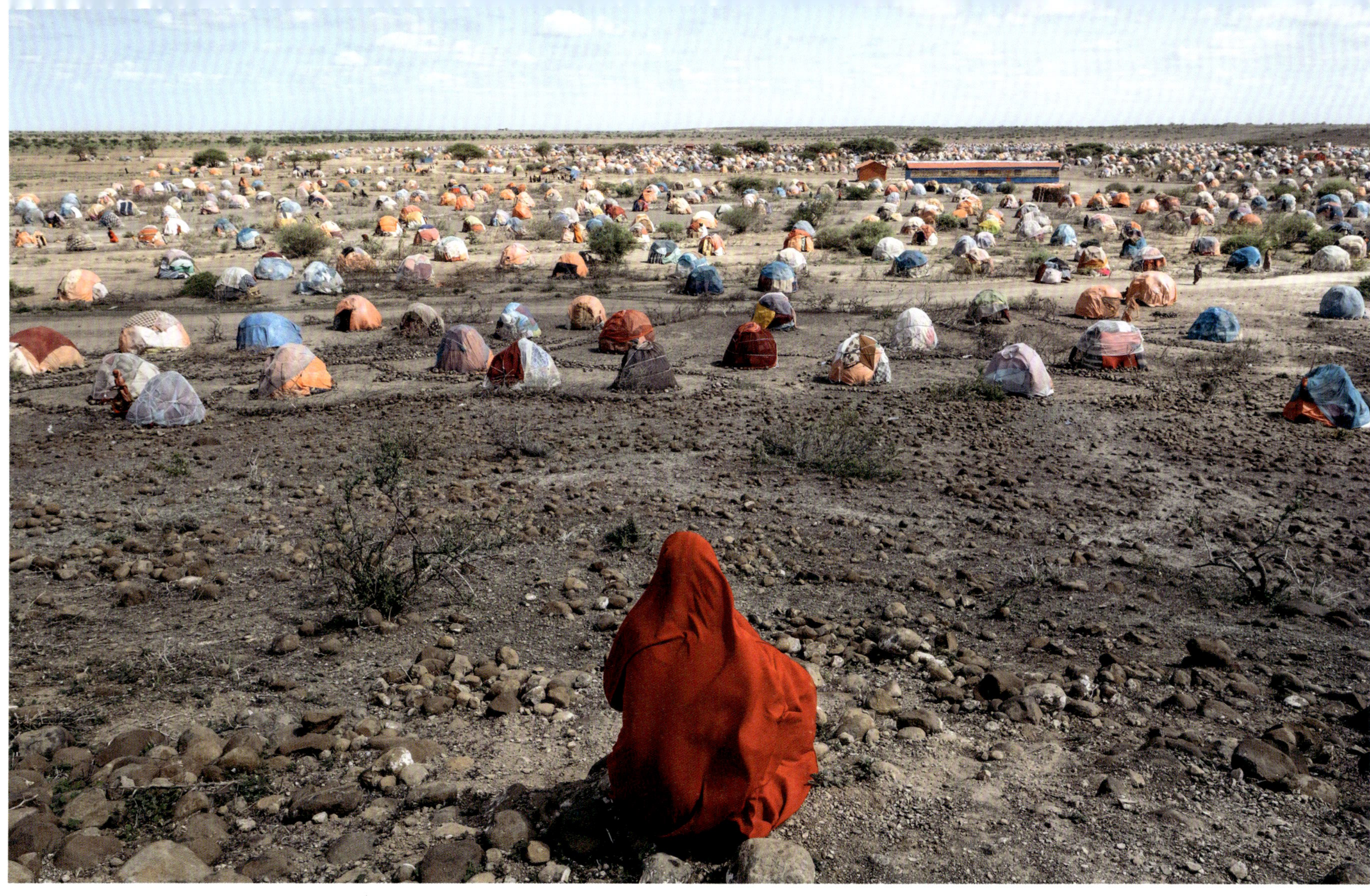

Samira (16) looks out onto Qolodo camp near Gode in the Somali Region, Ethiopia, on 16 May 2022. Her family owned 45 goats and 10 camels, all of which died during recent droughts.

# Africa

—

Angela Jimu
Africa Jury Chair

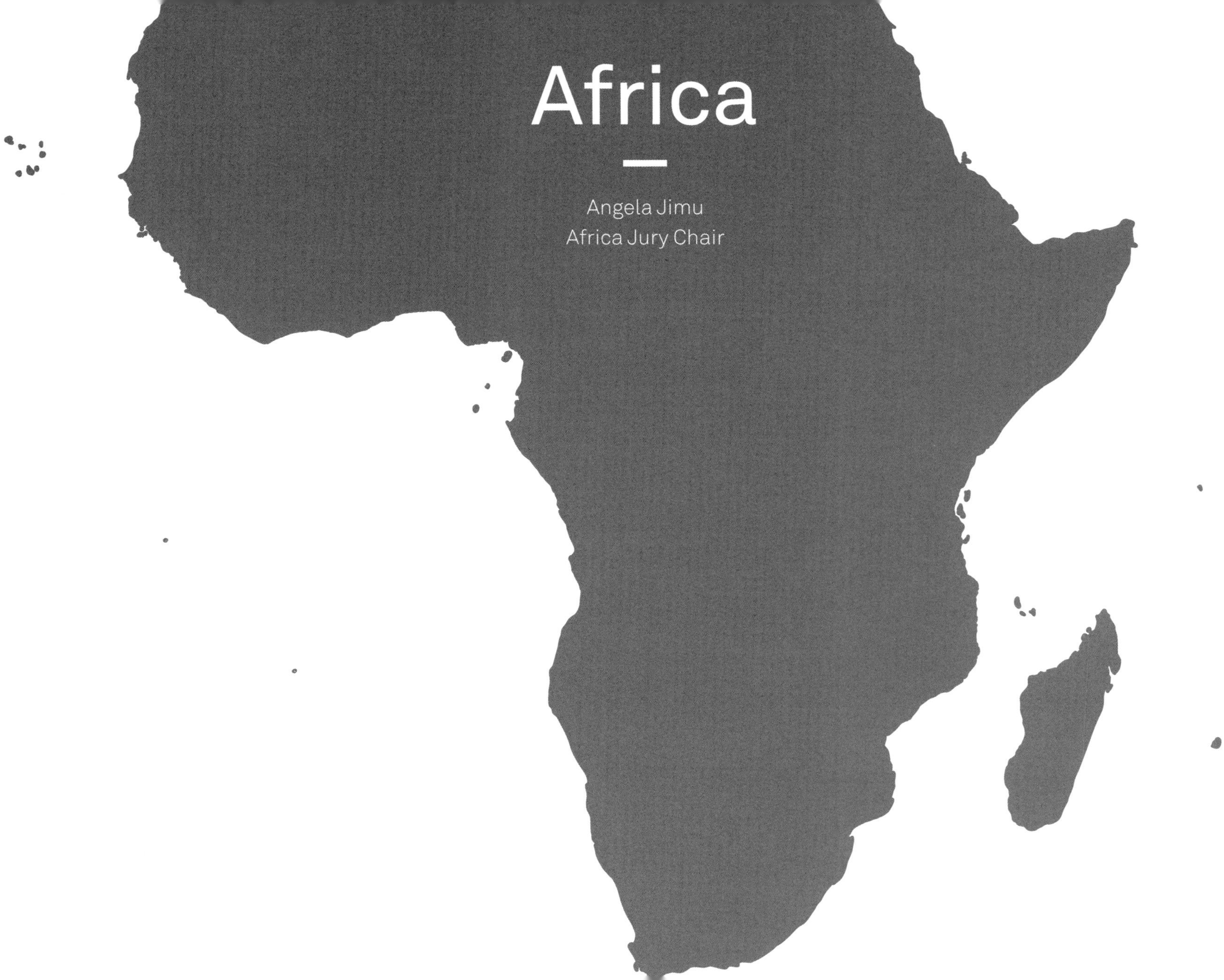

Being the Africa Jury chair for the 2023 World Press Photo Contest was an amazing and yet challenging experience. My own biases and prejudices were called into question. I also had to seriously consider through whose lens I was seeing the world, reflecting on the cautionary words of Nigerian author Chimamanda Ngozi Adichie on the dangers of telling a single story.

Although I have often spoken of and been a proponent of "shifting narratives", the entire process had me rethinking what this term meant in terms of the African continent. The results of the process culminated in a more open mind, as I became more aware of myself and the issues that confront us on the continent when it comes to visual storytelling.

Overall, certain themes kept recurring – themes such as identity, climate crisis, migration, trafficking, and conflict were common throughout entries from the continent's different regions.

My personal vision for the contest related to its capacity to show the human condition, particularly the effects of the climate crisis. This urgent issue needs to be addressed, and images have a particular power to elicit a response. We could not miss the opportunity to highlight an issue that has affected the entire continent.

I was saddened to note how relatively few entries there were from local photographers, and from photographers identifying as female, especially in view of World Press Photo's recent introduction of a regional model, which increases the chances of local visual journalists winning. This raises the question of how we can encourage participation from these groups in next year's contest.

One of the Africa Jury's most crucial discussion points was the politics of identity. We reached the consensus that we were more concerned about a photographer's intentions than their nationality.

The jury agreed that Africa is not homogeneous and that issues in different parts of Africa had to be represented, as issues were not of equal importance across different regions. And we concurred that some issues of great importance are underreported and need to be talked about. However, we were not willing to present images that spoke of important issues, and yet were badly executed.

As a jury, we needed to address a key issue: What is the Africa we want to show to the world? How do we strike a balance between showing the realities of the continent – realities such as the effects of the climate crisis or armed conflict – without reinforcing stereotypes?

When sitting on the global jury, I quickly realized fundamental differences in our paradigms. However, despite these fundamental differences, the truth remained that an image that is well executed speaks for itself.

# Jury

–

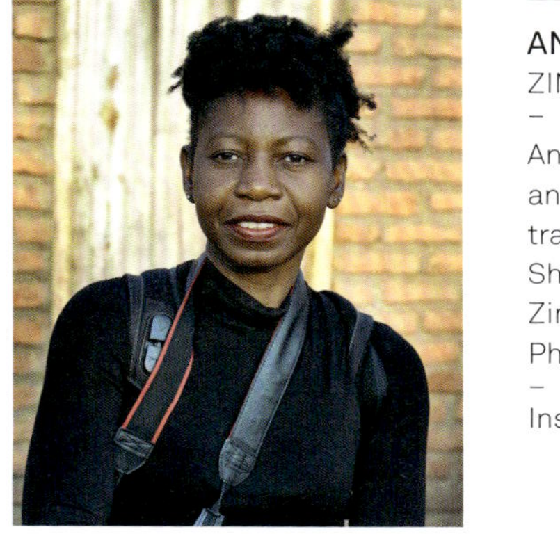

BON MSUNJE

**ANGELA JIMU** / CHAIR
ZIMBABWE/MALAWI

–

Angela Jimu is a storyteller using both text and images, a mentor, and a visual literacy trainer, living between Malawi and Zimbabwe. She is co-founder and director of the Zimbabwe Association of Female Photographers.

–

Instagram: @angjimu

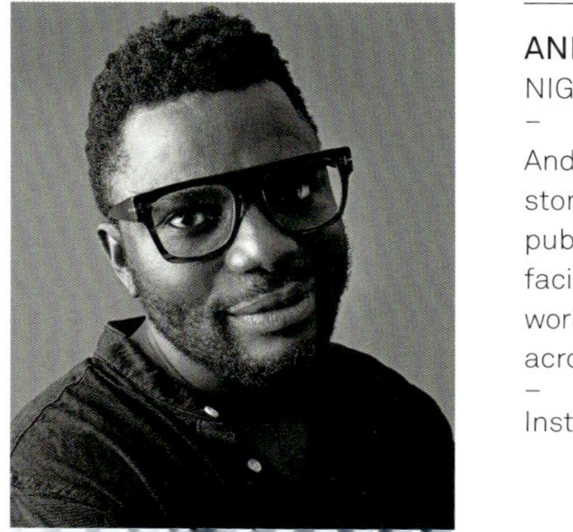

GODSON UKAEGBU

**ANDREW ESIEBO**
NIGERIA

–

Andrew Esiebo is an award-winning visual storyteller, whose works have been widely published and exhibited worldwide. He is a facilitator at StoryMi Academy, developing world-class storytellers and investigators across Africa.

–

Instagram: @andrewesiebo

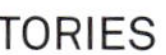

# Winners

–

## SINGLES

**LEE-ANN OLWAGE**
SOUTH AFRICA, 1986

–

Lee-Ann Olwage is a visual storyteller from South Africa. Her work explores themes of identity, transitions and universal narratives through long-term projects. She is a member of Native, Women Photograph, and African Women in Photography.

–

Instagram: @leeannolwage

GORDON DE BRUIN

## STORIES

**NICK HANNES**
BELGIUM, 1974

–

Nick Hannes is a photojournalist and documentary photographer based in Ranst, Belgium. His photography reflects on major contemporary themes such as migration, globalization, urbanization and crisis. Hannes is represented by Panos Pictures.

–

Instagram: @nick.hannes

ANJA PEETERS

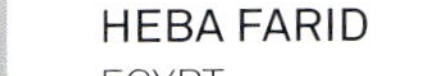

BARRY IVERSON

## HEBA FARID

EGYPT

–

Heba Farid is an artist, curator, researcher, and educator in photography, based in Cairo. She is a co-founder of TINTERA photographic art consultancy in Cairo.

–

## PAUL BOTES

SOUTH AFRICA

–

Paul Botes is an award-winning picture editor for *The Mail & Guardian* and *The Continent*. His work focuses primarily on issues of social justice and inequality.

–

Instagram: @paulbotes

CHERILYN BECKLES

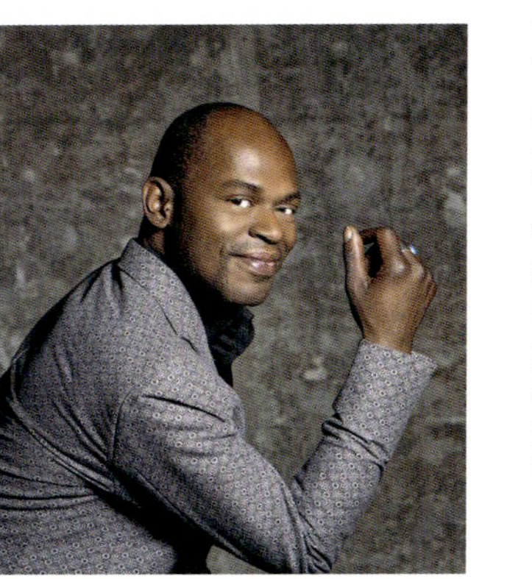

L'ATELIER & BEYOND

## YVES CHATAP

FRANCE/CAMEROON

–

Yves Chatap is a curator, publisher, and art critic, based between Paris and Yaoundé, engaged with institutional and experimental organizations. He is the author of multiple text contributions to trade magazines, exhibition catalogues, and monographs.

–

Instagram: @ychatap

# LONG-TERM PROJECTS

## M'HAMMED KILITO

MOROCCO, 1981

–

M'hammed Kilito is a documentary photographer and National Geographic Explorer based in Casablanca, Morocco. His practice focuses on the relationship between people and their environment, focusing on issues such as cultural identity and climate change.

–

Instagram: @mhammed_kilito

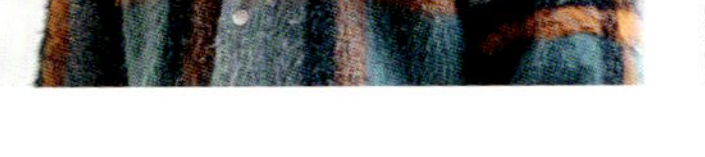

LADIMIR GHEORGHIU

# OPEN FORMAT

## MOHAMED MAHDY

EGYPT, 1996

–

Mohamed Mahdy is a visual storyteller based in Alexandria, Egypt. His work concentrates on the hidden and often unseen communities in Egypt, tackling diverse cultural and social issues.

–

Instagram: @mohamedmahdyph

RALITSA BELCHEVA

# Asia

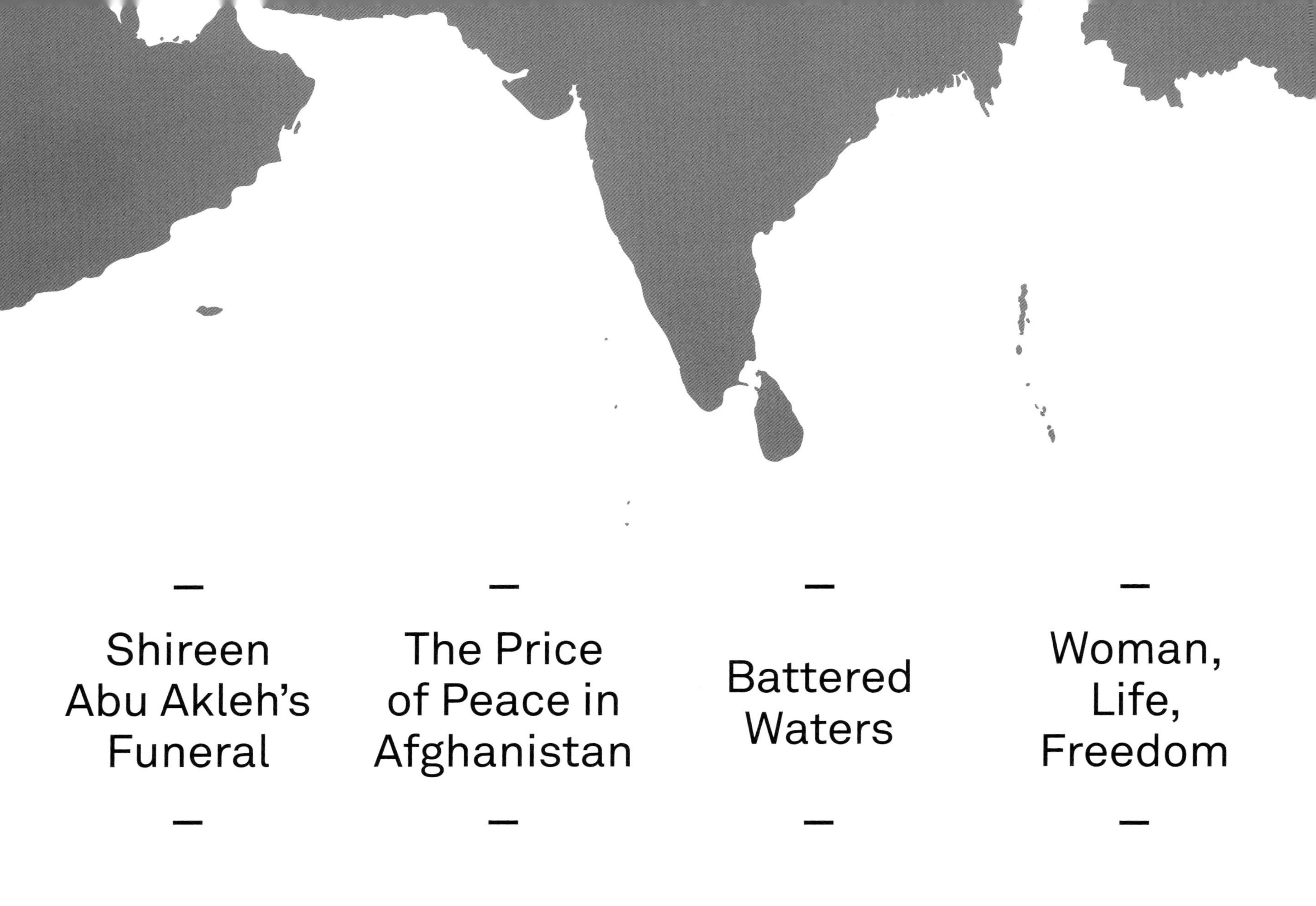

—
Shireen Abu Akleh's Funeral
—

—
The Price of Peace in Afghanistan
—

—
Battered Waters
—

—
Woman, Life, Freedom
—

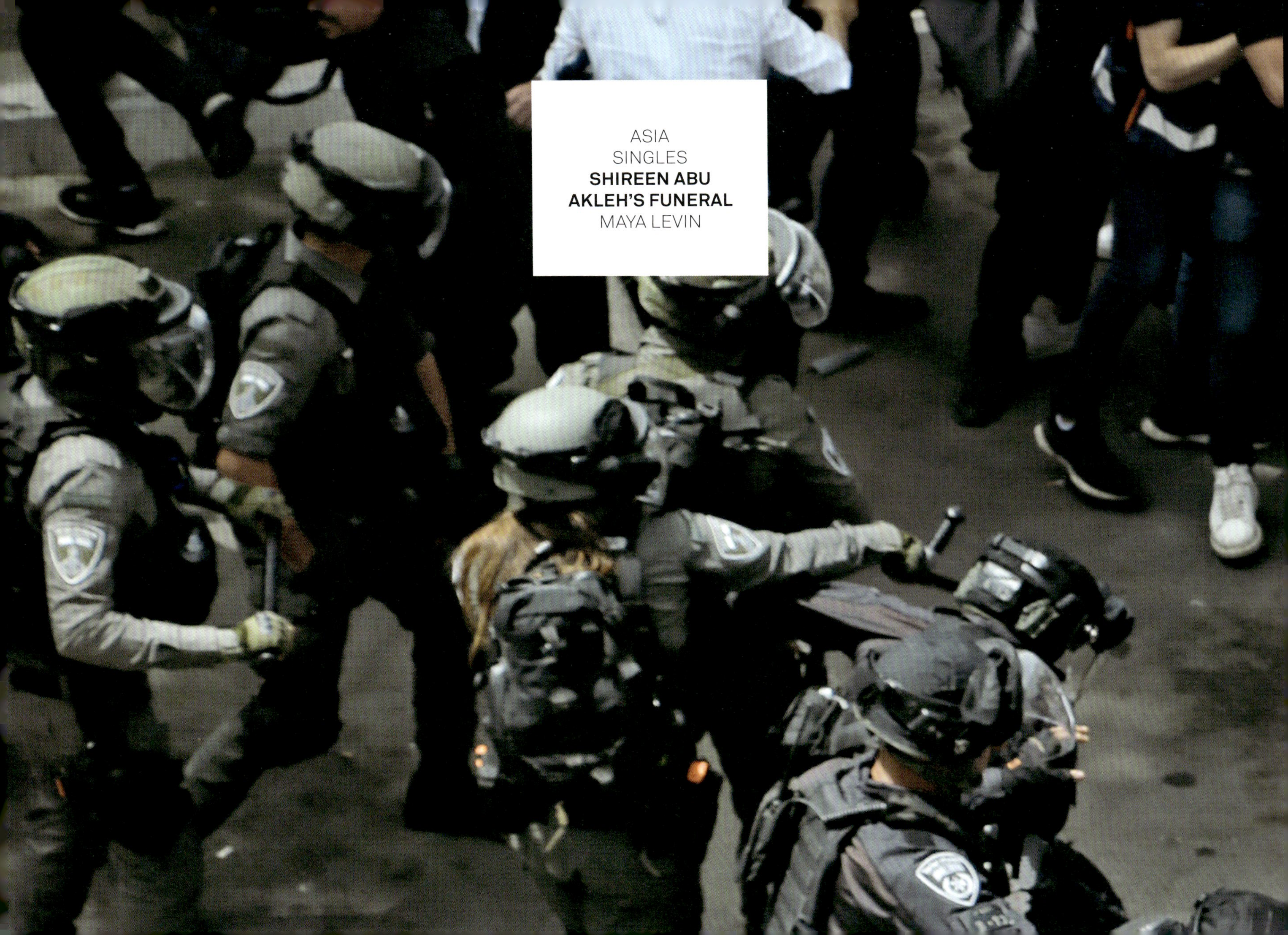

ASIA
SINGLES
**SHIREEN ABU AKLEH'S FUNERAL**
MAYA LEVIN

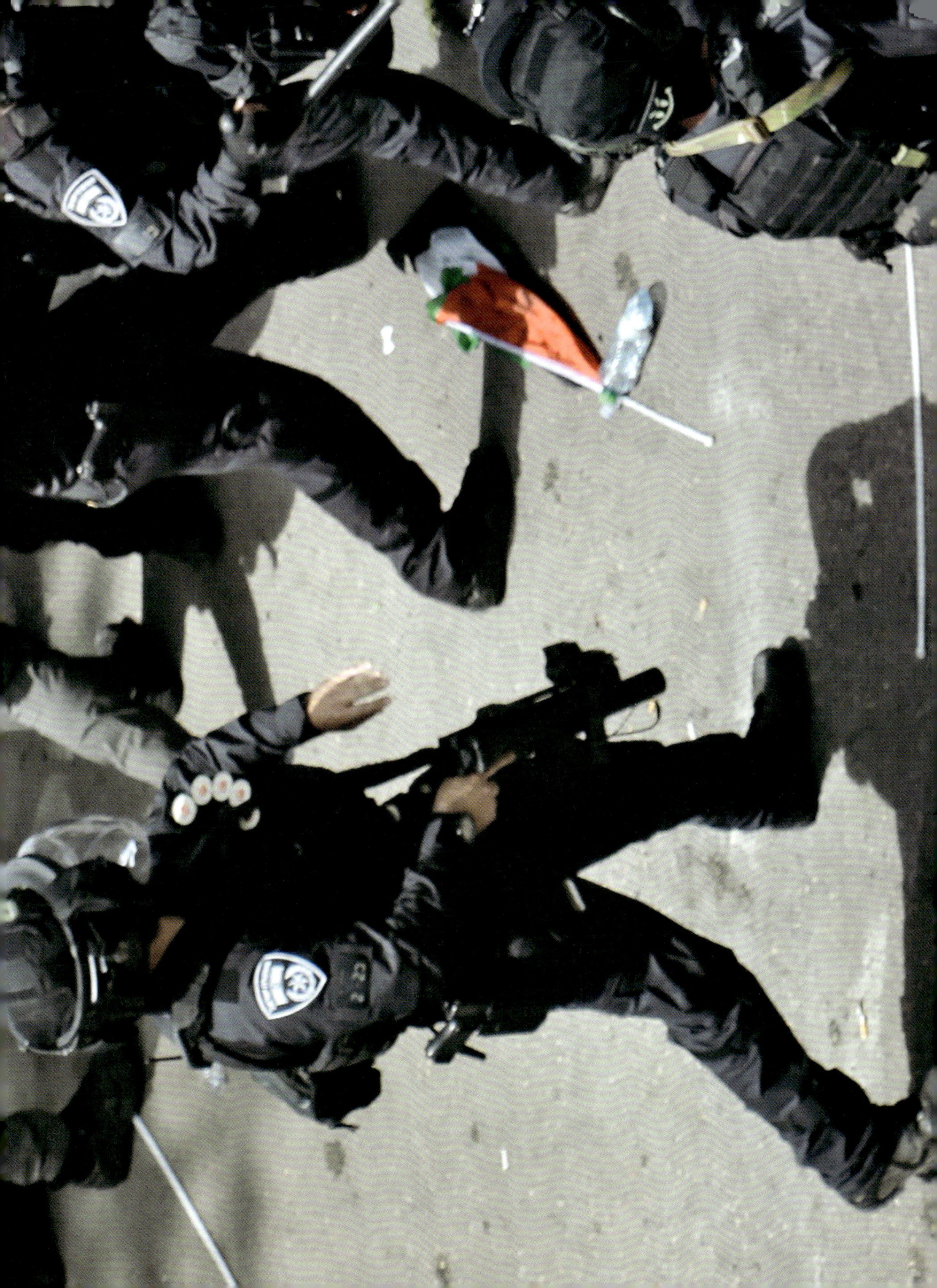

# Shireen Abu Akleh's Funeral

Israeli police beat mourners accompanying the coffin of Al Jazeera journalist Shireen Abu Akleh to her funeral, in East Jerusalem, on 13 May 2022. Police prohibited people from carrying the coffin on foot through the city, which is customary for notable deaths, as mourners chanted "We sacrifice our soul and blood for you, Shireen."

Abu Akleh, a veteran reporter of the Palestinian-Israeli conflict, was shot two days earlier while covering an Israeli military raid in Jenin, West Bank. Another journalist was wounded at the scene. After initial denials, the Israeli military has since admitted there was a "high possibility" Abu Akleh was shot by an Israeli soldier.

Maya Levin photographed this image on assignment for Associated Press.

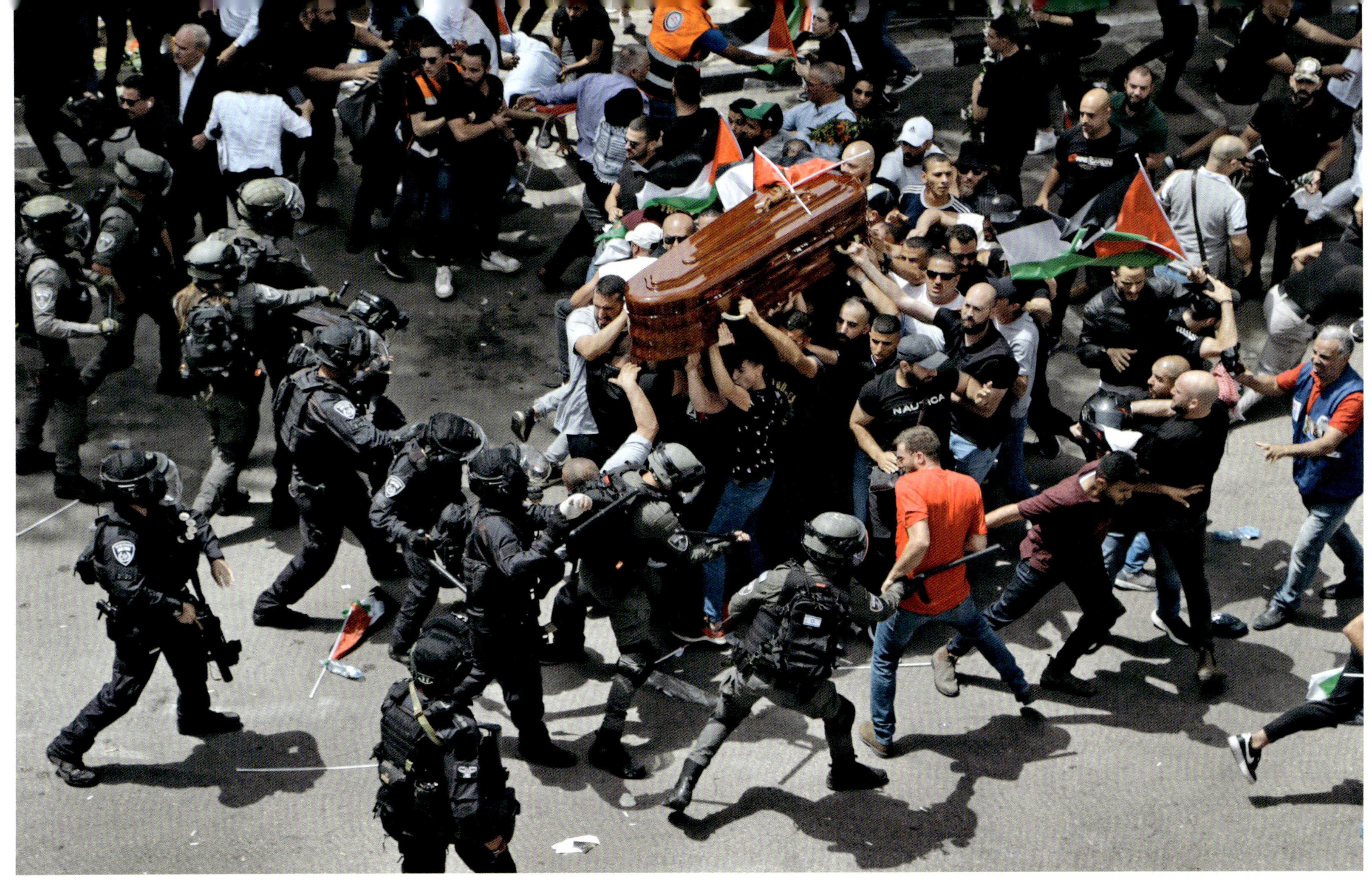
NAUTICA

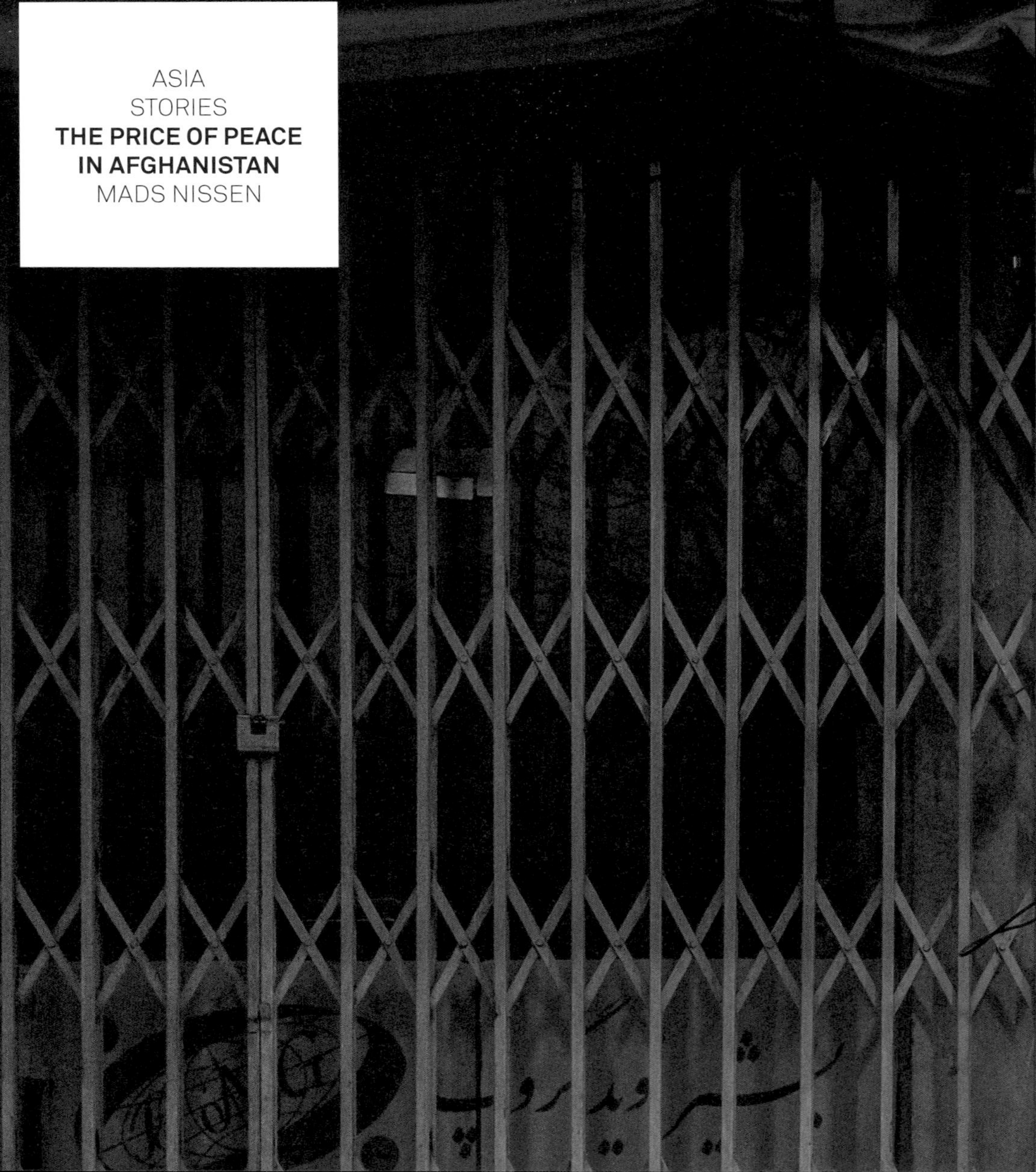

ASIA
STORIES
**THE PRICE OF PEACE IN AFGHANISTAN**
MADS NISSEN

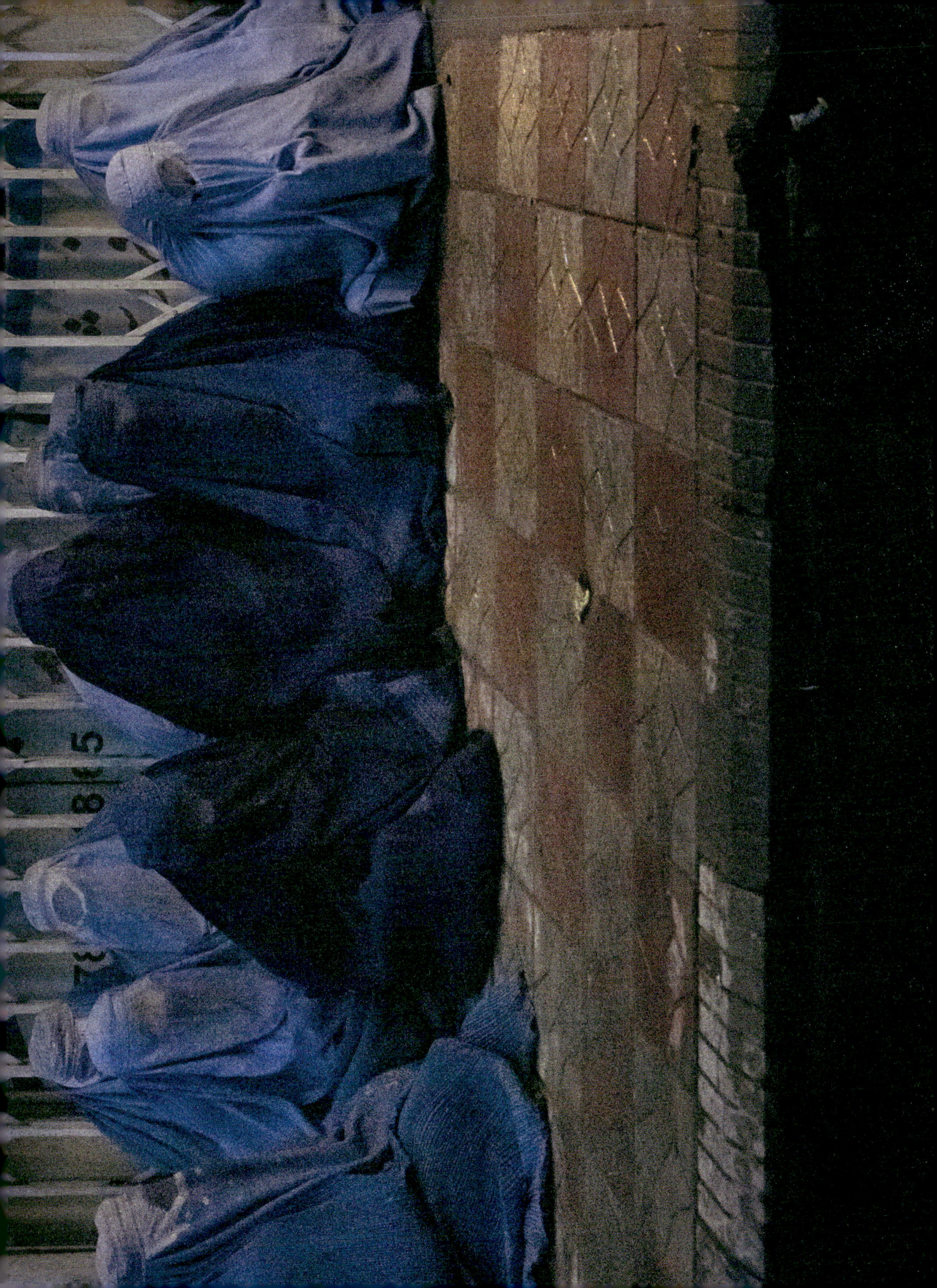

# The Price of Peace in Afghanistan

After the withdrawal of US and allied forces from Afghanistan in August 2021, the Taliban returned to power. In response, other nations stopped providing foreign aid and froze billions of dollars of government reserves deposited abroad. Intense droughts in 2022 exacerbated the economic crisis; currently half of the country's population do not have enough to eat and over a million children are severely malnourished according to the UN. This story captures the many difficulties Afghan people face in their daily lives.

Mads Nissen photographed these images on assignment for *Politiken*.
He is a member of Panos Pictures.

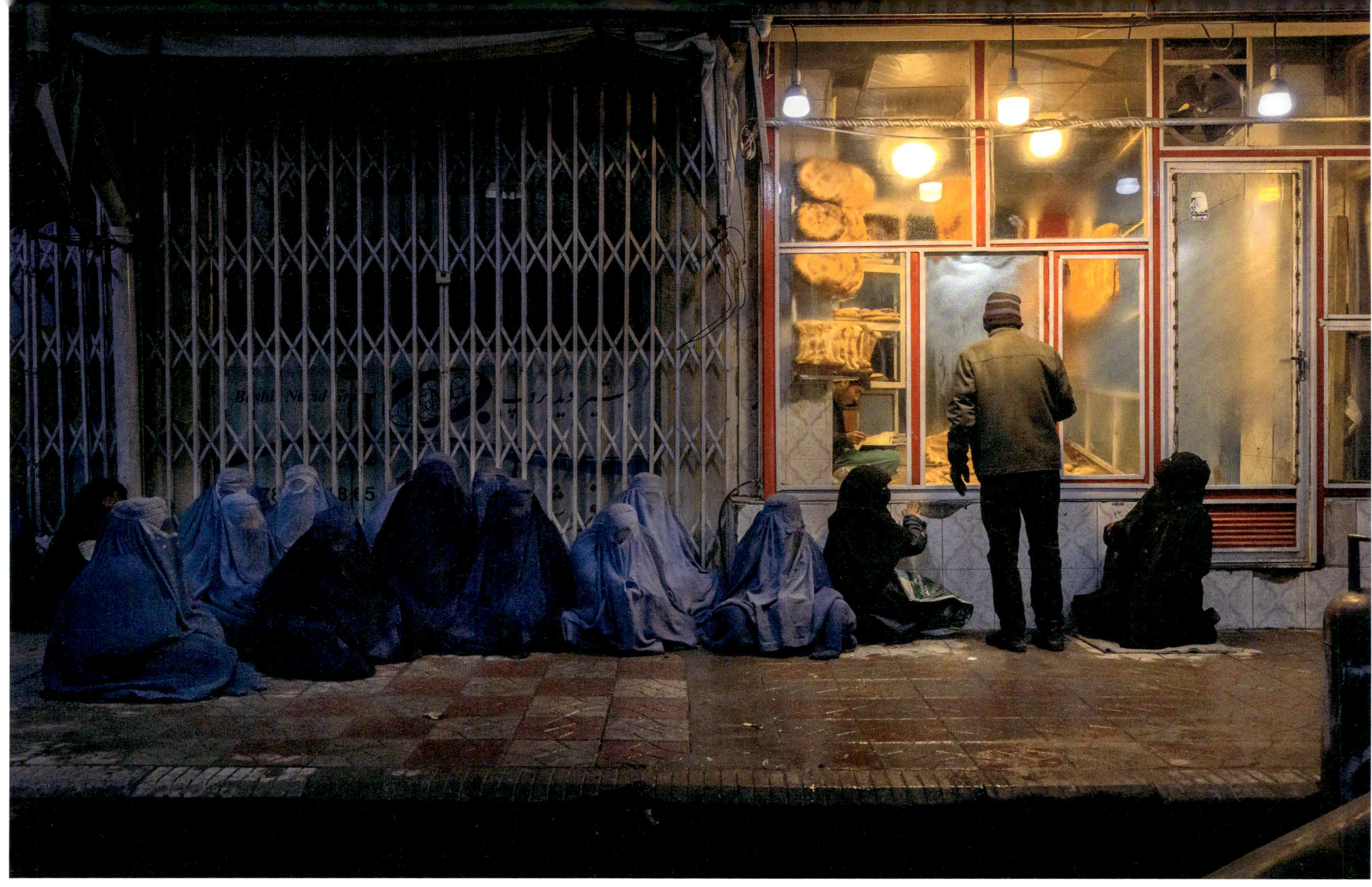

Women and children beg for bread outside a bakery in central Kabul, Afghanistan, on 14 January 2022

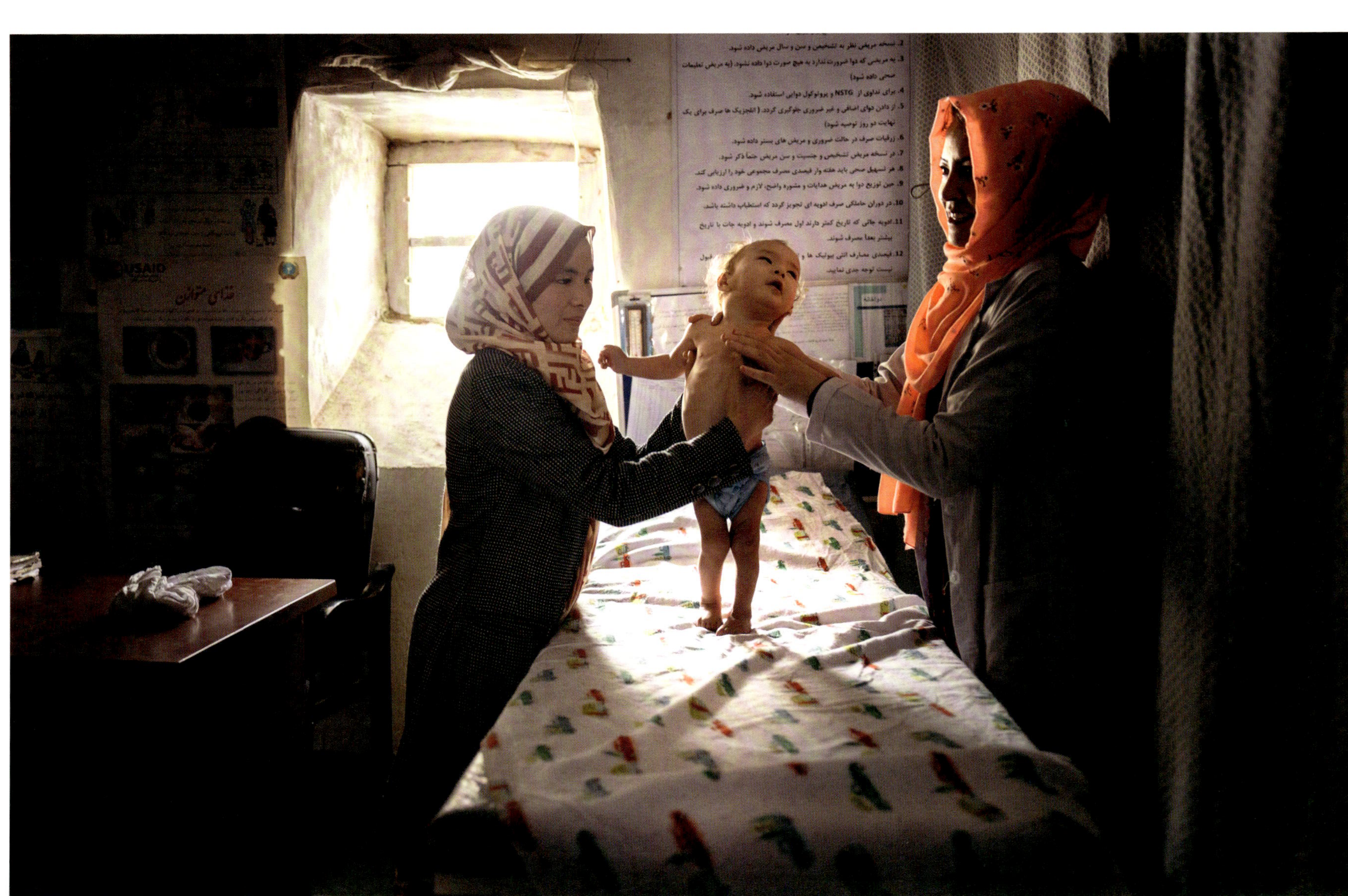

Hojatullah (11 months old) is examined at a small clinic in Alibeg, Afghanistan, on 12 January 2022. He is already suffering from severe malnutrition, a common problem in this village where most survive on a daily diet of white bread and tea.

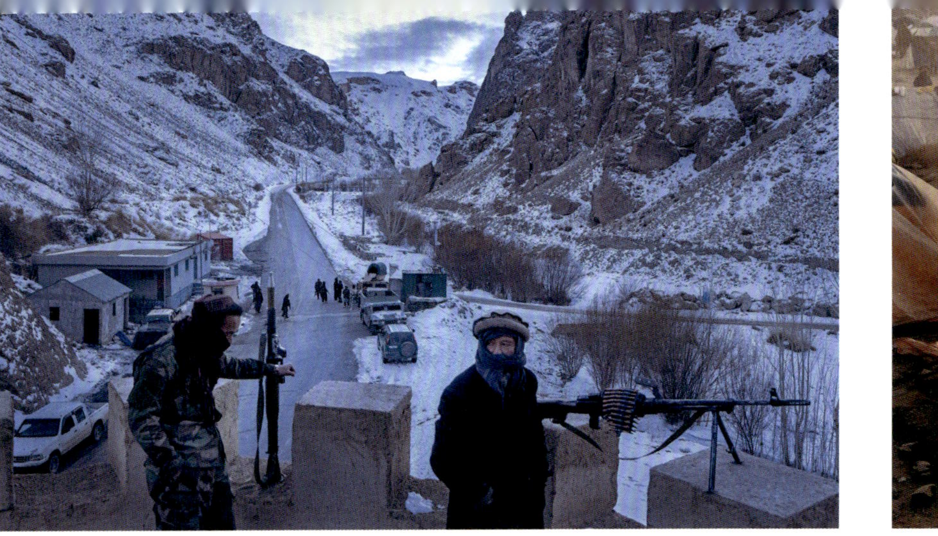

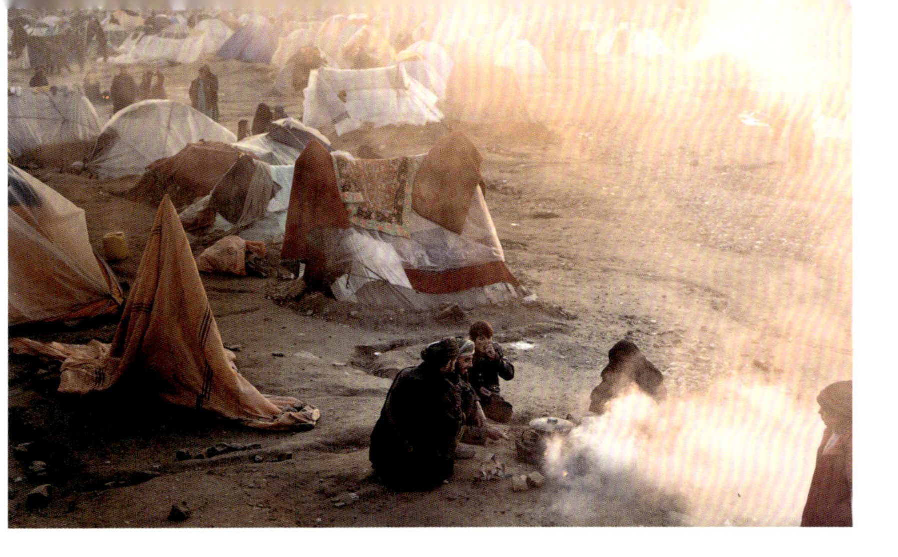

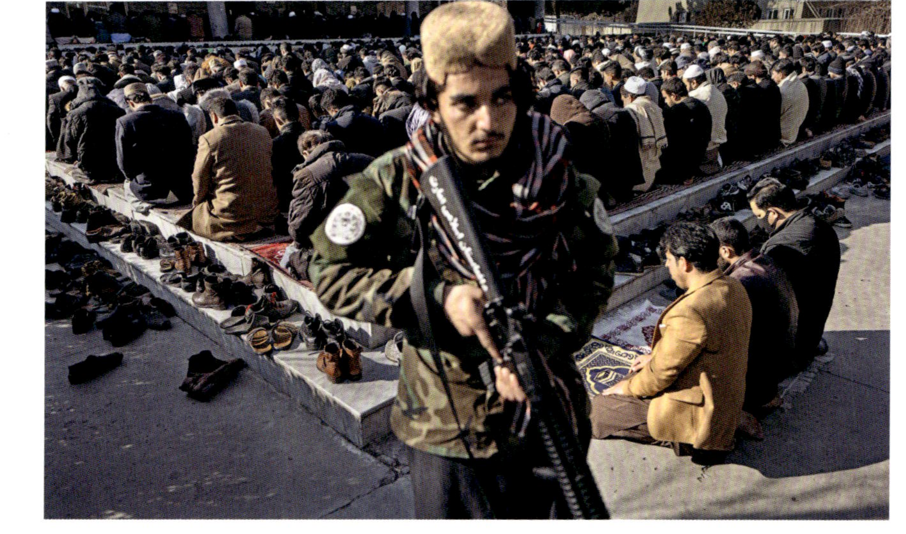

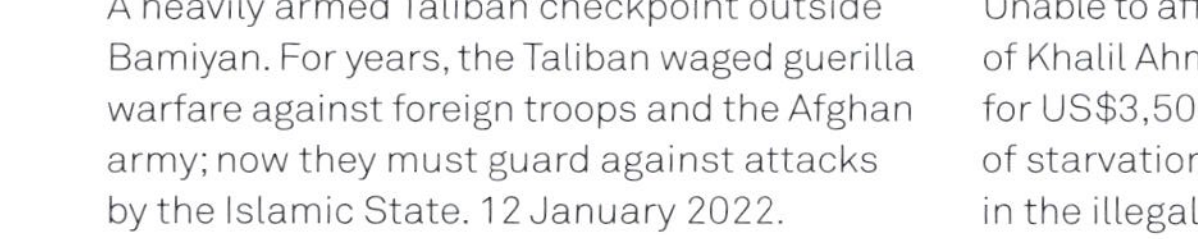

A heavily armed Taliban checkpoint outside Bamiyan. For years, the Taliban waged guerilla warfare against foreign troops and the Afghan army; now they must guard against attacks by the Islamic State. 12 January 2022.

Unable to afford food for the family, the parents of Khalil Ahmad (15) decided to sell his kidney for US$3,500. The lack of jobs and the threat of starvation has led to a dramatic increase in the illegal organ trade. Herat, Afghanistan, 19 January 2022.

A family cooks over a fire made with plastic, in a camp on the outskirts of Herat, Afghanistan, on 19 January 2022. Thousands of people moved into informal camps as a result of the food crisis, according to Amnesty International.

Sohalullah Hejrat (19) stands guard over Friday prayer at Sher Shah Suri Mosque in Kabul, Afghanistan, 14 January 2022. He has been with the Taliban for three years.

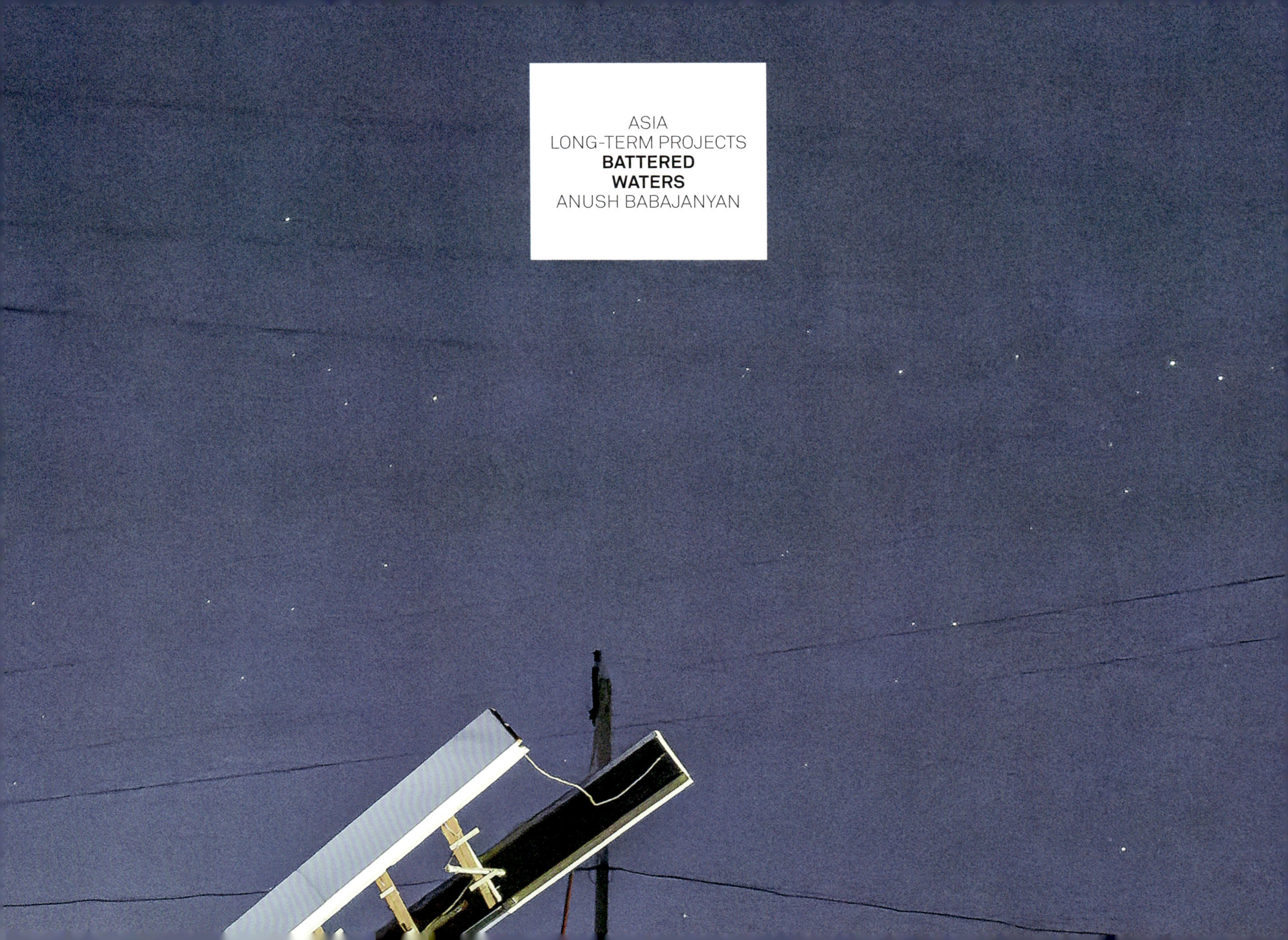

ASIA
LONG-TERM PROJECTS

**BATTERED WATERS**

ANUSH BABAJANYAN

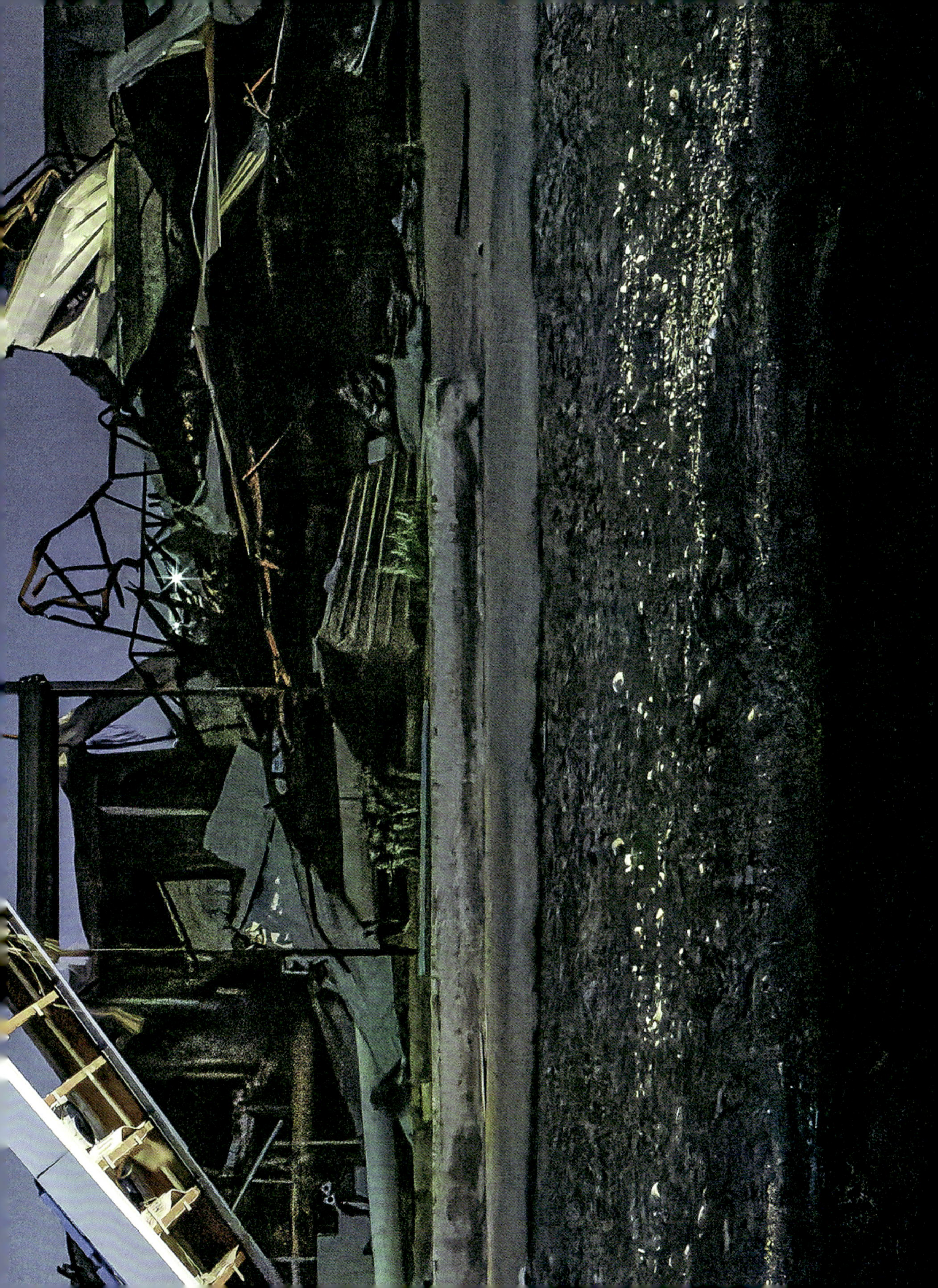

# Battered Waters

Four landlocked Central Asian countries are struggling with the climate crisis and lack of coordination over the water supplies they share. Tajikistan and Kyrgyzstan, upstream on the Syr Darya and Amu Darya rivers, need extra energy in winter. Downstream, Uzbekistan and Kazakhstan need water in summer for agriculture.

Historically, the countries seasonally traded fossil-fuel energy for water released from upstream dams, but since the fall of the USSR and the rise of privatized industries, this system has become imbalanced. Unsustainable use of water and recent intense droughts compound the challenges.

Anush Babajanyan is a member of VII Photo Agency and photographed this story with the support of the National Geographic Society.

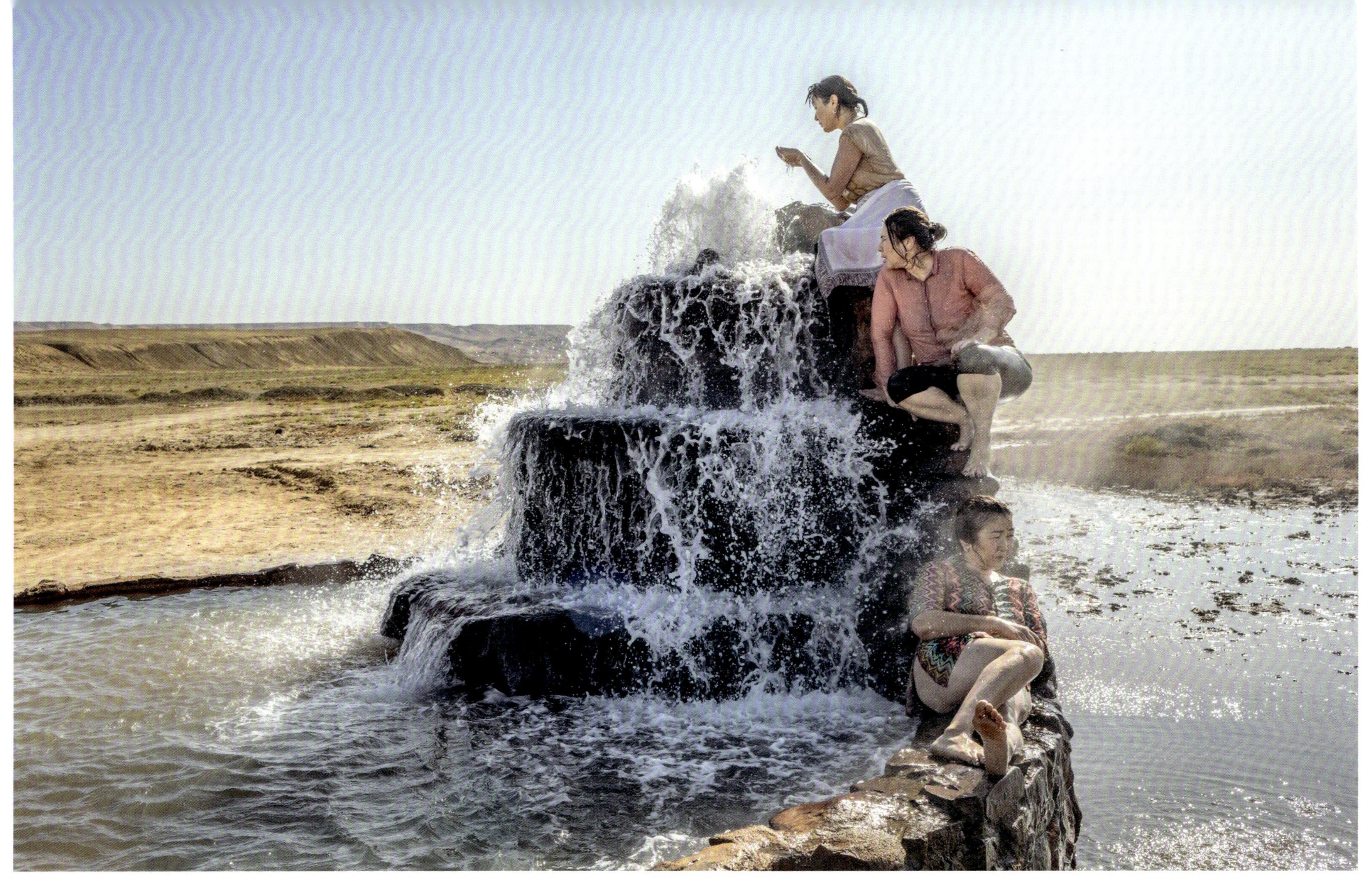

Women visit a hot spring that has emerged from the dried bed of the Aral Sea, near Akespe village, Kazakhstan, on 27 August 2019. Once the world's fourth-largest lake, the Aral Sea has lost 90 percent of its content since river water has been diverted.

Buildings lie in ruins on the Kyrgyzstan side of the Kyrgyzstan-Tajikistan border, on 15 July 2021. Disagreements over a water distribution source had turned into cross-border violence some weeks earlier.

Sonunbek Kadyrov pilots his water taxi, serving the village of Kyzyl-Beyit, Kyrgyzstan, on 16 March 2021. Local access to the main road was blocked by flooding during construction of the Toktogul Dam in the 1960s.

Visitors photograph the Rogun Dam, being built in eastern Tajikistan to provide hydroelectric power, on 22 March 2022. The 335-meter-high dam is due for completion in 2028-2029.

Girls cross a street in Norak, Tajikistan, on 21 March 2022. The Norak Hydroelectric Station provides 70 percent of the country's electricity. Dam water levels fell by four meters in 2021.

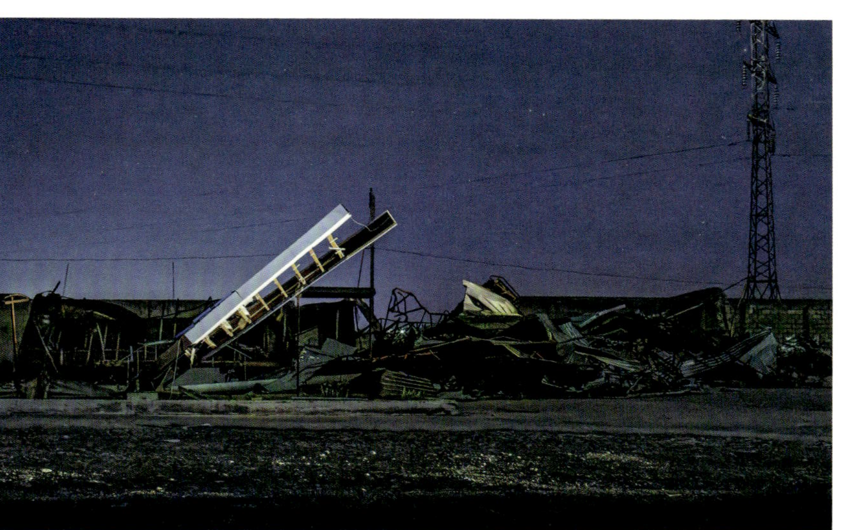

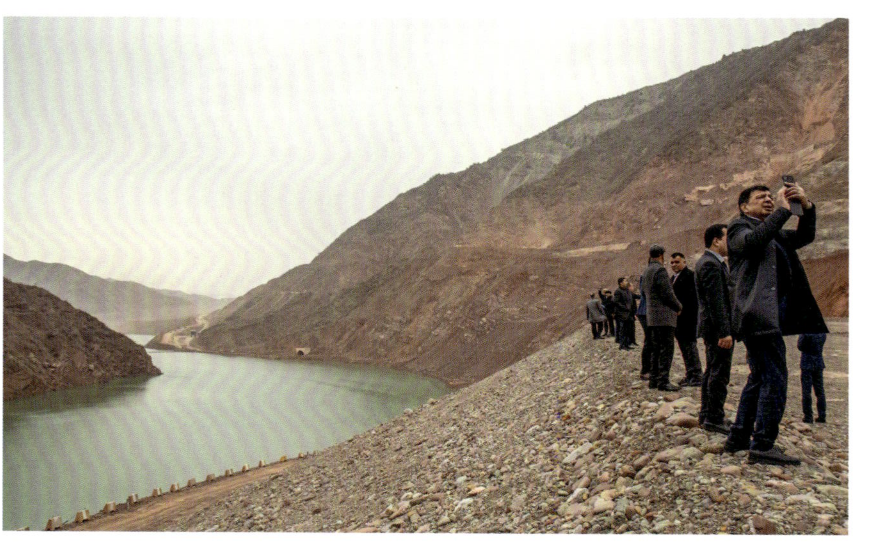

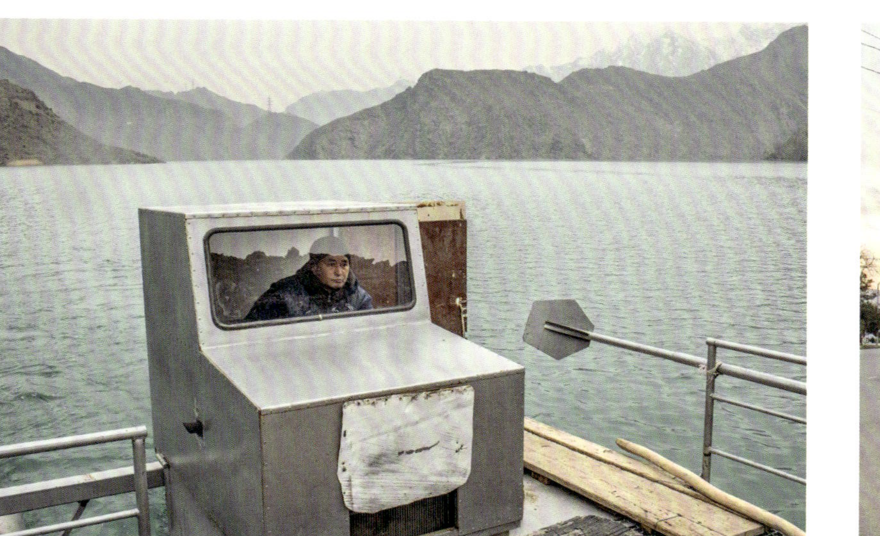

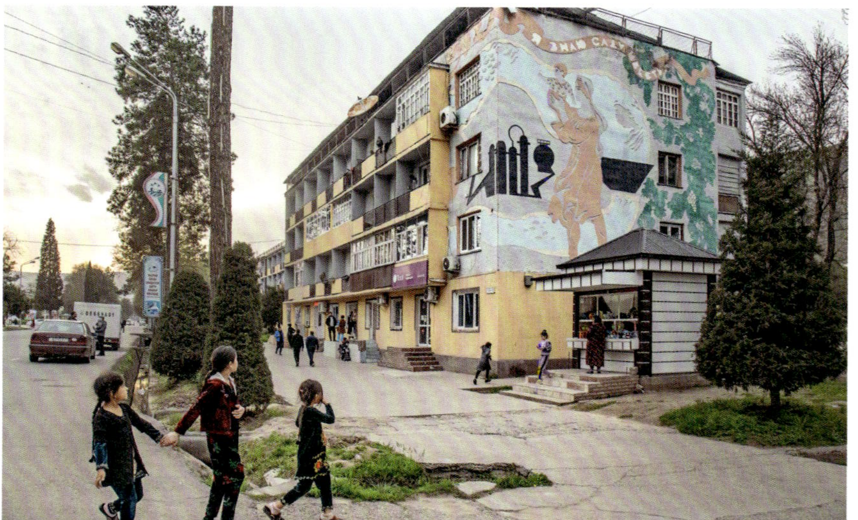

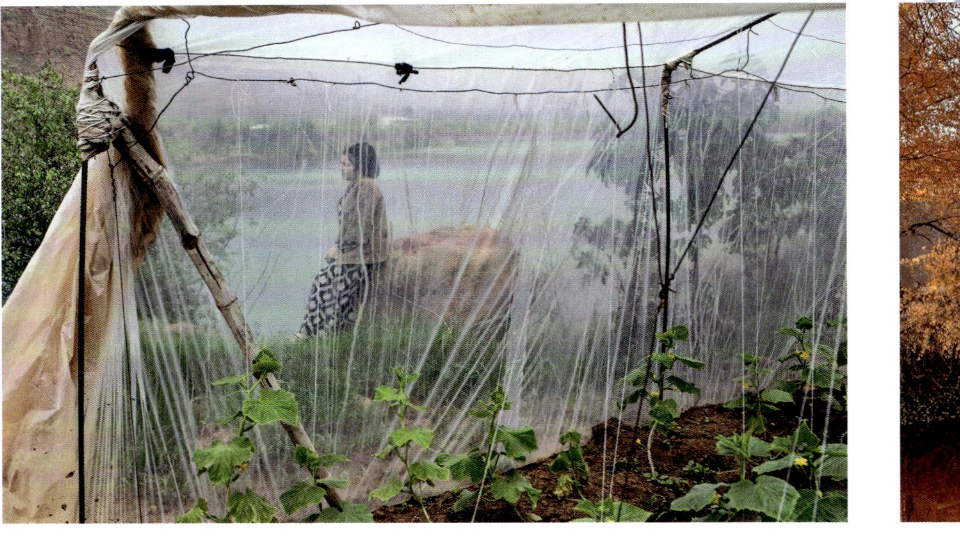

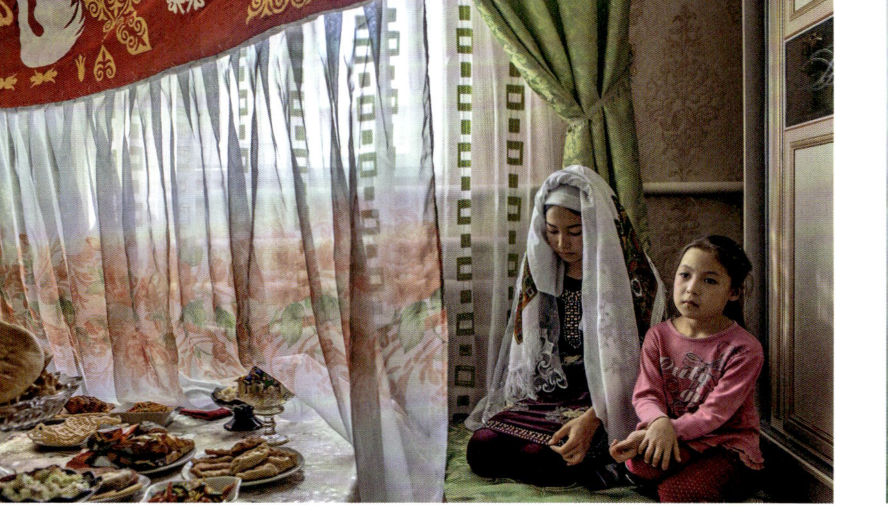

An inhabitant of the village Istiqlol, Tajikistan, rests beside her greenhouse on the River Vakhsh, a tributary of the Amu Darya, on 23 March 2022. She uses river water to irrigate her cucumbers.

Dinara (18) sits with a relative on her wedding day in Muynak, Uzbekistan, on 27 October 2019. Once a port on the Aral Sea, Muynak is now more than 150 kilometers from the coast. Dinara's father and new husband travel there to work as shrimp farmers.

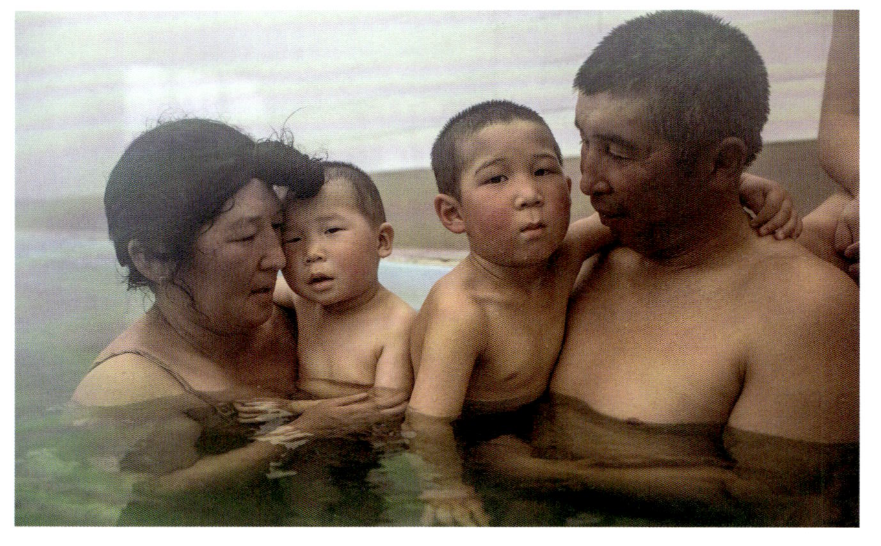

Silt in the Amu Darya in Uzbekistan gives the water a dark red color, as water levels in the river continue to decrease. 28 October 2019.

Jaynagul Brjieva and her family enjoy an outing to a hot spring in Kaji-Say, Kyrgyzstan, on 9 March 2021. The waters are thought by some to have healing properties.

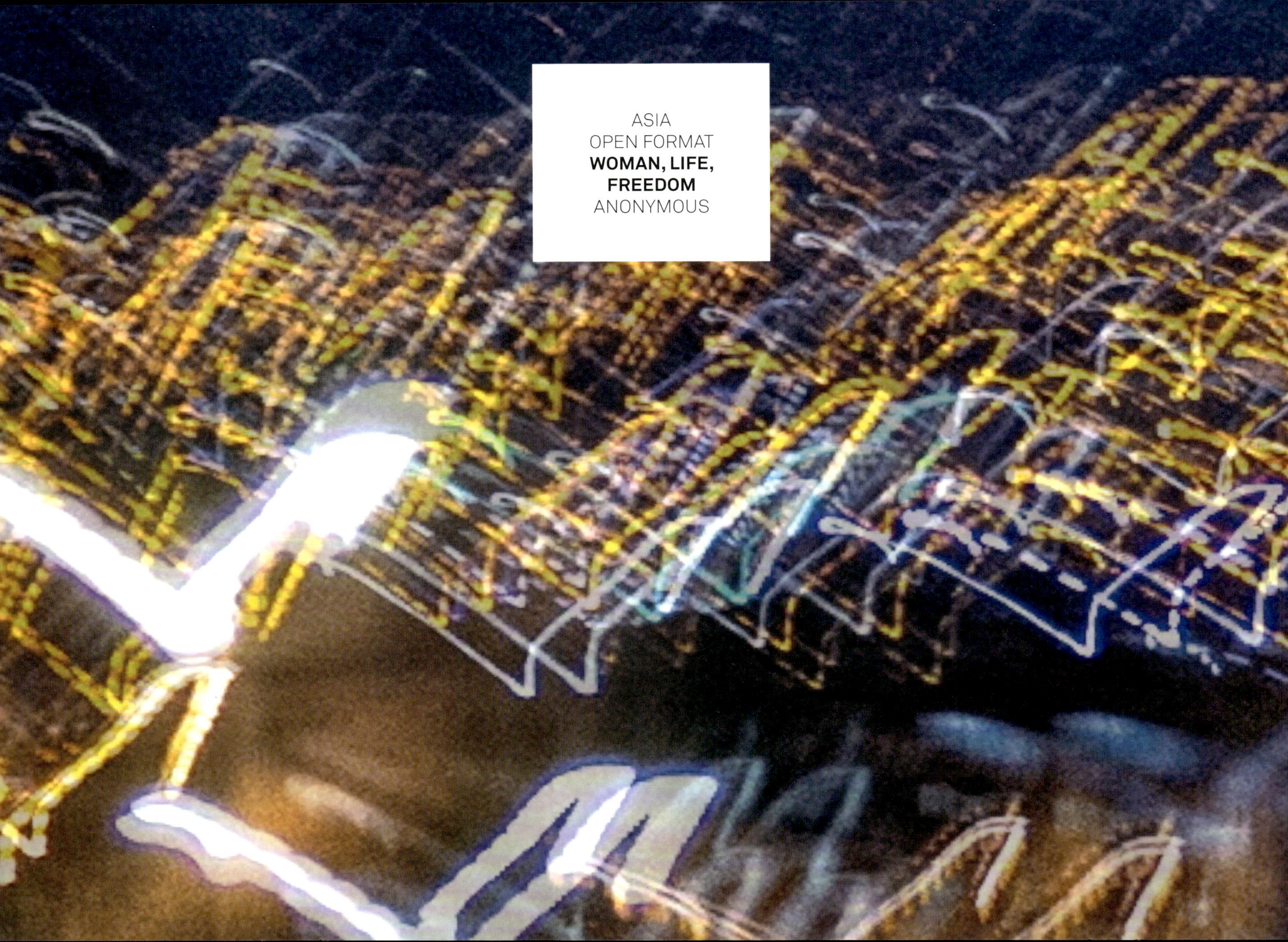

ASIA
OPEN FORMAT
**WOMAN, LIFE, FREEDOM**
ANONYMOUS

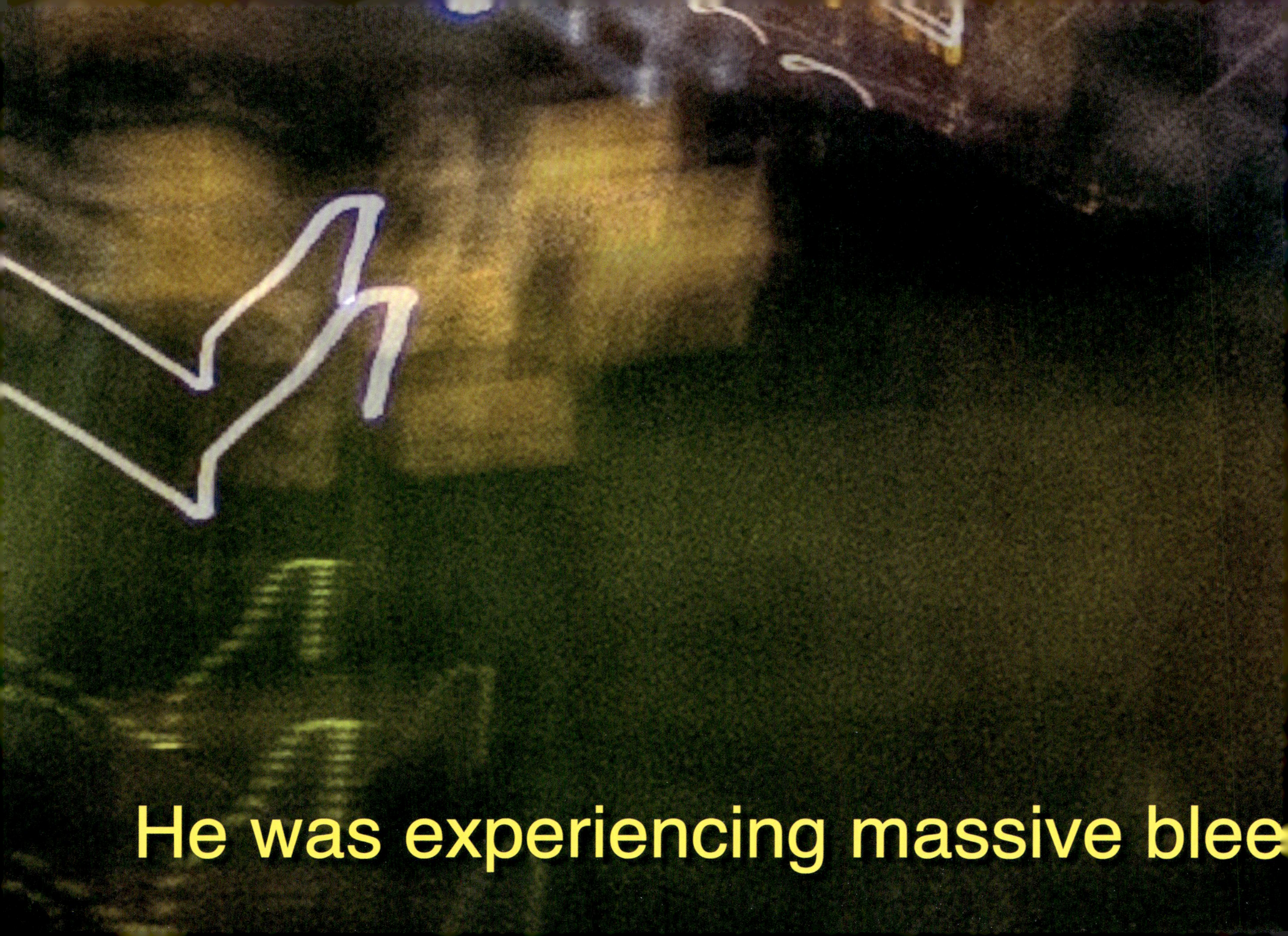
He was experiencing massive blee

Scan the QR code to watch the video.

# Woman, Life, Freedom

This photo-based video project narrates one chaotic night in the life of an Iranian nurse as she saves the life of a young protester named Reza. It offers a rare glimpse into the dangers faced by protestors on the streets of Iran today. On 16 September 2022, Mahsa "Jina" Amini, a 22-year-old Kurdish woman, died after she was arrested by Iran's morality police for allegedly violating the rules restricting the dress and conduct of women. The ensuing protests quickly intensified, spreading across the country. The Islamic Republic regime responded by disrupting internet access and violently repressing uprisings. Because hospitals are controlled by the regime, anyone injured in the protests risks arrest and further abuse upon seeking medical attention. Photographer Hossein Fatemi encountered the nurse in the video while providing support to local Iranian photographers covering the protests. Images and video for this project were captured by local photojournalists, the nurse herself, and a photographer on assignment to cover her story.

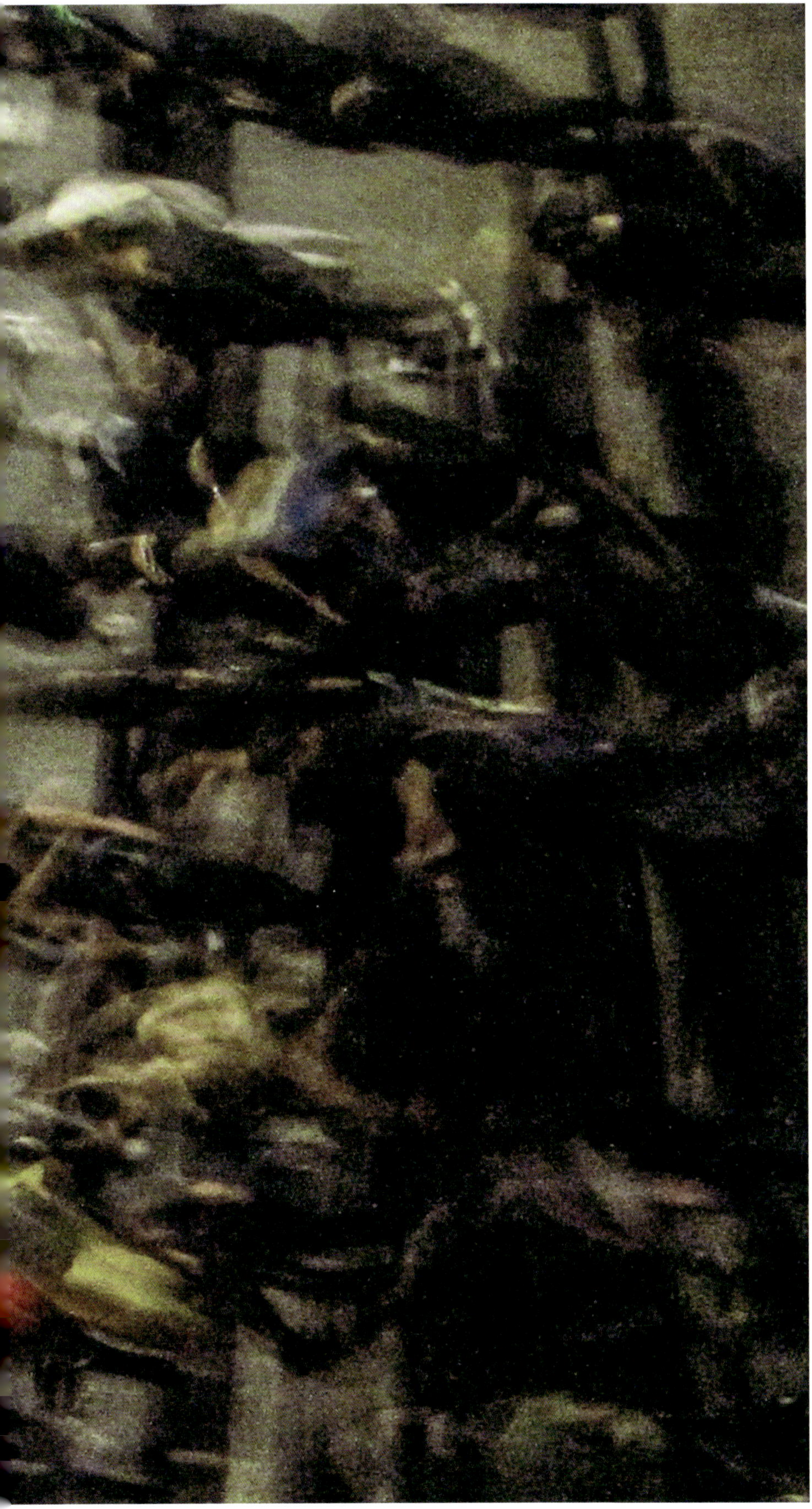

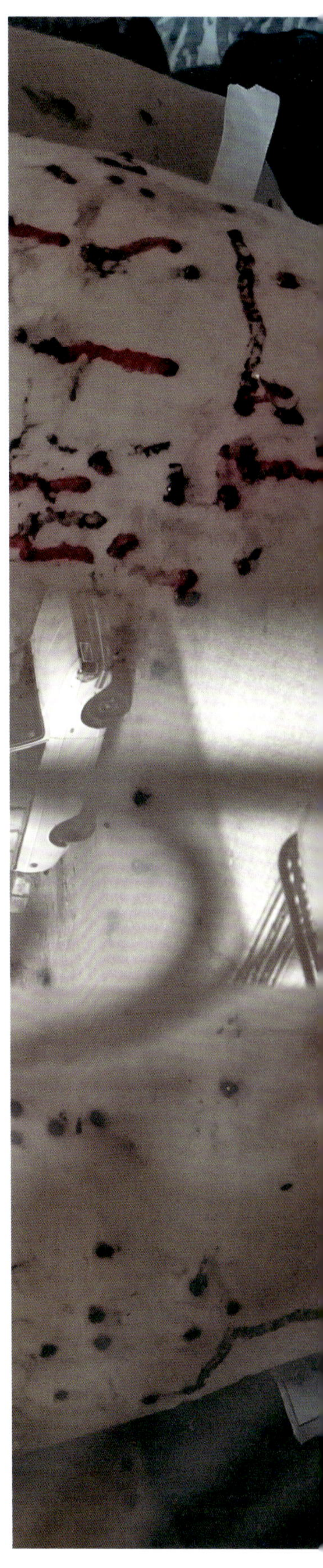

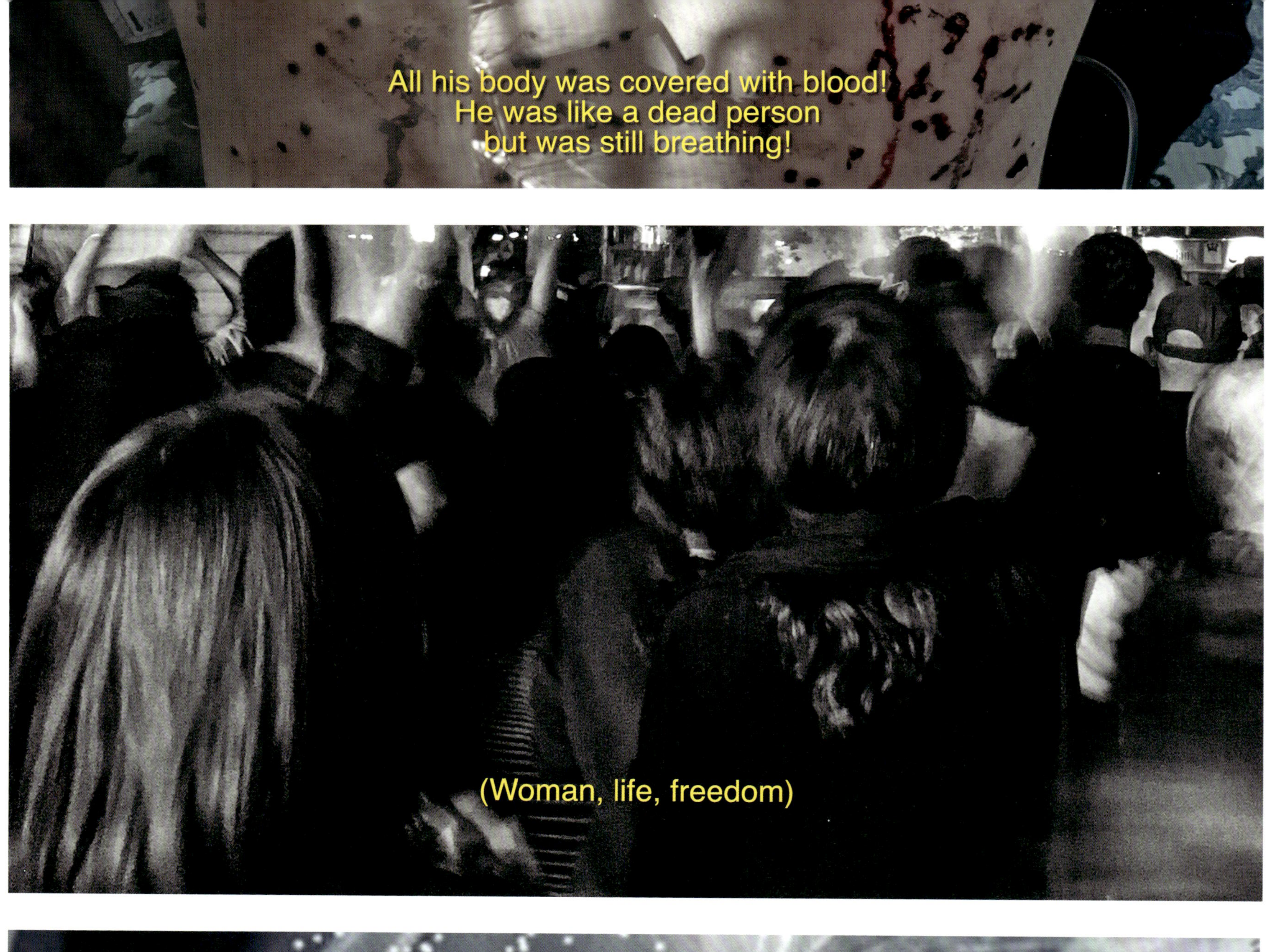
All his body was covered with blood!
He was like a dead person
but was still breathing!
(Woman, life, freedom)

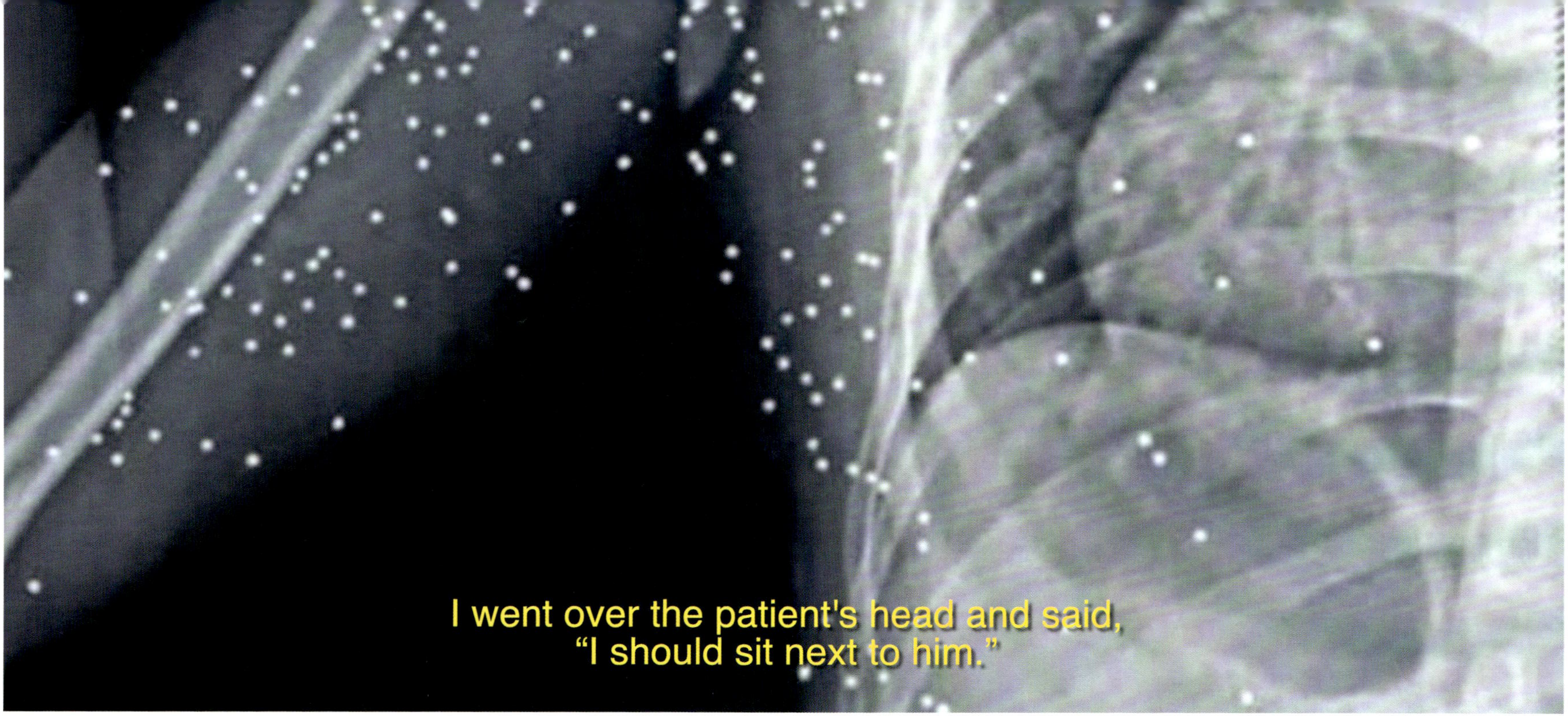

I went over the patient's head and said,
"I should sit next to him."

Journalists and photographers attempting to report on the protests face reprisals from the Iranian regime, ranging from intimidation to arrest and violent abuse. Due to these efforts, it is difficult to know what is really happening inside the country. Many of the photographers who captured the images seen here will remain anonymous for security reasons.

Story, Executive Producer: Hossein Fatemi / Editor: Hamid Reza
Producer: Q.S / Licence: Middle East Images/Iranwire
Photographers: 10 anonymous Middle East Images photographers

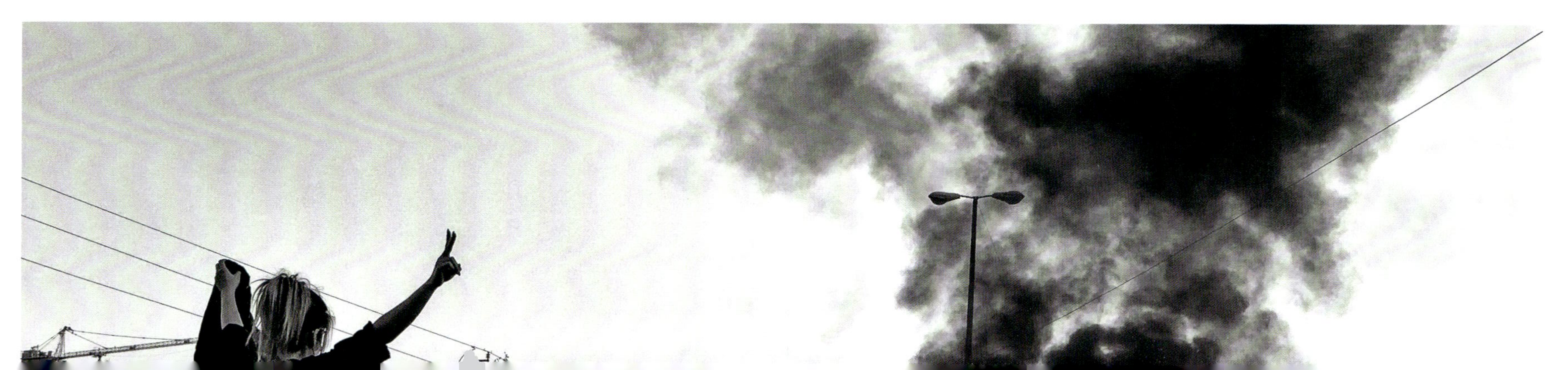

ASIA

# HONORABLE MENTIONS

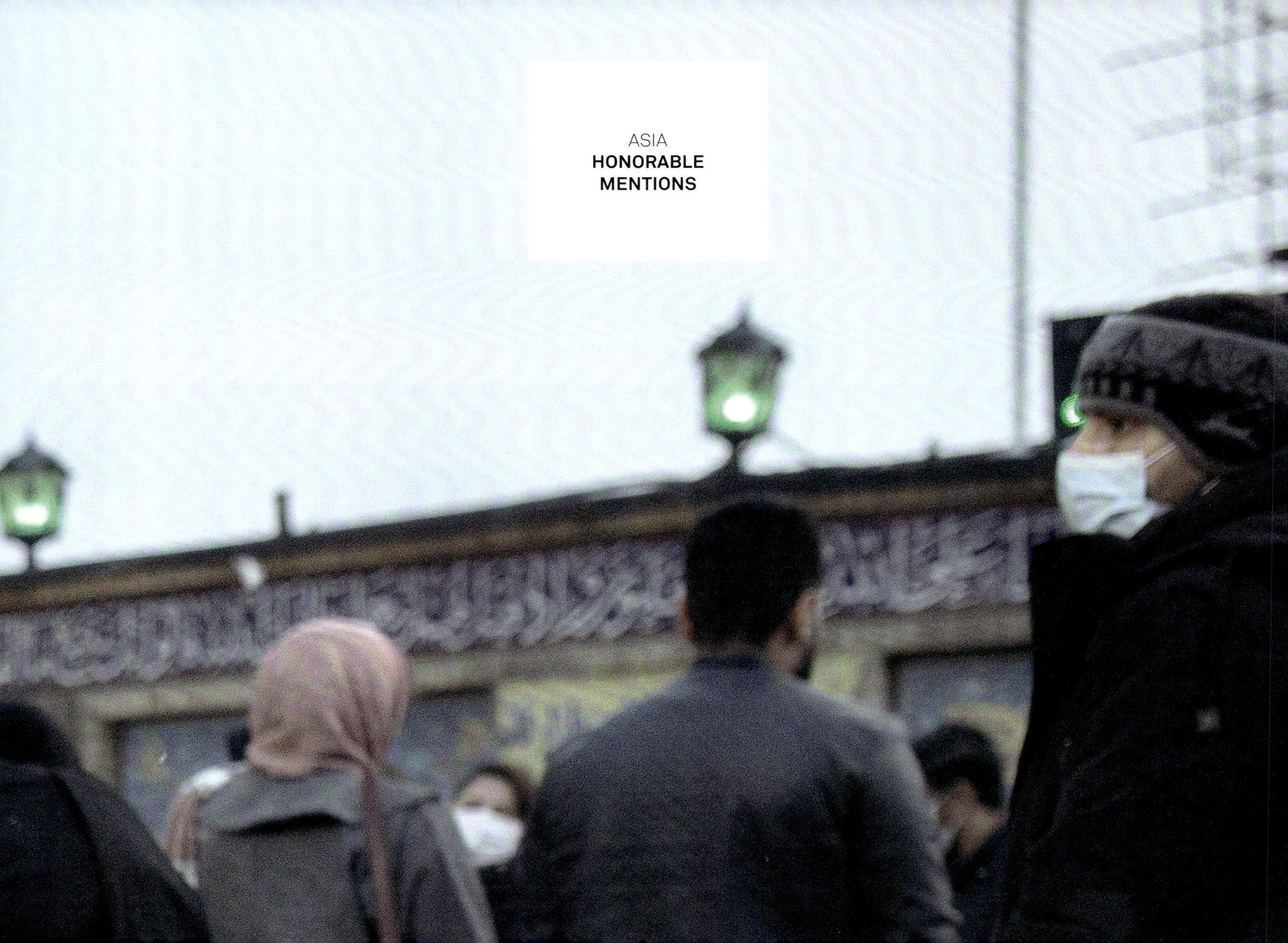

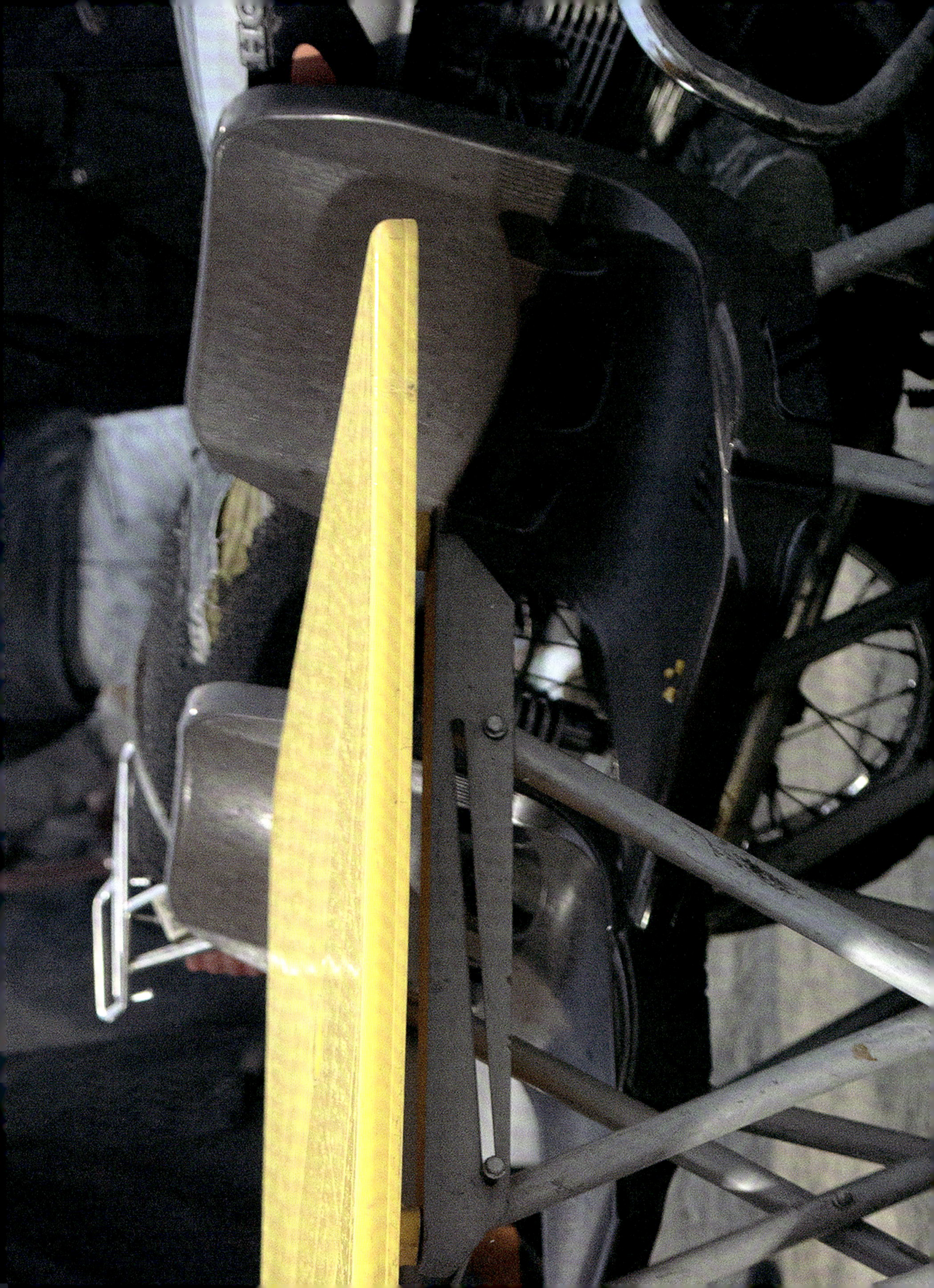

# Untitled

—

An Iranian woman sits on a chair in front of a busy square in Tehran, defying the mandatory hijab law, on 27 December 2022. “A few days after Mahsa’s death, I was walking past Keshavarzi Boulevard when I saw a massive crowd of men and women, young and old, chanting a slogan that I’ve never heard before: ‘Woman, Life, Freedom’. It enlightened me, it was moving,” she said.

Massive protests in Iran began after the arrest and death of Mahsa “Jina” Amini, a 22-year-old Kurdish woman who was taken into custody by the Islamic Republic’s morality police for allegedly violating the country’s mandatory hijab law. Despite the violent attacks on protestors, the protests spread rapidly to regions across the country, encompassing all age groups and social classes. To demonstrate their opposition to the government, women in Iran have been going out in public without wearing a hijab, turning everyday life into an act of civil disobedience.

Ahmad Halabisaz
Iran, 1984
–
Ahmad Halabisaz is a freelance photojournalist and visual storyteller who focuses on social issues, personal projects and documenting the impact of conflict, mostly in the Middle East.
–
Instagram: @Ahmad.halabisaz

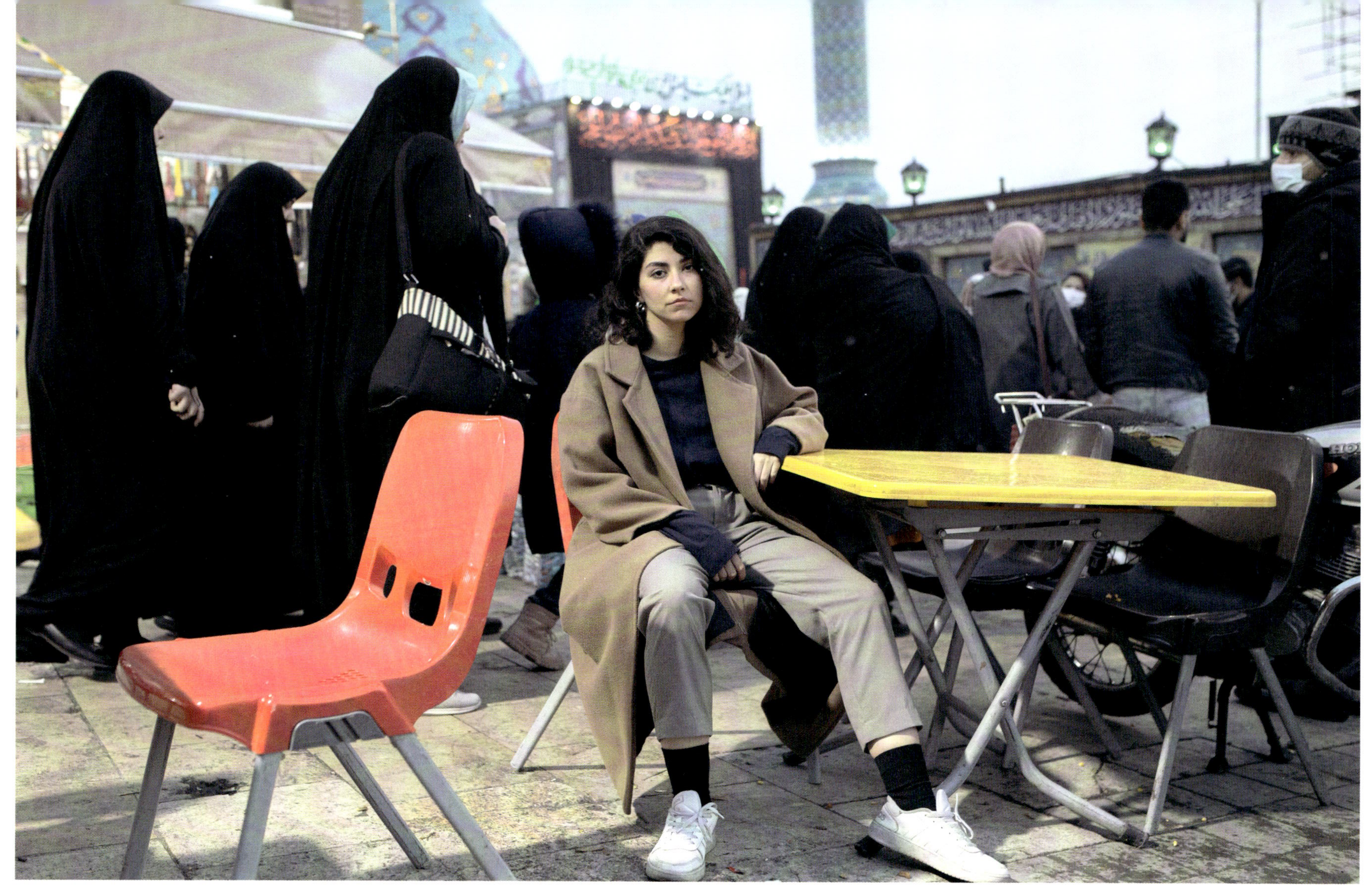

# Faint Light in the Unfinished Building

—

These simple, quiet images tell a complex story of the suffering that the real estate market crisis has caused for ordinary people. Chinese households invest up to 70 percent of their wealth into real estate. Demand for home ownership has created a decade-long boom in residential property construction and financing. However, a presale system led to a debt crisis for housing developers. Financing developments became more difficult and construction on many homes was halted. Although they ended up owning homes that may never be completed, these buyers still need to repay their mortgages. The fallout from this crisis has rippled through the domestic banking sector and the world's markets.

Weimin Chu
China, 1990

–

Weimin Chu is a professional photographer based in Chongqing, China. His works document changing landscapes and the effect this has on people's lives, focusing on long-term projects in Greenland and China.

–

Instagram: @thomaschuphoto

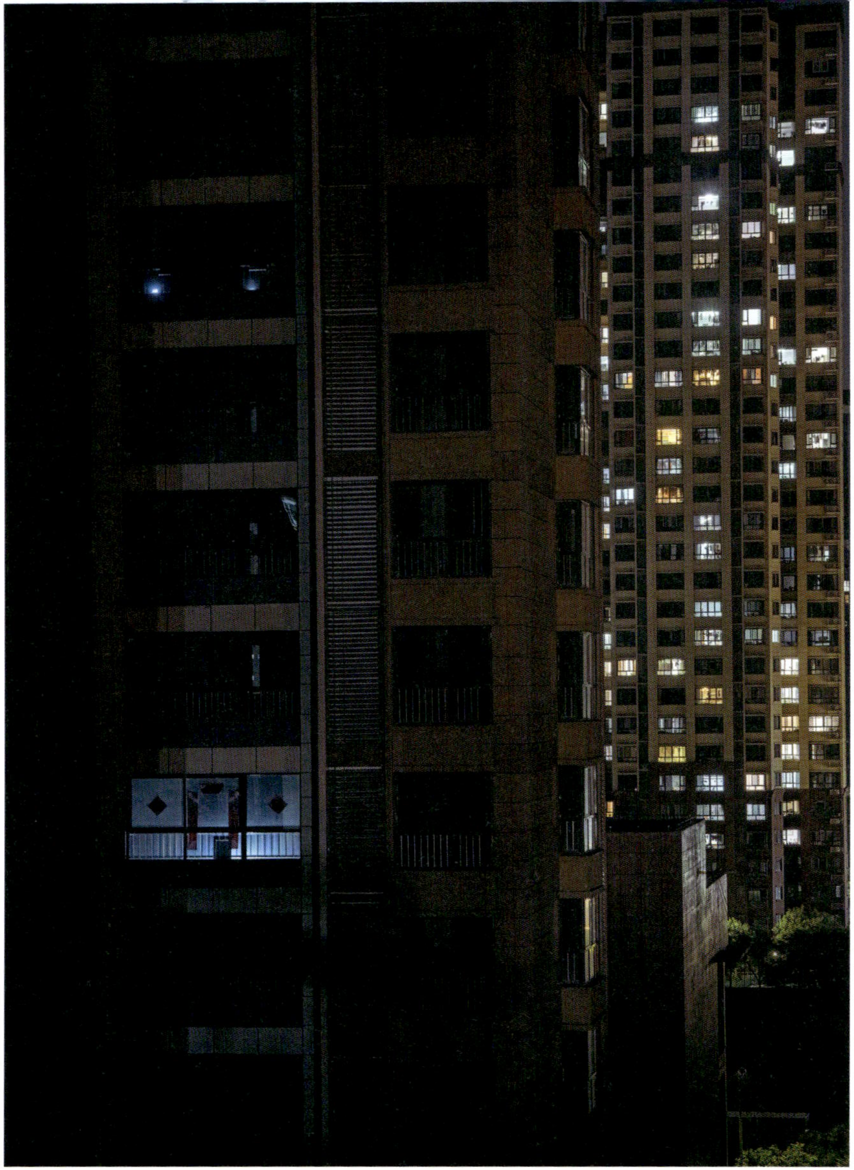

A solar-powered light illuminates an unfinished apartment in the city of Xi'an, on 14 June 2022. By some estimates, as many as 5% of new residential developments in major Chinese cities have not been completed, affecting hundreds of thousands of homeowners.

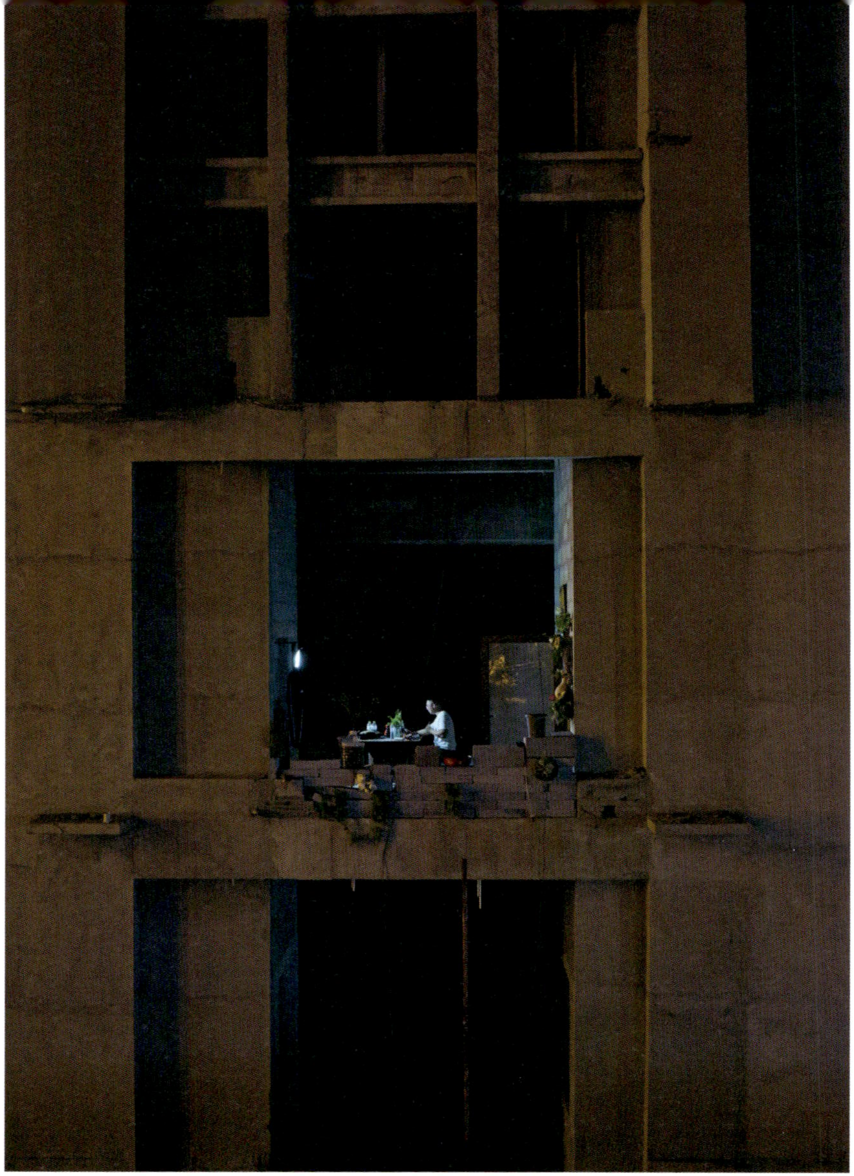

A homebuyer records a live webcast inside his unfinished home in the city of Qingdao, on 22 July 2022. Although live streams are often throttled or blocked, many people continue to find ways to attract attention to their situations online.

# Asia

Hideko Kataoka
Asia Jury Chair

A journey that began in Dhaka, Bangladesh, and continued for about a month, reached its final day in Amsterdam in late February. The Asia and then the global juries had been working sincerely with each photo, going through rounds and discussions among jurors, seeking deeper layers and meanings in works. Sometimes I had to endure emotions that spontaneously overflowed, as I reflected on my own experiences and background mirrored in the photographs.

Countries such as Iran, Afghanistan, India, and Sri Lanka (where violent civil protests led to the president fleeing the country) were shaken by complex, entangled events in 2022. Among the many submissions from the Asia region, we received a number of excellent projects depicting the rise of authoritarianism, power vacuums, climate change and more. Some of these photos made the front pages of a range of media outlets, while other projects received little media coverage. Some of the work defied local stereotypes by photographing themes seen from a foreigner's point of view, a completely different perspective than from inside the community. Other work presented the narrative power of the citizens themselves, through creative representation.

The story of Kashmir, a territory that is the subject of dispute between India and Pakistan, stood out in all categories, even though, in the end, it did not number among the winners. The region of Jammu and Kashmir, stripped of its 70-plus years of autonomy in 2019, continued to be held under high alert by the Indian government. In this situation, photographers carried on reporting while exposing themselves to danger. This courage is crucial because the world needs to recognize this dangerous conflict, and to know the pain endured by those on the ground. As a native of Japan, the only country to experience the hostile use of an atomic weapon, I have a further significant concern because both India and Pakistan are nuclear powers.

Some of the submissions from the Asia region were courageous in their protest against authoritarian dictatorship. In contrast, others made me think about a country itself, the tragedy and strife caused, for example, by the power vacuum after a strong power left. And, as always, it is the citizens who suffer.

I also wonder why, although citizens across the region protested  against coercive governments, so few pictures of the demonstrations were submitted for consideration. This absence raises a concern about the increasing infringement of freedom of speech being practiced by new and old authoritarian regimes alike. For the Honorable Mentions of the Asian region, the jury selected quiet civil protests as a sign of solidarity.

Our selection of these photographs is not merely a record of a point in the past, but is presented to create discussions about the future that emerges from them. I hope they will generate a rich conversation to create a better future for the world.

# Jury

—

TOMOHISA TOBITSUKA

**HIDEKO KATAOKA** / CHAIR
JAPAN
–
Hideko Kataoka is a photo editor, curator, and educator, and is director of photography at *Newsweek Japan*. A lecturer at Tokyo Polytechnic University, she also serves as a member of the External Review Committee at Tokyo Photographic Art Museum.
–
Twitter: @Hideko_Kataoka

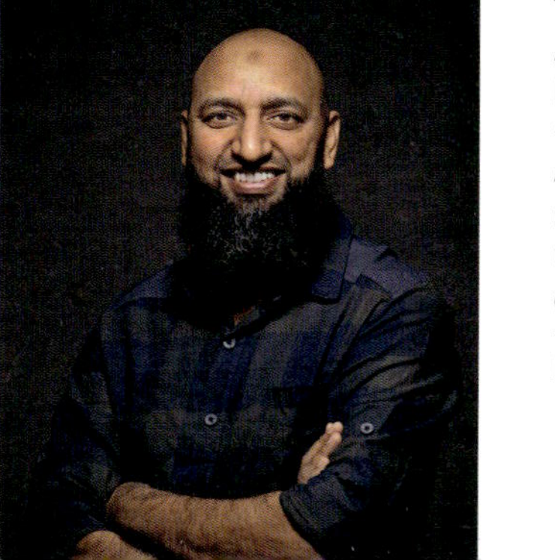

IDRIS AHMAD

**ALTAF QADRI**
INDIA
–
Altaf Qadri is an award-winning photojournalist, currently working with the Associated Press. Based in New Delhi, India, he is founder of the Visual Photo Academy.
–
Instagram: @altafqadri

# Winners

—

## SINGLES

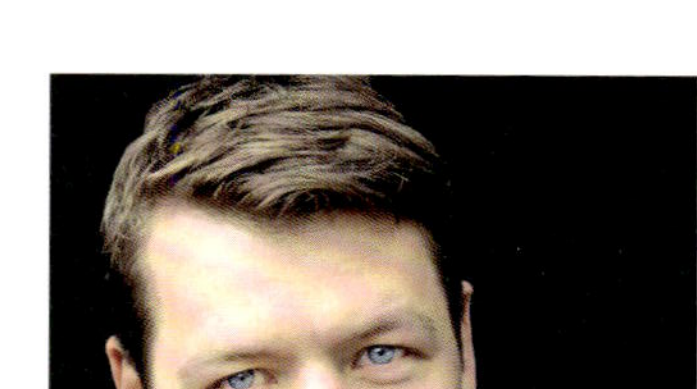

**MAYA LEVIN**
UNITED STATES, 1984
–
Maya Levin is an independent photographer focusing on community-driven stories. Since 2004, Levin has covered the Egyptian revolution, the Syrian refugee crisis on the Turkey border, and daily life in Israel and the Palestinian territories.
–
Instagram: @mayalevinphotography

## STORIES

**MADS NISSEN**
DENMARK, 1980
–
Mads Nissen is a photographer based in Copenhagen, Denmark. To him, photography is all about empathy – creating understanding while confronting contemporary social issues such as inequality, human rights violations, and our destructive relationship with nature.
–
Instagram: @madsnissen

ORTEN RODE

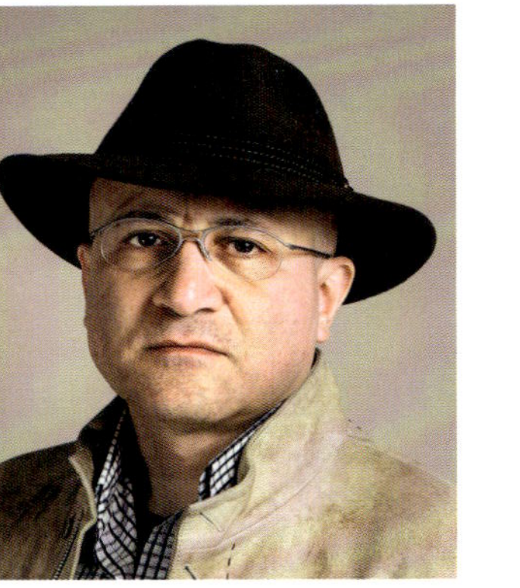

KOOS BREUKEL

## ISSA TOUMA
SYRIA
–
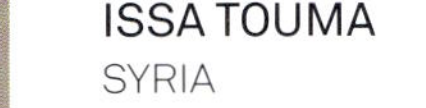

Issa Touma is a photographer and film director based in Aleppo, Syria, and 2016 winner of the European Film Award for Best Short Film. Work in international collections includes the Victoria & Albert Museum (London), and FOMU (Antwerp).
–
Instagram: @issa_touma

MYRIAM BOULOS

## MYRIAM BOULOS
LEBANON
–
Myriam Boulos is a Lebanese photographer, co-founder, and photo editor of *Al Hayya* magazine. She uses photography to explore, defy and resist society. In 2021, she joined Magnum Photos as a nominee.
–
Instagram: @myriamboulos

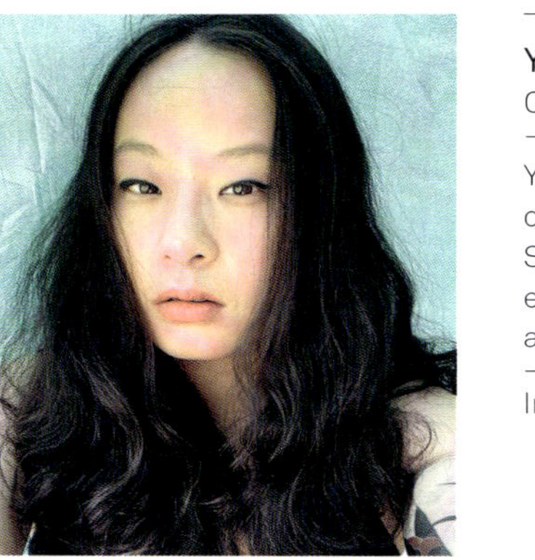

YINING HE

## YINING HE
CHINA
–
Yining He is a leading curator and researcher of photographic arts, and is based in China. She has curated more than 40 cross-cultural exhibitions for museums, art institutions, and photography festivals across Eurasia.
–
Instagram: @yininghe

# LONG-TERM PROJECTS

## ANUSH BABAJANYAN
ARMENIA, 1983
–
Anush Babajanyan is a photographer whose work focuses on social narratives and personal stories. She is a member of VII Photo Agency and a National Geographic Explorer.
–
Instagram: @anushbabajanyan

JOHN STANMEYER

# OPEN FORMAT

## HOSSEIN FATEMI
IRAN, 1980
–
Hossein Fatemi's work concentrates on capturing political and social events in his native Iran. He is accepting the award on behalf of the anonymous photographers who took the images in *Woman, Life, Freedom*.
–
Instagram: @hosseinfatemi

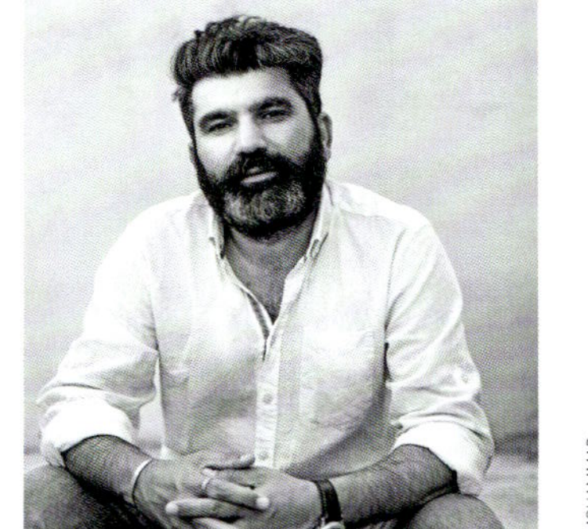

YOUNES MOHAMMAD

# Europe

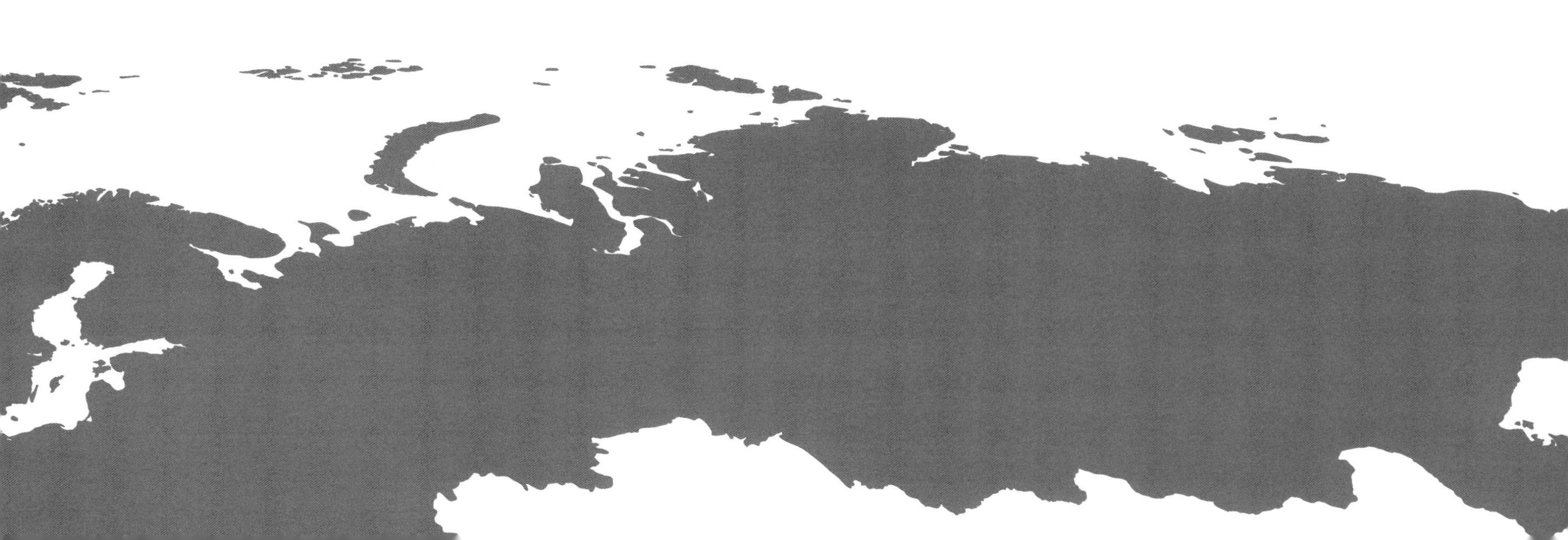

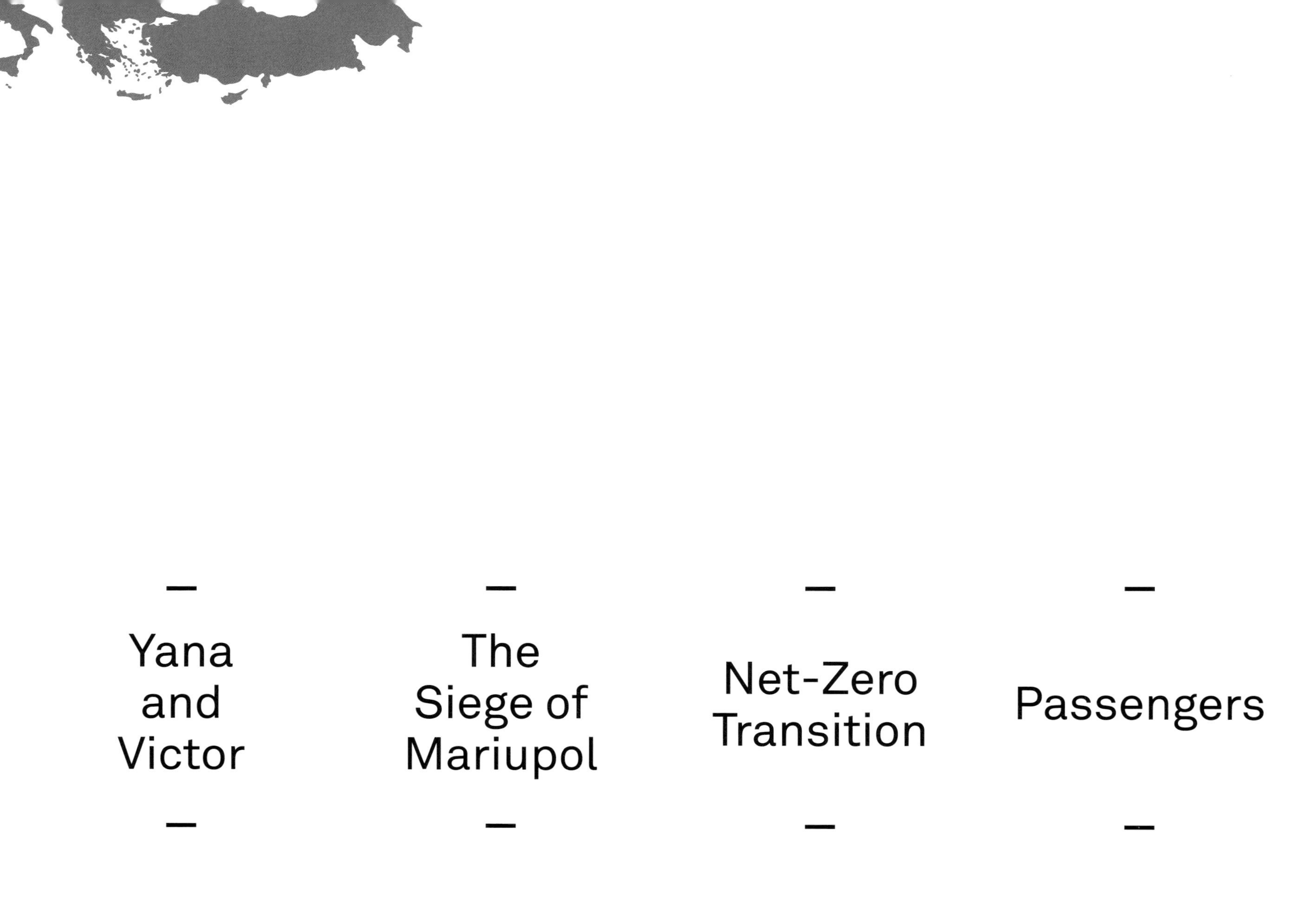

Yana and Victor

The Siege of Mariupol

Net-Zero Transition

Passengers

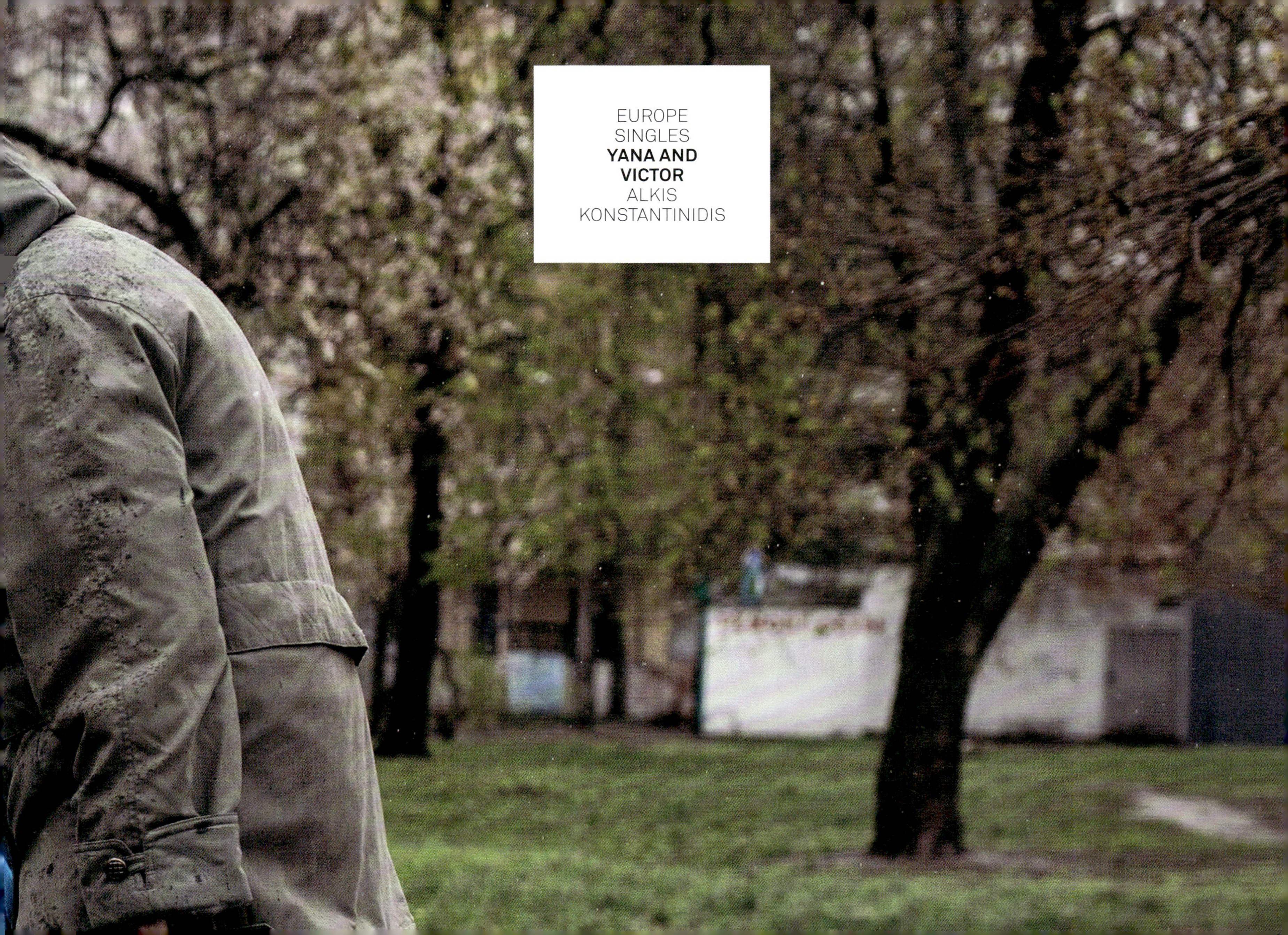

EUROPE
SINGLES
**YANA AND VICTOR**
ALKIS KONSTANTINIDIS

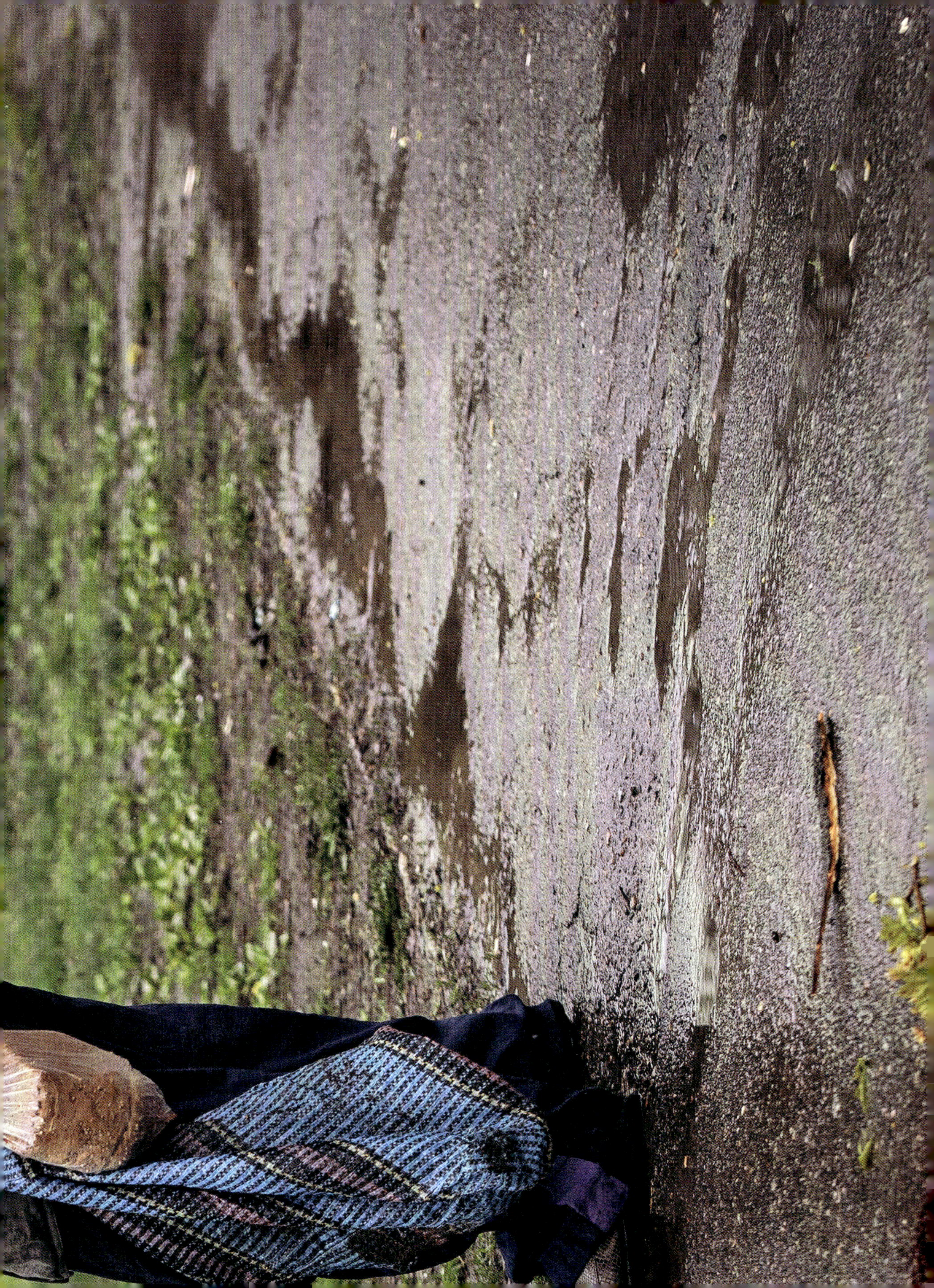

# Yana and Victor

Consoled by her partner Yevgeniy Vlasenko and her mother Lyubov, Yana Bachek cries over the body of her father Victor Gubarev (79), killed while buying bread during the shelling of Kharkiv, Ukraine, on 18 April 2022. Russian forces began advancing towards Kharkiv, Ukraine's second-largest city, just after their full-scale invasion on 24 February. Throughout March and April, the city was partially encircled and remained under heavy shelling. In May, Ukraine forced a Russian withdrawal from the immediate surroundings of Kharkiv. The jury felt this image encapsulated the grief and horror that Ukrainian civilians endure on a daily basis since Russia's invasion.

Alkis Konstantinidis took this photograph on assignment for Reuters.

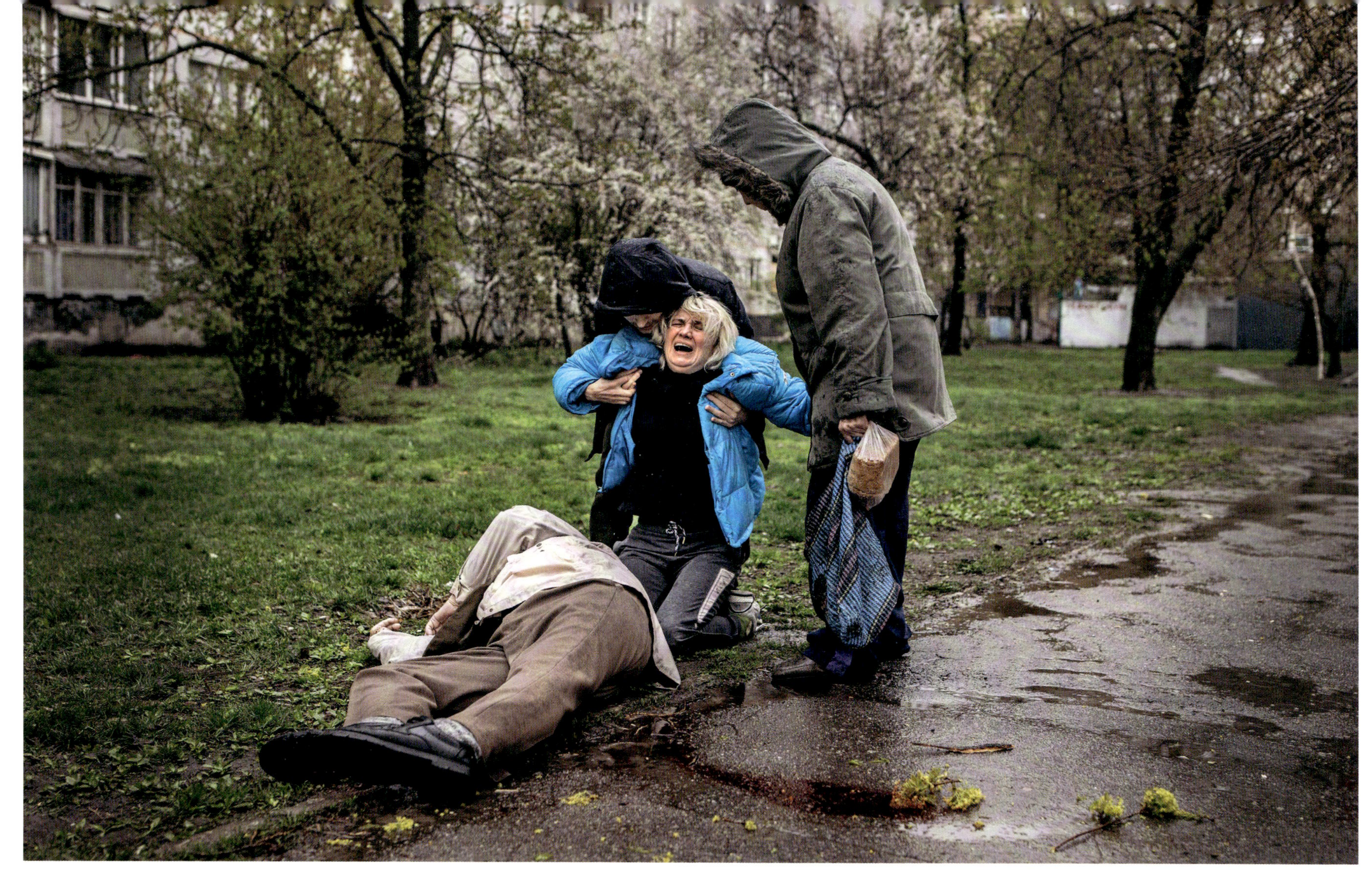

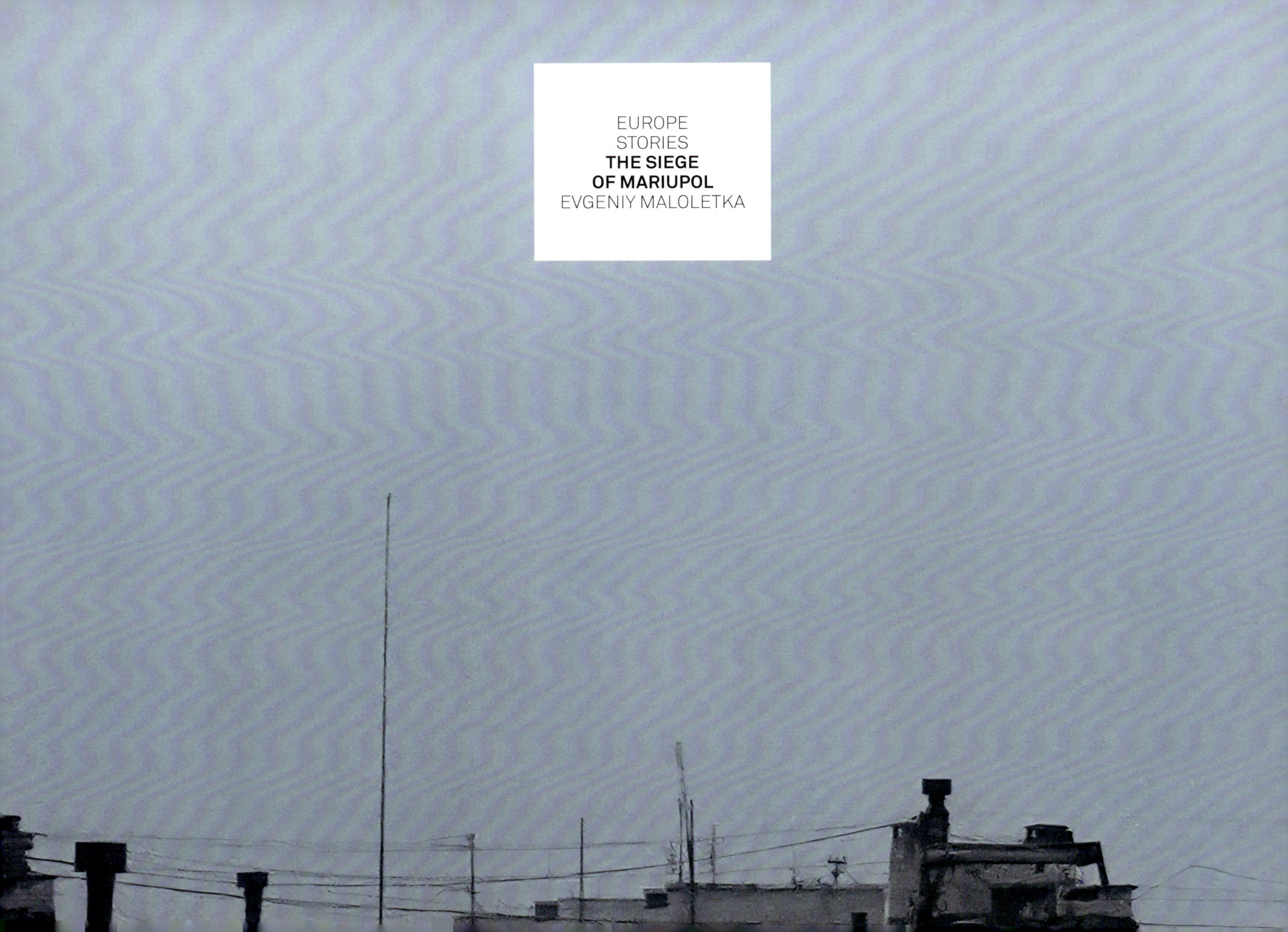

EUROPE
STORIES
**THE SIEGE
OF MARIUPOL**
EVGENIY MALOLETKA

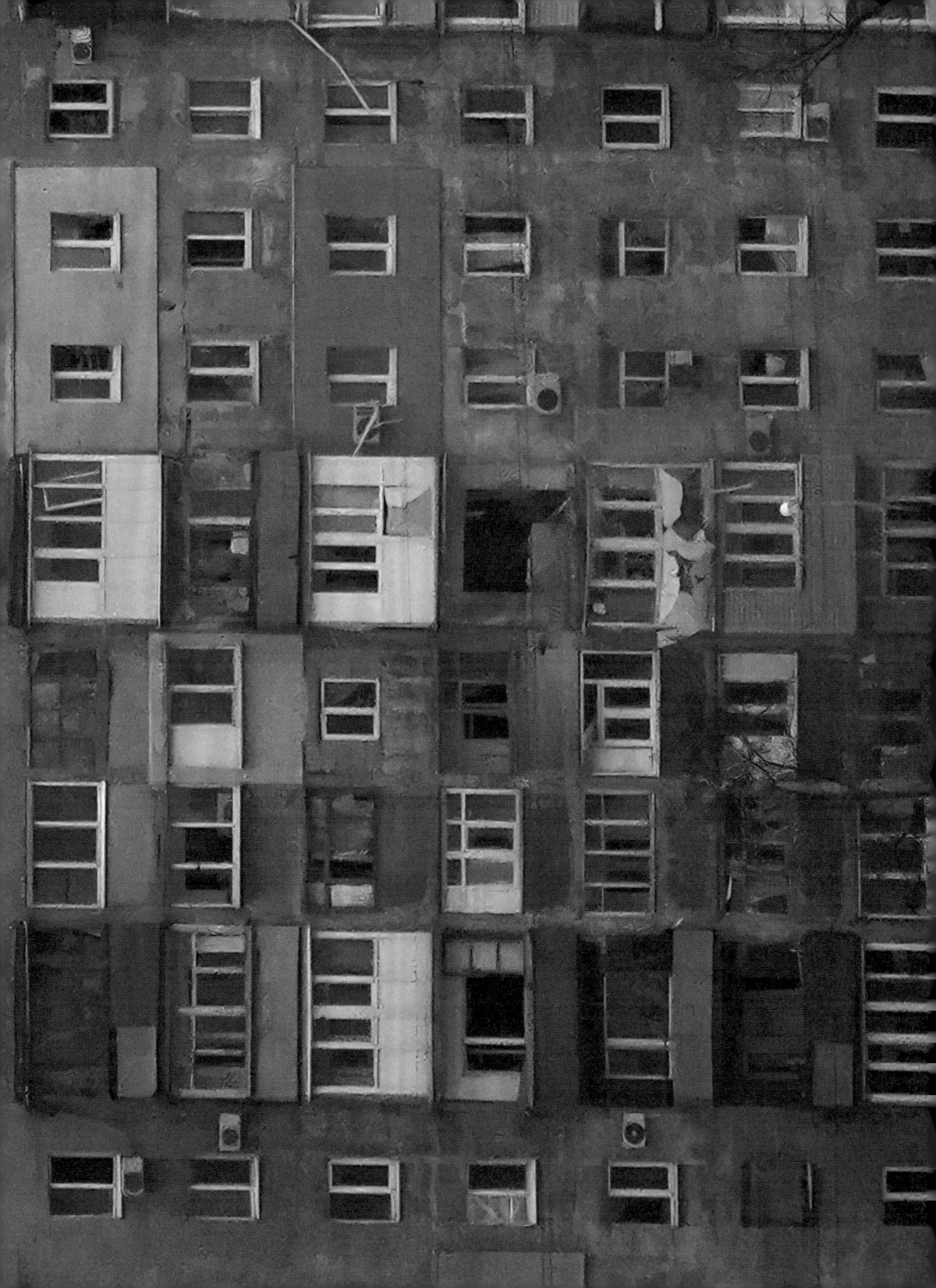

# The Siege of Mariupol

When Russian forces invaded Ukraine on 24 February 2022, they immediately targeted the strategically important port of Mariupol on the Sea of Azov. By 20 May, Russia gained full control of the city, which had been devastated by shelling, and tens of thousands of civilians had fled or been killed. Maloletka was one of the very few photographers documenting events in Mariupol at that time. The jury felt his story communicated the horror of the war for civilians; they praised the photographer's resilience while working under immense pressure and imminent threat.

Evgeniy Maloletka photographed these images on assignment for Associated Press.

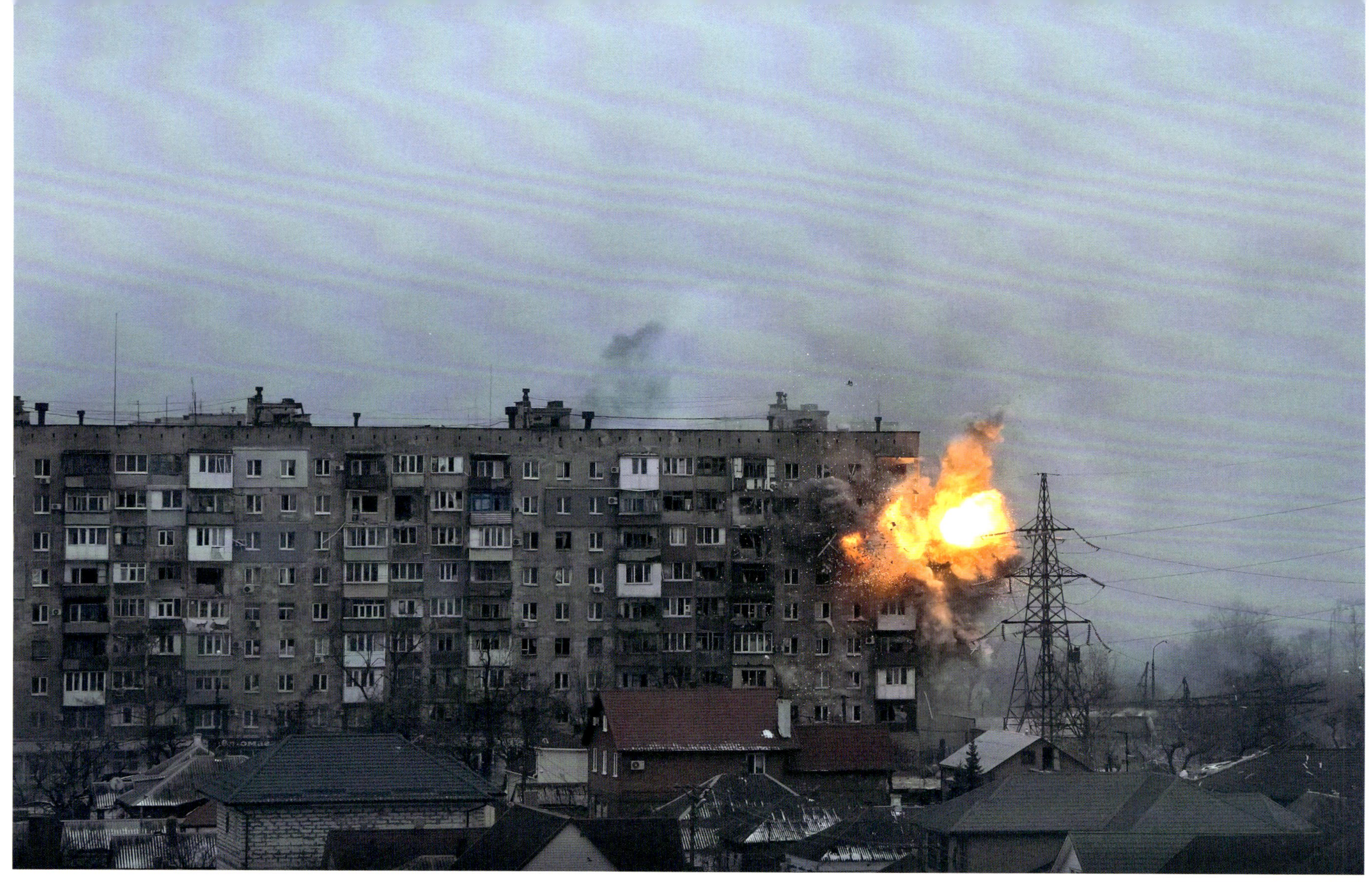

An explosion erupts from an apartment building on Mytropolytska Street, Mariupol, after fire from a Russian army tank, on 11 March 2022.

Russian army tanks move through a street on the outskirts of Mariupol, on 11 March 2022.

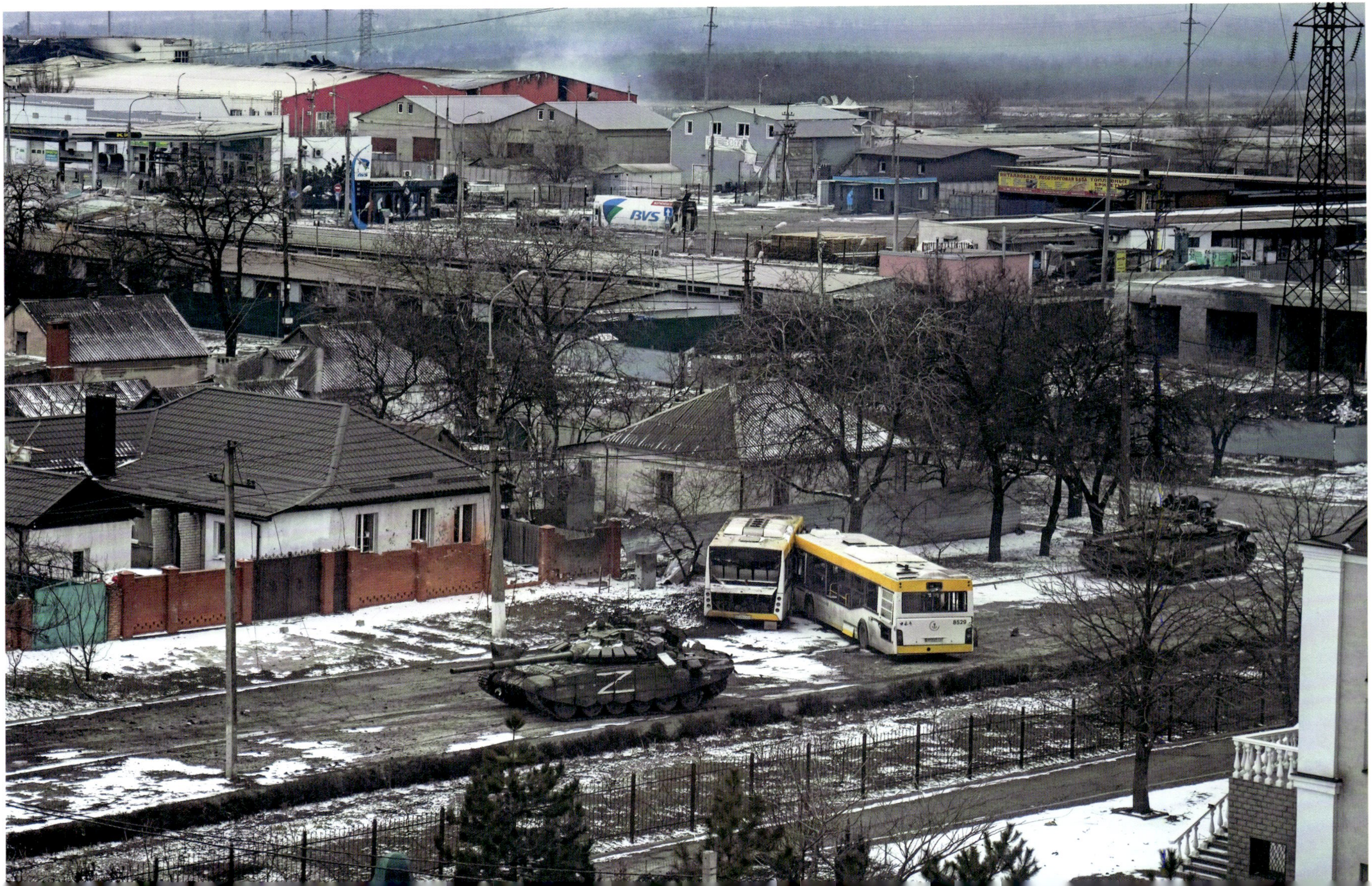

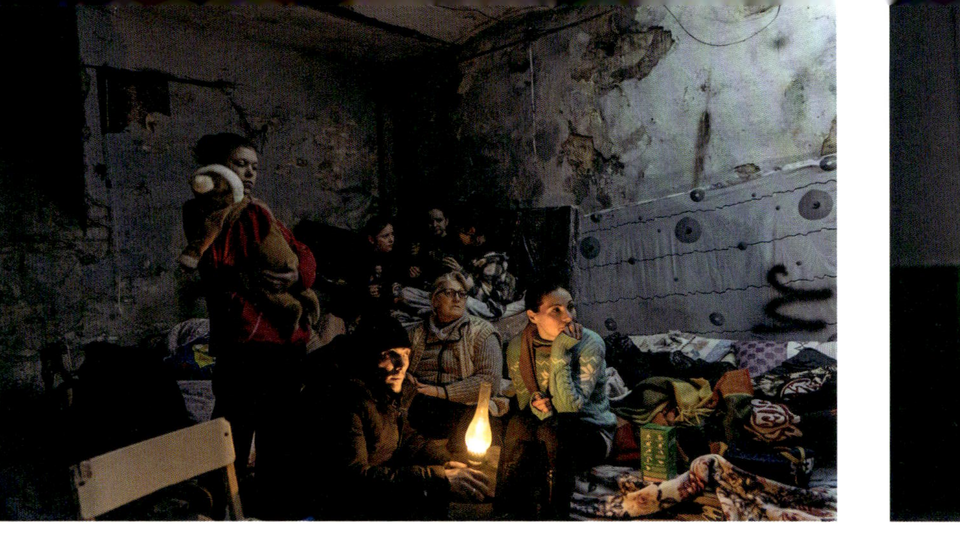

Zhanna Goma (right) and her neighbors settle in a bomb shelter in Mariupol, on 6 March 2022.

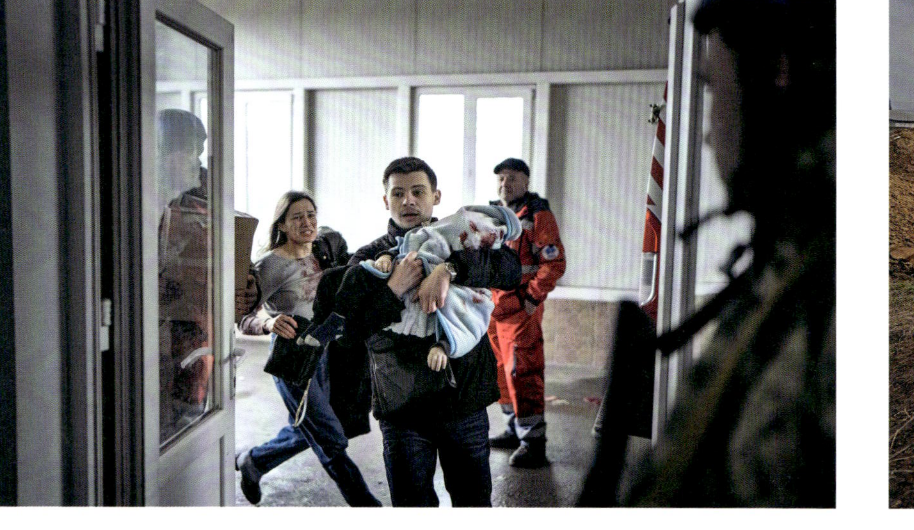

Marina Yatsko and her boyfriend Oleksandr Kulahin bring her 18-month-old son Kirill, fatally wounded during shelling, to a hospital in Mariupol, on 4 March 2022.

Serhiy Kralya, a civilian injured during shelling by Russian forces, rests after surgery at a hospital in Mariupol, on 11 March 2022.

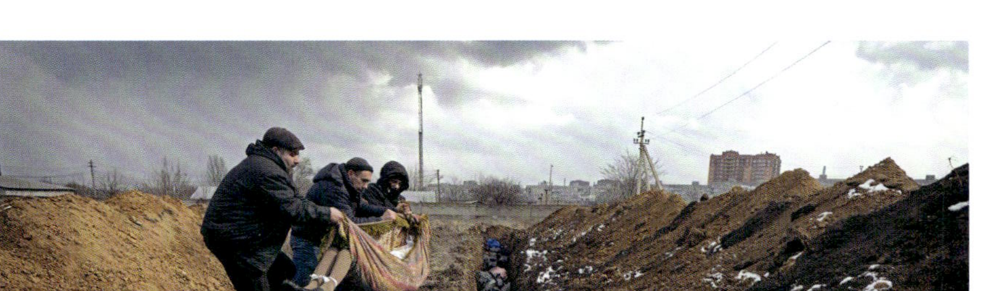

People place dead bodies in a mass grave in an old cemetery in Mariupol, on 9 March 2022. According to the BBC, on some days, up to 150 people a day were buried in mass graves during periods of heavy Russian shelling.

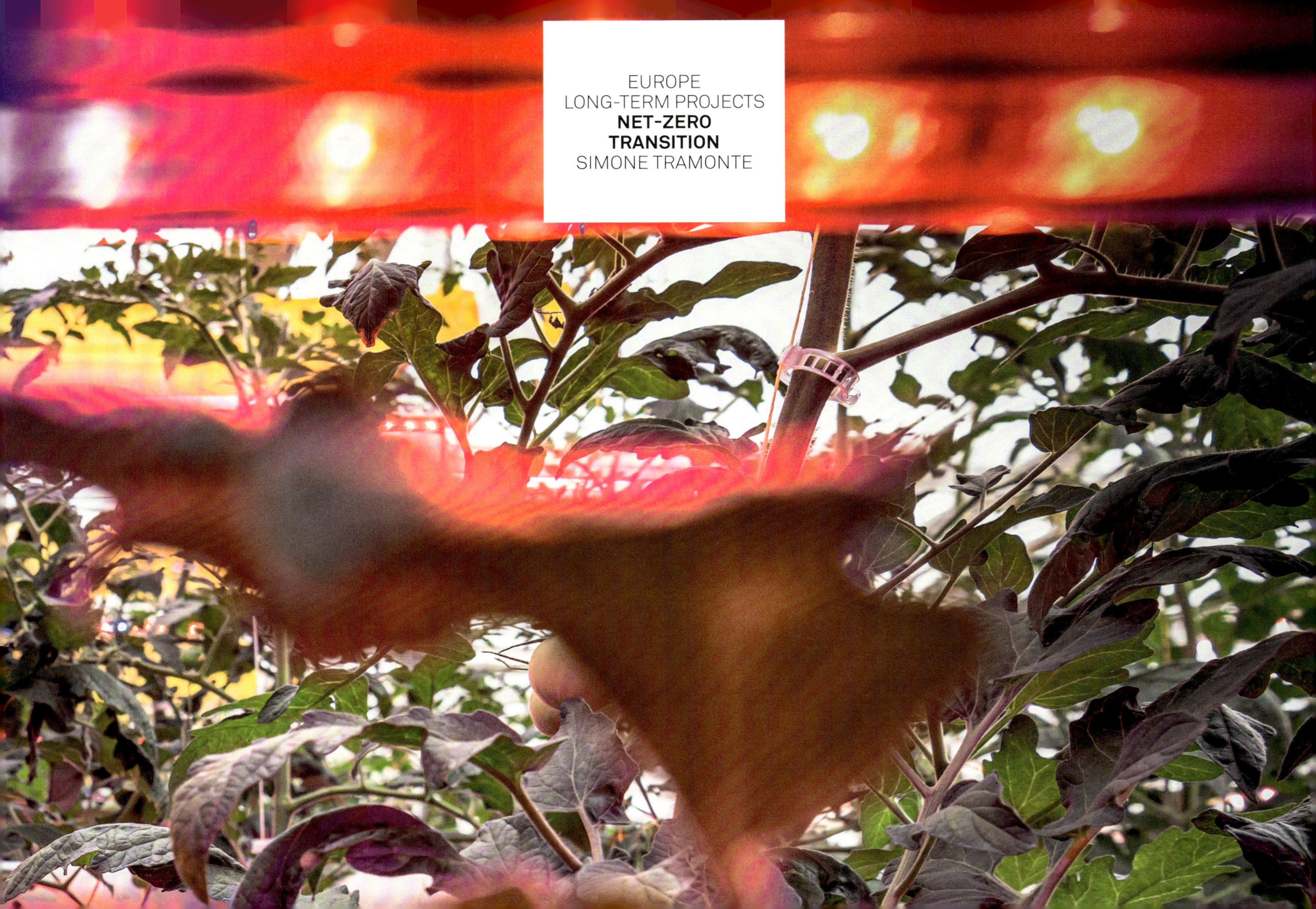

EUROPE
LONG-TERM PROJECTS
**NET-ZERO TRANSITION**
SIMONE TRAMONTE

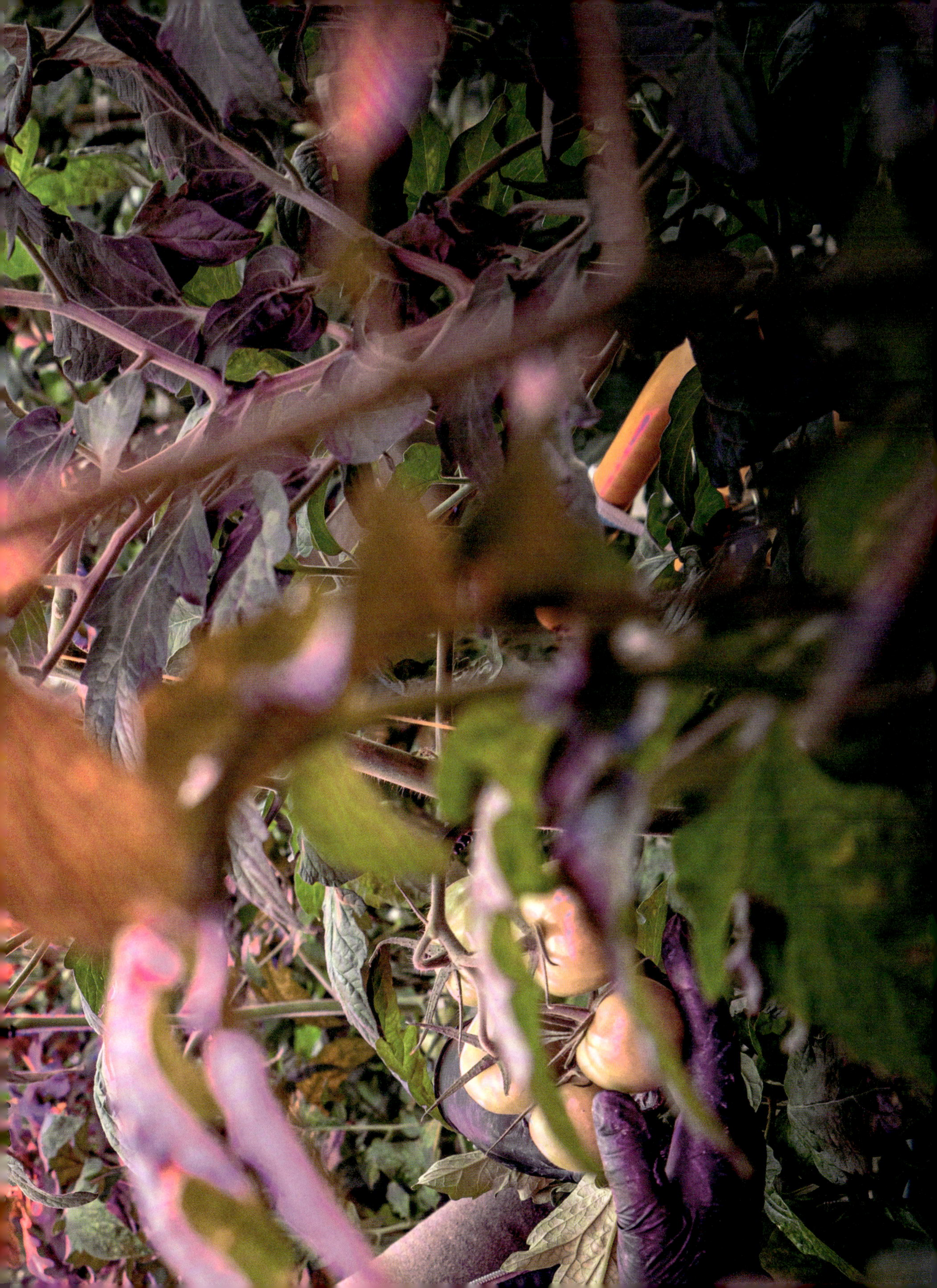

# Net-Zero Transition

Renewable energies, new technologies for food production, and the circular economy can be seen as key directions among European companies seeking a green transition. Human-induced climate change is the largest, most pervasive threat to the natural environment and society that the world has ever experienced, according to the OCHR. This prompted the European Union to establish targets to cut greenhouse emissions by at least 55 percent by 2030 and to reduce them to net-zero by 2050. The photographer documents innovative technologies that offer possible routes to these goals.

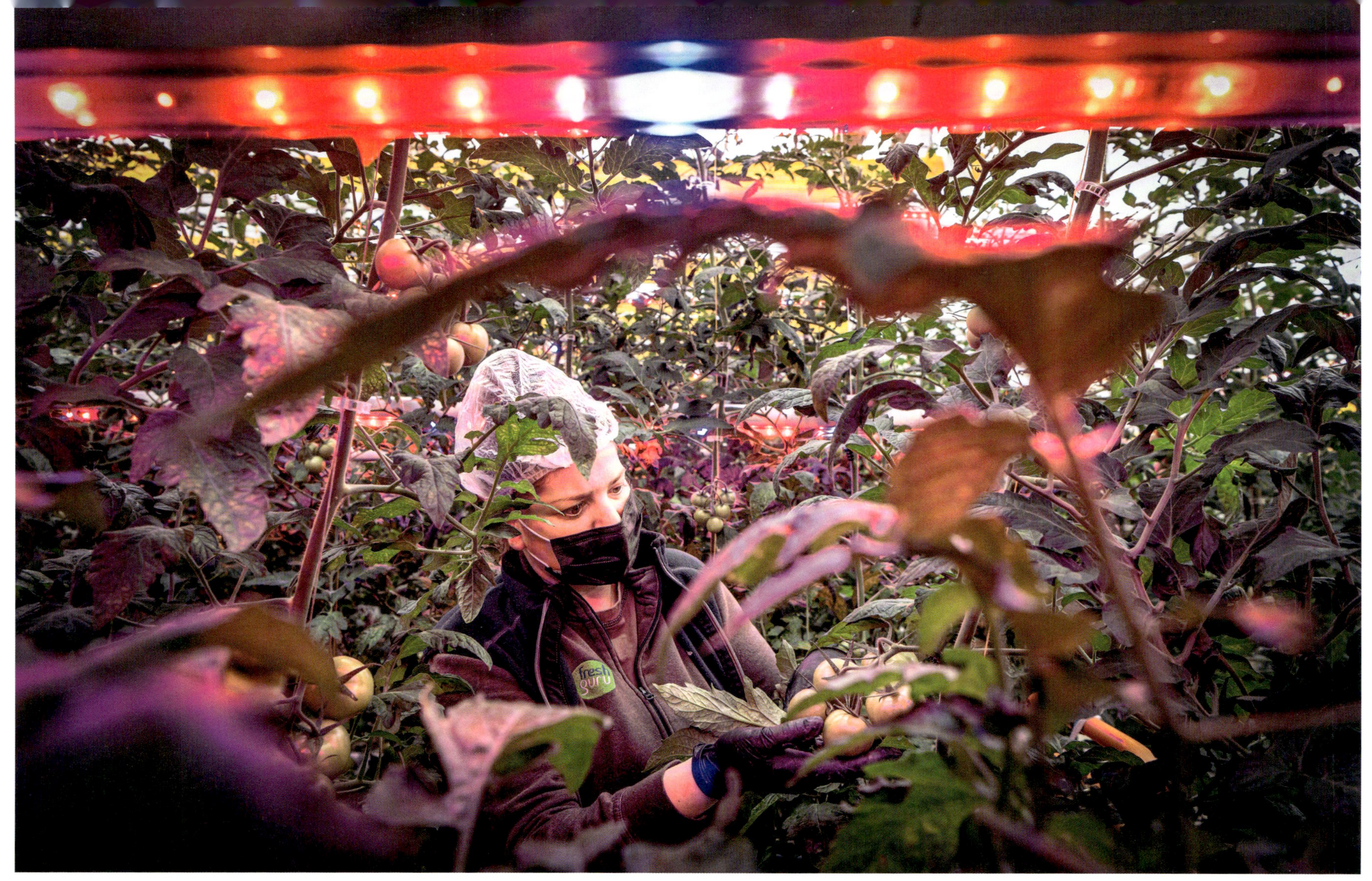


A worker harvests tomatoes in a greenhouse in Ostellato, Italy, on 22 February 2021.
High-efficiency LED lights using 100 percent green energy ensure sustainable year-round production.

Workers monitor seedling growth at a vertical farm, near Milan, Italy, on 10 November 2022. Crops grown in vertical stacks increase efficiency of land use, and reduce water consumption.

Kristinn Haflidason monitors a photobioreactor at a microalgae production facility in Hellisheiði, Iceland, on 14 July 2020. The company cultivates omega 3-rich algae using waste and geothermal power.

An operator runs a routine check of a photobioreactor at a microalgae facility in Reykjanesbær, Iceland, on 13 July 2020. The company uses algae to produce a food supplement rich in antioxidants.

Greenhouse operations in Ostellato, Italy, pictured on 22 February 2021, are based on a circular economy. Plant waste fuels the biogas (renewable fuel) plant that powers the greenhouse.

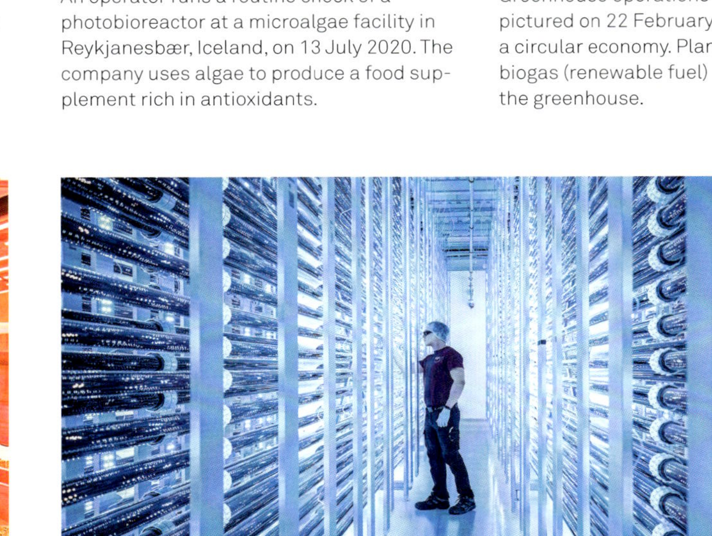

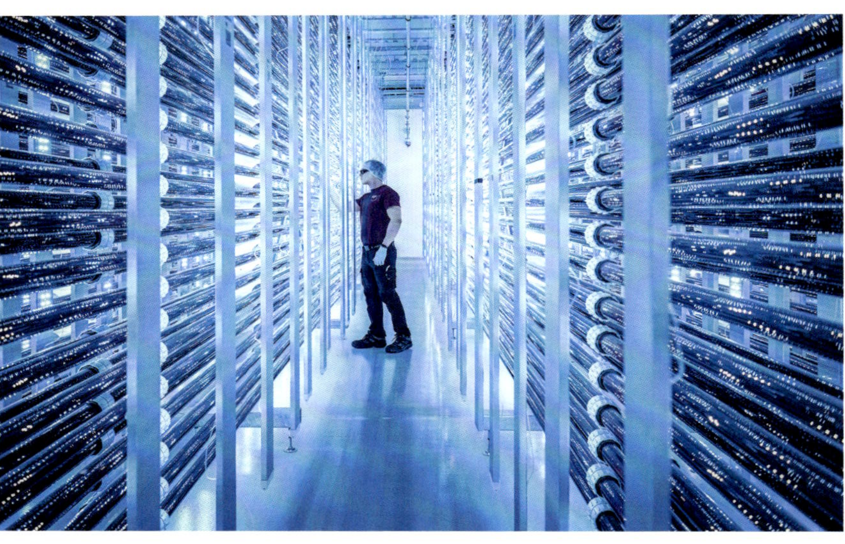

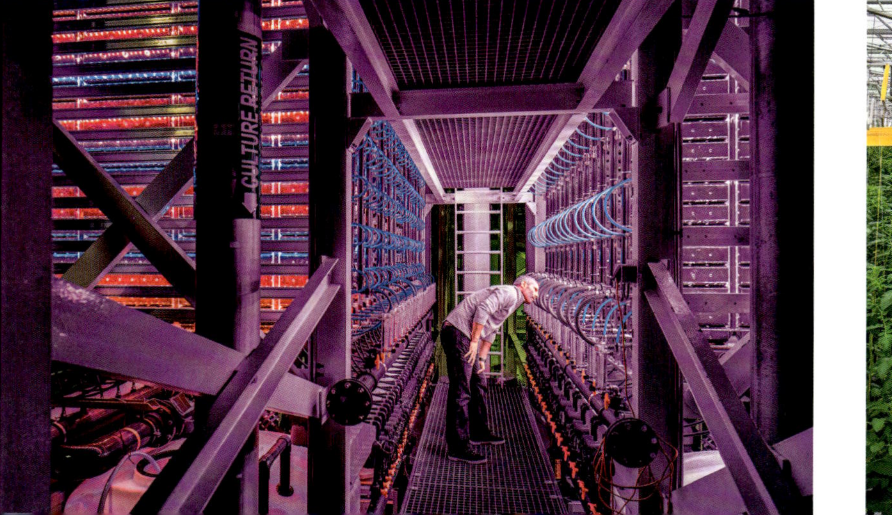

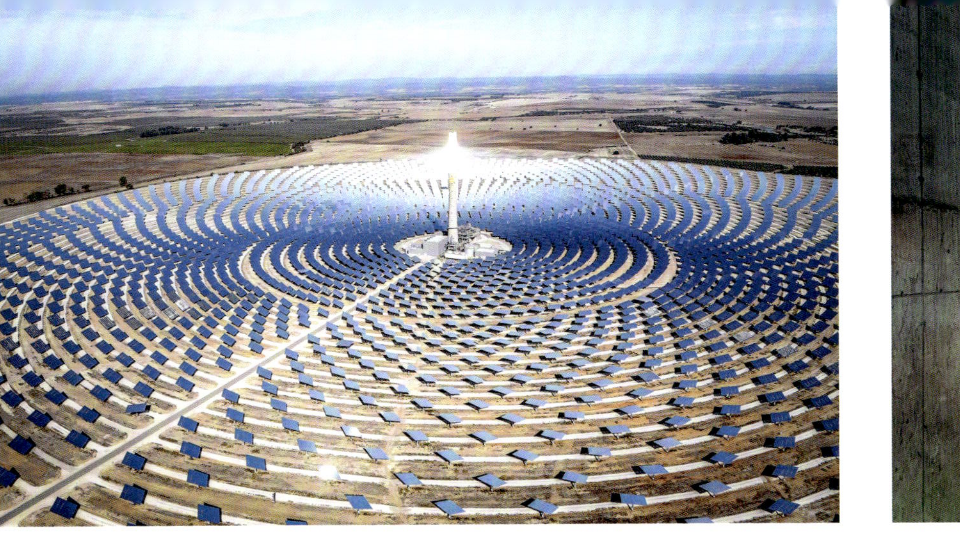

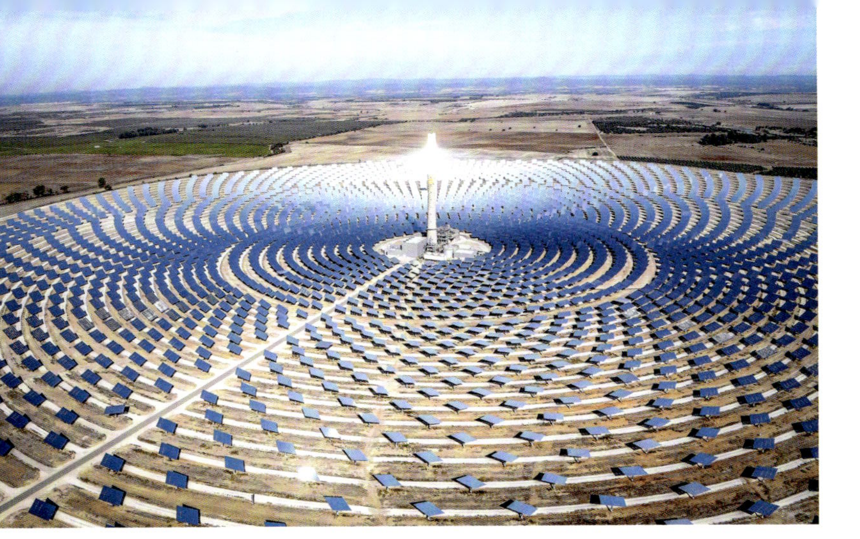

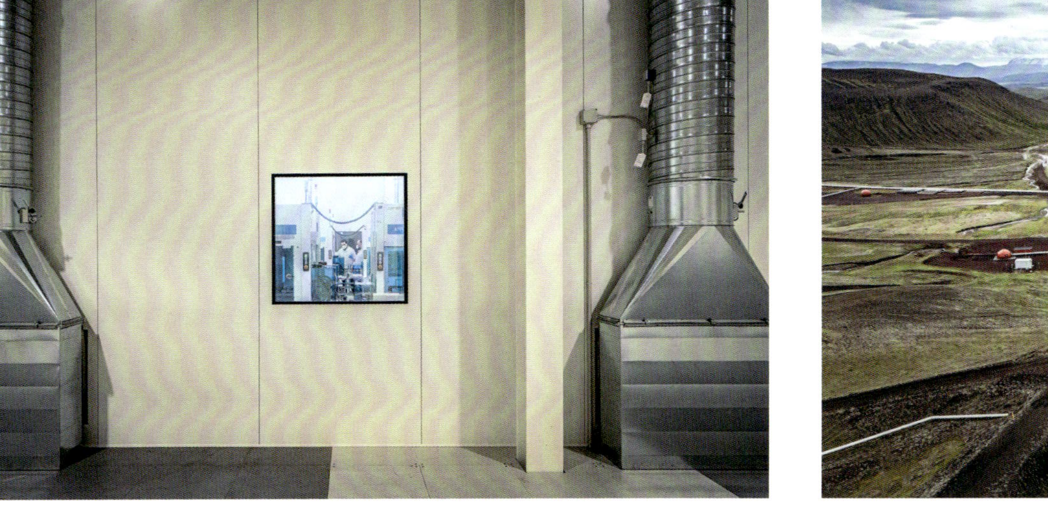

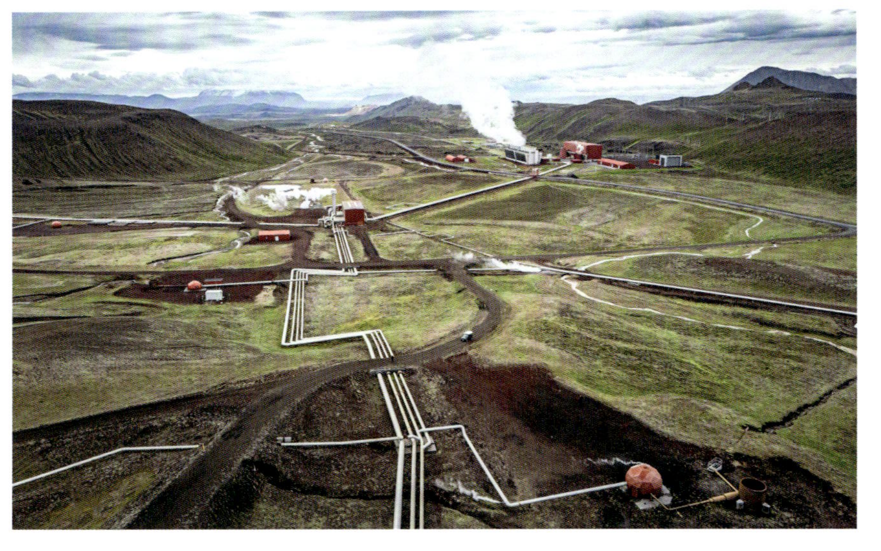

This solar plant in Fuentes de Andalucía, Spain, pictured on 17 October 2021, can supply uninterrupted power. Instead of sunlight, it uses solar heat (which is more easily stored) to generate electricity.

This "gigafactory" in Catania, Italy, pictured on 11 March 2021, was the first in Europe to manufacture photovoltaic panels that produce solar energy from both sides.

The collection chamber of a waste-to-energy plant, pictured in Turin, Italy, on 26 May 2021, powers the largest district-heating network in Italy, serving around 9,300 homes and more than 500,000 citizens.

Carbon emissions from a geothermal power station, pictured in Iceland, on 19 July 2020, are reinjected into geothermal wells to minimize their environmental impact.

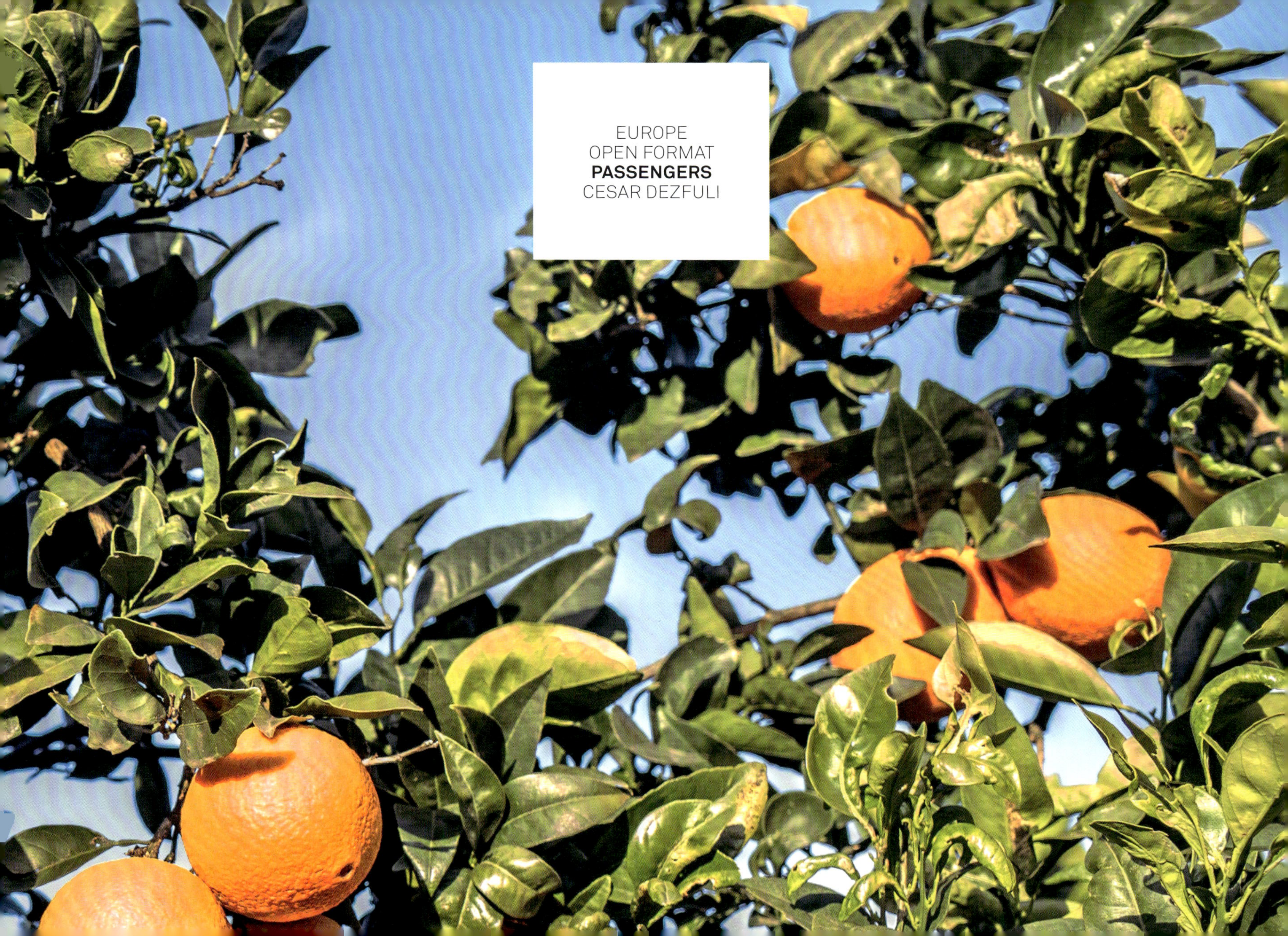

EUROPE
OPEN FORMAT
**PASSENGERS**
CESAR DEZFULI

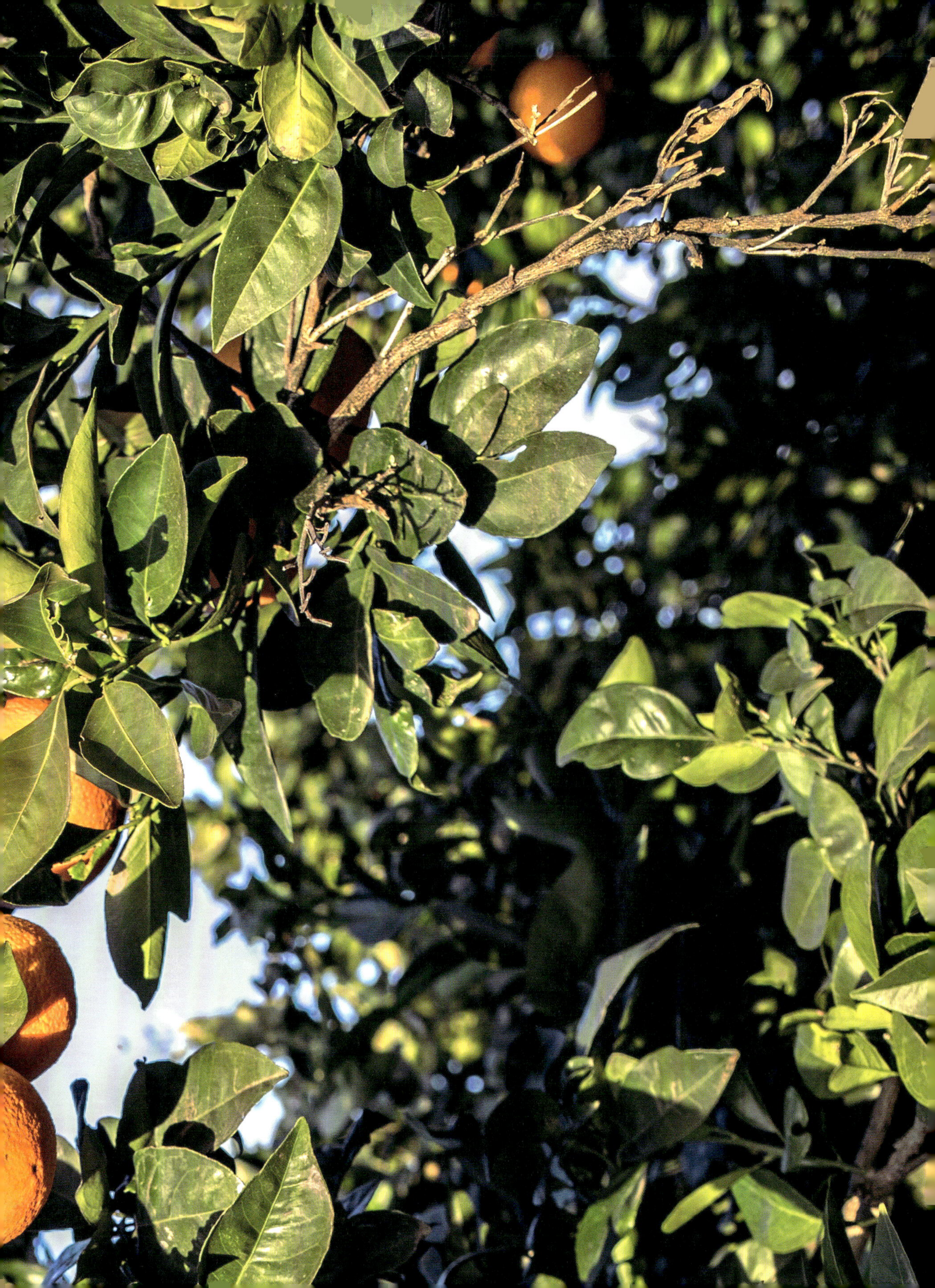

Scan the QR code to experience the interactive website

# Passengers

Since 2015, the influx of migrants, refugees, and asylum seekers from Africa to Europe has been covered in European news media as either a series of humanitarian crises or as a set of abstract statistics. On 1 August 2016, a boat carrying 118 people was found drifting off the coast of Libya, one of hundreds that required rescue in the past years. What happened to these individuals after their arrival in Europe? The *Passengers* project, presented as a multimedia website for *De Volkskrant*, highlights several personal stories from the people who were on that boat in 2016 as they seek to establish new lives across the continent.

Supported by *De Volkskrant*/Catchlight.

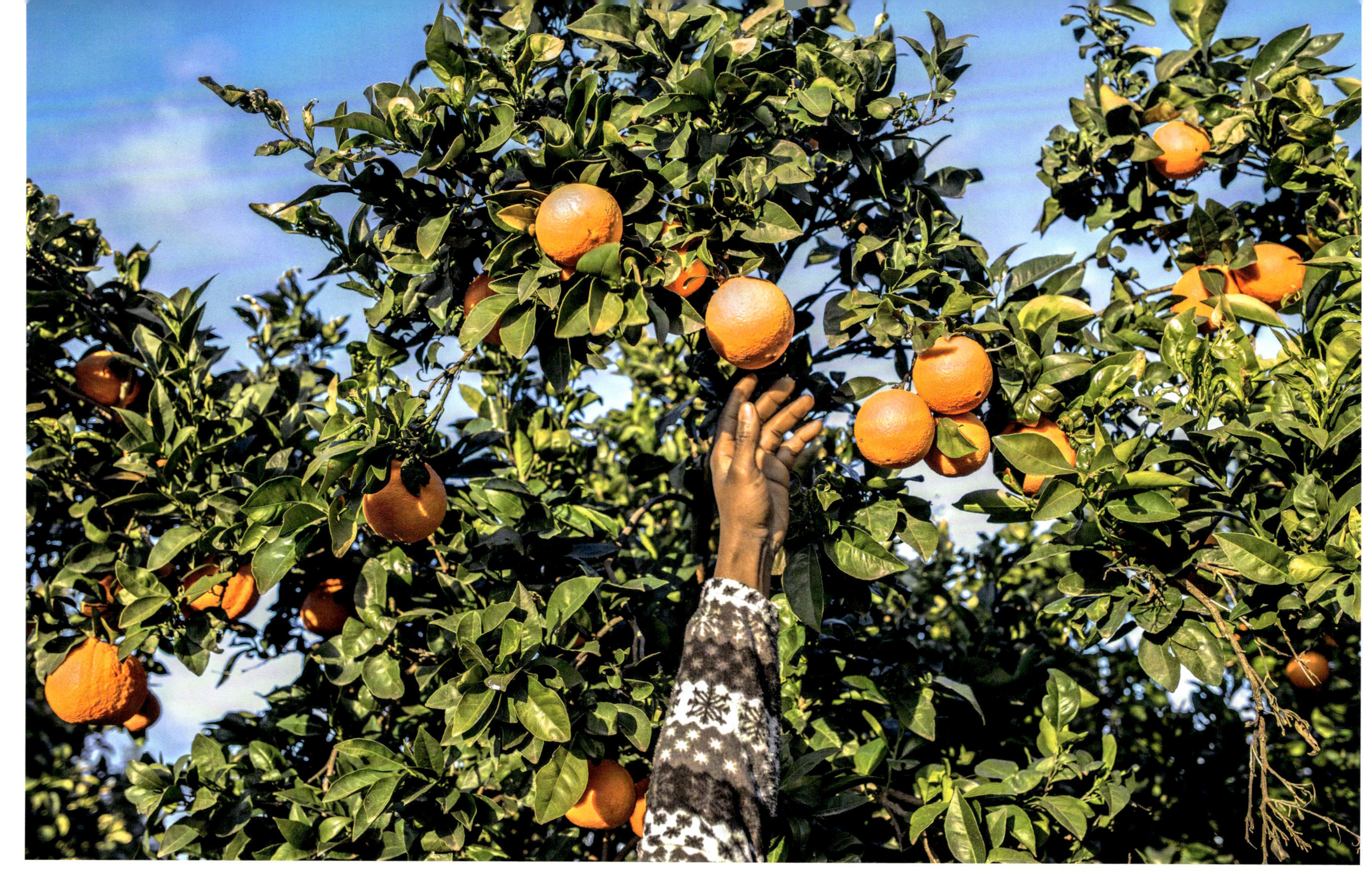

Alpha Oumar is from Guinea, where he studied writing and literature. Due to lack of economic opportunity, he decided to migrate to Europe. In August 2016, he was placed in a shelter in Brindisi, Italy after a long journey that took him through Mali, Algeria, and Libya. Eventually, he was granted a residence permit by Italian authorities and found a job picking fruit in Palagiano, Italy. He dreams of reuniting with his wife in Italy and pursuing further studies in literature.

Photographer: Cesar Dezfuli
Text: Maartje Bakker
Design: Titus Kneгtel
Editing: Gabriel Eisenmeier
Code: Martijn Eerens

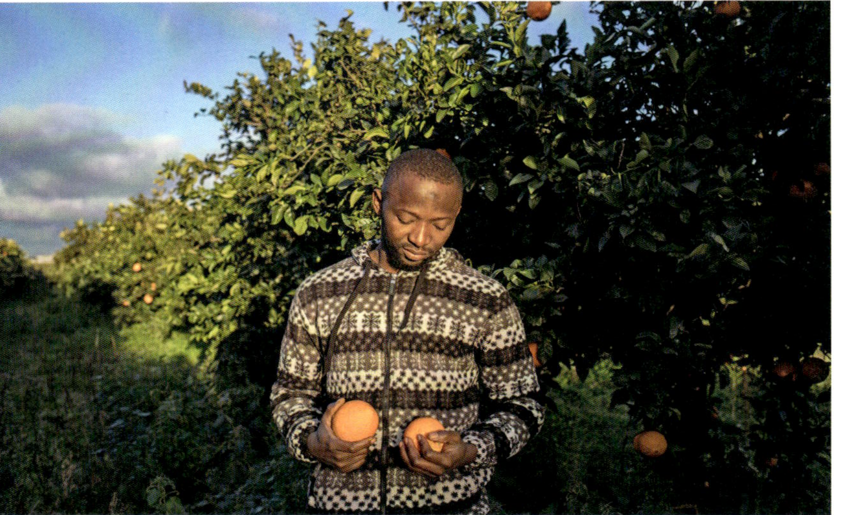

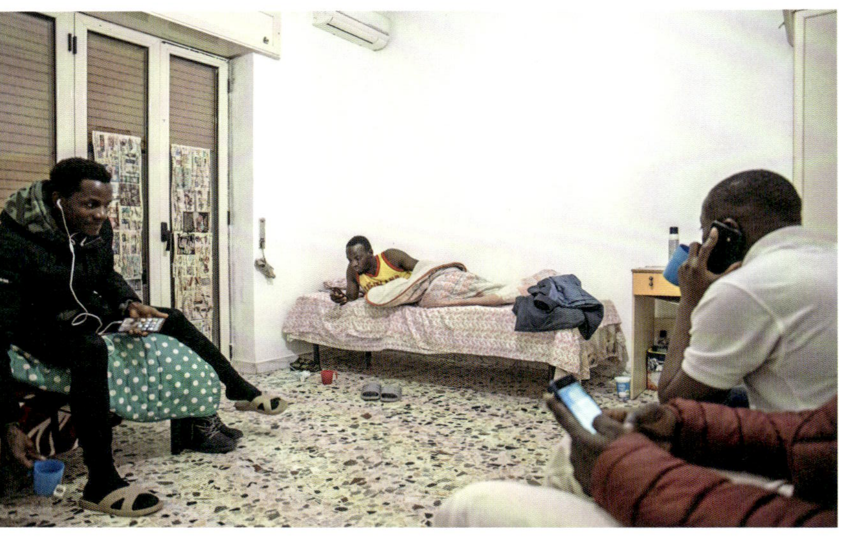

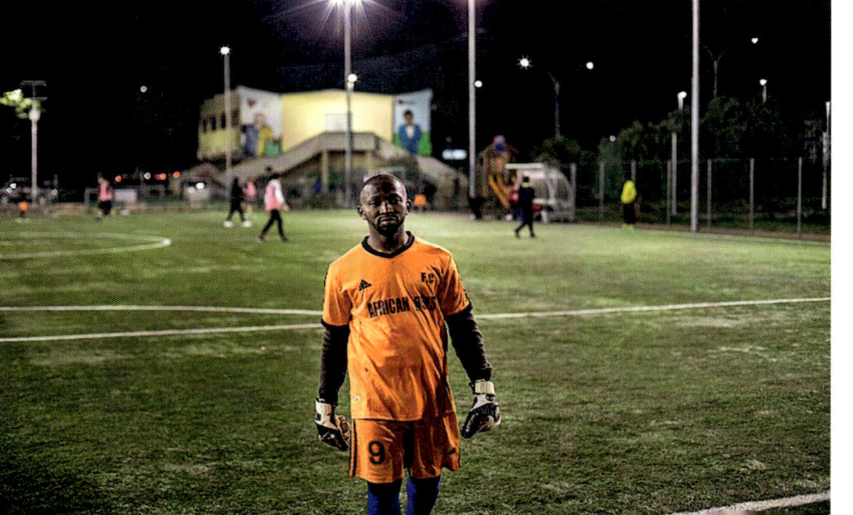

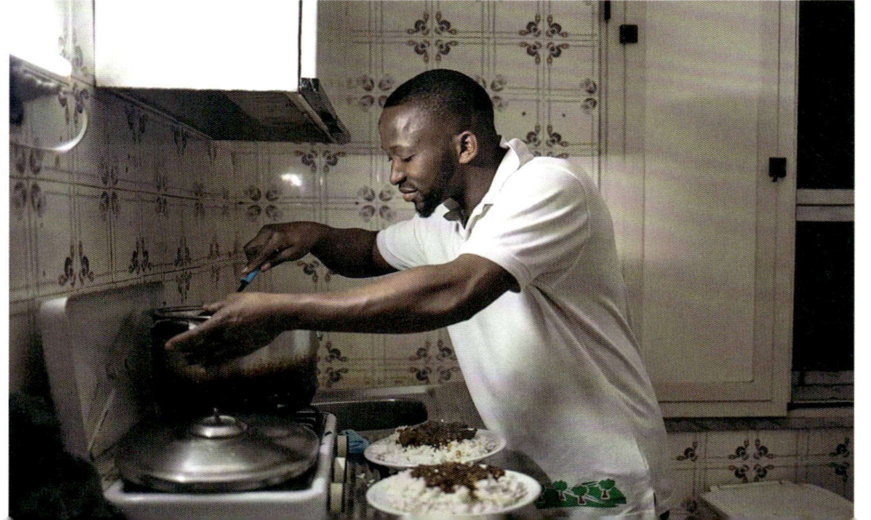

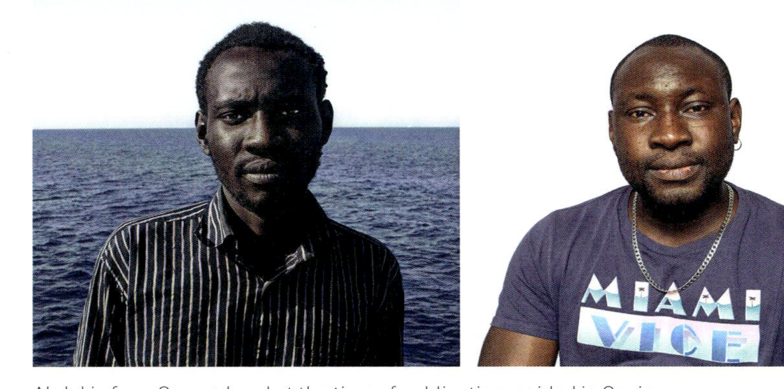

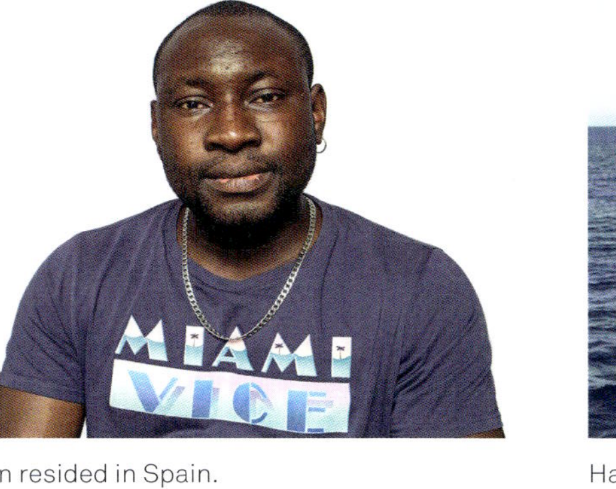


Abdul is from Senegal and at the time of publication resided in Spain.

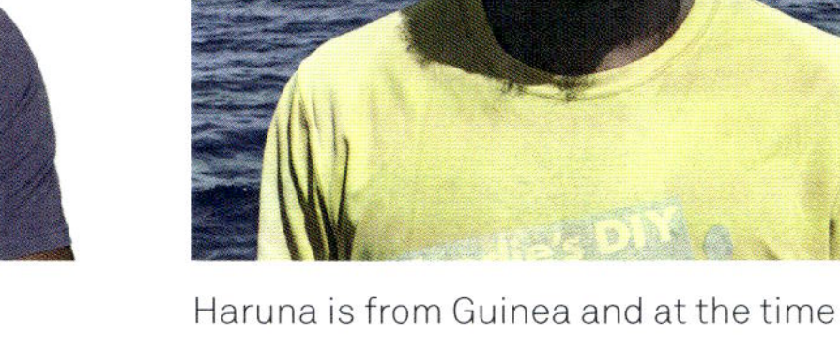

Haruna is from Guinea and at the time of publication resided in Kiel, Germany.

Neboth is from Nigeria and at the time of publication resided in Matera, Italy.

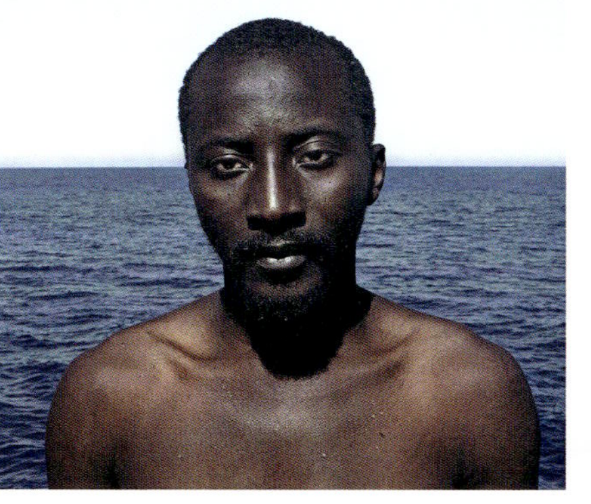

Modou is from Senegal and at the time of publication resided in La Fuliola, Spain.

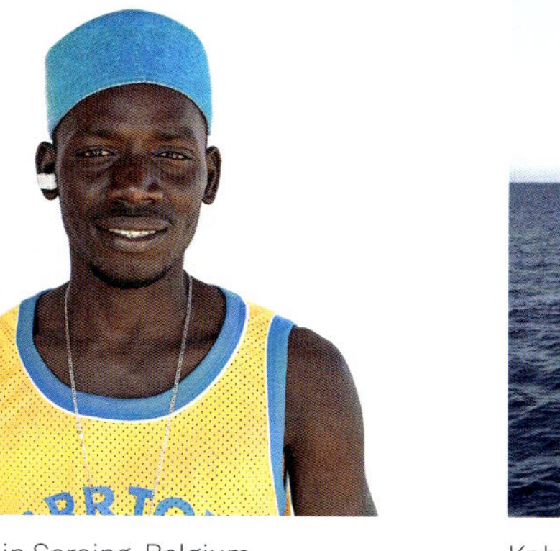

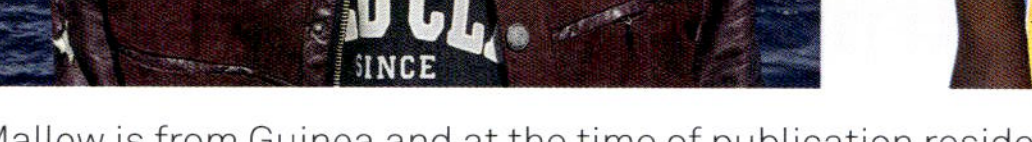

Mallow is from Guinea and at the time of publication resided in Seraing, Belgium.

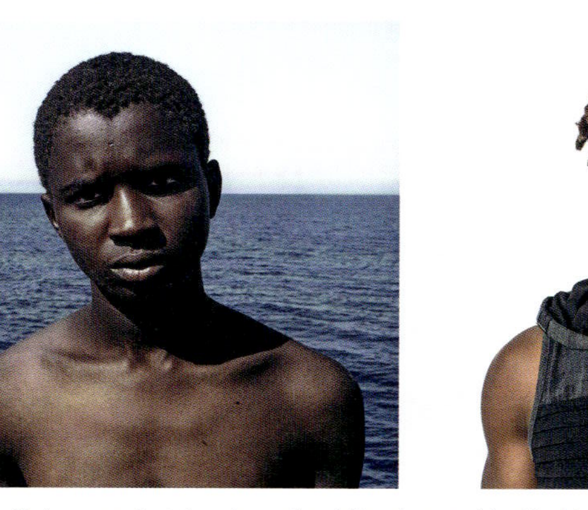

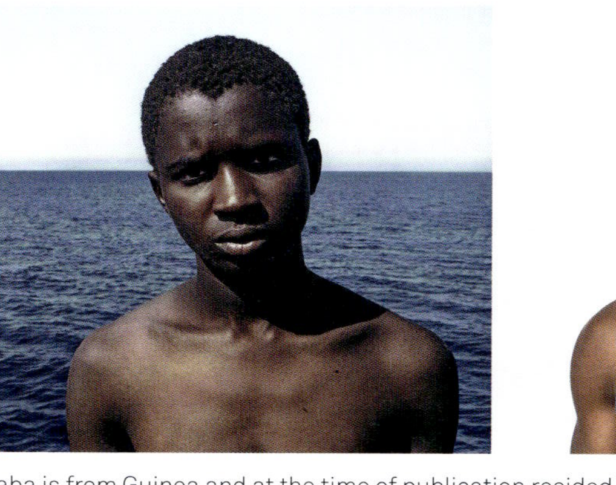

Kaba is from Guinea and at the time of publication resided in Montauban, France.

EUROPE
# HONORABLE MENTIONS

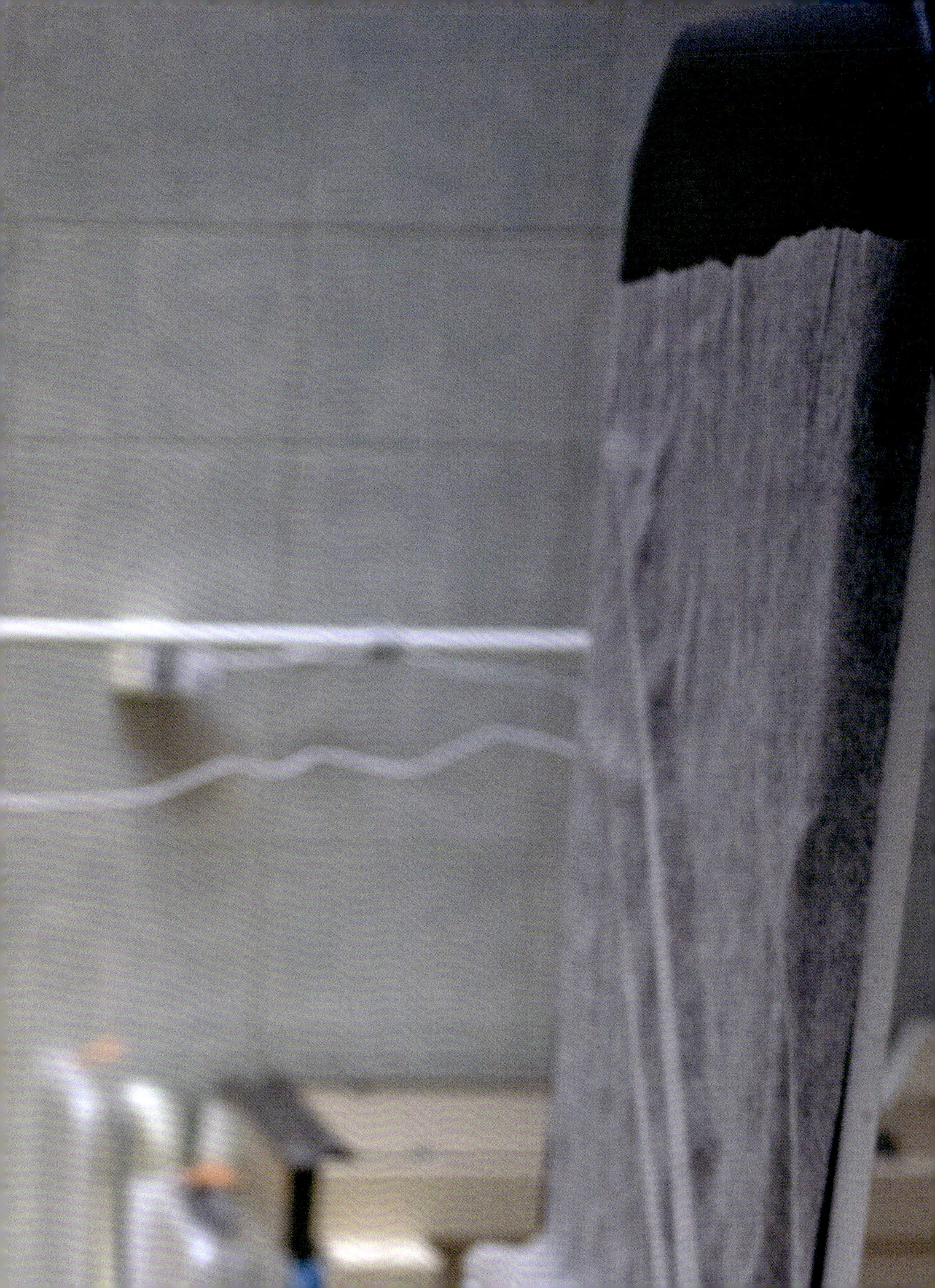

# War Wounds

—

This project portrays people who have undergone amputations as a result of the Russian invasion of Ukraine, which started in February 2022. The photographer, who lost a leg reporting in Afghanistan, feels a camaraderie with the amputees, and strives to depict the cruelty of war behind the front lines. While territory can be surrendered and regained, the loss of a limb, like the loss of a life, is permanent. The jury commented on the sympathy and empathy with which the story was handled.

Emilio Morenatti
Spain, 1969

–

Emilio Morenatti is a photojournalist working for the Associated Press (AP) agency based in Barcelona, Spain. Morenatti also runs AP's photography department in Spain and Portugal.
He photographed this image on assignment for AP.

–

Instagram: @emilio_morenatti

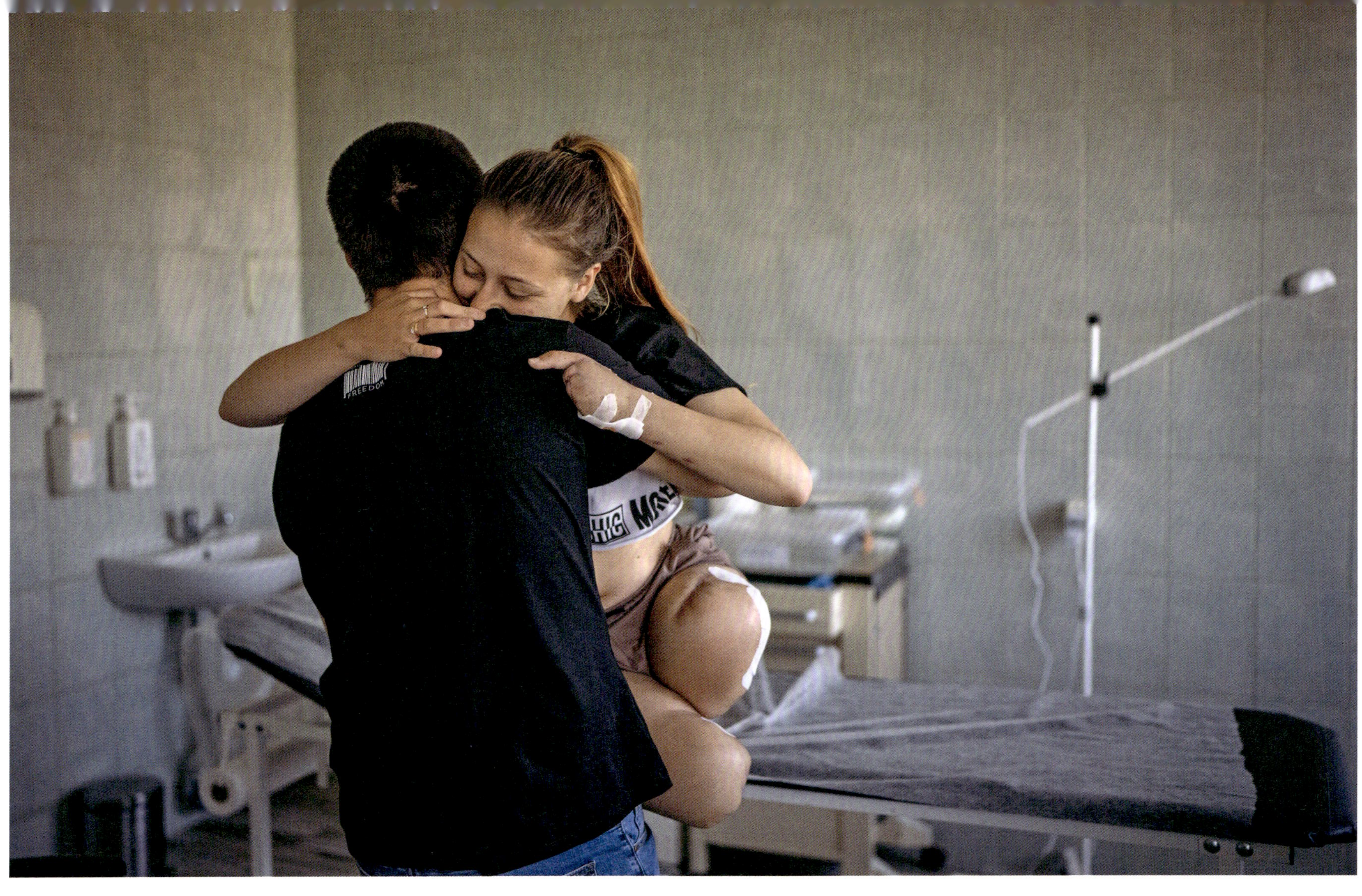


Viktor (23) carries his wife Oksana Balandina (23) in a Lviv hospital, on 14 May 2022. The couple married while Oksana was in the hospital, and Viktor carried her like this for their first dance.

# Europe

—

Kateryna Radchenko,
Europe Jury Chair

The impressive number of applications from Europe inspired us to research and learn more about the lives and stories of people in countries across the continent. Diving into them every day took us on a virtual journey through the events of 2022. Stories about the destinies of migrants (their attempts to cross borders in boats on the open sea; living in unsanitary conditions in forests, or in temporary shelters on long-awaited European land, but behind barbed fences) sat alongside images of natural disasters and the consequences of climate change (dried-up rivers and lakes; outbreaks of forest fires that destroyed everything in their path; people's fight for every piece of nature still habitable). Alongside these were private, intimate family stories (of motherhood, love and hate, relationships), coverage of sports and political events (protests, clashes with the police, tear gas), and stories about the latest inventions, or the disappearance of small regional villages.

As I looked through the applications, one event gave way to another. Images of vivid moments streamed by, but my eyes would linger on photos from Ukraine. Most stories submitted in 2022 dealt with the war in Ukraine – images of pain, loss, death, and destroyed cities. They were breathtaking, but one's mind refused to believe that such atrocities against civilians could happen in the 21st century. Ukraine has attracted documentary photographers and photojournalists from all over the world, so many stories came up again and again: faces behind the windows of trains and buses; goodbyes filled with grief; the wounded and the killed; churned-up landscapes; destroyed houses; exhumations; burned-out military vehicles; doctors and volunteers at work; empty, grief-stricken looks.

Every day, at every online session, our panel of judges tried to answer the most important question: "What really matters? What is worth showing and sharing from 2022?" We could not and did not want to avoid shocking images, because the Russia-Ukraine war had become the topic of the year, so events in Ukraine had to be shown as they really were.

The Long-Term and Open Format projects really impressed us because of their authors' systematic research and the way they immersed themselves in their subjects, giving the viewers access to unexpected stories, to large industrial facilities, to boats that transport migrants, to private homes, and gated communities. This closeness brings the audience almost face-to-face with the heroes of the stories, allowing them to feel their experiences, their pain, and their worries.

Choosing the winners is a very intense and responsible process. Each time you try to balance the narrative and visual components of the project. Each time you think about the impact that an image and its author can have. The great power of World Press Photo is in the opportunity it provides to collect and show images that matter to the whole world, and to demonstrate the unity between communities, countries, and people in their intention to solve common problems.

# Jury

–

KATERYNA RADCHENKO / CHAIR
UKRAINE
–
Kateryna Radchenko is a Ukrainian curator, artist, and photography researcher. She is the founder and director of the Odesa Photo Days festival in Odesa, Ukraine, and author of several international publications.
–
Instagram: @radchenko_ua

OKSANA KANIVETS

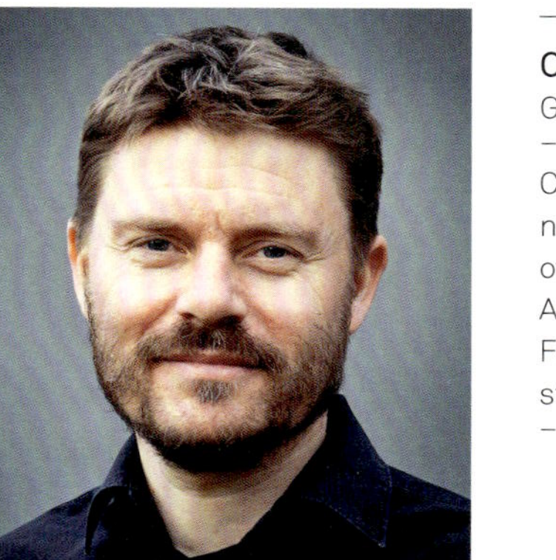

CHIHO BANGERT

CHRISTOPH BANGERT
GERMANY
–
Christoph Bangert is a German photojournalist, author, and educator. He is a professor of photography at the Hannover University of Applied Sciences and Arts, and founder of the Fotobus Society, one of the largest non-profit student photography projects worldwide.
–

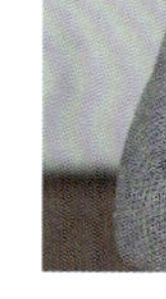

# Winners

–

SINGLES

ALKIS KONSTANTINIDIS
GREECE, 1984
–
Alkis Konstantinidis is a photojournalist based in Athens, Greece. He joined Reuters in 2014. Throughout his career, Konstantinidis has covered major stories around the world.
–
Instagram: @alkisk_

PETROS GIANNAKOURIS

STORIES

EVGENIY MALOLETKA
UKRAINE, 1987
–
Evgeniy Maloletka is a Ukrainian war photographer, journalist and filmmaker. Since 2014, he has been covering the war in Ukraine and other major events such as the Euromaidan Revolution, the protests in Belarus, and the Nagorno-Karabakh war.
–
Instagram: @evgenymaloletka

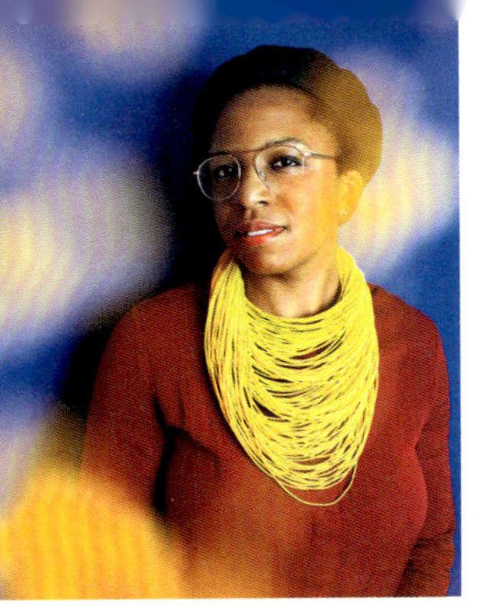

MARGUERITE BORNHAUSER

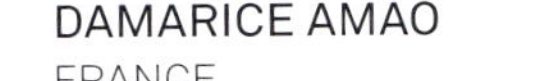

### DAMARICE AMAO

FRANCE

–

Damarice Amao is a photography historian, and an associate curator for photography at the Musée National d'Art Moderne/Centre Pompidou.

–

Instagram: @damariceamao

OLIVIA HARRIS

### GABRIELLE FONSECA JOHNSON

UNITED KINGDOM

–

Gabrielle Fonseca Johnson is the editor of *The Wider Image*, Reuters' award-winning multimedia storytelling imprint. She leads a team commissioning stories from photographers and multimedia journalists around the world.

–

Instagram: @gfonsecajohnson

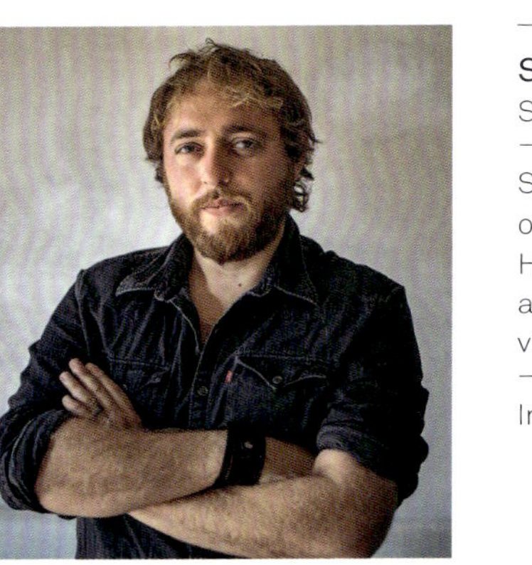

MARIBEL IZCUE

### SANTI PALACIOS

SPAIN

–

Santi Palacios is a photojournalist focusing on migrations, conflicts, and human ecology. He is editor-in-chief of *Sonda Internacional*, a non-profit media outlet specializing in visual journalism and the climate crisis.

–

Instagram: @santipalacios

## LONG-TERM PROJECTS

### SIMONE TRAMONTE

ITALY, 1976

–

Simone Tramonte is a photographer focusing on documenting social and environmental contemporary issues. His work aims to document how innovative technologies can shape a more sustainable future.

–

Instagram: @simonetramonte

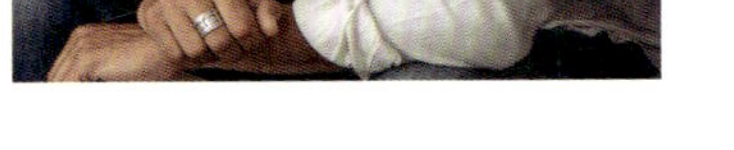

## OPEN FORMAT

### CESAR DEZFULI

SPAIN/IRAN, 1991

–

Cesar Dezfuli is a freelance photojournalist focusing on human rights and international affairs. Since 2015, his focus has been on the migrant crisis at the borders of Europe, in particular the Central Mediterranean migration route.

–

Instagram: @dezfuli

CESAR DEZFULI

# North and Central America

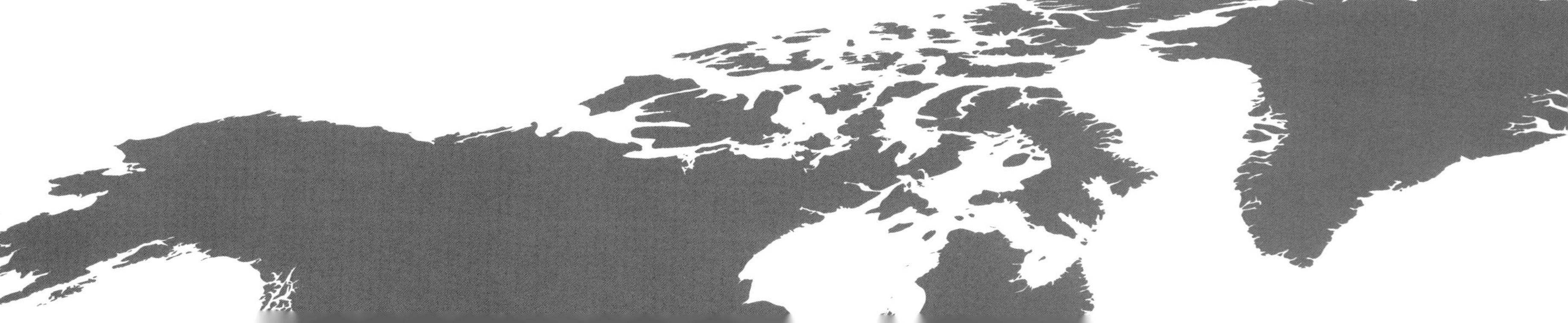

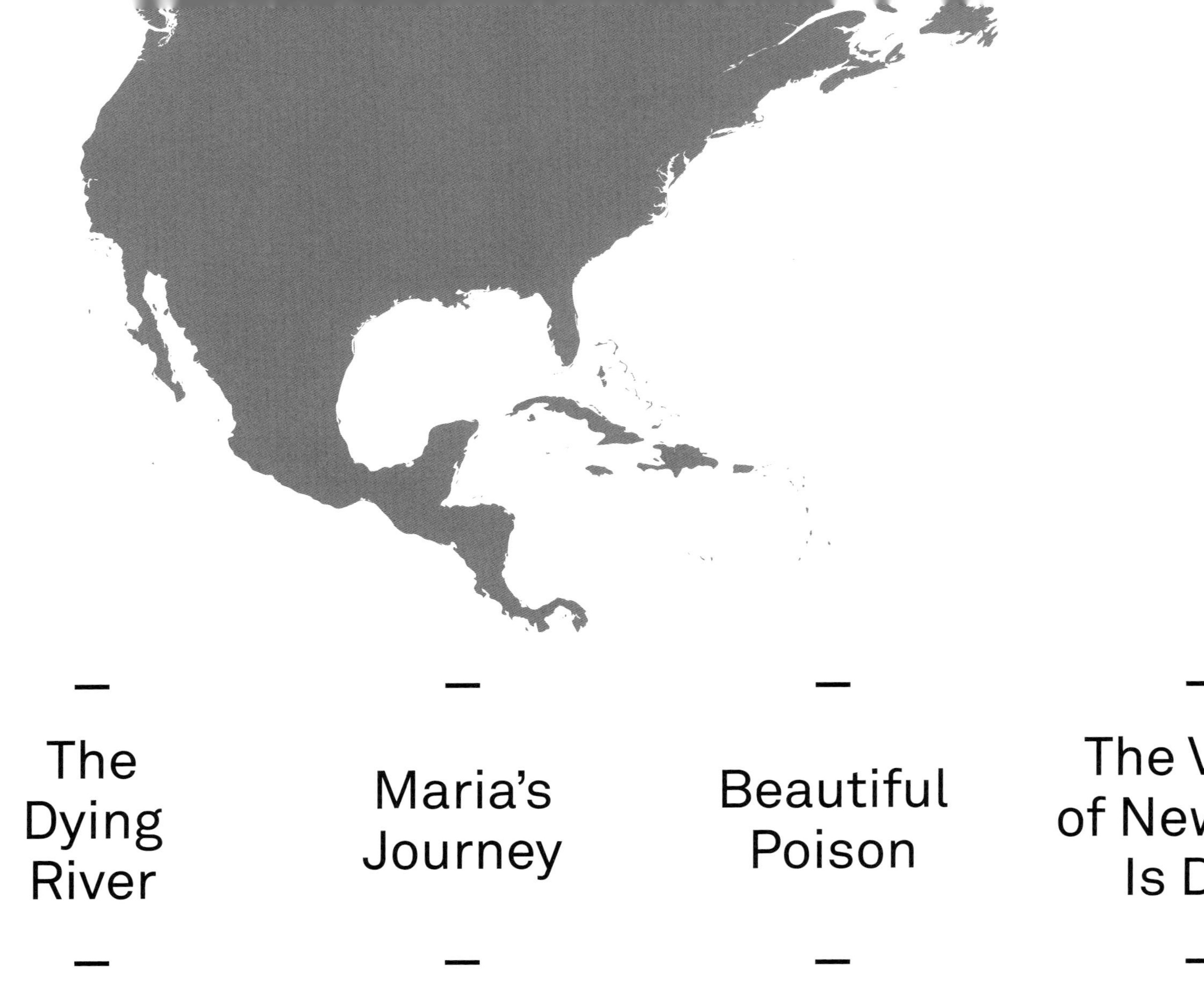

The Dying River

Maria's Journey

Beautiful Poison

The Voice of New York Is Drill

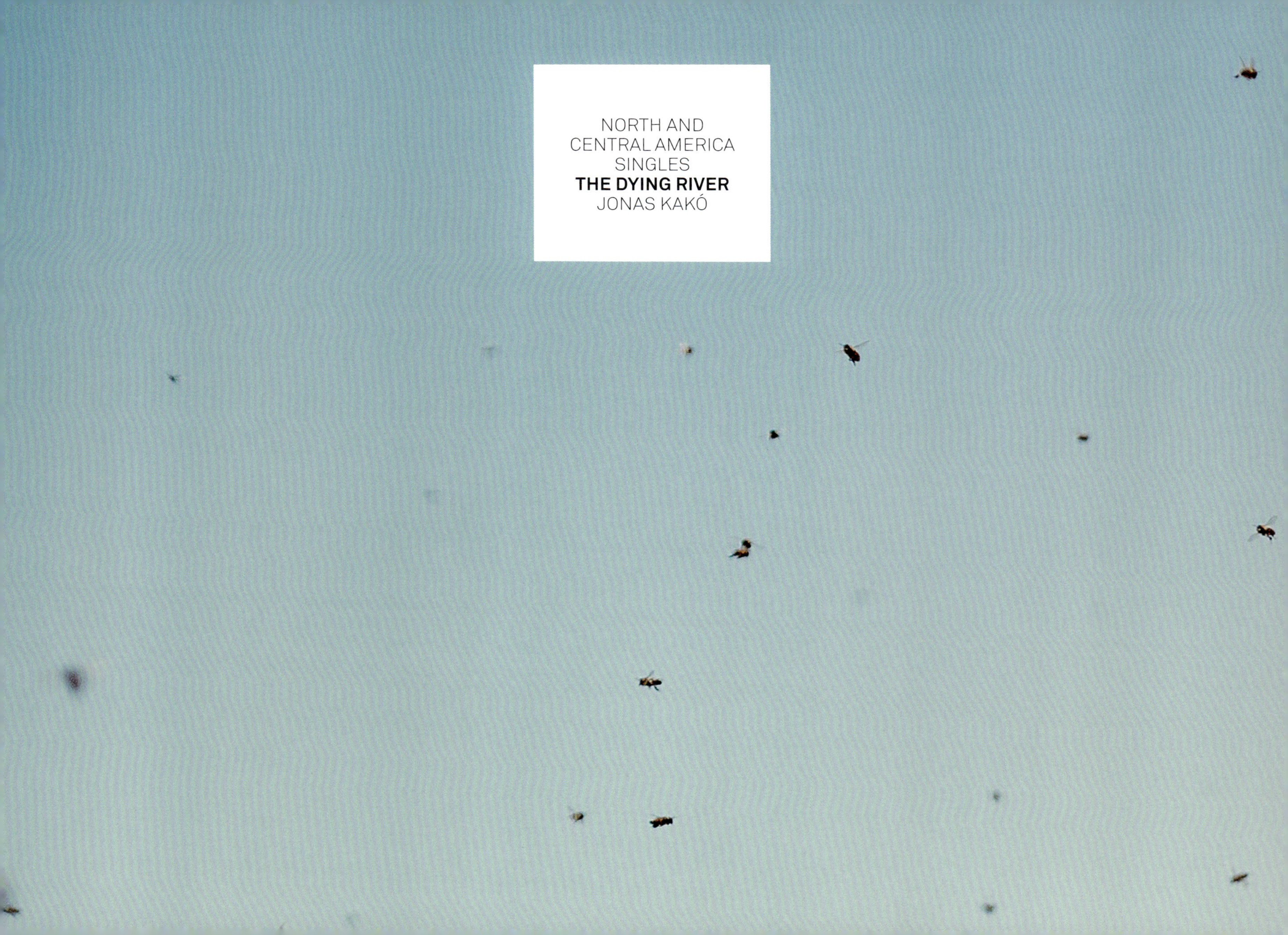

NORTH AND
CENTRAL AMERICA
SINGLES

**THE DYING RIVER**

JONAS KAKÓ

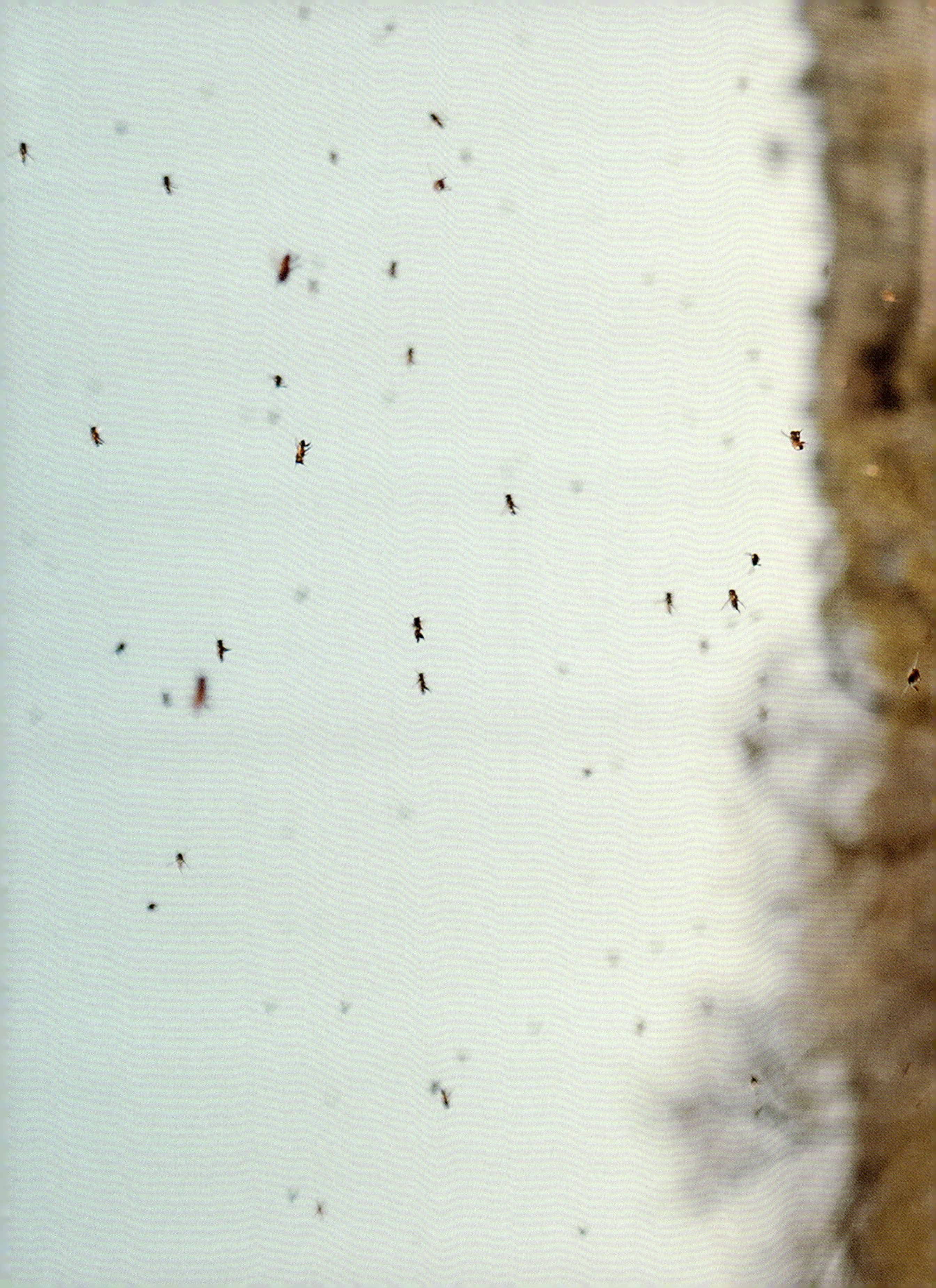

# The Dying River

Alfredo, Ubaldo, and José tend beehives near Wenden in the Arizona desert, United States, on 11 March 2022. A substantial decrease in flow of the Colorado River, caused by lack of rain and increasing demand for water upstream, now requires these workers to provide water for the bees in troughs. Heat and drought weakens bees, making them more susceptible to pathogens and parasites, and impacts the plants from which they feed. Between 2019 and 2020, colonies of bees – vital for pollinating crops – declined by 43.7 percent across the US. The jury felt this understated portrait invites reflection on an environmental issue that resonates at a global level.

Jonas Kakó is a member of Panos Pictures.

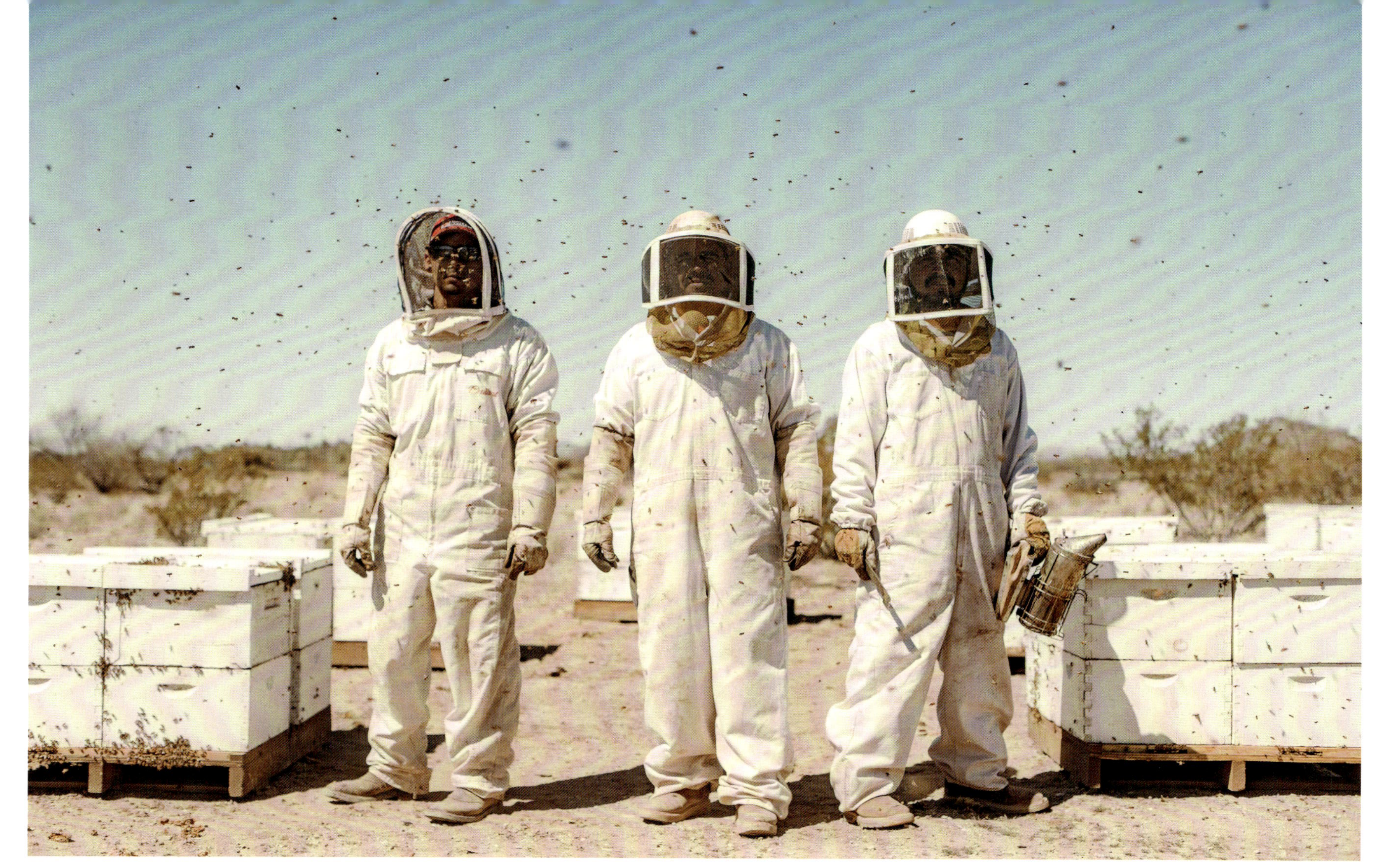

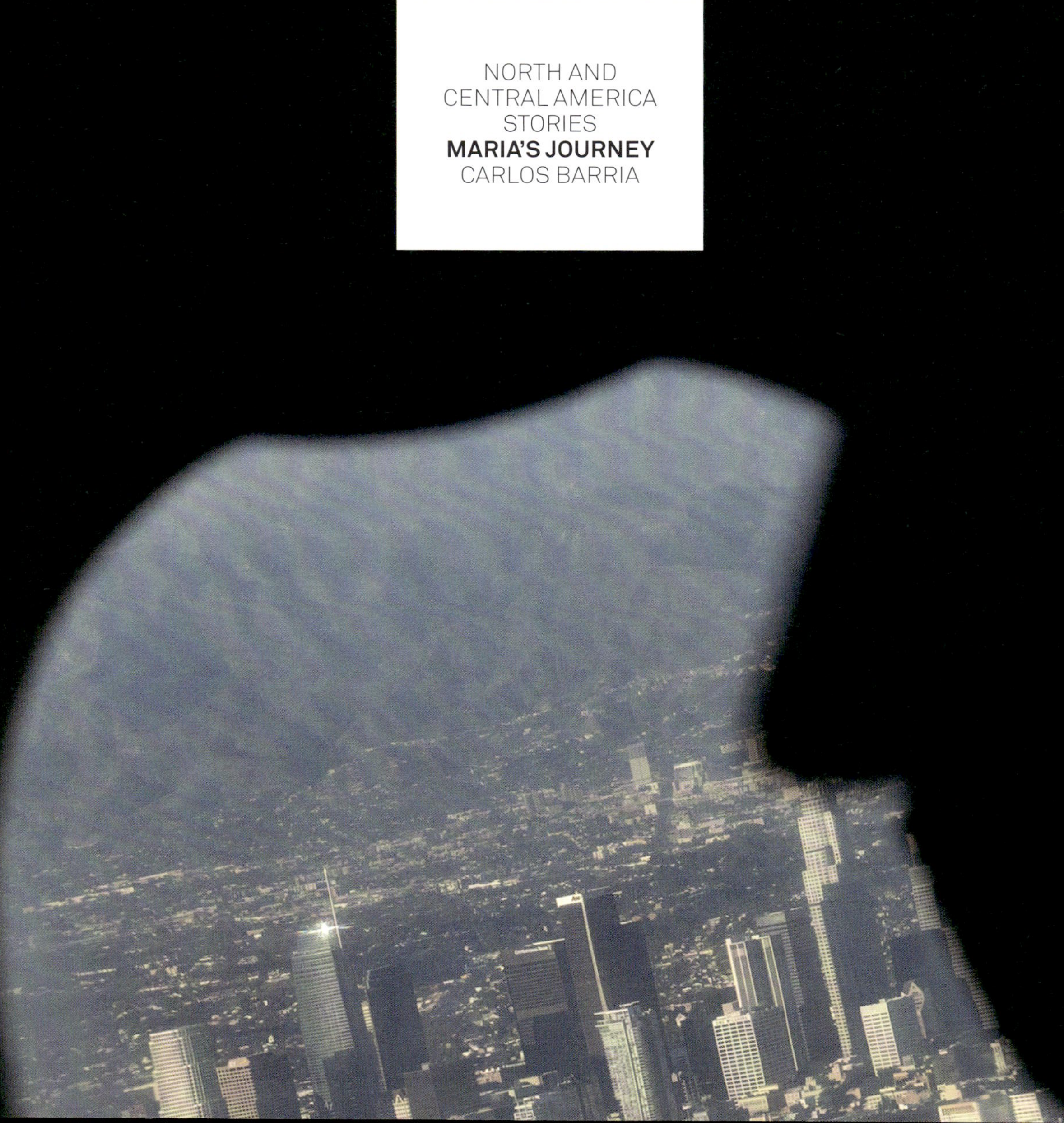

NORTH AND
CENTRAL AMERICA
STORIES
**MARIA'S JOURNEY**
CARLOS BARRIA

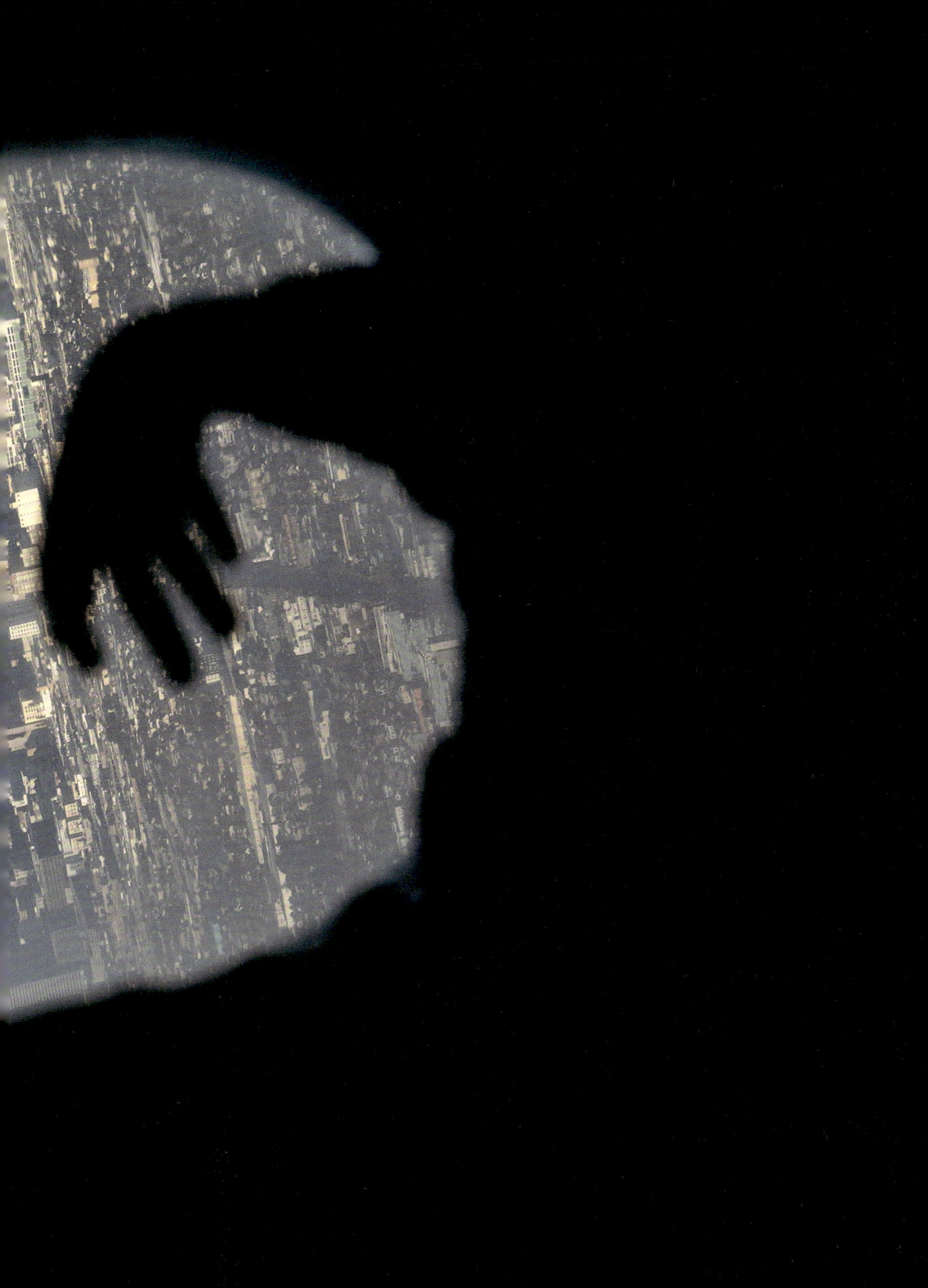

# Maria's Journey

Upon arriving in the United States from Honduras in 2017 in search of asylum, Maria Hernandez and her two daughters, aged eight and three, were apprehended. Border authorities deported Maria, but her children remained behind. At first, they stayed in a children's shelter; later, they went to live with Maria's adult son, who was already in the US. In 2022, Maria returned under an asylum program, and was reunited with her family in Los Angeles, California. The jury appreciated how this story visualizes the complications that immigrants often encounter when assimilating in a new country.

Carlos Barria photographed these images on assignment for Reuters.

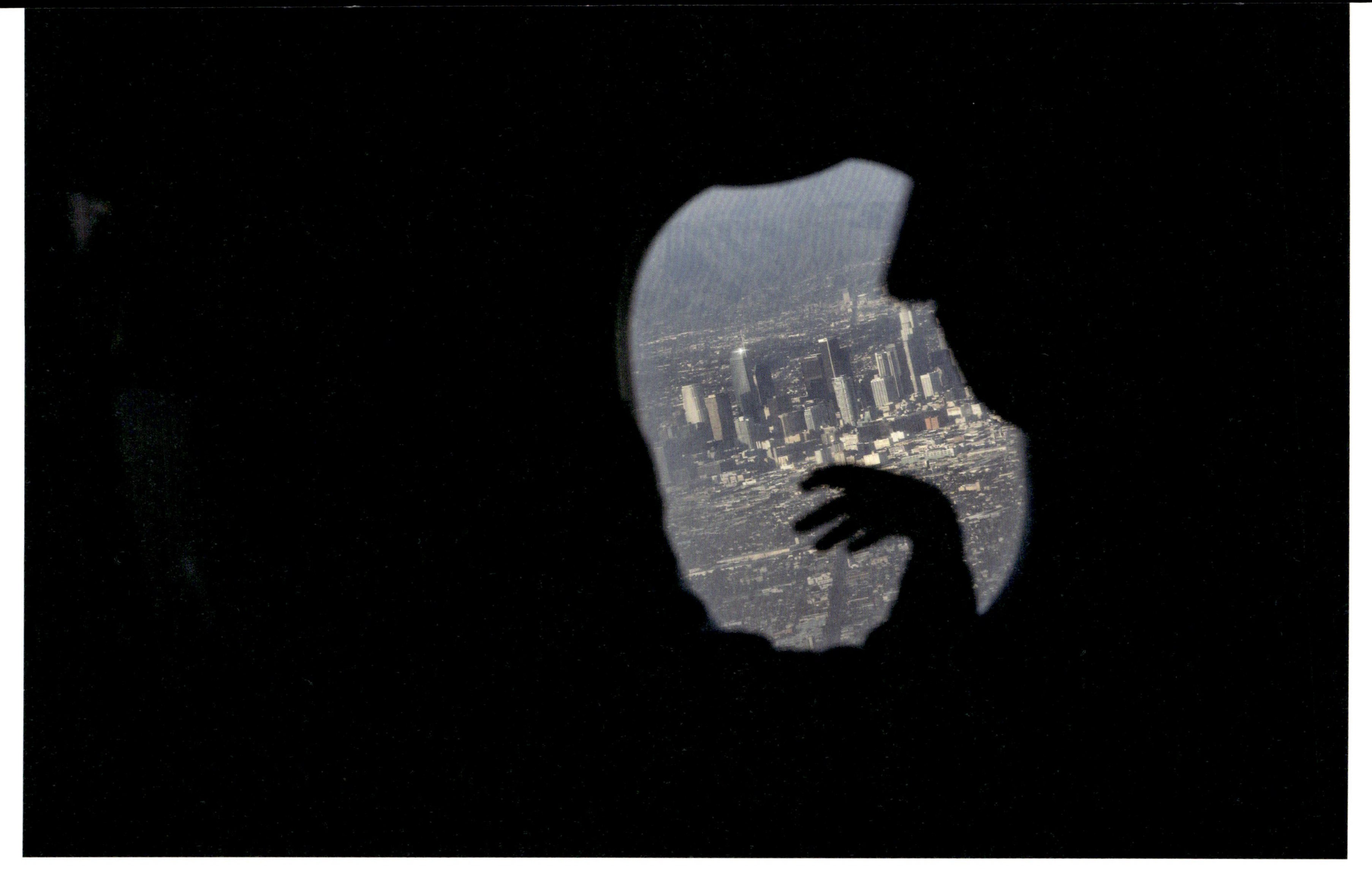

Maria Hernandez and her grandson Aron look out at the city of Los Angeles, United States, from an airplane window as they arrive to reunite with their family, on 11 January 2022. Maria had raised Aron since his mother relocated to the US years earlier in search of opportunities.

Maria Hernandez arrives to work on a banana plantation, in San Pedro Sula, Honduras, on 25 June 2021.

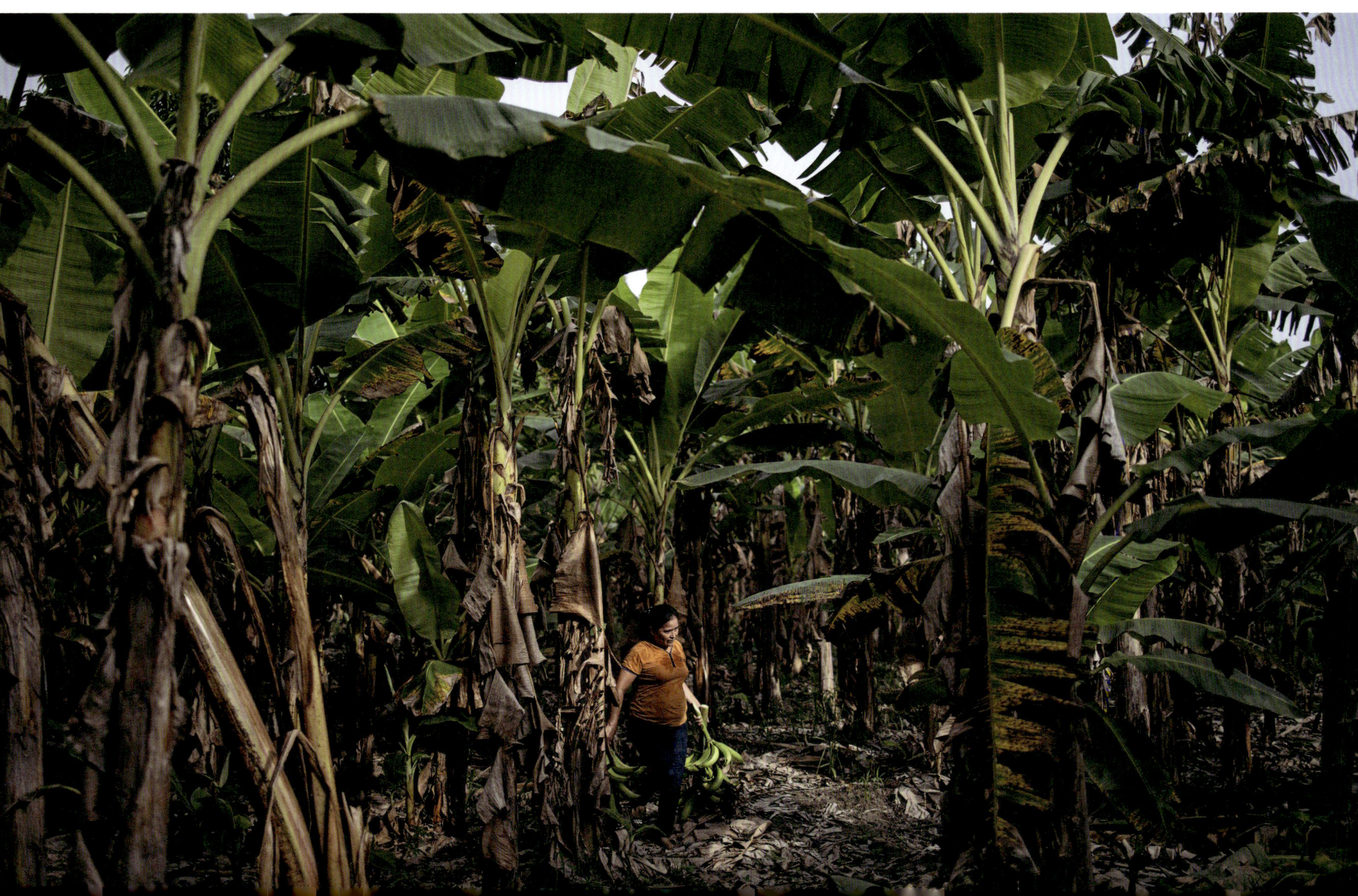

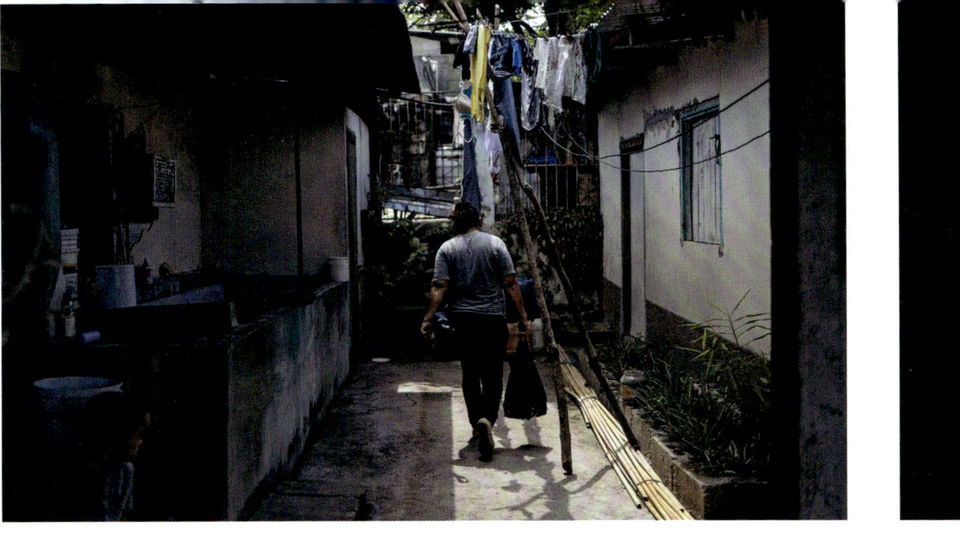

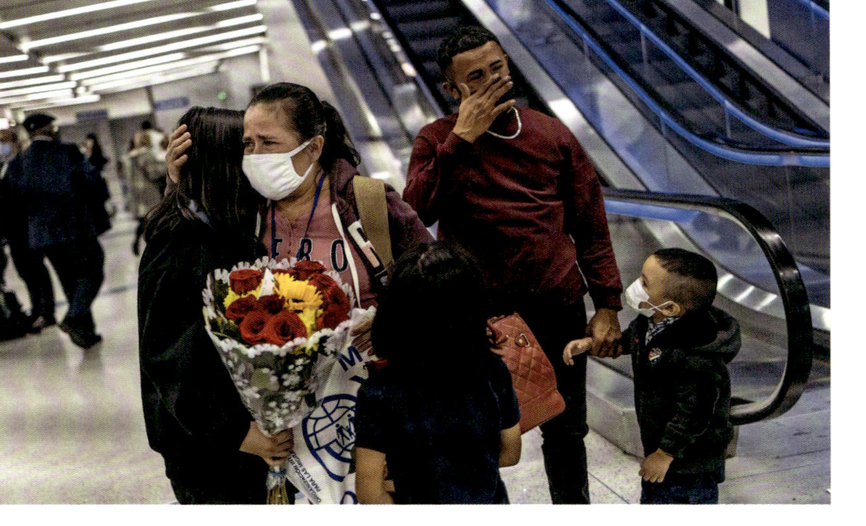

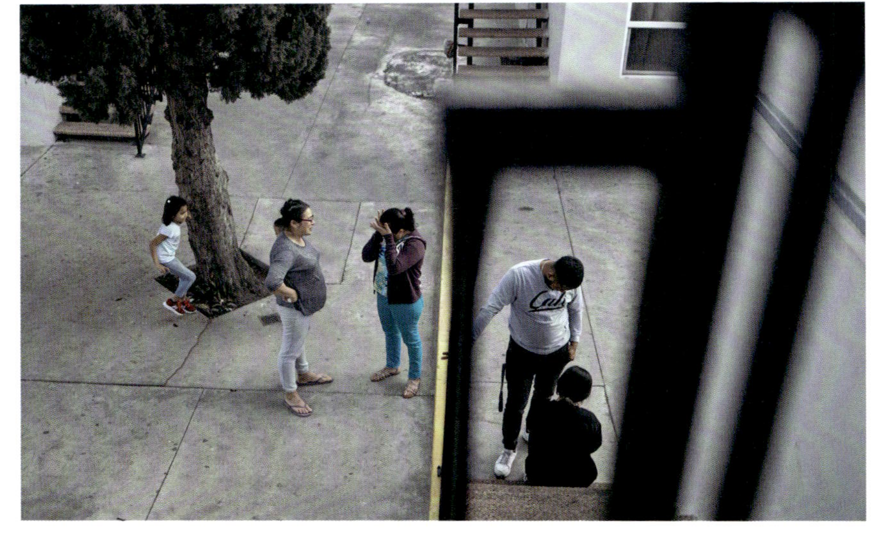

Maria Hernandez walks home from shopping in San Pedro Sula, on 23 June 2021, while awaiting a decision on her immigration case.

Maria Hernandez hugs her daughter Michelle, while her son Maynor is overcome with emotion, during their family reunion at Los Angeles International Airport, on 11 January 2022.

Maria Hernandez rides in a pickup truck on the way to work at a banana plantation, in San Pedro Sula, on 24 June 2021.

Maria Hernandez cries as she chats with her friend Marta after viewing a potential apartment to rent in Los Angeles, on 12 January 2022. Without a credit history or sufficient documentation to open a bank account, she initially struggled to rent accommodation.

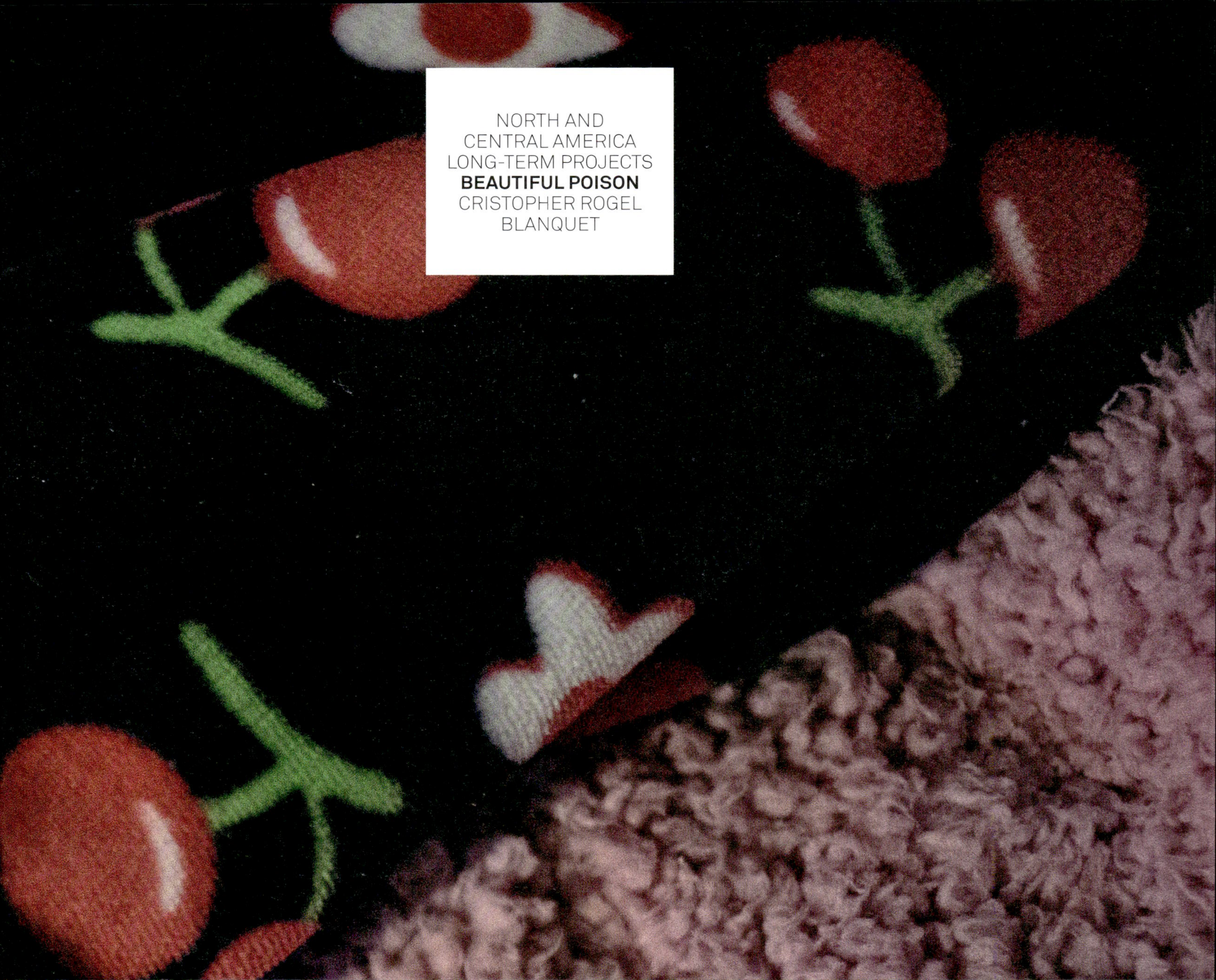

NORTH AND
CENTRAL AMERICA
LONG-TERM PROJECTS

**BEAUTIFUL POISON**

CRISTOPHER ROGEL
BLANQUET

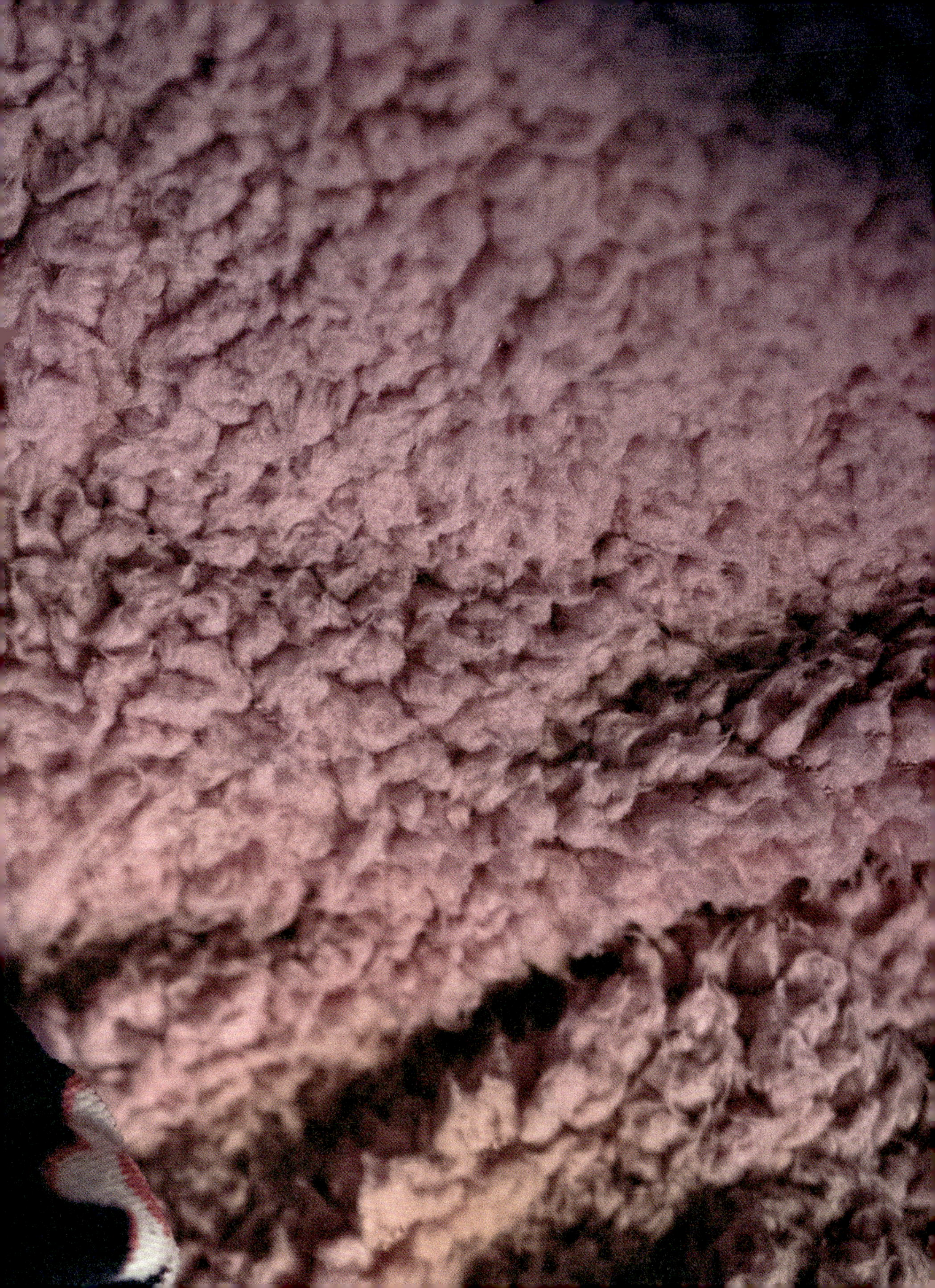

# Beautiful Poison

The EU, China, the US, and other countries that have banned certain agrichemicals due to health and environmental risks still sometimes legally sell these substances to countries where labor is cheap and then import the products grown abroad. Although the Mexican government has begun to take steps against such double standards, some toxic pesticides remain on the market, and guidelines for their use are not always enforced. The photographer sought to document flower-growing families in Villa Guerrero in order to raise awareness of the environmental and human impact of agrichemicals in the Mexican flower belt and portray the authorities' neglect of health-care in the region, as well as to call attention to consumers' responsibilities when buying flowers.

Cristopher Rogel Blanquet is supported by a W. Eugene Smith Grant and the National System of Art Creators FONCA. He is a stringer for Getty Images.

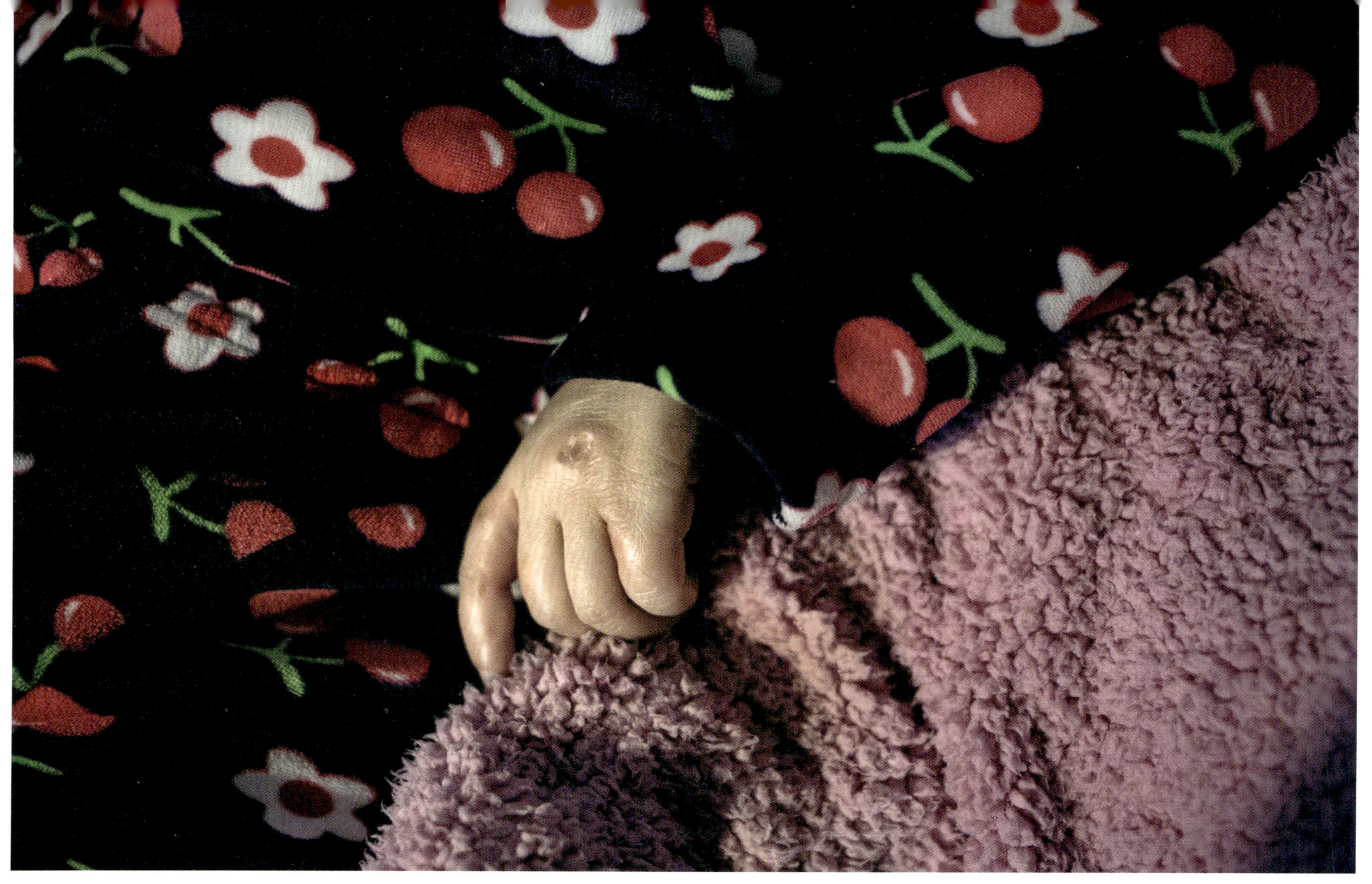

Carmelita (16), who lives with encephalomalacia (softening of the brain tissue), sits in her room in Villa Guerrero, Mexico, on 21 November 2021. Although a direct causal relationship is difficult to prove, certain agrichemicals have been linked to congenital conditions, stillbirth, and cancer.

Floriculture greenhouses (pictured on 1 October 2022) cover hundreds of hectares in Villa Guerrero. The surrounding state is responsible for most of the country's greenhouse-grown cut flower production.

Sebastián (18), who was born with hydrocephalus, holds on to his mother, Doña Petra, after she has bathed him, in Villa Guerrero, on 18 March 2020. Doña Petra died of kidney failure during the pandemic.

Carmelita (16) lies on her bed on 21 November 2021. Photosensitivity caused by encephalomalacia gives Carmelita such pain that she cannot go out into the light.

Sebastián (18) bathes with the help of his father Don Tino, on 21 March 2020. He is dependent on his parents for most daily activities.

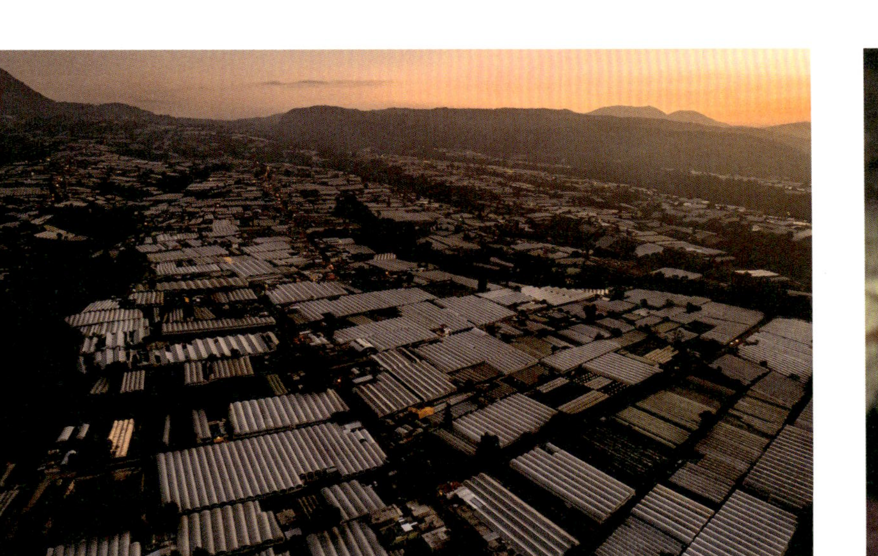

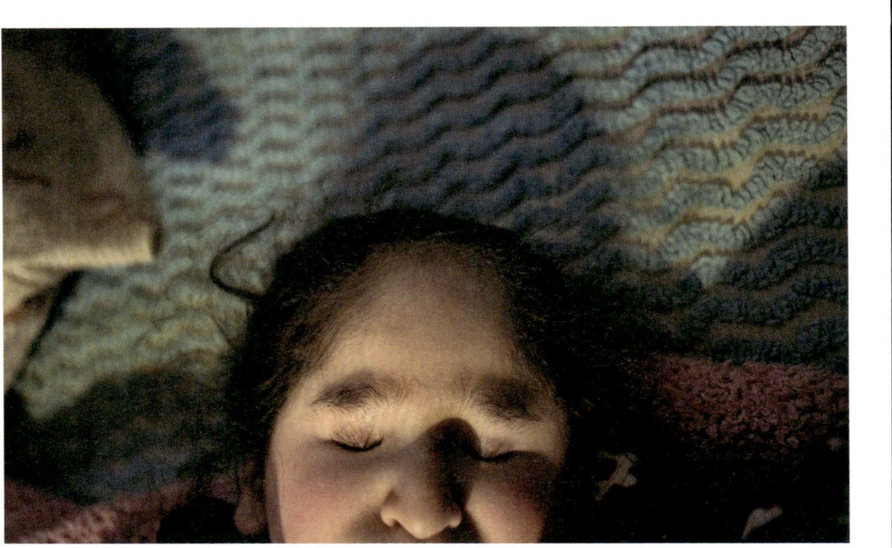

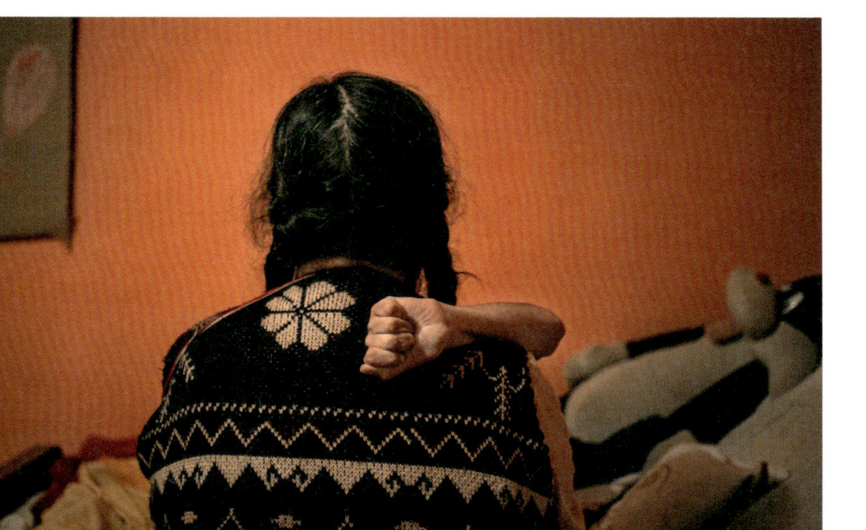

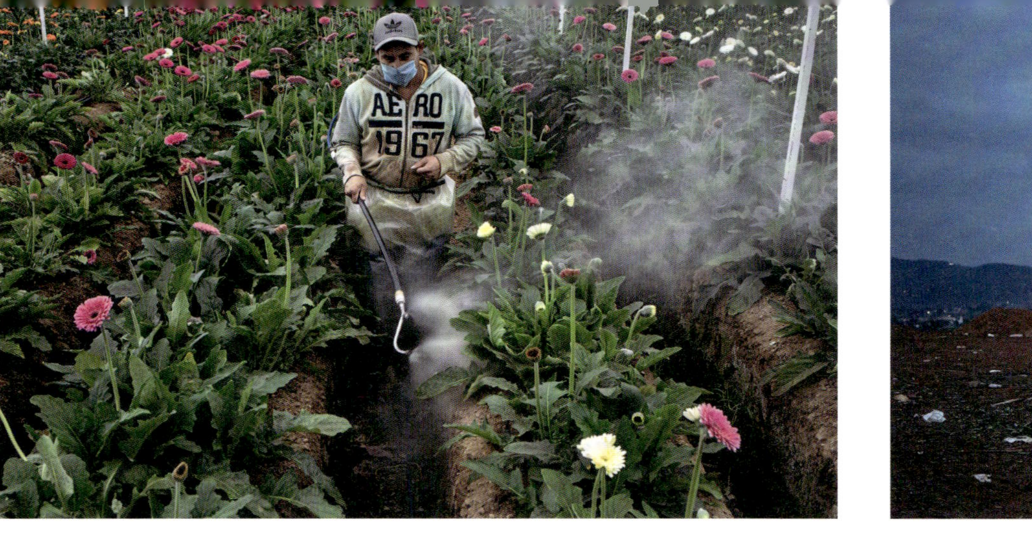

A worker fumigates gerberas inside a Villa Guerrero greenhouse, on 21 March 2020.

A man sells flowers from his car at the Villa Guerrero flower market, on 16 May 2021. Most flowers sold at the market are shipped around the country or exported.

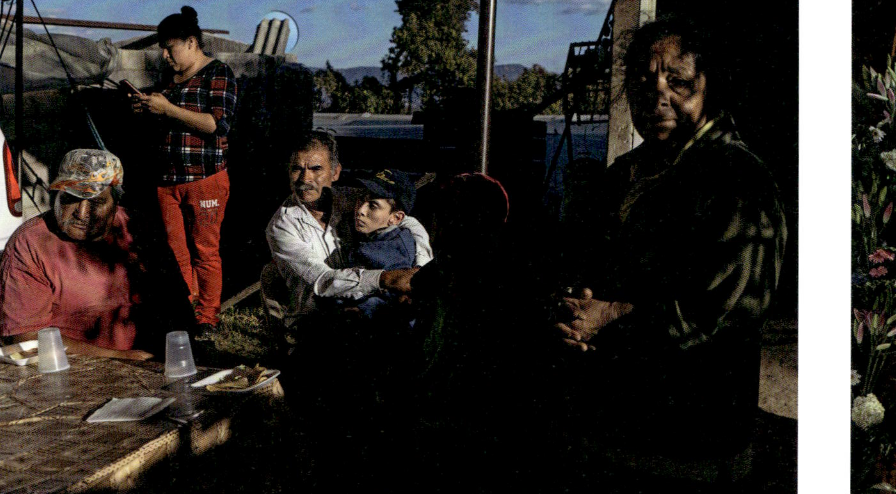

Don Tino holds Sebastián (18) at a family reunion, on 3 February 2022. Marisela (looking at cell phone) has experienced two stillbirths, and other family members live with conditions possibly linked to agrichemicals.

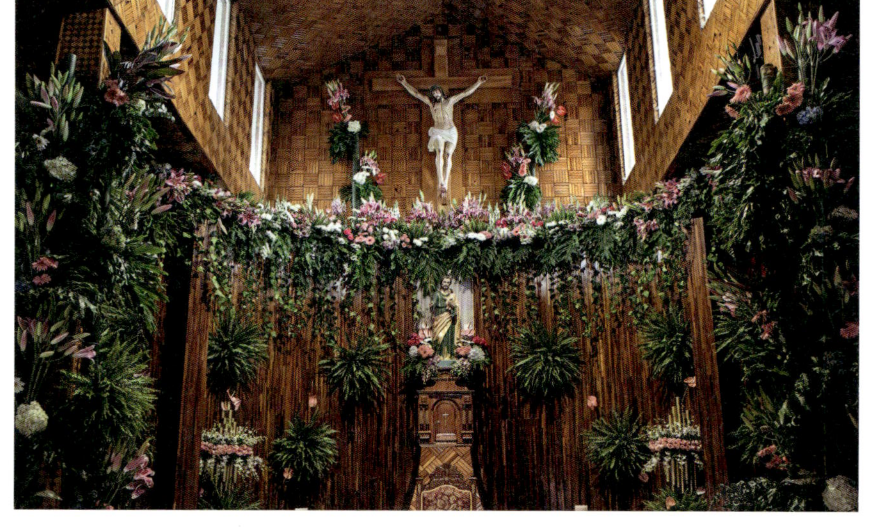

Local flowers adorn the church of San Miguel in Villa Guerrero, on 19 March 2020.

NORTH AND
CENTRAL AMERICA
OPEN FORMAT

# THE VOICE OF NEW YORK IS DRILL

ASHLEY PEÑA

Scan the QR code to listen to the artists featured in this story on Spotify

# The Voice of New York Is Drill

Drill, a musical genre that originated in Chicago, United States, may be the most recent wave of rap music to achieve massive global success, but its story is not new to hip-hop. Even as their hit songs top charts, New York drill artists are targeted by New York City Police Department (NYPD) investigators who comb their lyrics and music videos for evidence of gang-related crimes. Concerts are shut down and artists face indictments, all while success brings rivalry and jealousy among peers out on the streets. This series offers an intimate look at several members of this new generation of young men and women drill artists striving to realize their dreams.

Ashley Peña photographed these images on assignment for *New York Magazine*.

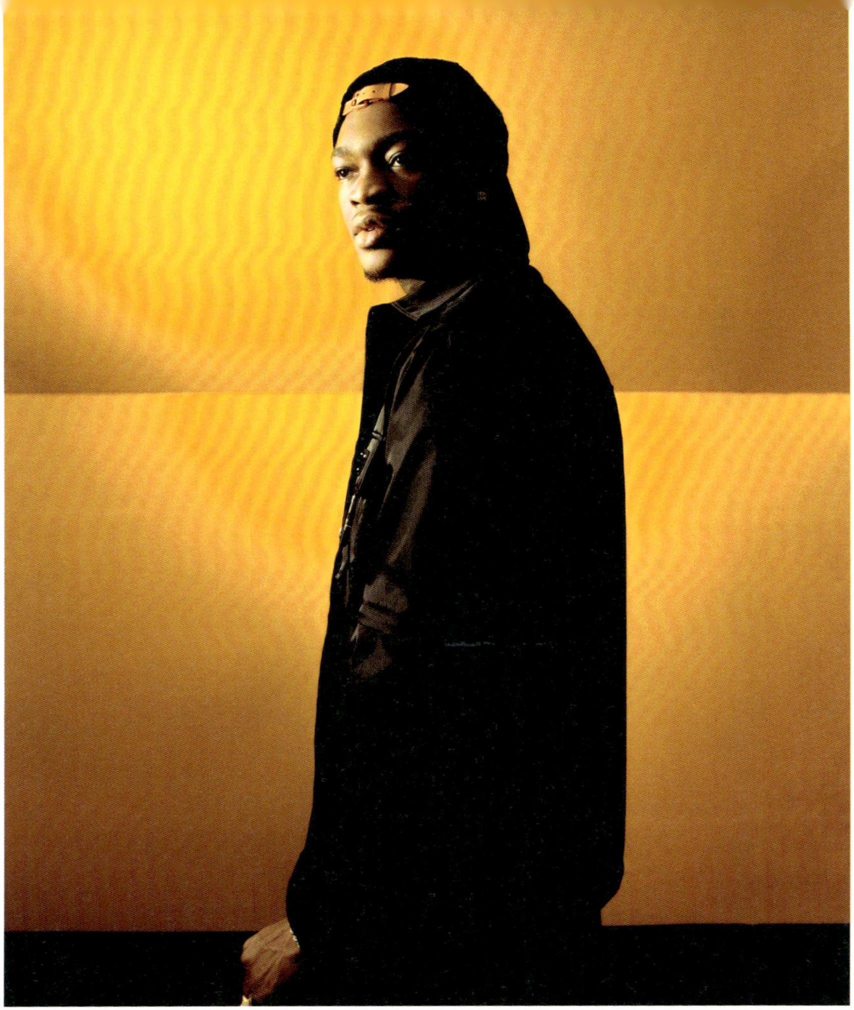

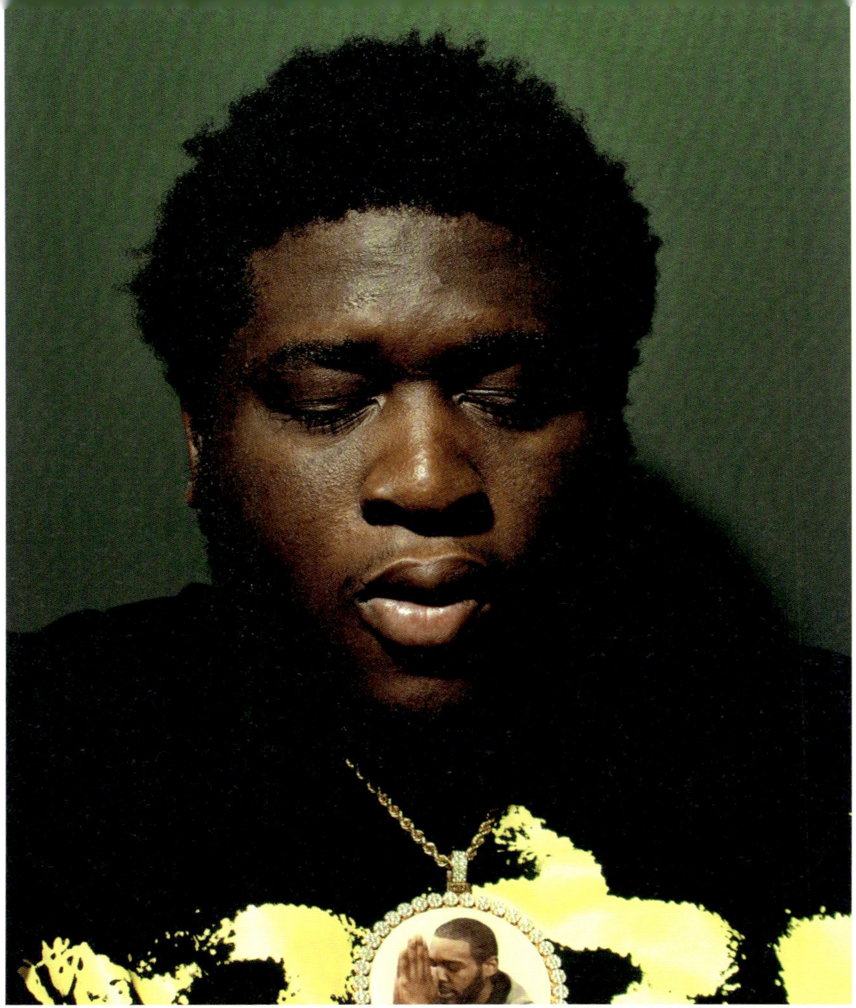

26AR (23) was sentenced to four years in prison at the age of 16 on gang conspiracy charges. While incarcerated, he began his career as a rap artist. Crown Heights, New York, United States, 21 July 2022.

Cash Cobain (24) is a self-taught producer and rapper from the South Bronx who has produced for musical superstars like Lil Yachty. South Bronx, New York, 15 July 2022.

B-Lovee (21) is a South Bronx native who has turned local renown into global success by going viral on video sharing platforms like TikTok. South Bronx, New York, 11 July 2022.

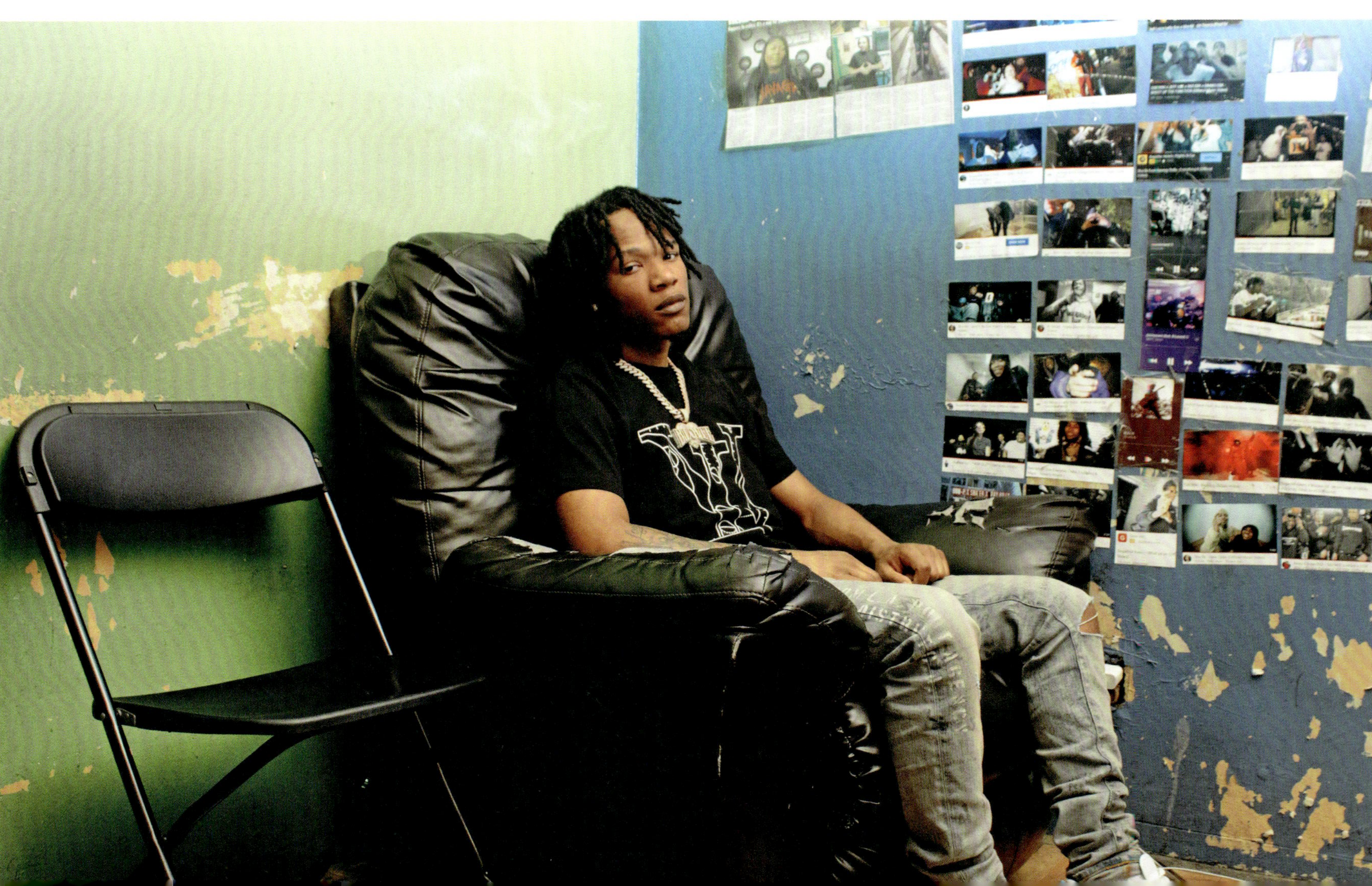

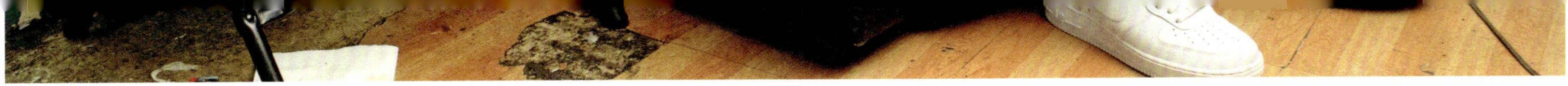

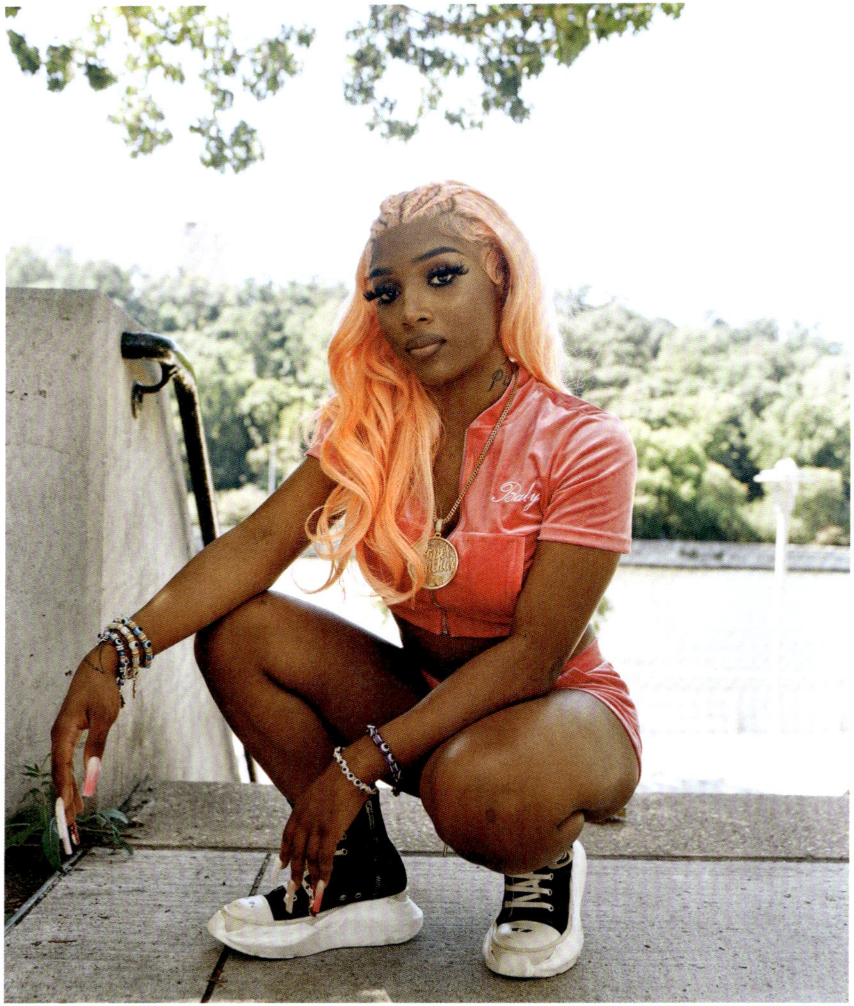

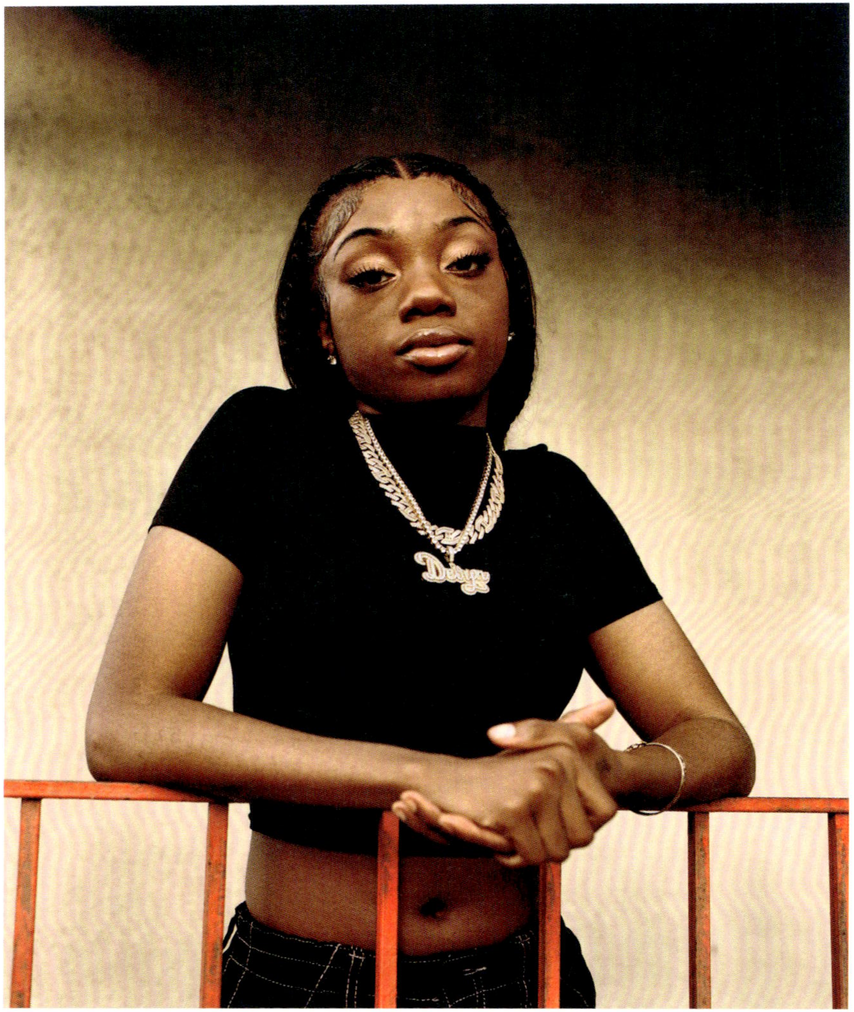

Kenzo B (18) is one of the young up-and-coming artists in the Brooklyn drill scene. The Bronx, New York, on 4 August 2022.

Young Devyn (20) is inspired by her Caribbean heritage and dreams of making space for women in the drill scene. New York, 30 July 2022.

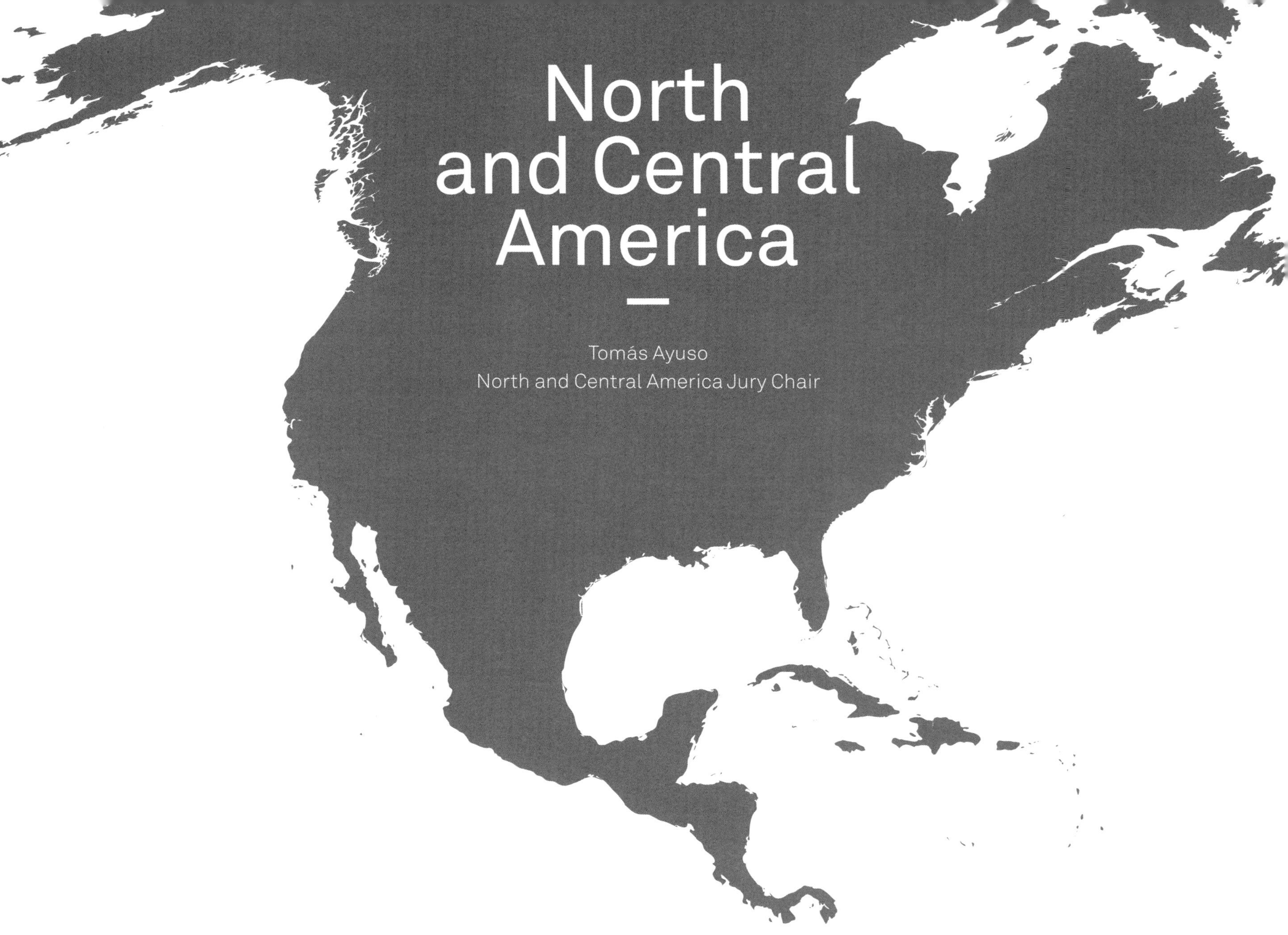

# North and Central America

—

Tomás Ayuso

North and Central America Jury Chair

The visual work produced by the North and Central America region photographers in 2022 was as varied as the region itself. From the deep-blue melt dripping off Greenland's glaciers, to the rusted red earth powdering everything across the vast US–Mexico borderlands, and all the way to the pale-green fronds of Central America's cloudy rainforests, this year's entries stunned the jury with their superb variety and sheer technical prowess.

But it was the visual narrative and quality of the storytelling that truly stood out across the region. The submissions reflected not only the ever-shifting news cycle, but also the inner preoccupations of the region's people. Entries traced migration from source to sanctuary; navigated the fallout from further encroachment on women's rights across communities; and honored the stories of individuals' struggles to determine their identity on their own terms.

This year's contestants went beyond reflection by peering into the shape of stories to come. For instance, as the climate crisis left no country unpunished, photographers composed visual stories that presaged possible tumult – and solutions – yet to come. Given our region's permanent state of motion, issues which are front and center one year might be supplanted by more pressing continental concerns in another. In addition, core issues seldom if ever stay static, fluctuating along with the people whose lives they affect. The 2023 World Press Photo entrants managed, almost without exception, to assemble impressive bodies of work that presented the interlinked past, present, and future of regional issues, and the states of mind of our people.

Similarly, contestants found ways to innovate on oft-told stories, avoiding derivative tropes of the past. As the regional model evolves and grows more well-known among a pool of potentially interested photographers, the space for photographers from nearly every corner of the region to participate broadens. Notably, female-identifying and non-binary winners reached near parity with the number of their male peers this year, and the ratio of local to foreign photographers was evenly balanced. Compared with past years, more people from less-represented communities and countries now feel empowered to tell the stories of their communities, in ways only someone who grew up surrounded by the tragedies and celebrations of home ever could.

With this year's cultural and historic moments so perfectly captured, our jury struggled to choose from the wealth of entries. We were constantly struck by the sheer strength and subtle introspection of submissions, apparent as our shortlist ultimately emerged. As a jury, we arrived at one undeniable consensus: whether it's an image capturing the continent's zeitgeist in a single still, or a long-term project weaving together the complex instances of a person's life over an extended period of time, the future of North and Central America's visual storytelling is safe in the hands of a multitude of photographers, shining incandescently bright.

# Jury

–

PATRICK MACLEOD

TOMÁS AYUSO / CHAIR
HONDURAS
–
Tomás Ayuso is a Honduran writer and documentary photojournalist. He focuses on forced displacement, and urban dispossession in Latin American conflict, seeking to weave threads of disparate communities into the story of the Western Hemisphere.
–
Instagram: @tomas_ayuso

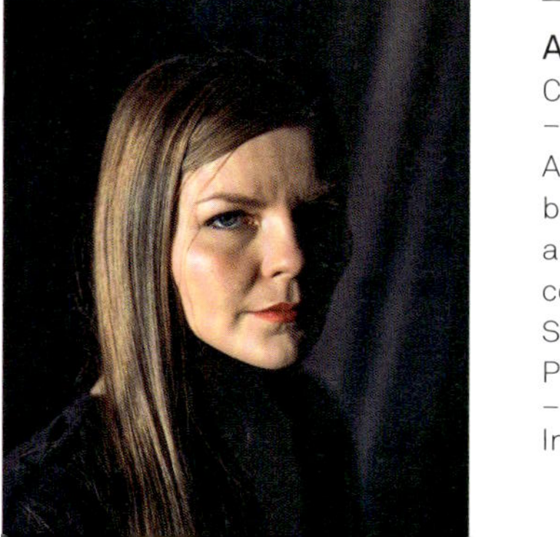

ASON FRANSON

AMBER BRACKEN
CANADA
–
Amber Bracken is a freelance photojournalist based in Edmonton, Canada, working primarily across western North America to better connect to global issues in her own backyard. She was the winner of the 2022 World Press Photo of the Year.
–
Instagram: @photobracken

# Winners

–

## SINGLES

JONAS KAKÓ
GERMANY, 1992
–
Jonas Kakó is a documentary photographer based in Hannover, Germany. His work looks at the effects of the climate crisis, focusing on the individuals who already suffer from it and whose existence is threatened.
–
Instagram: @jonaskako

MAXIMILIAN VON LACHNER

## STORIES

CARLOS BARRIA
ARGENTINA, 1979
–
Carlos Barria is a senior photographer at Reuters, based in California, United States. Barria has spent more than 20 years with Reuters covering breaking news around the world.
–
Instagram: @carlosabarria

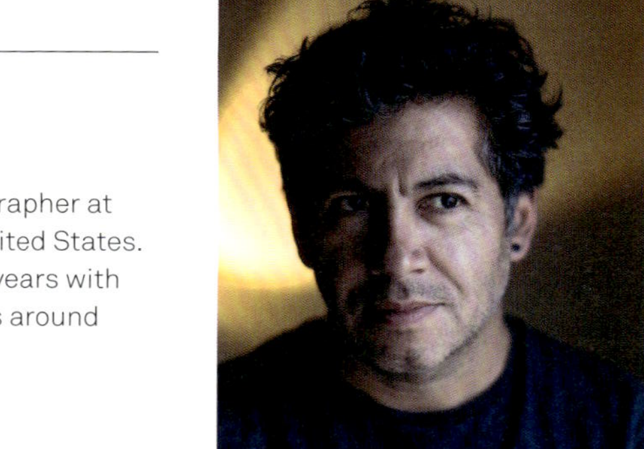

JTH MORRIS

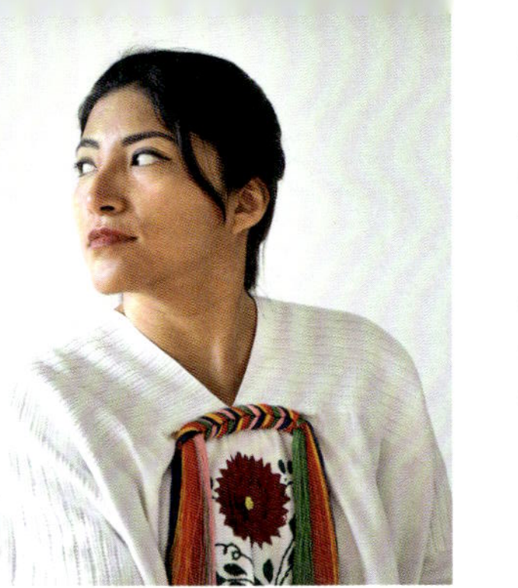

CITLALI FABIAN

## CITLALI FABIAN
MEXICO
–
Citlali Fabian is a documentary photographer from Yalalteca, Oaxaca, Mexico, now based in the United Kingdom. Her work explores ways of addressing indigenous identity in connection with territory, migration, and community bonds.
–
Instagram: @citlalifabian

DANIEL BEREHULAK

## KEITH BEDFORD
UNITED STATES
–
Keith Bedford is the international photo editor for the *Los Angeles Times*. Earlier he worked as a freelance journalist, frequently contributing to such publications as *The New York Times* and *The Wall Street Journal*.
–
Instagram: @keithbedford

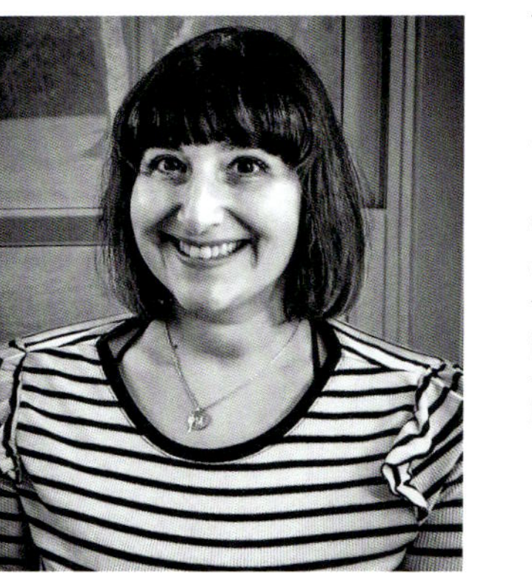

GRACE MONTELEONE

## MARIE MONTELEONE
UNITED STATES
–
Marie Monteleone is the North American deputy photo editor for Bloomberg News, overseeing the photo and video assignments for North America and the Caribbean. She is based in New York.
–
Instagram: @mountainlion6

# LONG-TERM PROJECTS

## CRISTOPHER ROGEL BLANQUET
MEXICO, 1984
–
Cristopher Rogel Blanquet is a documentary photographer and journalist whose work documents social conflict, torture, migration, human rights, and natural disasters.
–
Instagram: @rogelblanquet

ALAN CARRANZA

# OPEN FORMAT

## ASHLEY PEÑA
DOMINICAN REPUBLIC/UNITED STATES, 2000
–
Ashley Peña is an artist and image-maker based in New York. Peña uses her lens to document and tell stories with a focus on people across the African diaspora.
–
Instagram: @ashleyypenaa

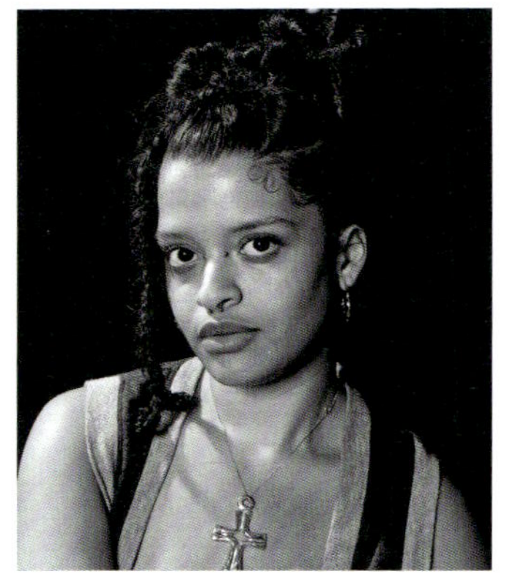

LAMAR KENDRICK

# South America

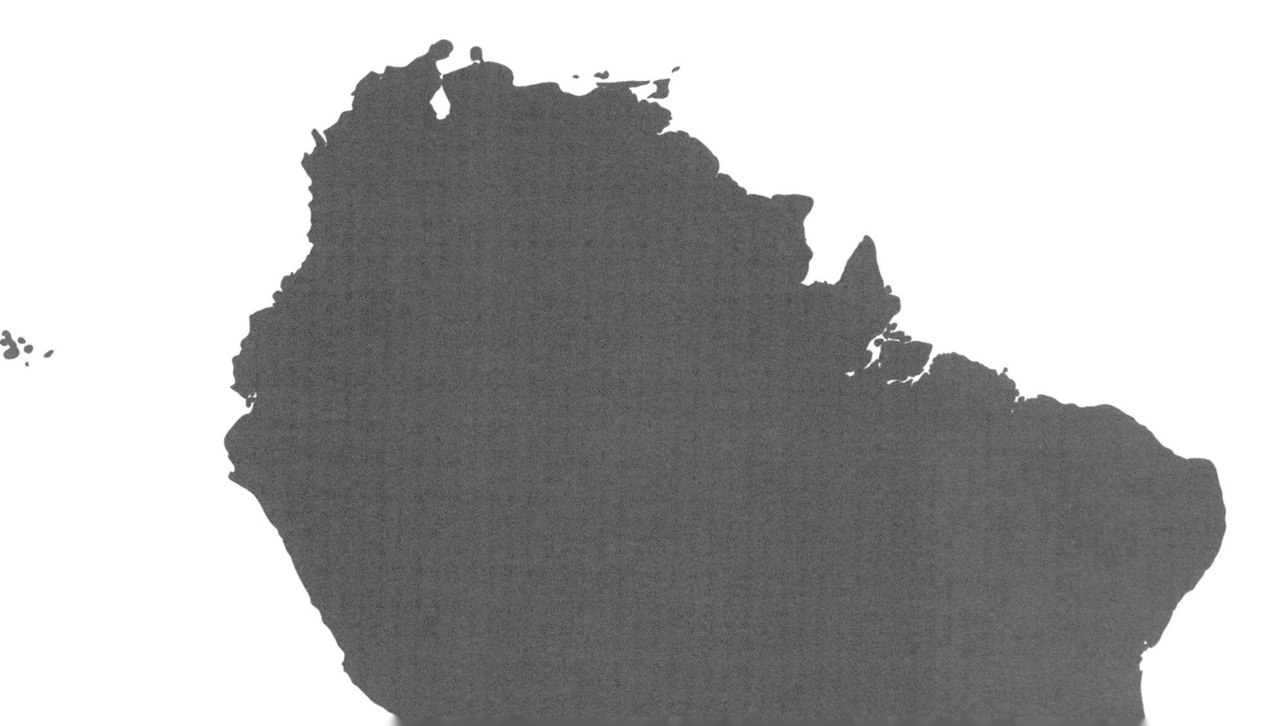

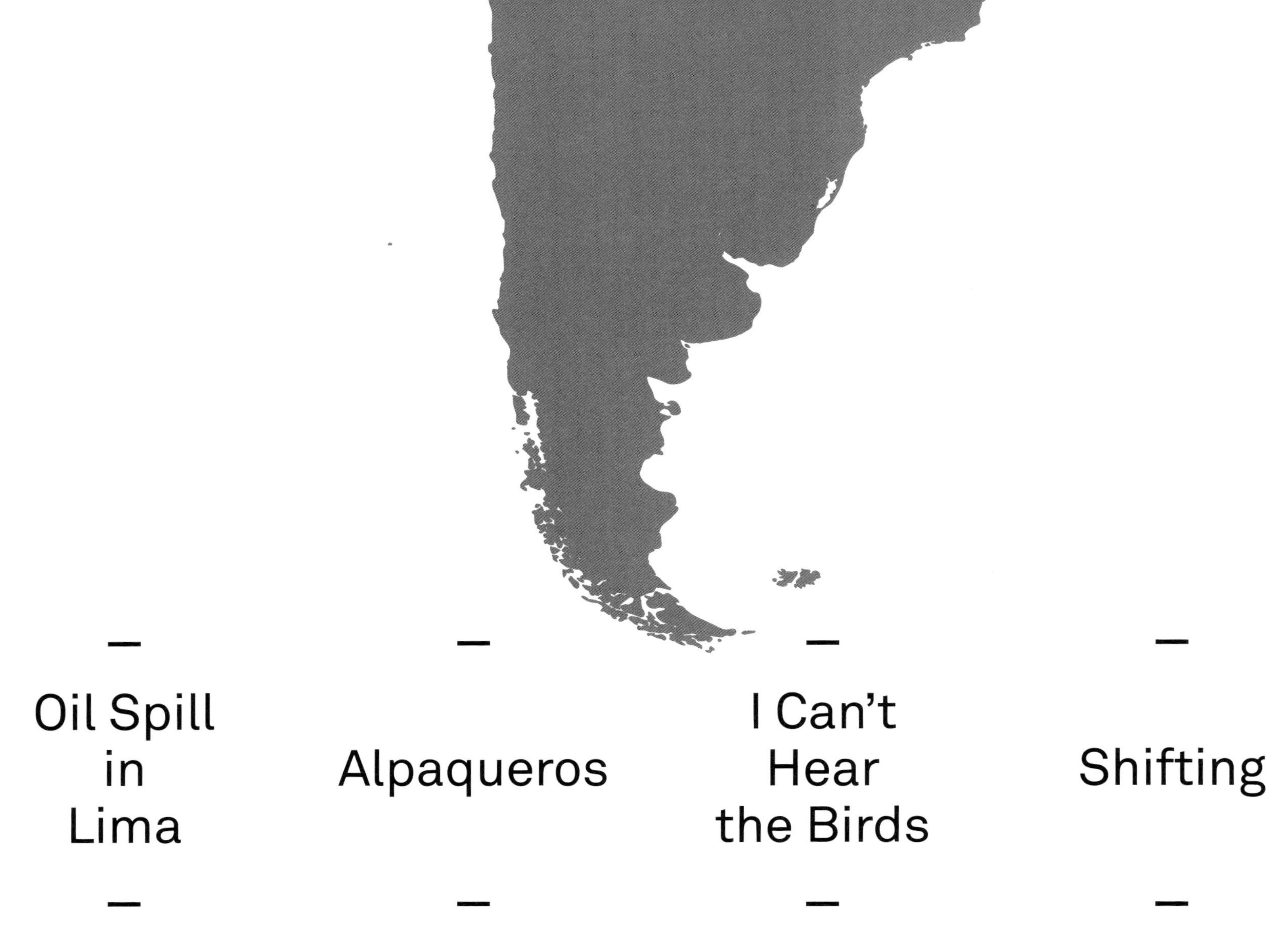

Oil Spill in Lima

Alpaqueros

I Can’t Hear the Birds

Shifting

SOUTH AMERICA
SINGLES

# OIL SPILL IN LIMA

MUSUK NOLTE

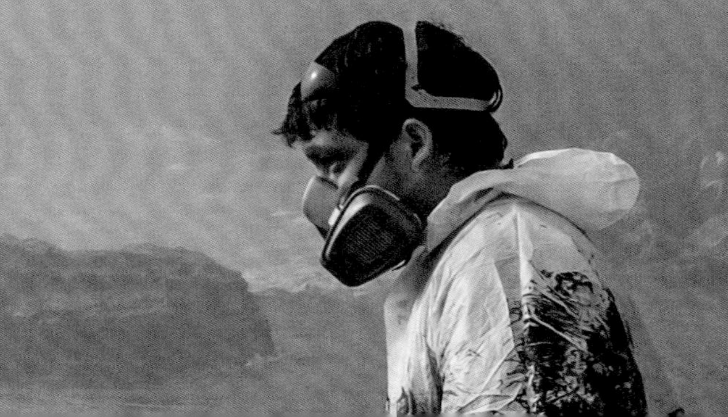

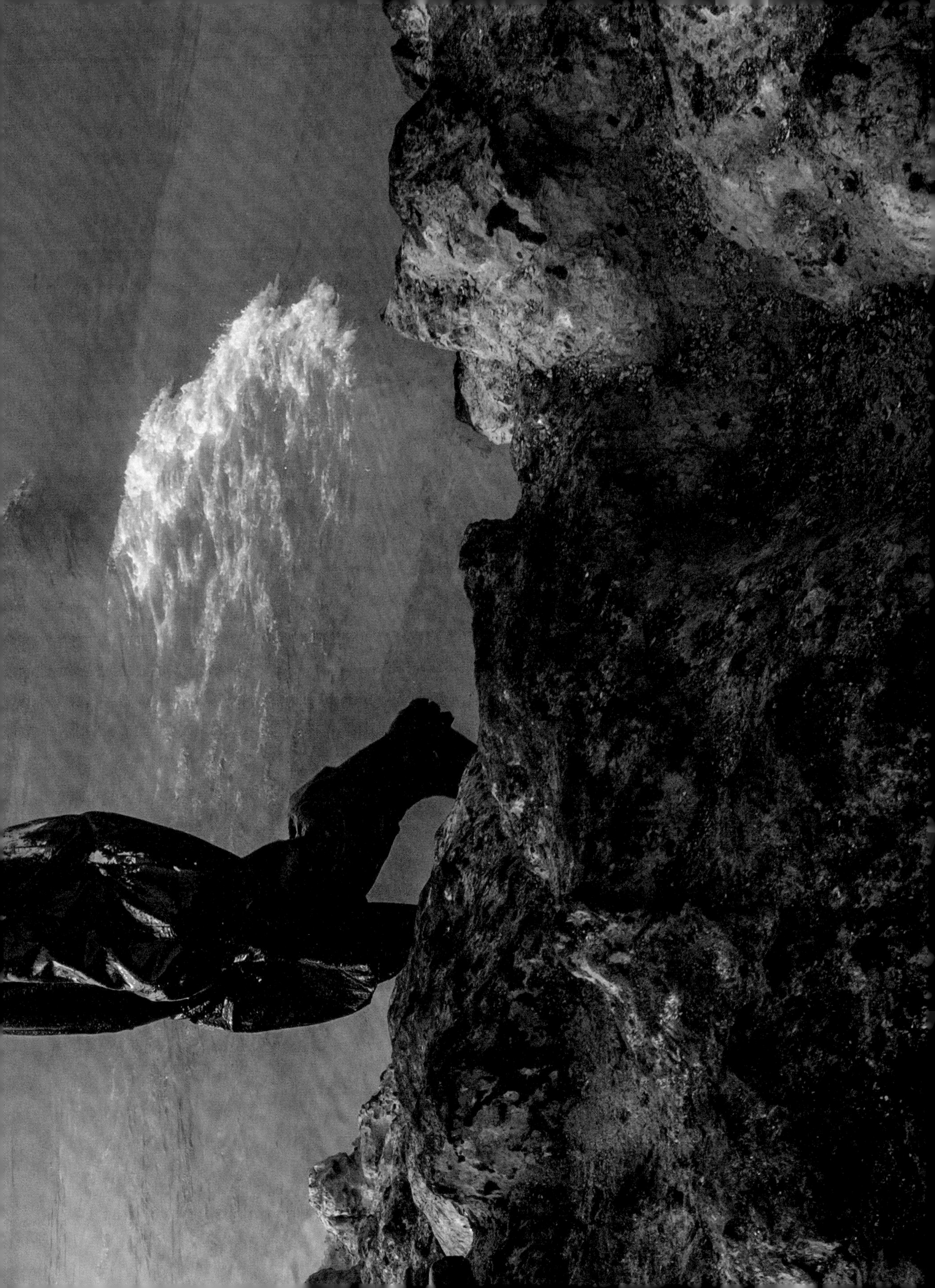

# Oil Spill in Lima

Workers deal with the environmental disaster caused by an oil spill at Repsol's nearby La Pampilla refinery at Playa Cavero, Peru, on 21 January 2022. On 15 January, nearly 12,000 barrels of crude oil spilled into the sea while a tanker was unloading at the Spanish transnational oil company's refinery. The spill extended over 7.13 square kilometers, polluting beaches, killing wildlife, and impacting livelihoods, in what the Peruvian government termed the country's worst ecological disaster in recent memory. UN experts believe its effects will last up to ten years. The jury felt the photo communicated the devastating ecological impacts of oil extraction in the region with subtlety and clarity.

Musuk Nolte took this photo as part of a project for the Bertha Foundation.

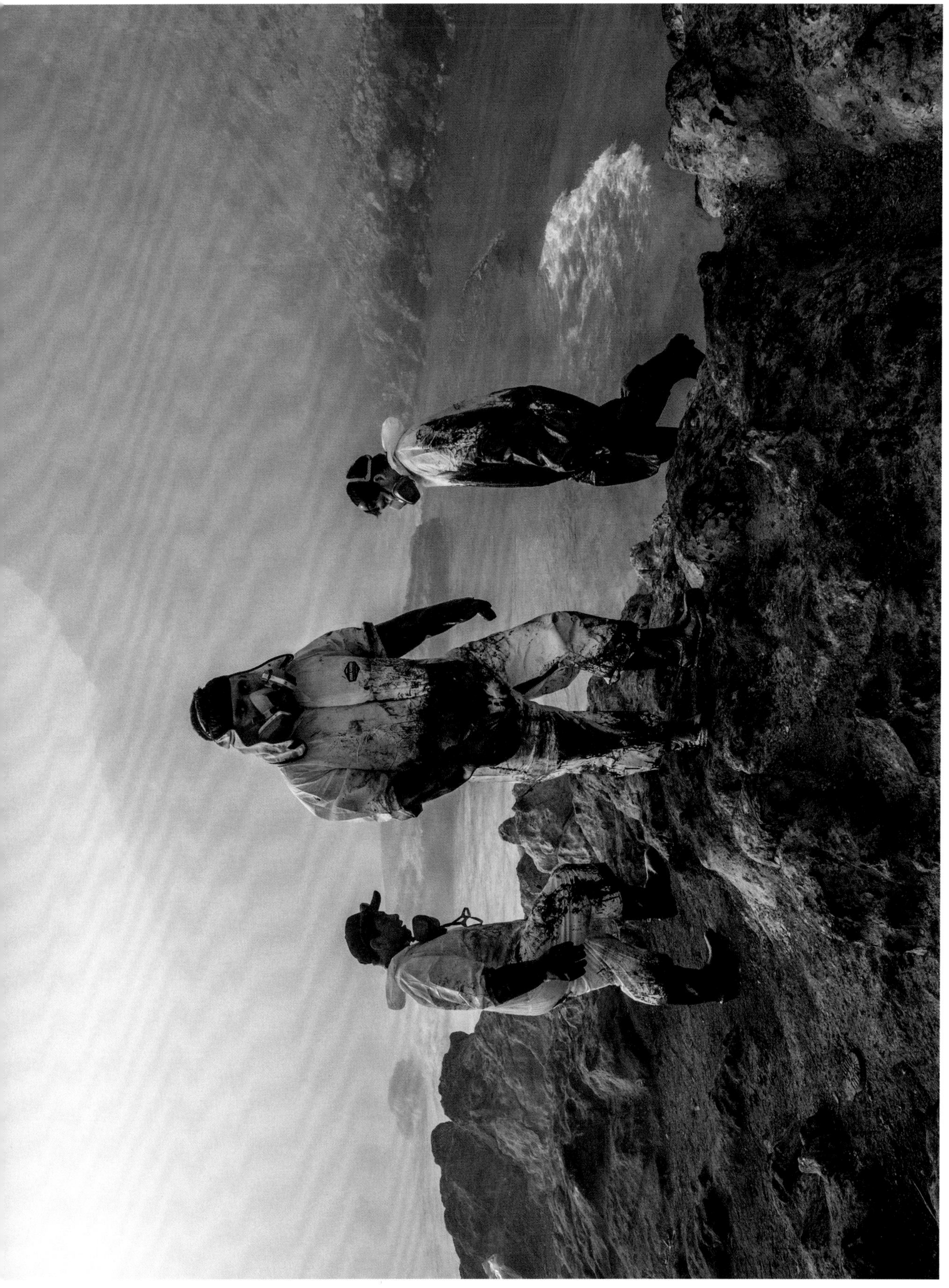

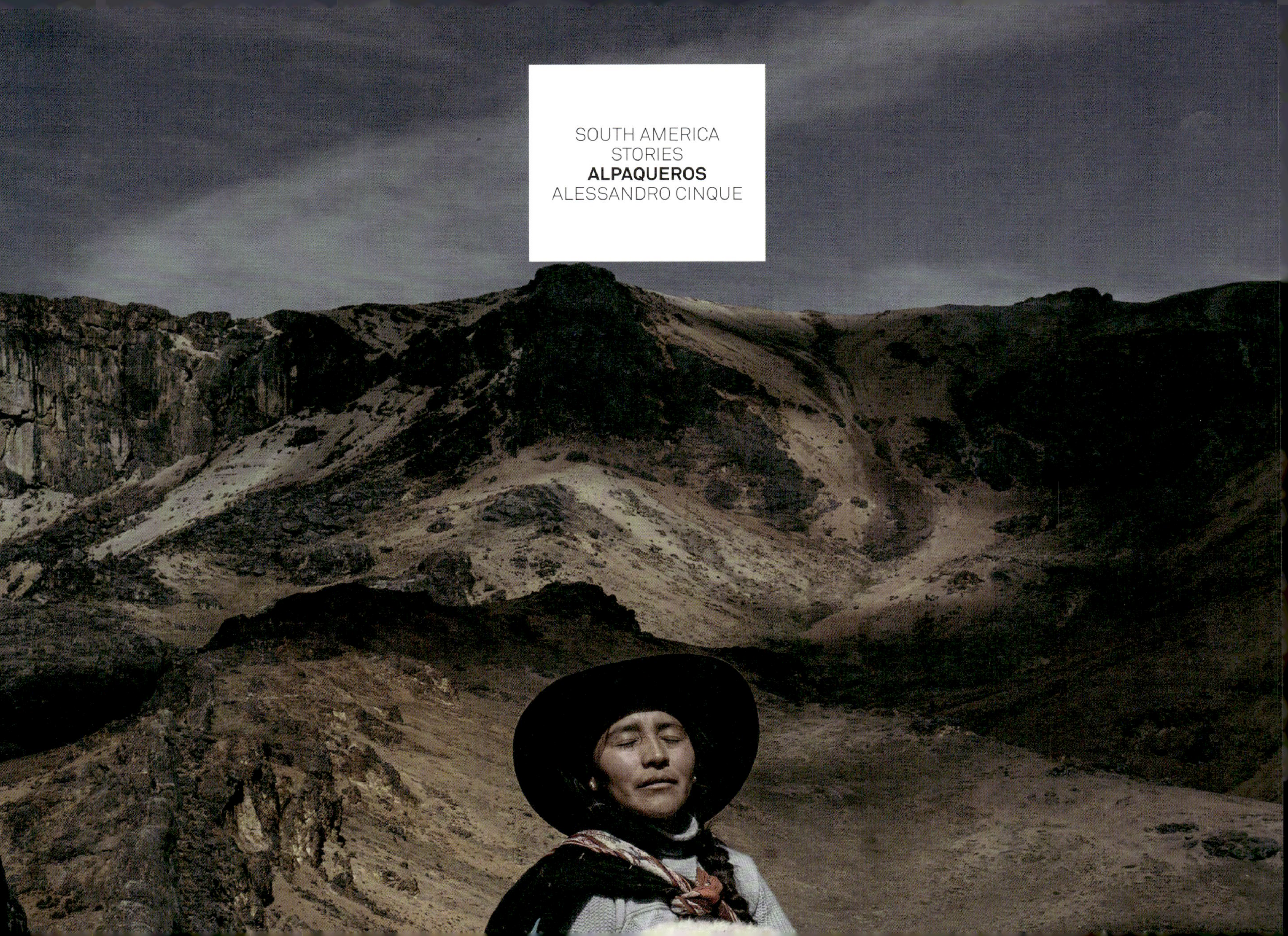

SOUTH AMERICA
STORIES
**ALPAQUEROS**
ALESSANDRO CINQUE

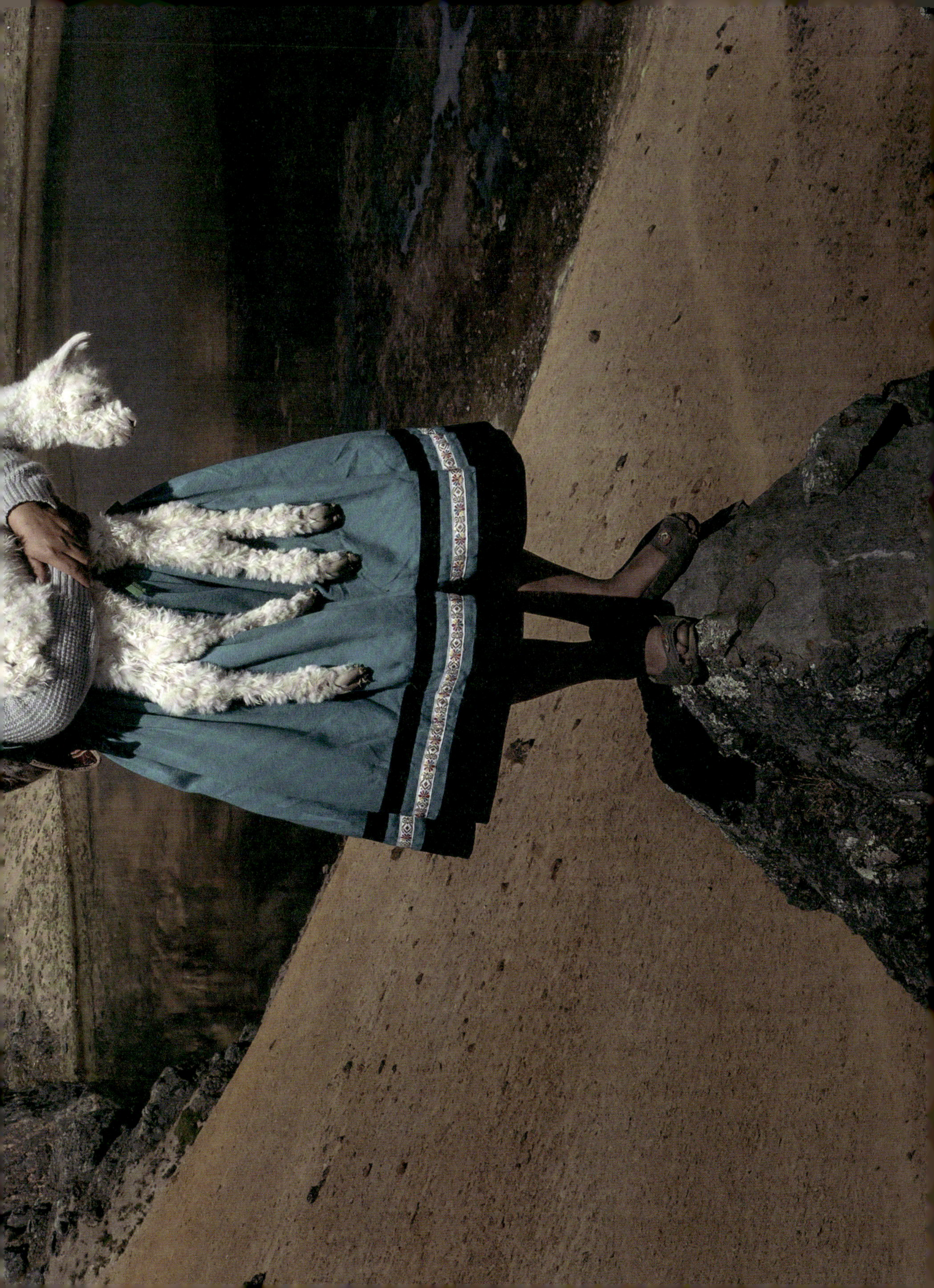

# Alpaqueros

Vital to the livelihoods of many people in the Peruvian Andes, alpacas face new challenges due to the climate crisis. With natural pastures shrinking and glaciers retreating, these animals increasingly struggle to graze and hydrate. *Alpaquero* (alpaca-farmer) communities in turn may be forced to move to higher altitudes or to abandon their lifestyles. To combat these difficulties, scientists hope to address the problem by creating breeds more resistant to extremes in temperature. The jury appreciated the way the story illuminates how culture and identity are deeply intertwined with the environment.

Alessandro Cinque's story was supported by *National Geographic* and the Pulitzer Center.

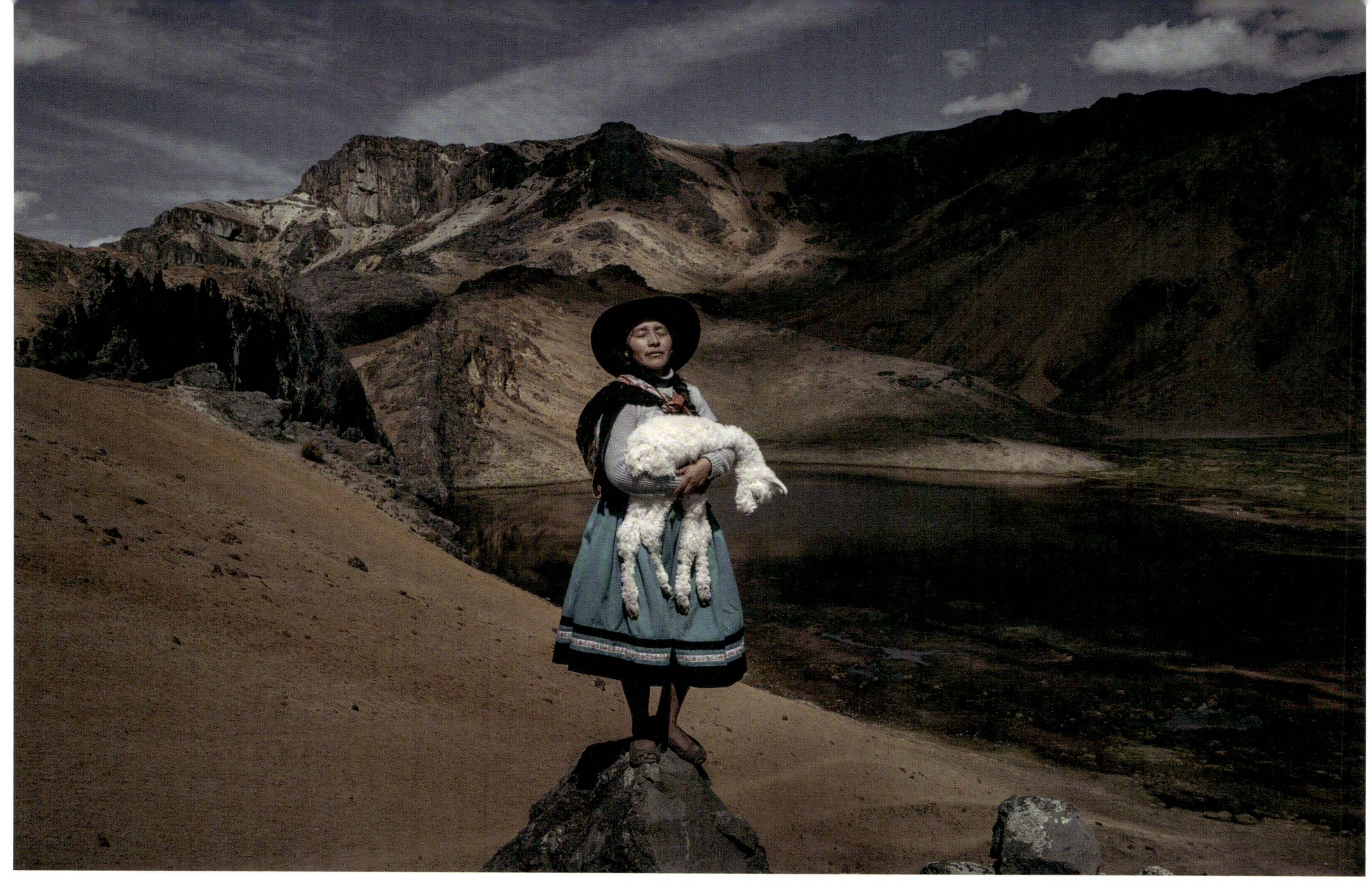

Alina Surquislla Gomez, a third-generation *alpaquera* (alpaca-farmer), cradles a baby alpaca on the way to her family's summer pastures, in Oropesa, Peru, on 3 May 2021.

Alpacas rest outdoors at night in Oropesa, on 2 May 2021. Many *alpaqueros* cannot afford to build shelters for their animals, despite freezing temperatures at high altitudes.

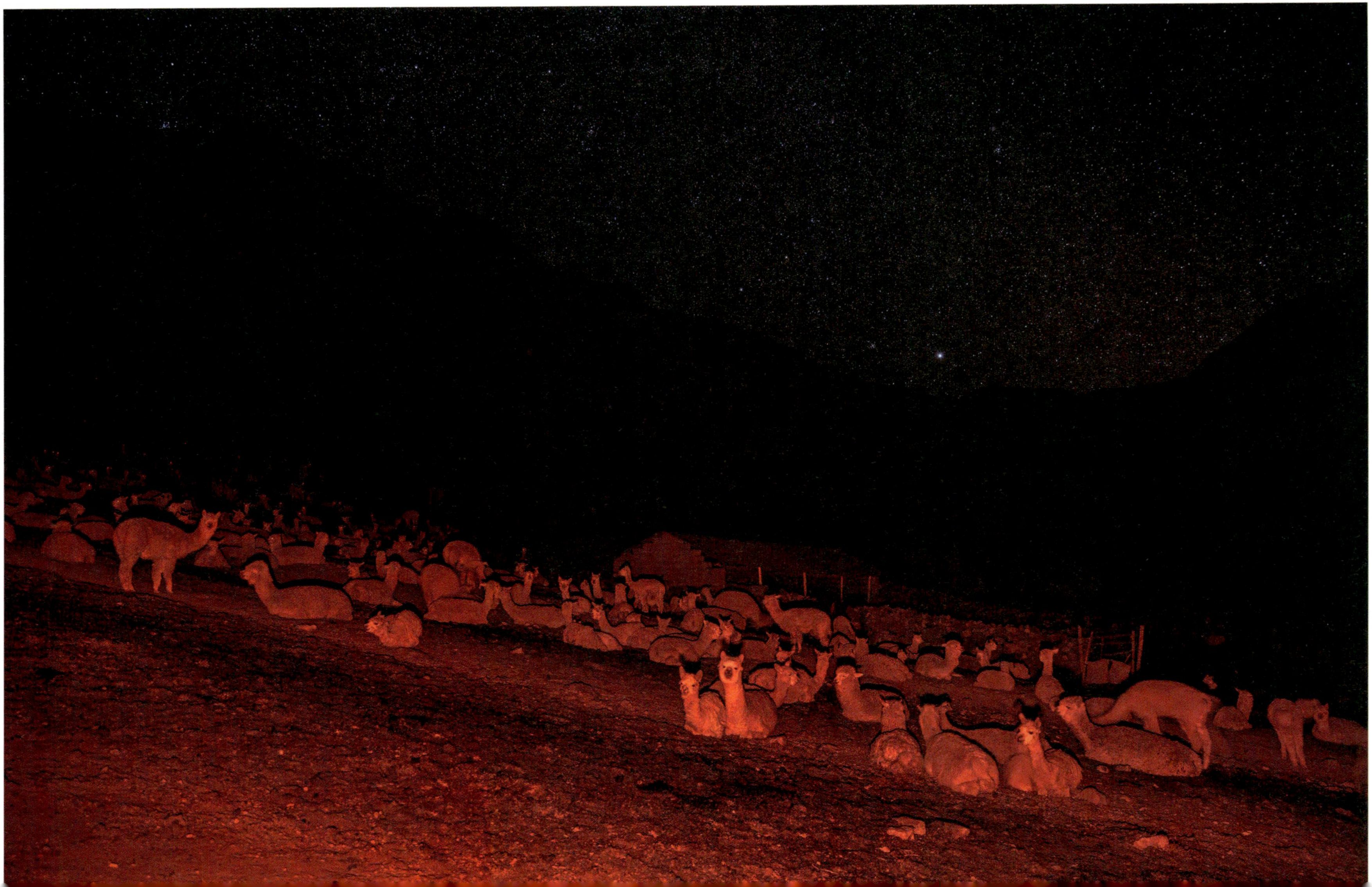

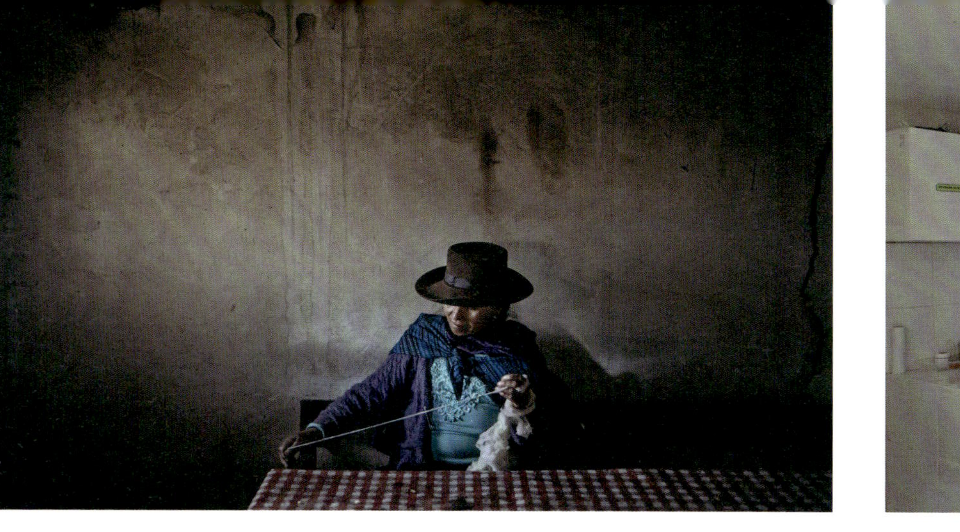

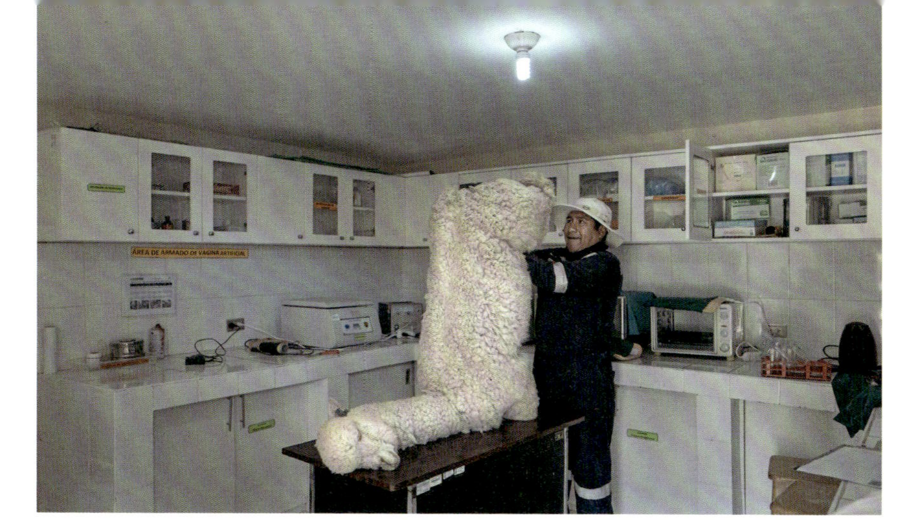

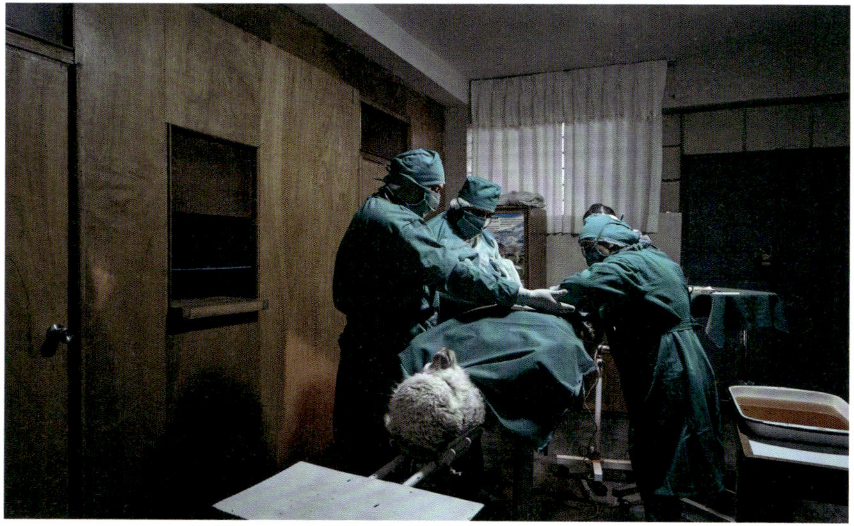

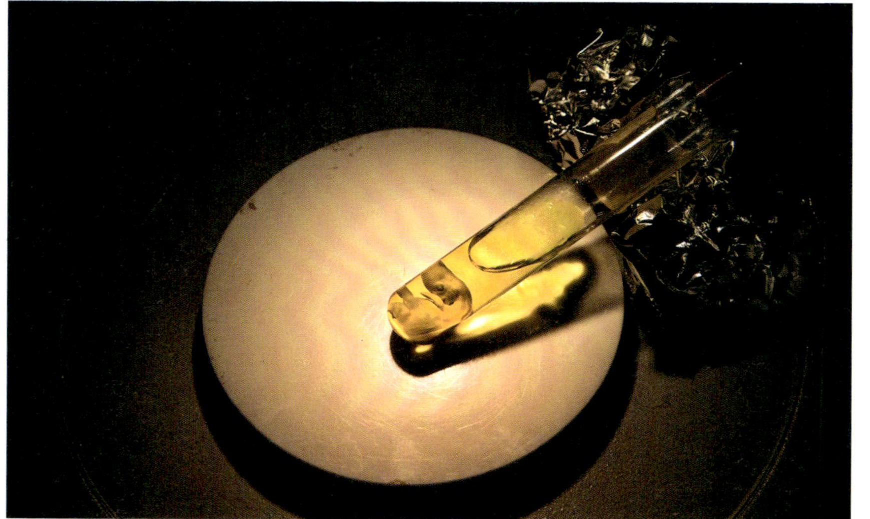

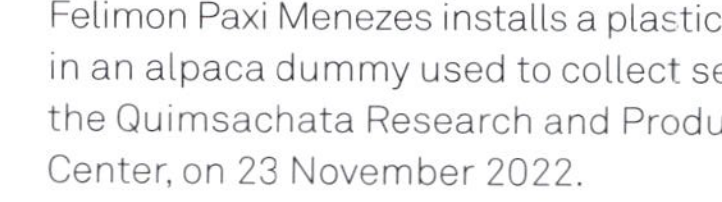

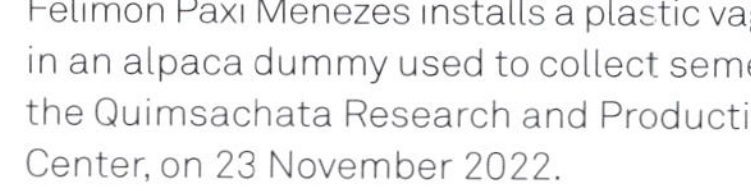

Margaret Pilsen makes handmade crafts from alpaca wool, in Cusco, Peru, on 28 April 2021.

A medical team prepares an alpaca for surgery to retrieve eggs for in vitro fertilization at Quimsachata Research and Production Center, on 23 November 2022. The center houses the largest genetic reserve of alpaca breeds in the world.

Felimon Paxi Menezes installs a plastic vagina in an alpaca dummy used to collect semen at the Quimsachata Research and Production Center, on 23 November 2022.

An alpaca fetus is analyzed at the Quimsachata Research and Production Center, on 22 November 2022. The center aims to create breeds more resilient to the climate crisis.

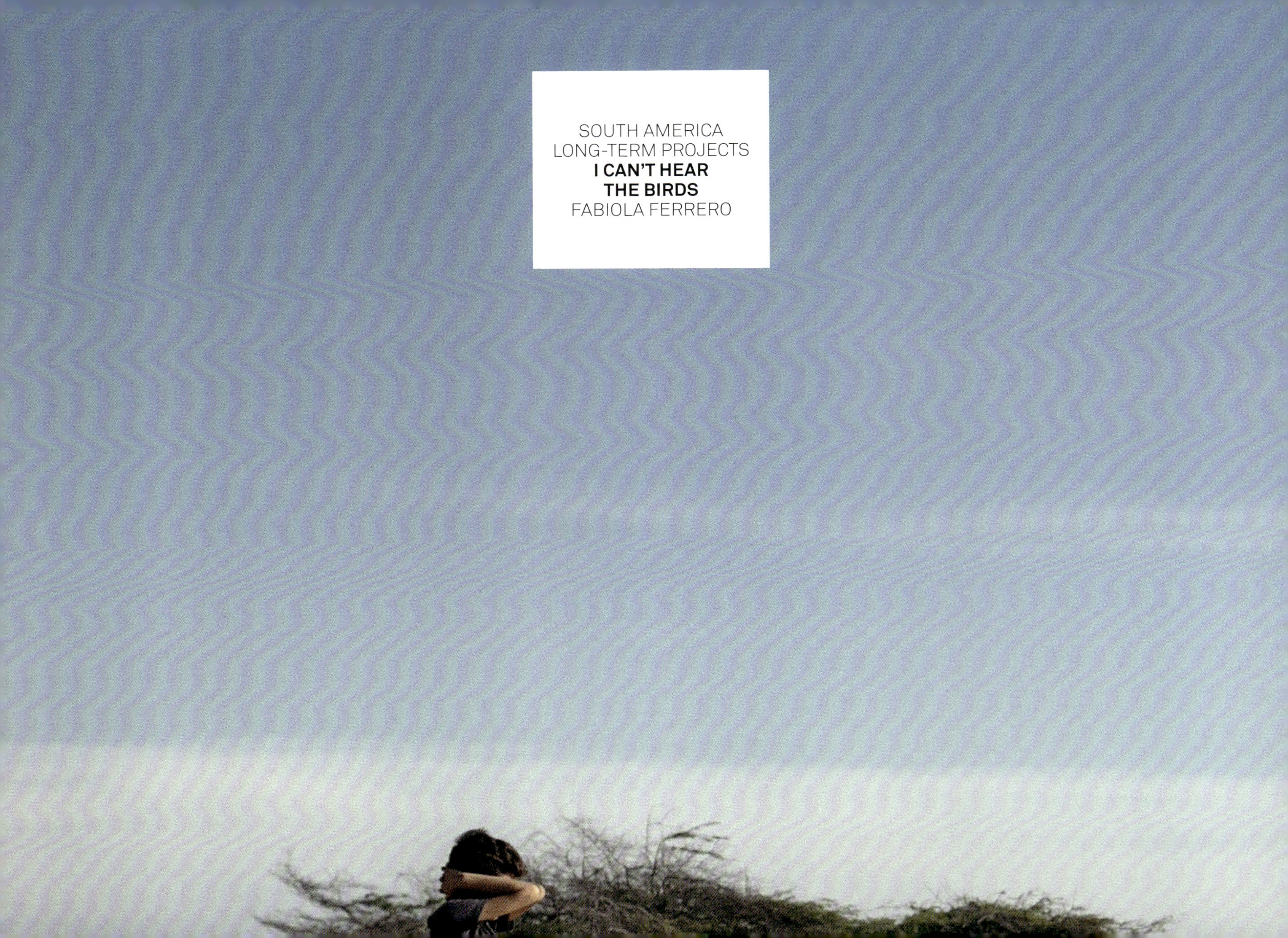

SOUTH AMERICA
LONG-TERM PROJECTS

**I CAN'T HEAR THE BIRDS**

FABIOLA FERRERO

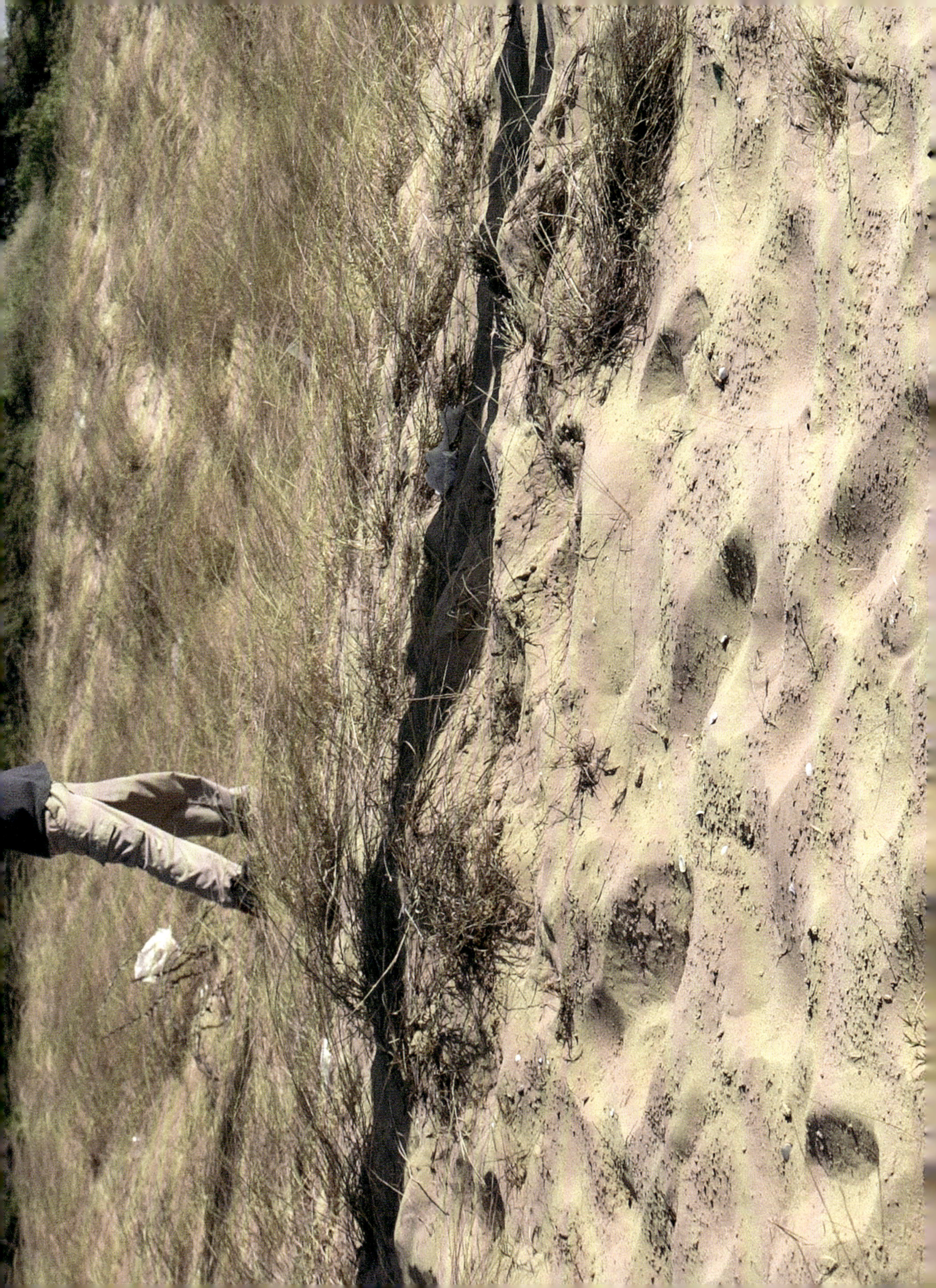

# I Can’t Hear the Birds

Seven million Venezuelans have left their country to live abroad, driven by economic collapse, political unrest, high unemployment, and extreme social inequality. Around the turn of the millennium, oil-rich Venezuela was prosperous, but its fortunes declined following plummeting oil prices, later economic mismanagement, and political instability. Young people, especially, began to leave. The photographer was one, but she returns to search for traces of the Venezuela of her memory. Her project combines images of migration and past political violence with those of present-day Venezuela, and of the decay and the resilience of people living within it.

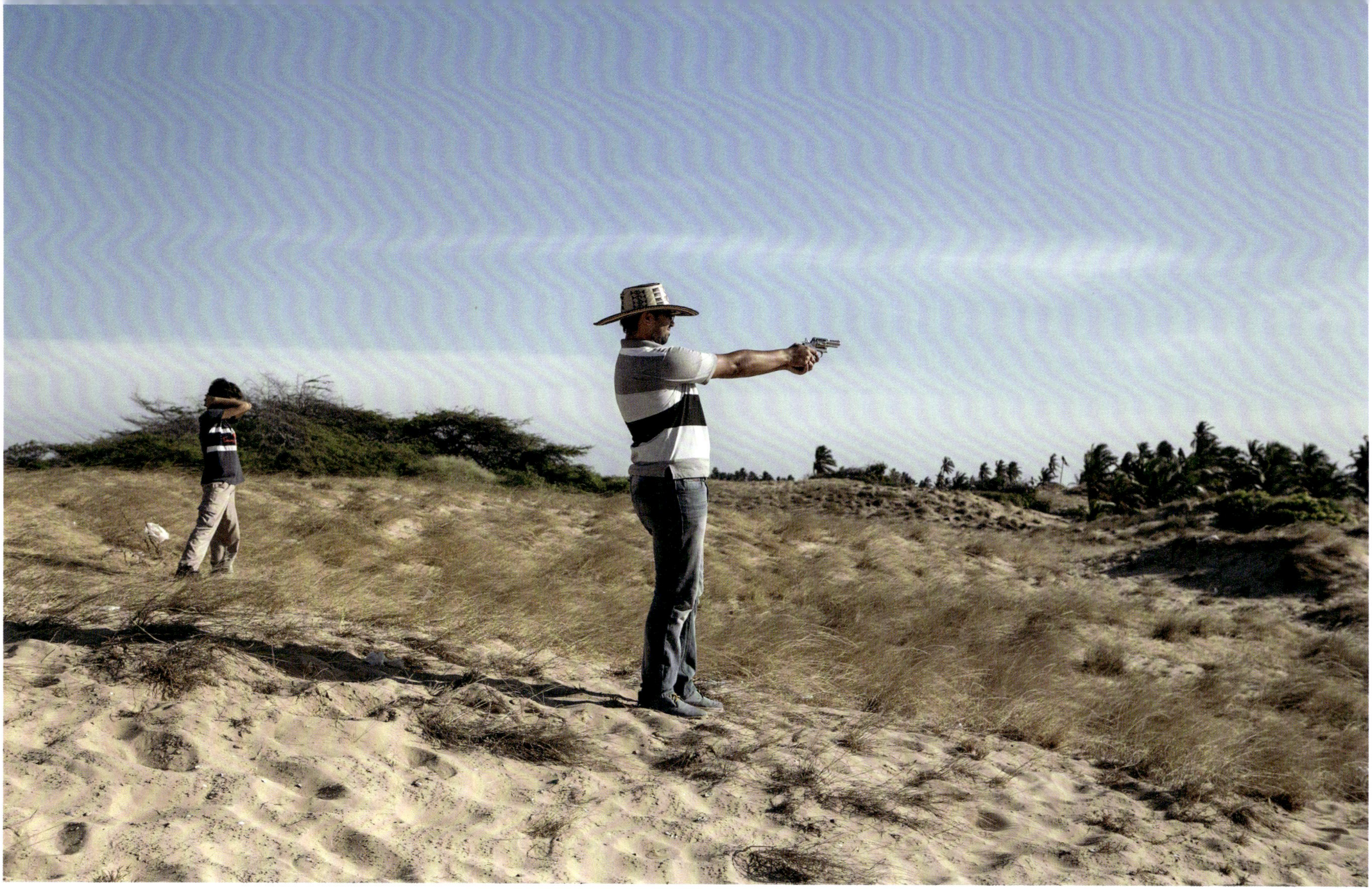

A man fires his gun to commemorate dead relatives, in a Wayuu ritual in the Guajira Desert, on the Venezuela-Colombia border, on 26 February 2017. The Wayuu Indigenous community straddles both countries, and doesn't recognize the border.

Members of the civilian Bolivarian Militia of Venezuela commemorate the fourth anniversary of President Hugo Chávez's death, in Cuartel de la Montaña, Caracas, where his body rests, on 5 March 2017.

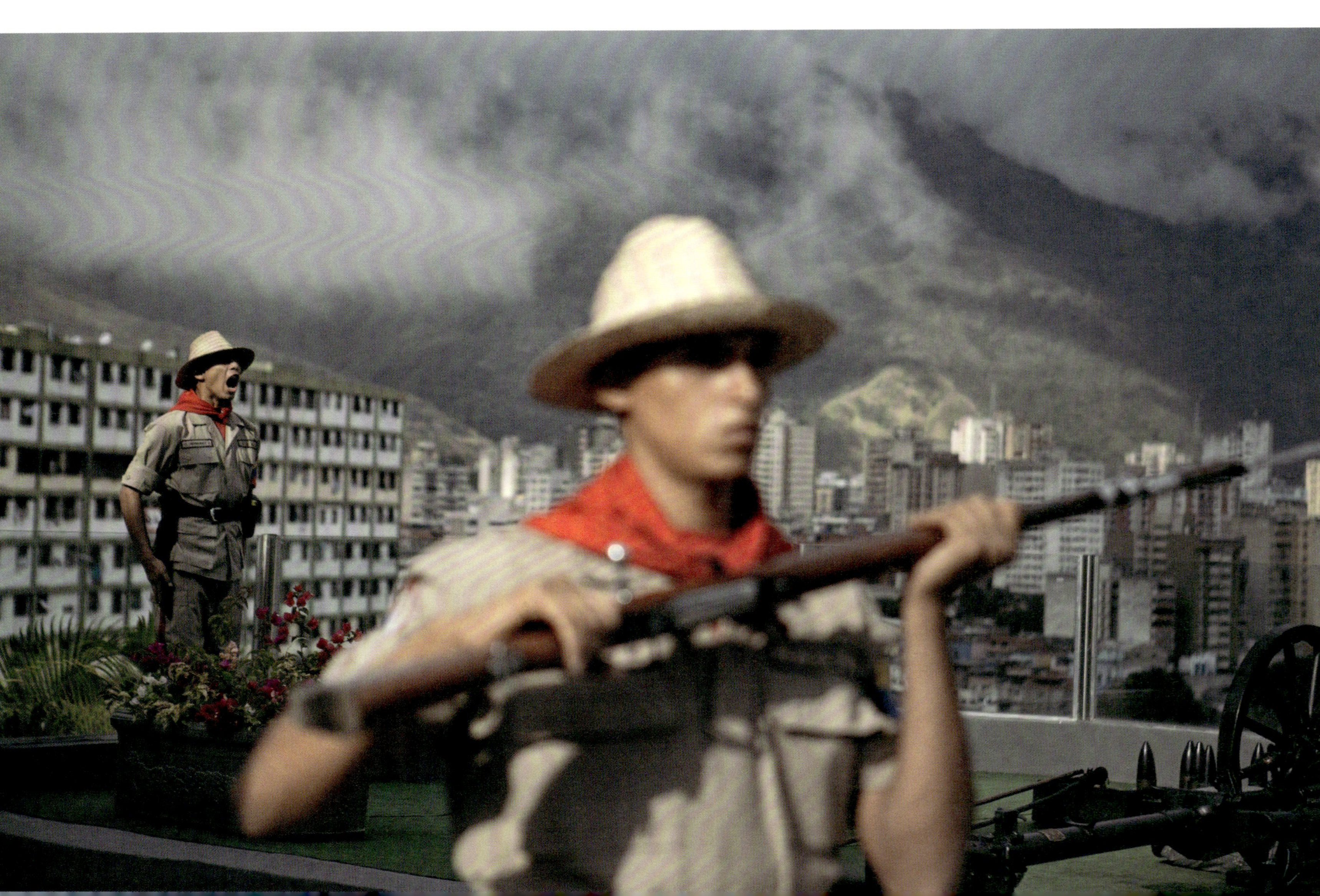

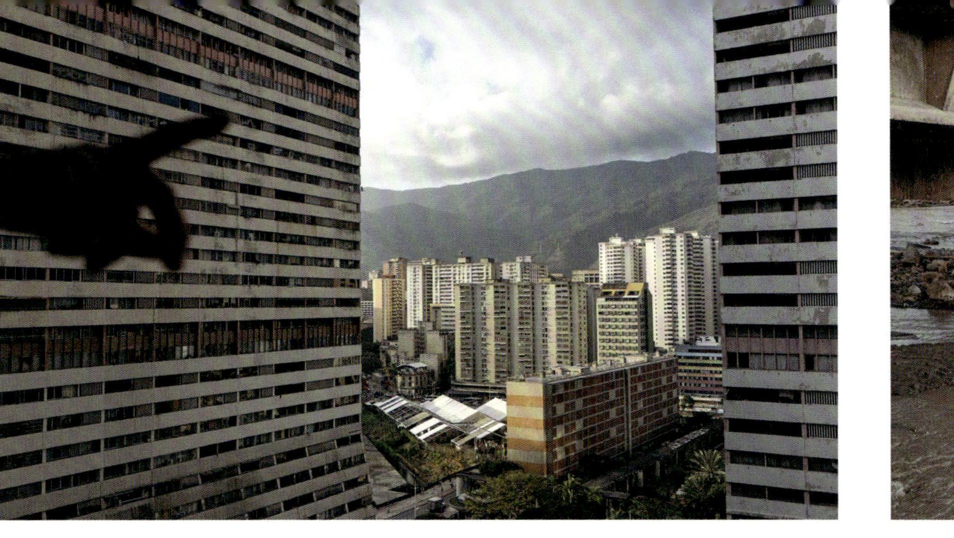

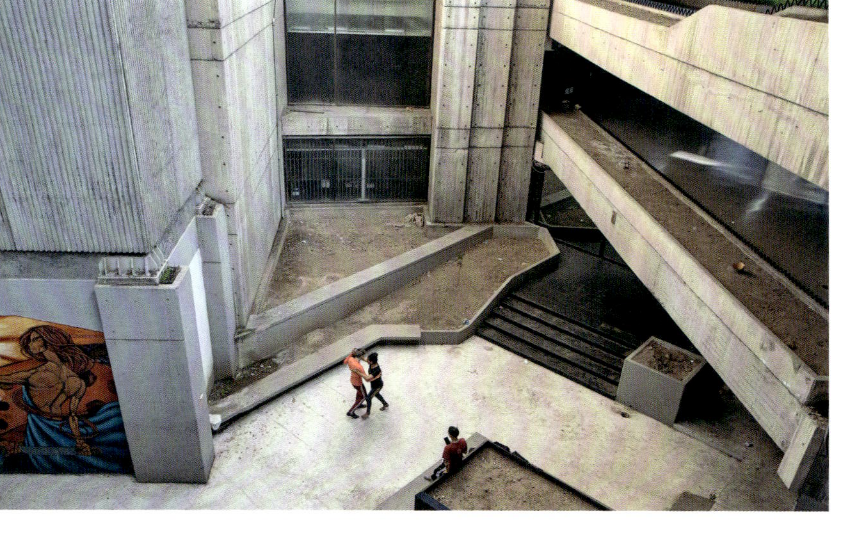

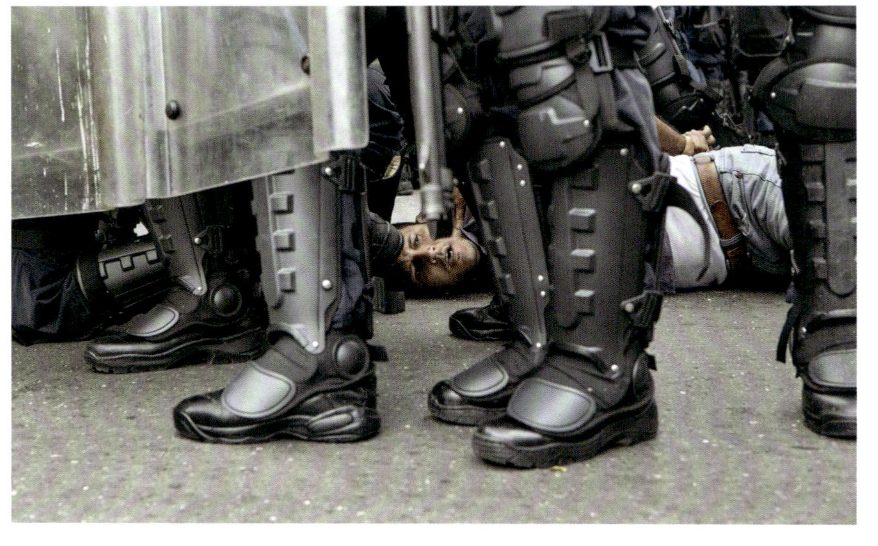

The Twin Towers of Parque Central in Caracas, pictured here on 17 March 2022, were a prestigious development that until 2003 held the title of tallest skyscrapers in Latin America.

A couple dances the tango in a Parque Central courtyard, on 17 August 2021. The complex now leaks, is badly maintained and insecure.

A man carries a woman across the Táchira River, which forms the Venezuela-Colombia border, on 16 November 2020. Bridges were closed due the COVID-19 pandemic.

Police arrest a man during a protest rally for a referendum to remove President Maduro from office, in Caracas, on 18 May 2016.

SOUTH AMERICA
OPEN FORMAT
**SHIFTING**
JOHANNA ALARCÓN

Scan the QR code
to watch the video.

# Shifting

Valentina is a 13-year-old who aspires to become a photographer and whose mother is in prison for marijuana possession. Ecuador's ongoing prison crisis and punitive drug sentencing policy means that the separation between parents and children has been especially harrowing. The video and imagery in this multimedia project center around the imagination and experiences of Valentina as a young artist, whose rich inner world is not defined by her mother's incarceration, even as she awaits their reunion.

Johanna Alarcón is a member of the Magnum Foundation and Panos Pictures.

Ecuador-based visual storyteller and photojournalist Johanna Alarcón became acquainted with Valentina and her mother while Alarcón was working with prisoners on artistic projects. Members of her own family have been incarcerated. Alarcón's deep personal connection to the subject makes possible this complex, collaborative, and multi-dimensional representation of Valentina's life story. The combination of analog and digital photography with video, animation, and audio gives a special look into the inner life of a young artist making sense of the world through her photography.

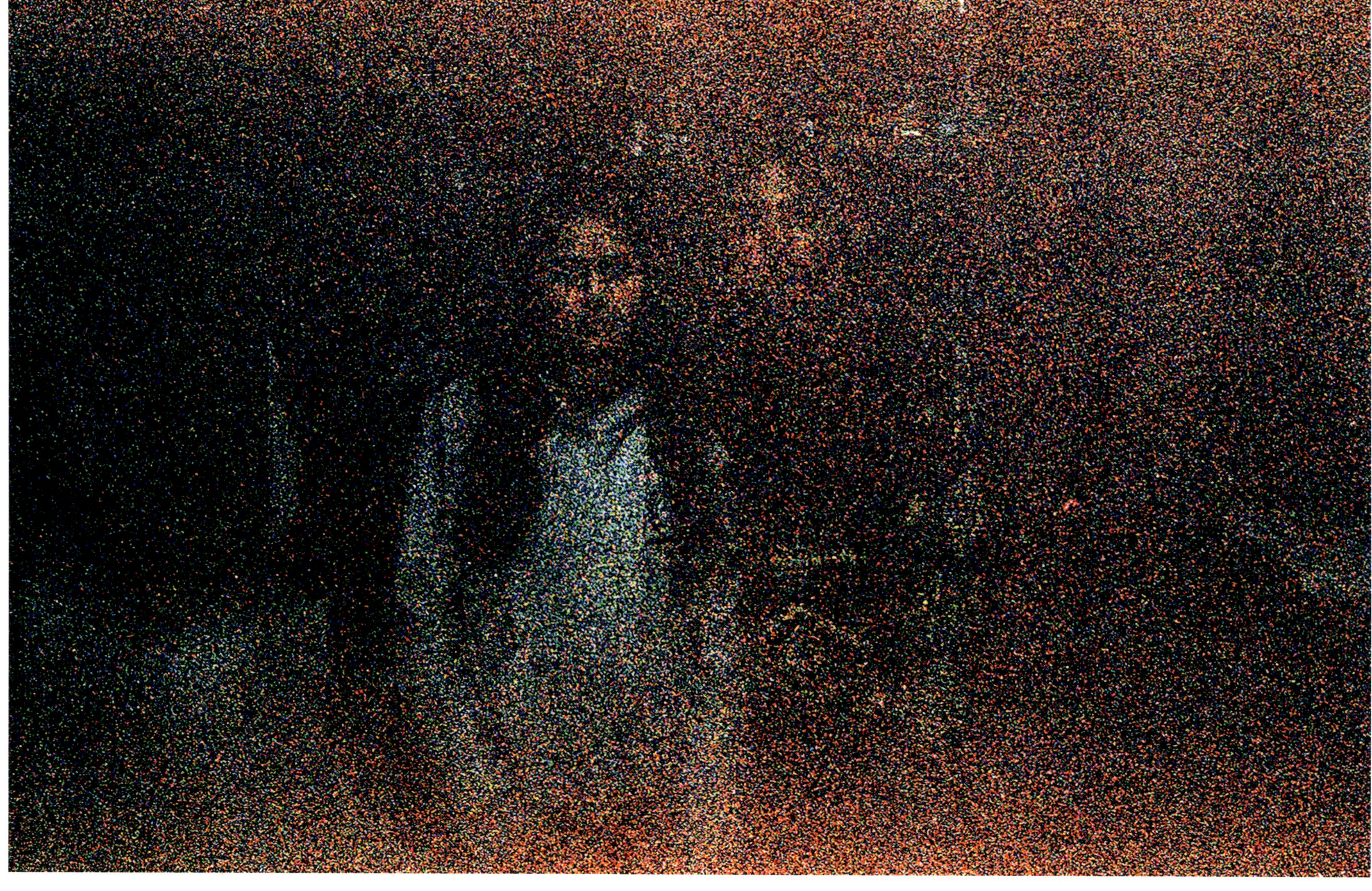

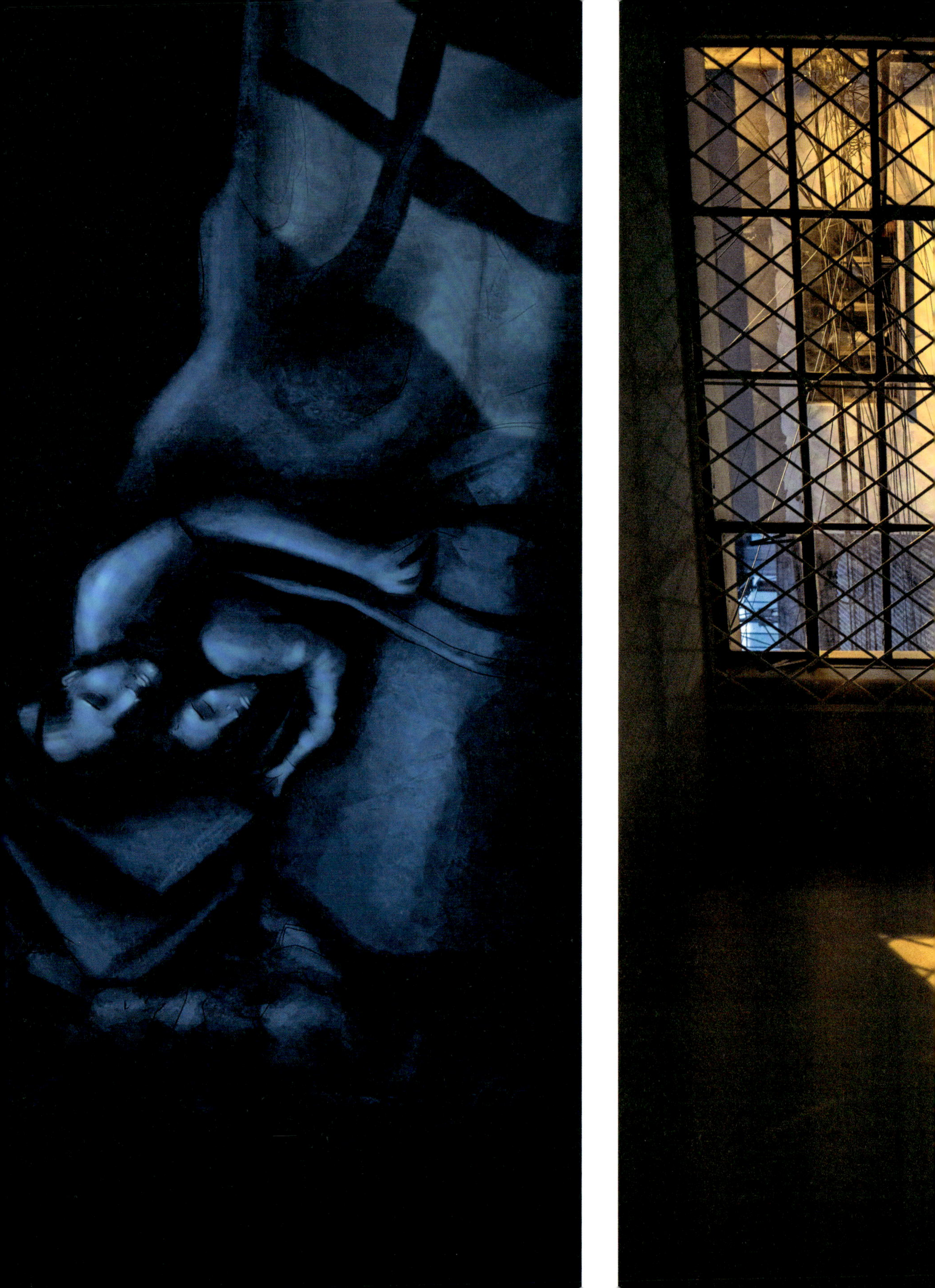

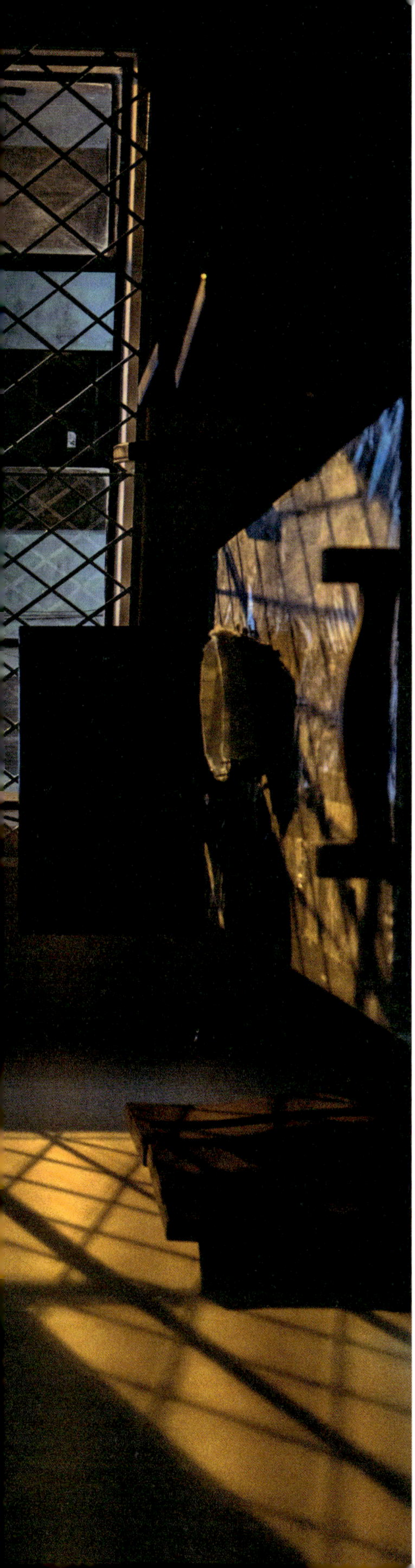

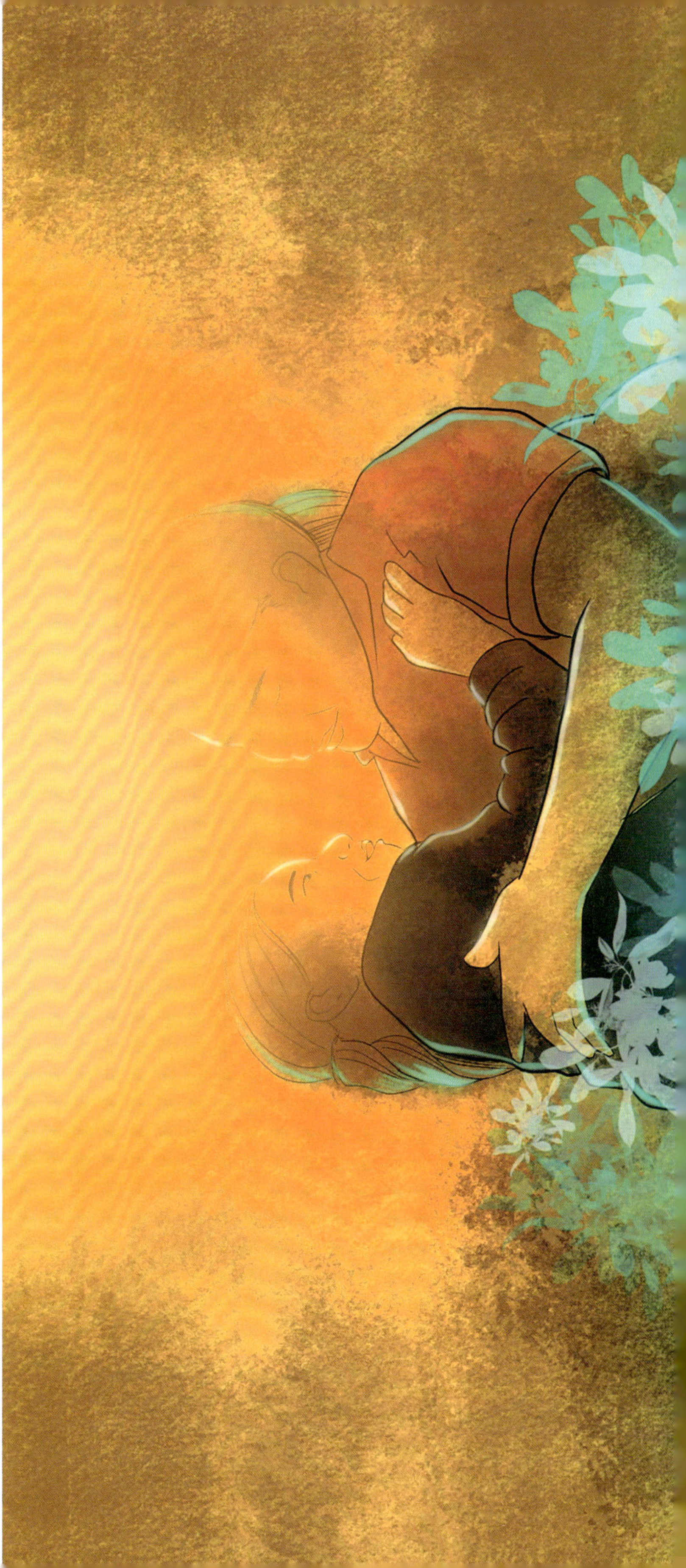

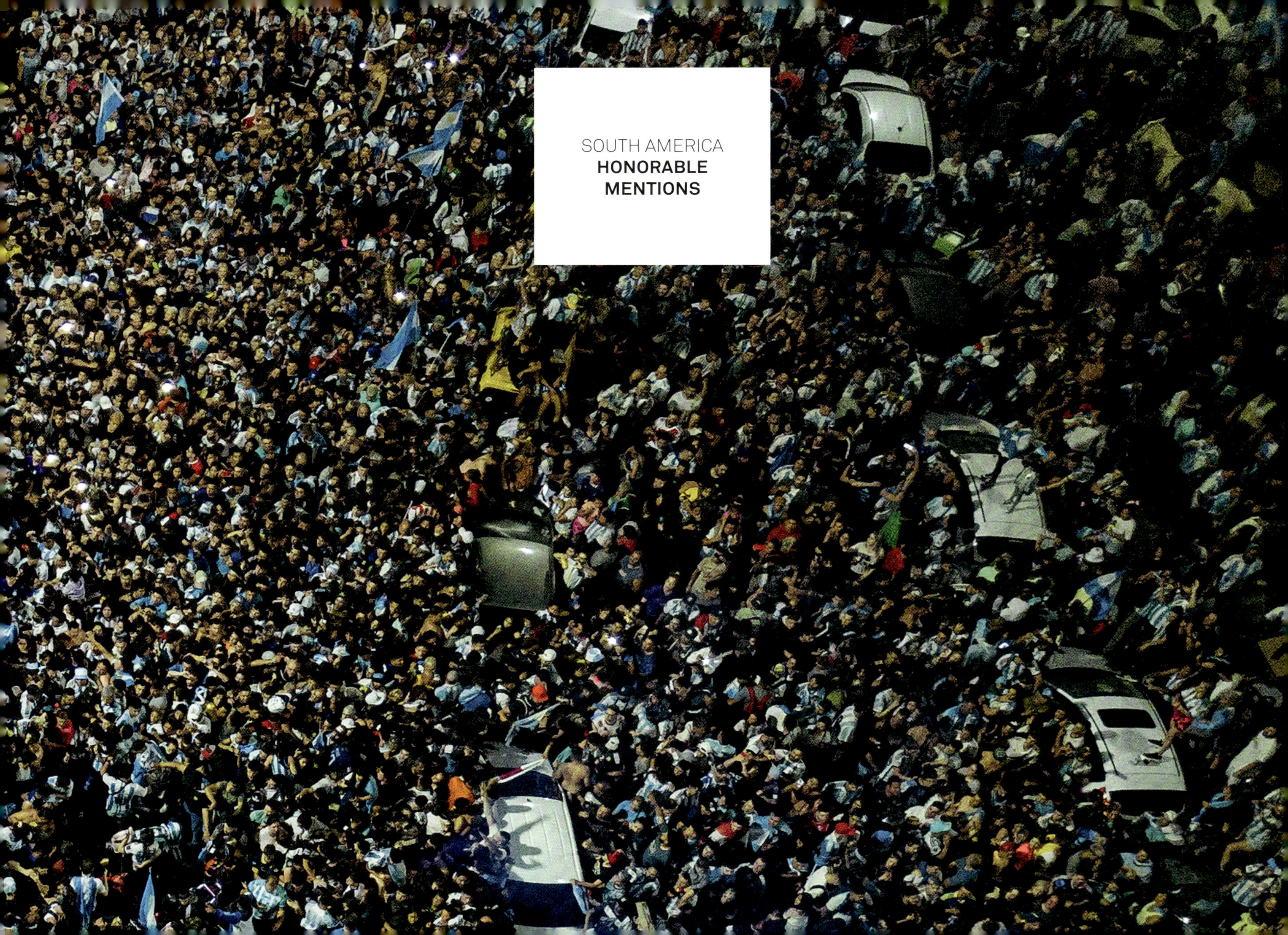

SOUTH AMERICA
**HONORABLE MENTIONS**

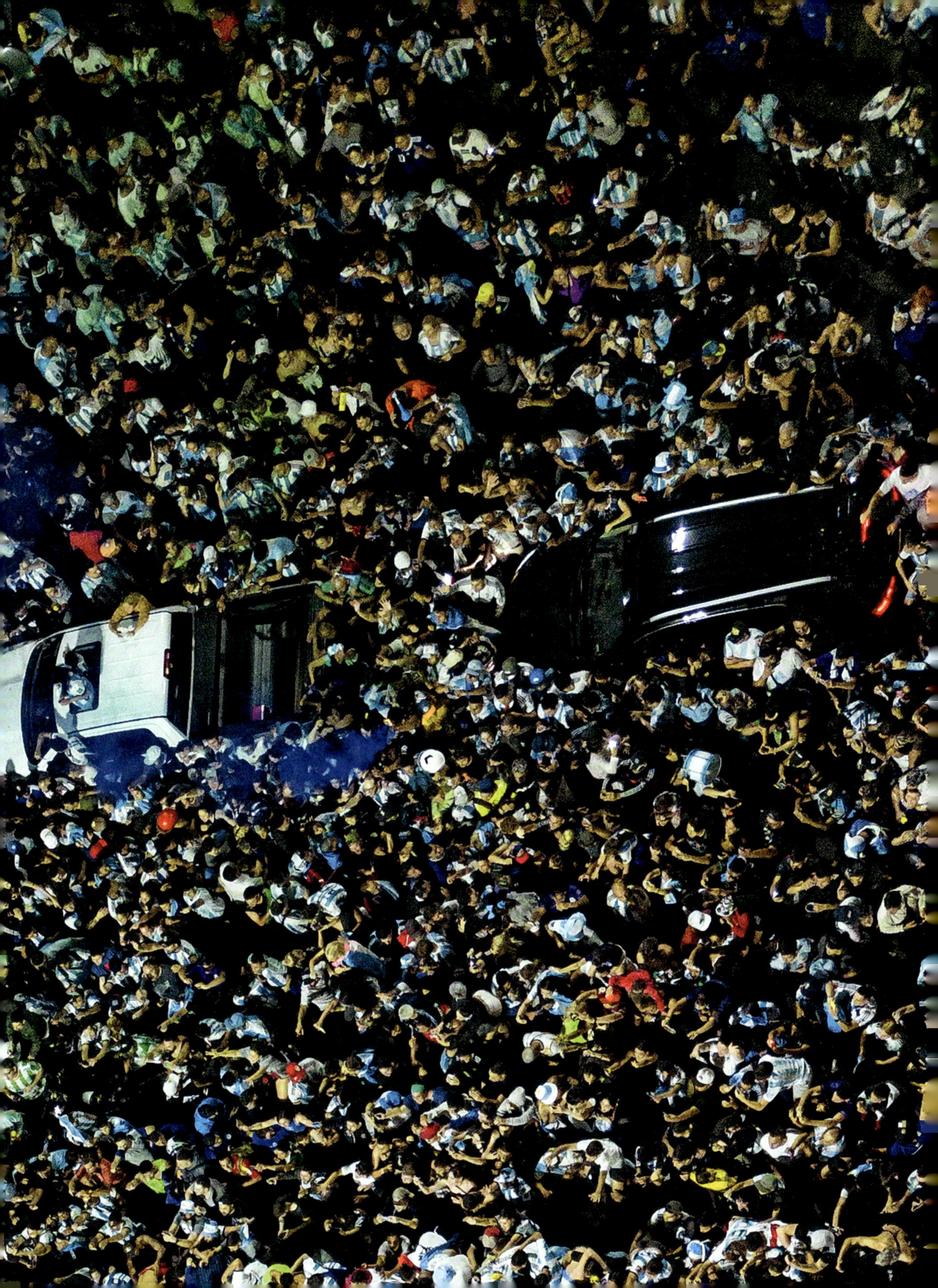

# World Champions

—

These images capture the celebratory scene in Buenos Aires after Argentina national football team's victory at the 2022 FIFA World Cup in Qatar. An estimated five million people took to the streets to participate in the parade and join the national team members in one of the greatest public demonstrations in Argentina's history. For striker and star player Lionel Messi, the win cemented his legacy as one of the greatest footballers of all time.

Tomás Francisco Cuesta
Argentina, 1996

–

Tomás Francisco Cuesta is a photo and video journalist focusing on press, sports, entertainment and documentary. He works for a variety of organizations including AFP, Getty Images, Reuters and *La Nacion*. He photographed this story on assignment for Agence France-Presse.

–

Instagram: @tomifcuesta

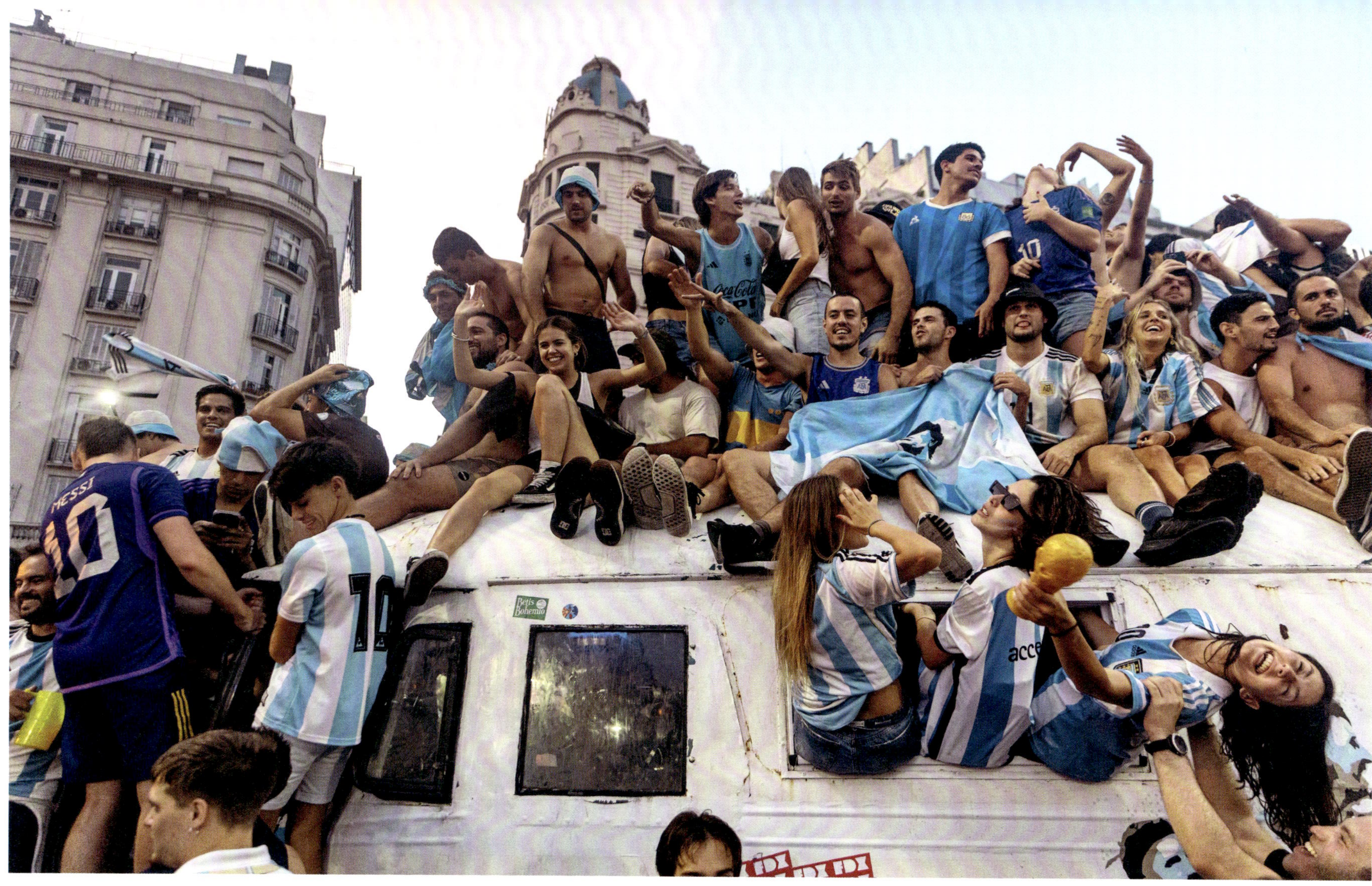


A scene of jubilation as Argentinians revel in their country's return to football world dominance. Buenos Aires, 18 December 2022.

# South America

—

Felipe Dana
South America Jury Chair

As members of the South American jury, we had a unique opportunity to concentrate on topics and stories that were relevant to our region, especially those that could contribute to narratives in meaningful ways and bring attention to issues that are often overlooked, and which may not have received the attention they deserved on a global stage. This was especially important in a year like 2022, when the news coverage was dominated by the war in Ukraine.

Our review of thousands of photographs gave us an extraordinary view of the region, as we navigated through a wide range of topics and emotions. We saw the celebration of Argentina's World Cup victory on the streets of Buenos Aires; violent protests across multiple countries; and the dangerous journeys thousands of migrants made traveling north through Colombia, fleeing years of economic decline in Venezuela, gang violence, and more. The region's visual journalists continued to document the impact of climate change and environmental exploitation, not only in the Brazilian Amazon, but also in the Atacama Desert in Chile, tropical glaciers in Peru, wildfires in Argentina, and floods, pollution, and natural disasters across the region. We also admired stories that shed new light on issues of identity, discrimination, and gender.

As we narrowed down the entries, the process of selecting winners became increasingly challenging. We had a diverse panel of judges, with different opinions and perspectives and that turned out to be a great learning process. I was often pushed out of my comfort zone, and it was difficult to select between so many important and diverse stories. It was interesting to hear from other jury members what topics and issues they thought were important for them, to compare our thought processes and share how each of us weighed our decisions when selecting possible winners.

World Press Photo's new regional format with fewer categories also presented challenges, and we could not help but think about all the important visual journalism that did not receive any awards. However, it is uplifting to know that each region now has a space in this important and global platform. I believe this is a strong step towards a more diverse and inclusive photojournalism industry.

# Jury

—

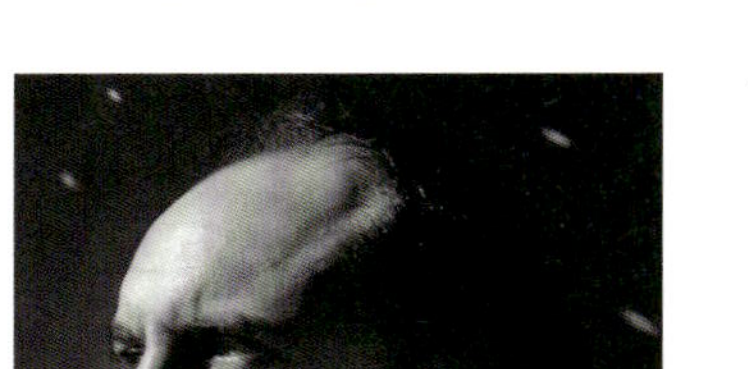

RENATA BRITO

**FELIPE DANA** / CHAIR
BRAZIL

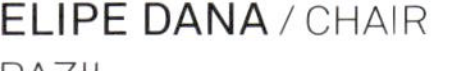

–

Felipe Dana is an award-winning Brazilian photojournalist, and an editor at the Associated Press, focusing on social issues and endemic violence in his native Rio de Janeiro. He has also covered conflicts across the world.

–

Instagram: @felipedana

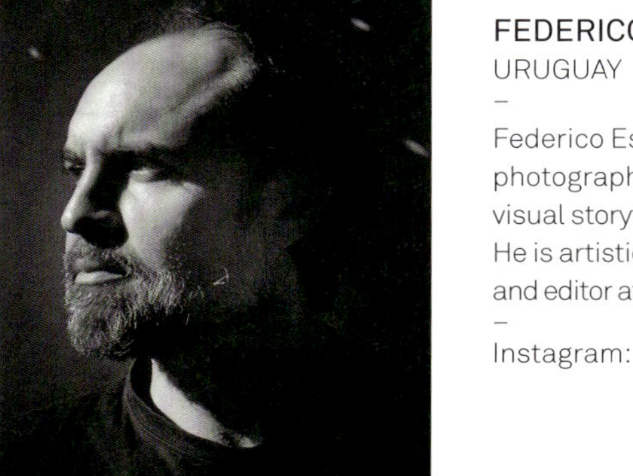

TORIA GALLARRETA

**FEDERICO ESTOL**
URUGUAY

–

Federico Estol is a Uruguayan artist and photographer, currently working as a socio-visual storyteller in the Latin American region. He is artistic director of San José Foto festival, and editor at El Ministerio Ediciones publishers.

–

Instagram: @federicoestol

# Winners

—

## SINGLES

**MUSUK NOLTE**
PERU/MEXICO, 1988

–

Musuk Nolte is a photographer, documentalist and editor. His work straddles documentary and artistic photography to approach social issues, such as memory and environmental depredation.

–

Instagram: @musukn

A. MUMENTHALLER

## STORIES

**ALESSANDRO CINQUE**
ITALY, 1988

–

Alessandro Cinque is a photojournalist based in Lima, Peru, whose work delves into the social and environmental issues affecting minorities, often focusing on the devastating impact of mining on Indigenous people and their lands.

–

Instagram: @alessandro.cinque

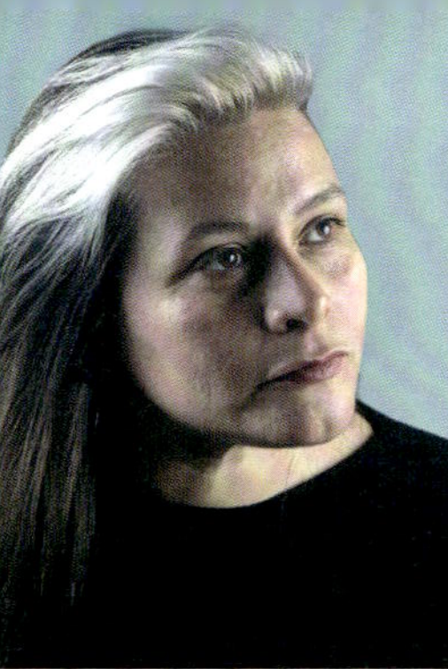

COOPERATIVE SUB

## GISELA VOLÁ
ARGENTINA

–

Gisela Volá is a photographer, teacher, curator, a co-founder of Cooperativa Sub, and a member of Vist projects. She lives in Argentina, and works in Latin America.

–

Instagram: @giselavola

## ISADORA ROMERO
ECUADOR

–

Isadora Romero is an Ecuadorian freelance visual storyteller based in Quito, Ecuador. She holds the 2022 World Press Photo Open Format Award, and is co-founder of Ruda Colectiva, a collective of Latin American women and non-binary photographers.

–

Instagram: @isadoraromerophoto

ANA MARÍA BUITRÓN

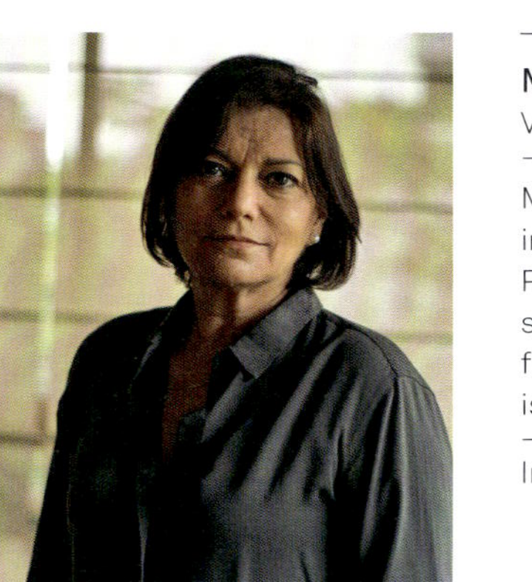

EZEQUIEL CRESPO

## MARIANELA BALBI
VENEZUELA

–

Marianela Balbi is a Venezuelan journalist, investigative reporter, and director of Instituto Prensa y Sociedad Venezuela (IPYS), a civil society organization that defends the right to freedom of expression, and promotes journalists' professional development.

–

Instagram: @nela.balbi

# LONG-TERM PROJECTS

## FABIOLA FERRERO
VENEZUELA, 1991

–

Fabiola Ferrero is a journalist and photographer born in Caracas, Venezuela. Ferrero develops long-term visual projects about South America, and especially Venezuela's crisis.

–

Instagram: @fabiolaferrero

STEFANO POZZEBON

# OPEN FORMAT

## JOHANNA ALARCÓN
ECUADOR, 1992

–

Johanna Alarcón is a freelance photojournalist and visual storyteller whose work focuses on social justice, human rights, identity and gender-related issues. Alarcón is a member of the Magnum Foundation and Panos Pictures.

–

Instagram: @johis.alarcon

ABUBAKR MOHAMED

# Southeast Asia and Oceania

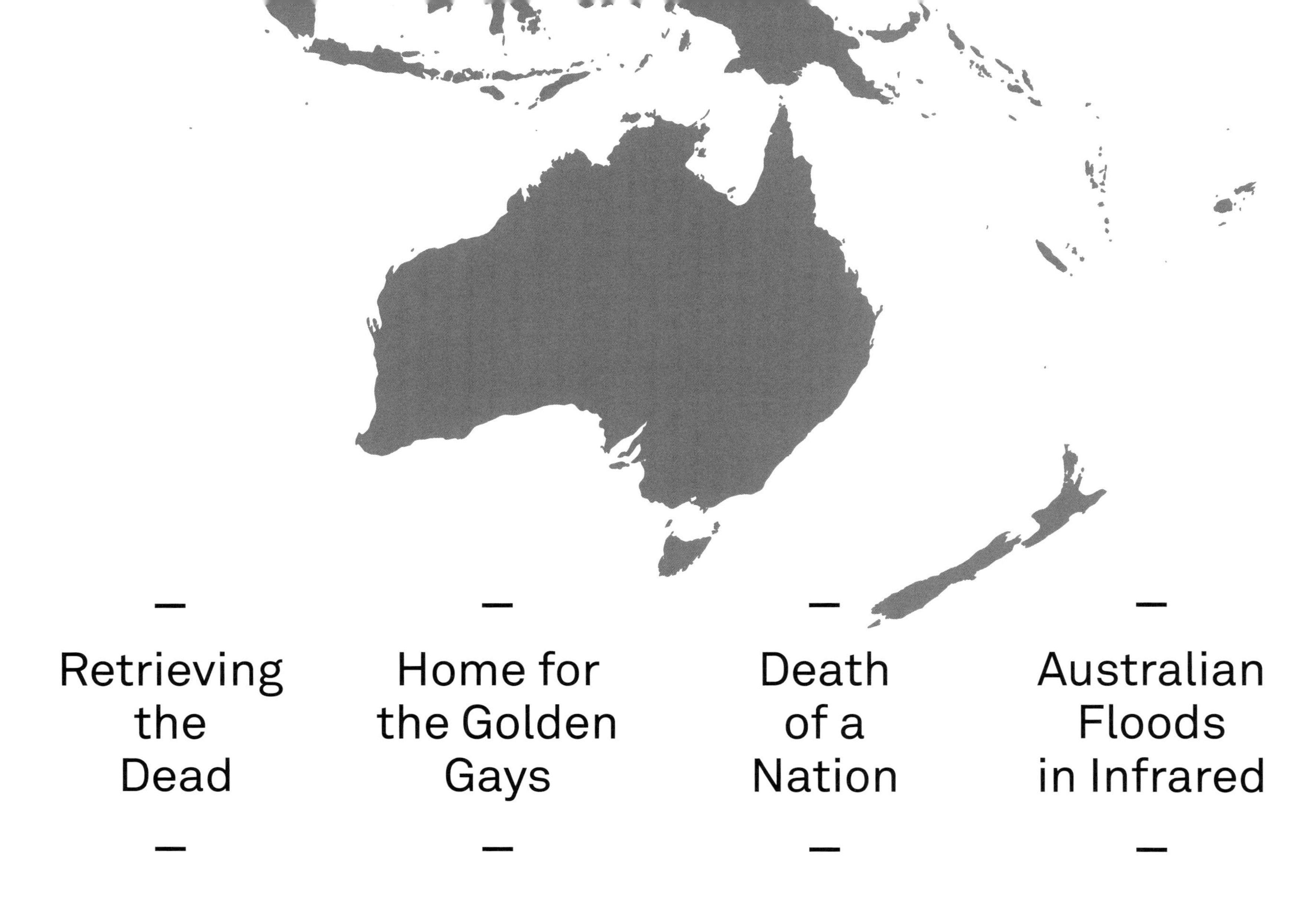
Retrieving the Dead
Home for the Golden Gays
Death of a Nation
Australian Floods in Infrared

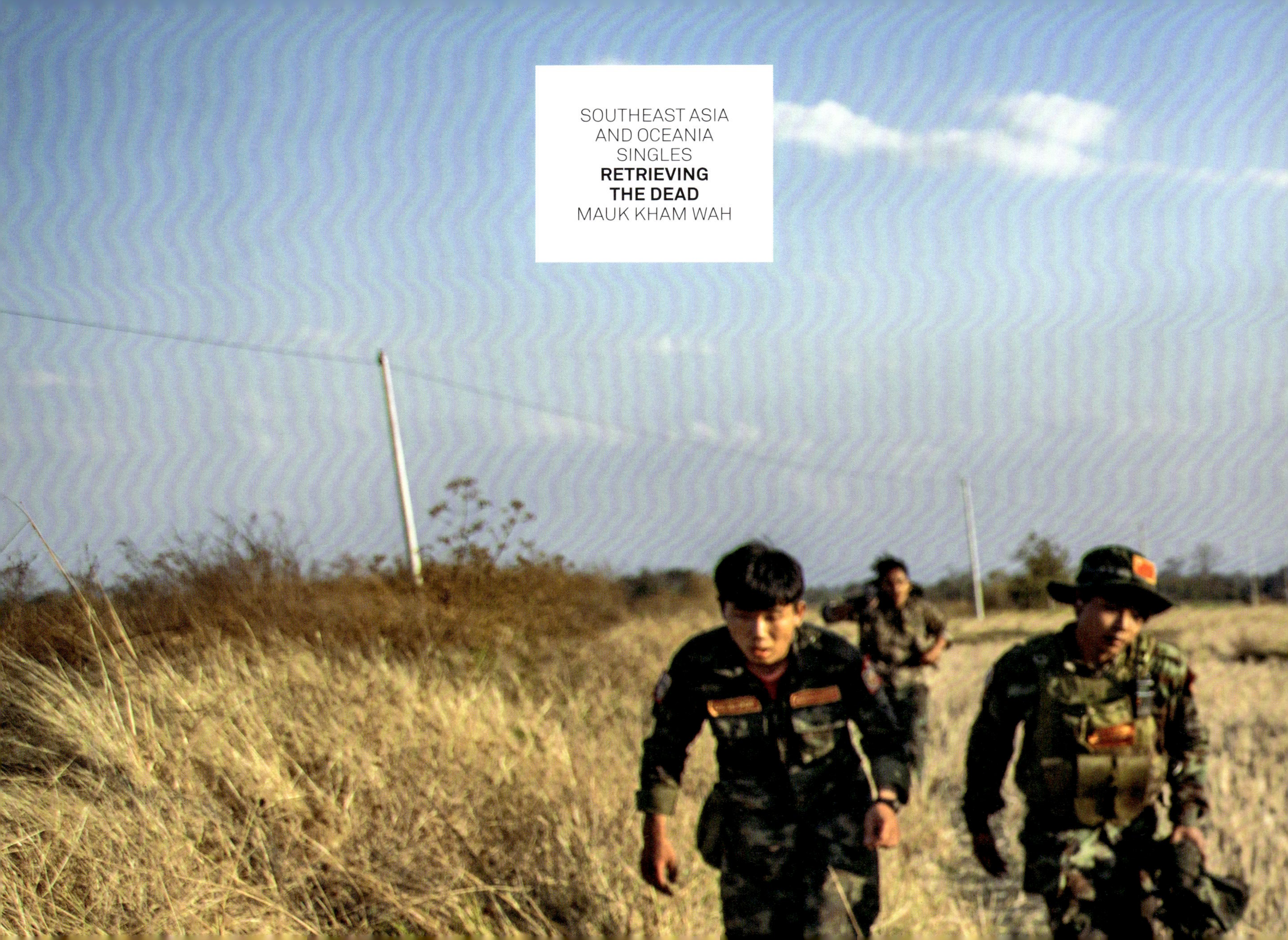

SOUTHEAST ASIA
AND OCEANIA
SINGLES

# RETRIEVING THE DEAD

MAUK KHAM WAH

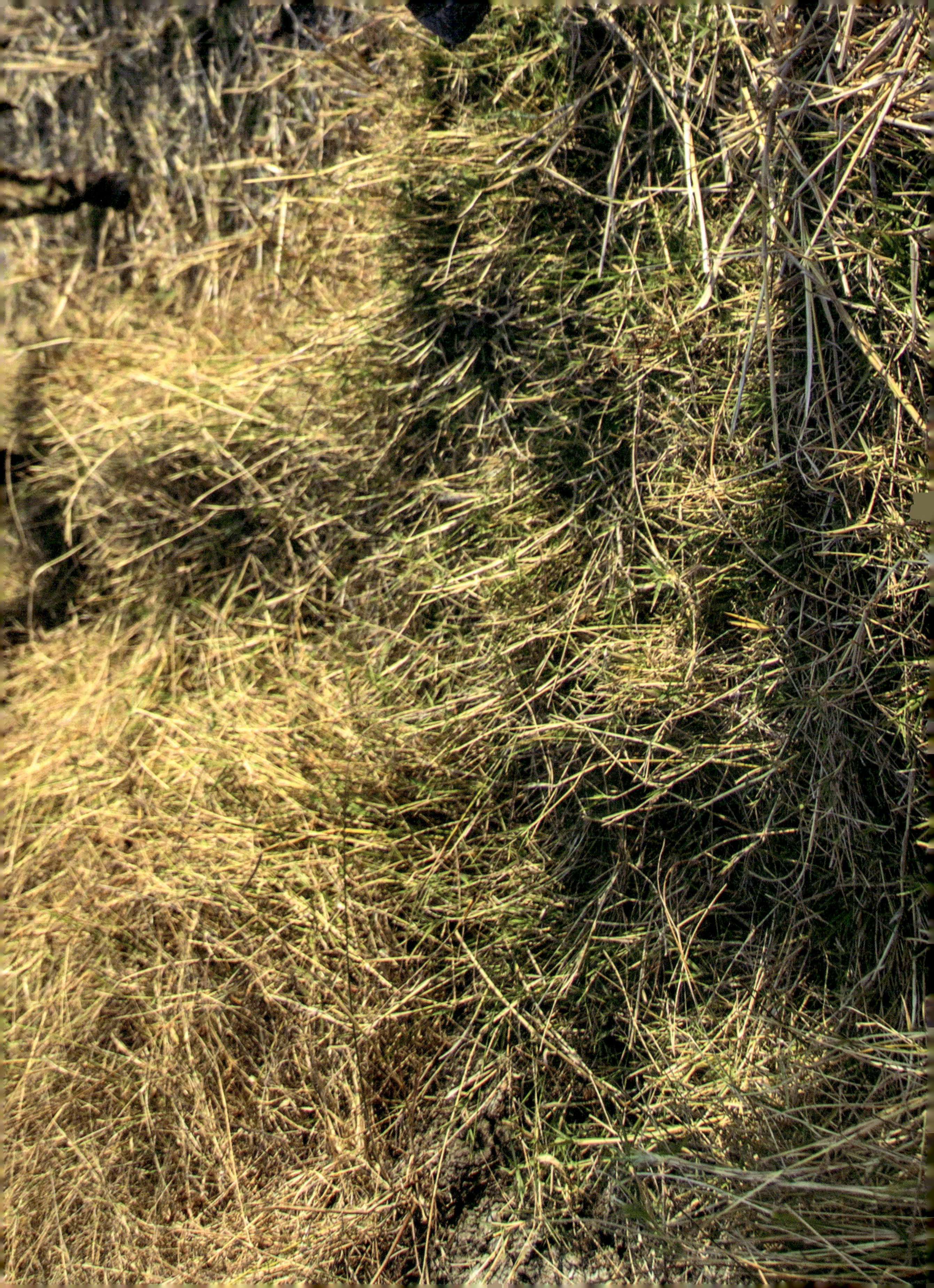

# Retrieving the Dead

Resistance fighters from the People's Defense Forces (PDF) retreat with the body of a comrade, following a clash with the Myanmar military, in Moe Bye, Kayah (Karenni) State, Myanmar, on 21 February 2022. Myanmar authorities had sent reinforcements to the region as fighting with local opposition groups intensified.

The PDF fights alongside regional and ethnic armed groups also opposed to Myanmar's military dictatorship. It is the armed wing of a parallel government that was formed primarily by ousted democratic lawmakers in the wake of a military coup in Myanmar in 2021. At great personal risk, the photographer spent a year with people who had joined this combined resistance movement.

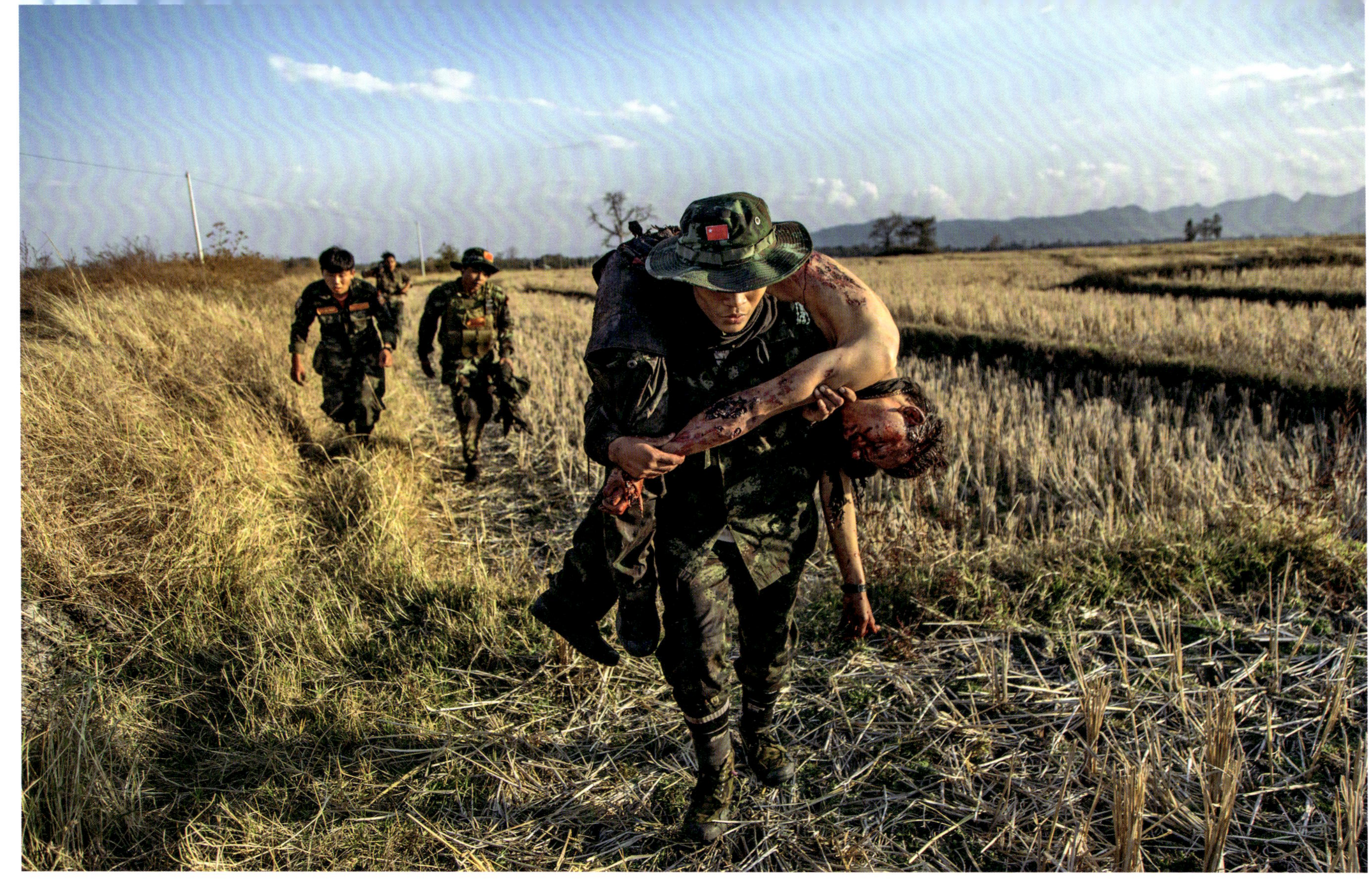

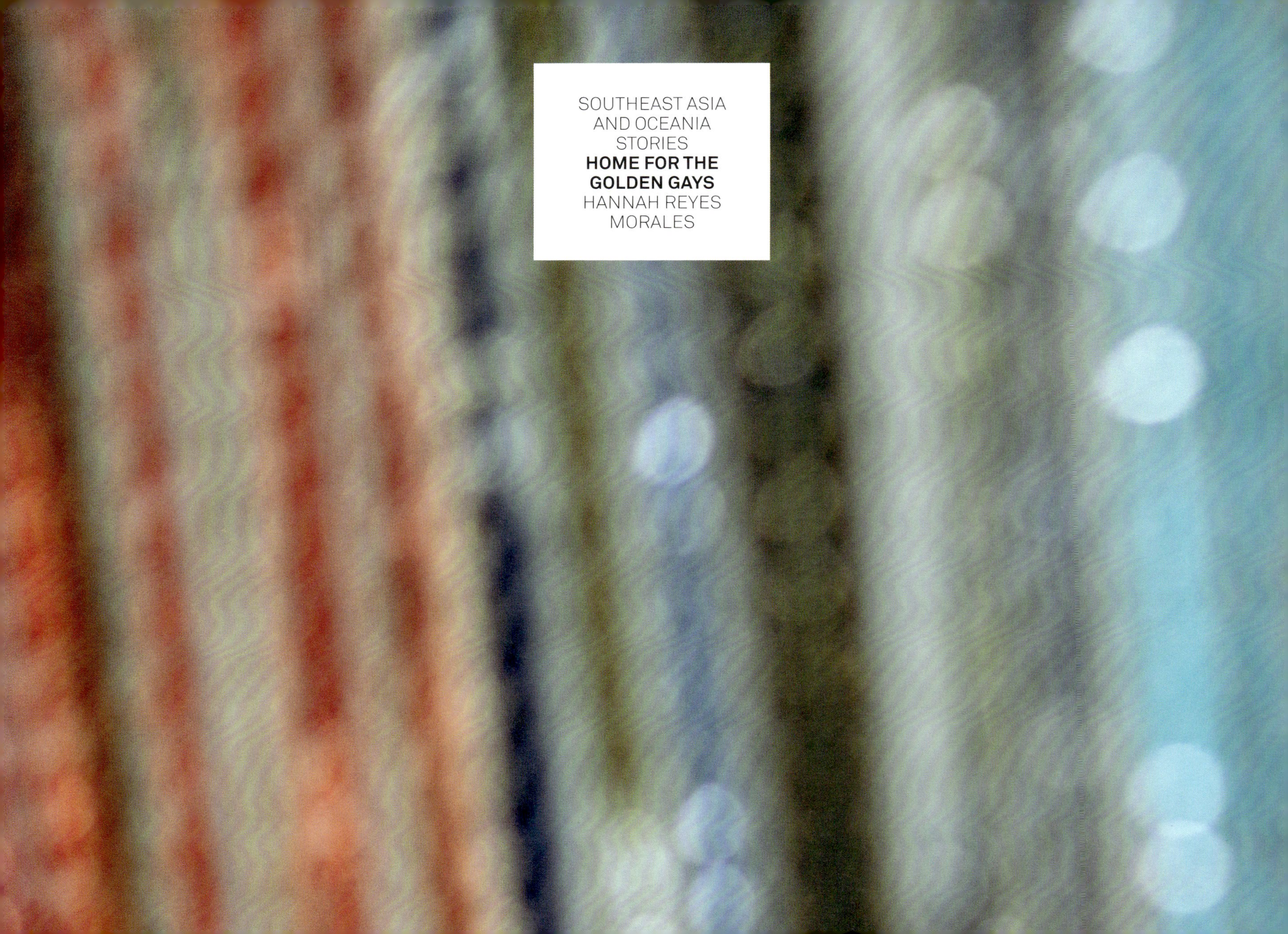

SOUTHEAST ASIA
AND OCEANIA
STORIES

# HOME FOR THE GOLDEN GAYS

HANNAH REYES
MORALES

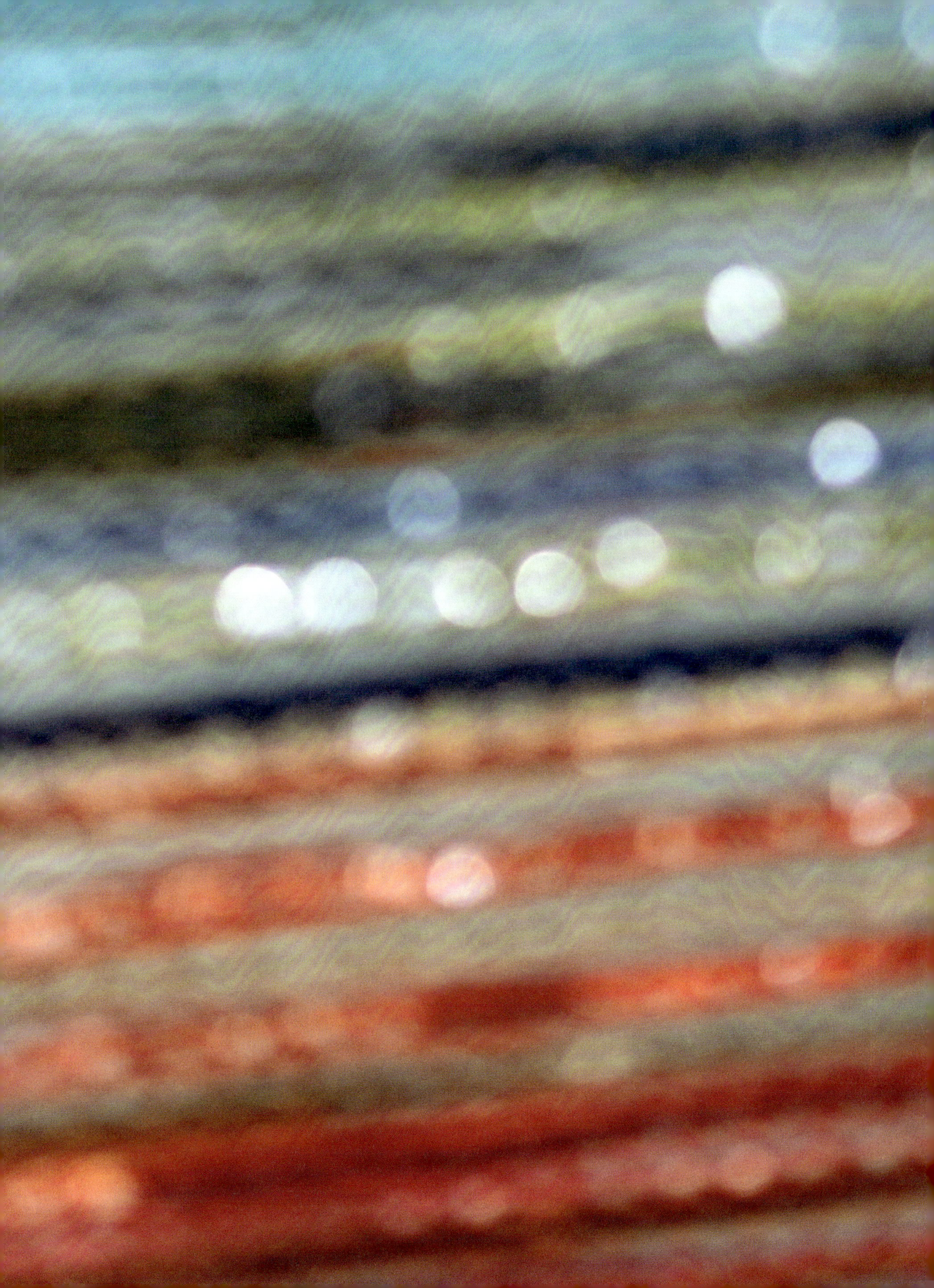

# Home for the Golden Gays

The Golden Gays are a community of older LGBTQI+ people from the Philippines who have lived together for decades and support each other. In a country where they face discrimination, prejudice, and challenges amplified by their age and socioeconomic class, the group came together and made a home, sharing care responsibilities and staging shows and pageants to make ends meet. When their founder died in 2012, the community were evicted and some experienced homelessness until 2018, when they began renting a house in Manila. The jury commended this story for portraying the warmth, joy, and dignity of the community.

Hannah Reyes Morales photographed these images on assignment for *The New York Times*.

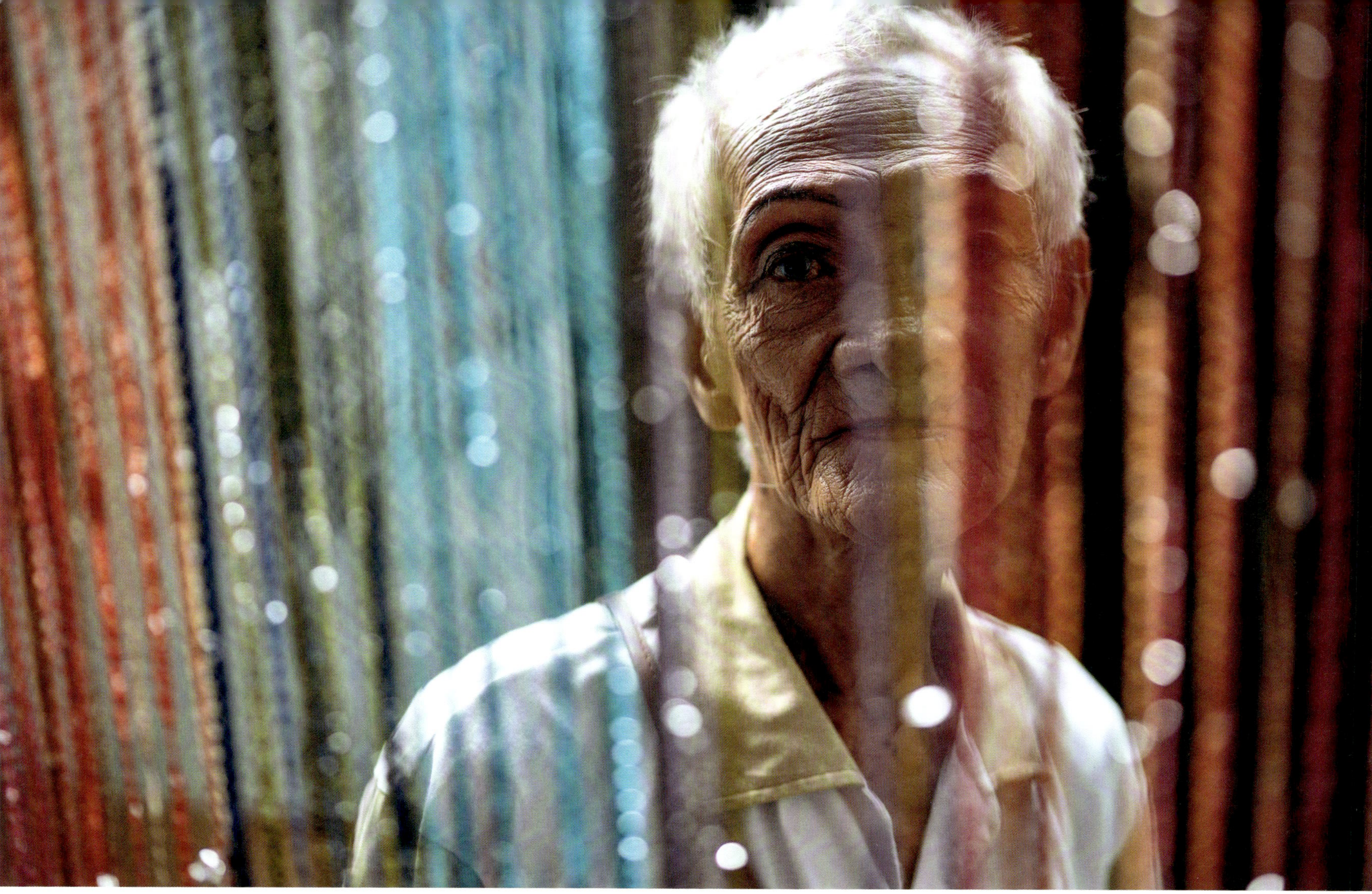

Al Enriquez (86) looks through a curtain in the Golden Gays' home in Manila, the Philippines, on 18 July 2022.

Odessa Jones (55), back home from a film audition, poses with flowers in Manila, on 18 July 2022.

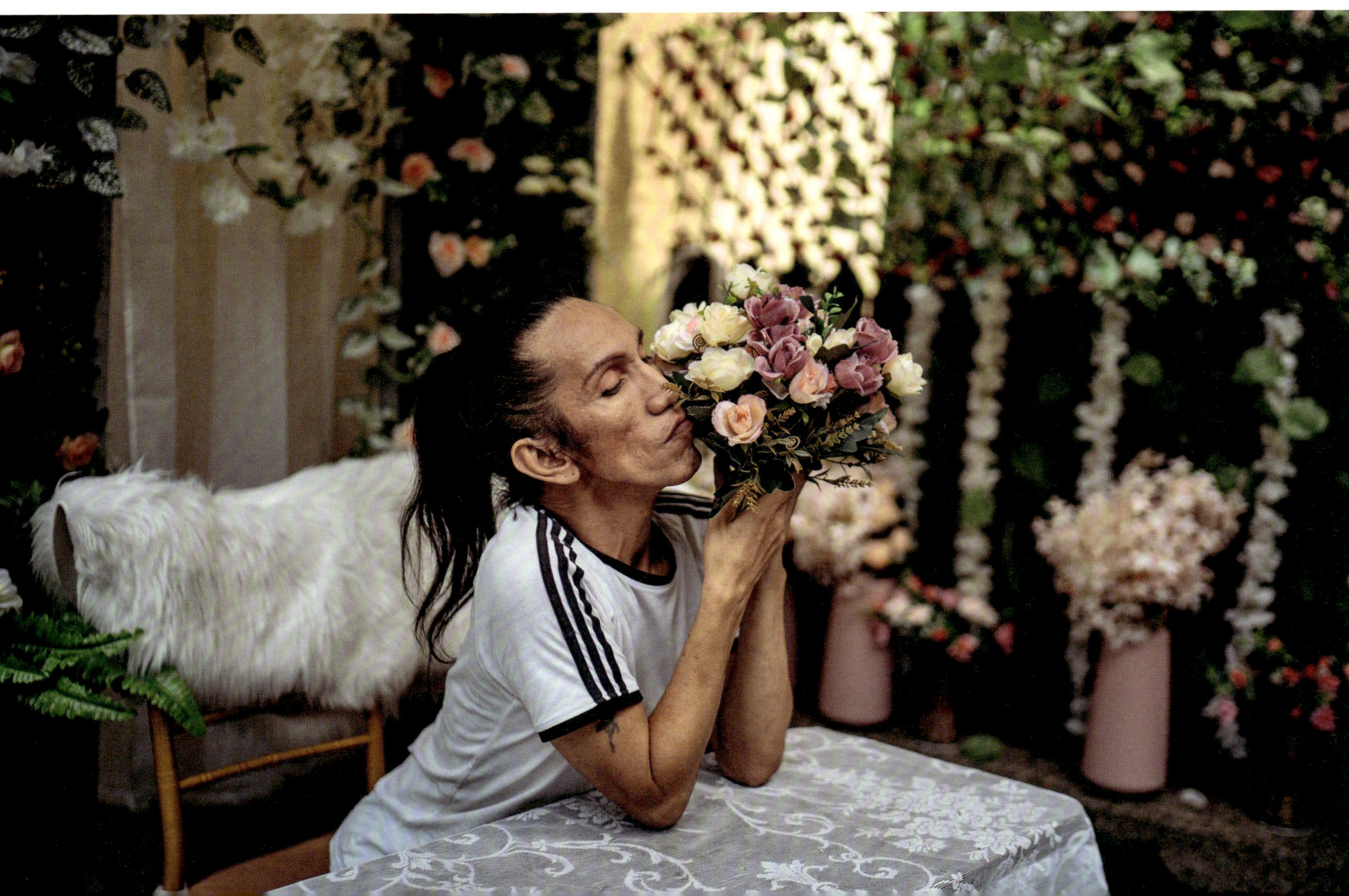

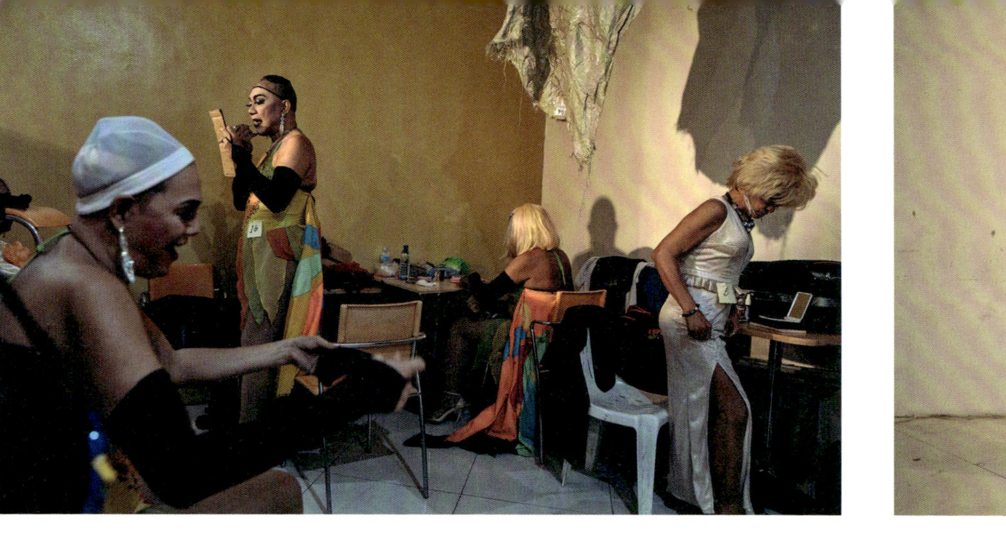

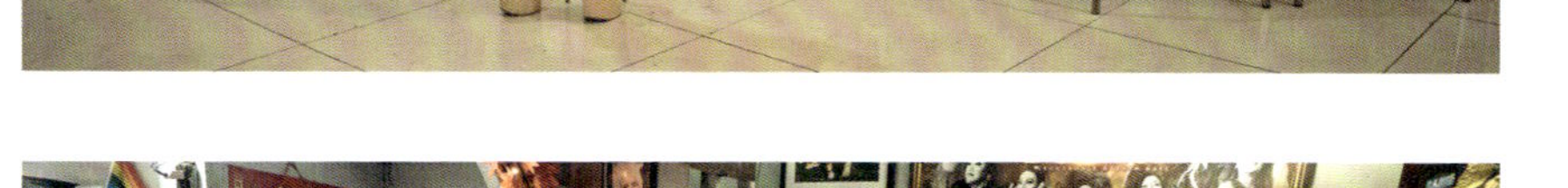

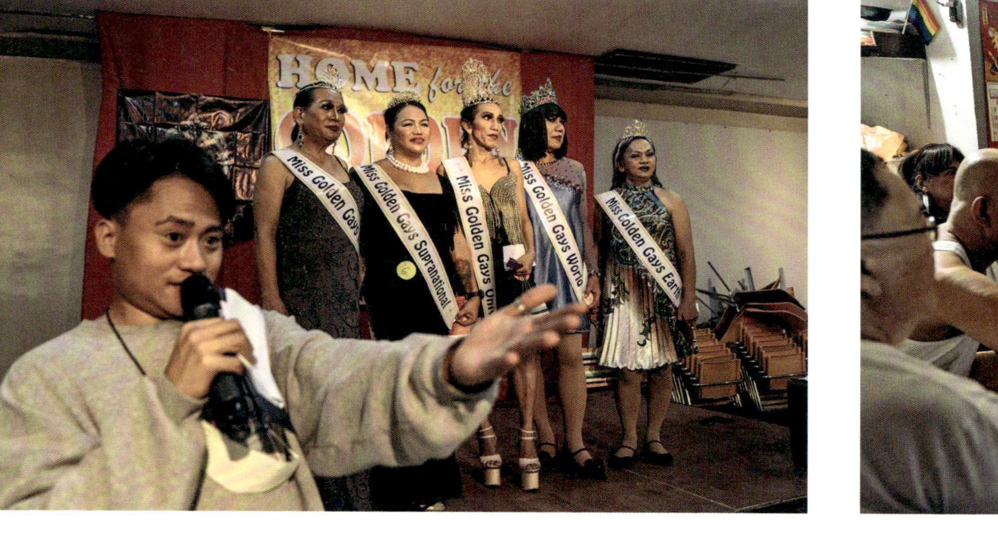


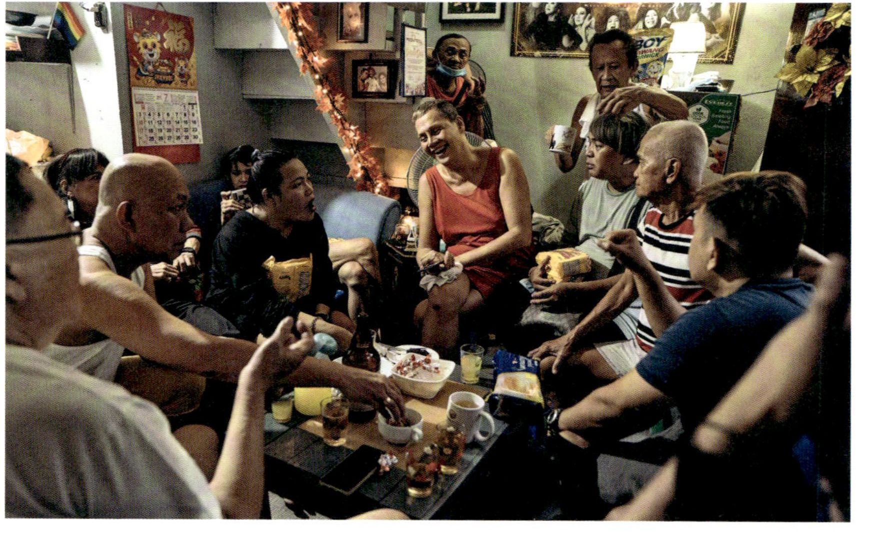

Members of the Golden Gays prepare for a show in Manila, on 26 June 2022.

Members of the Golden Gays perform in a talent and beauty pageant at a shopping mall in Manila, on 24 July 2022.

Odessa Jones (55) performs in a show for the Golden Gays' benefactors in Manila, on 24 July 2022.

Members of the Golden Gays community unwind at home after a show, in Manila, on 24 July 2022.

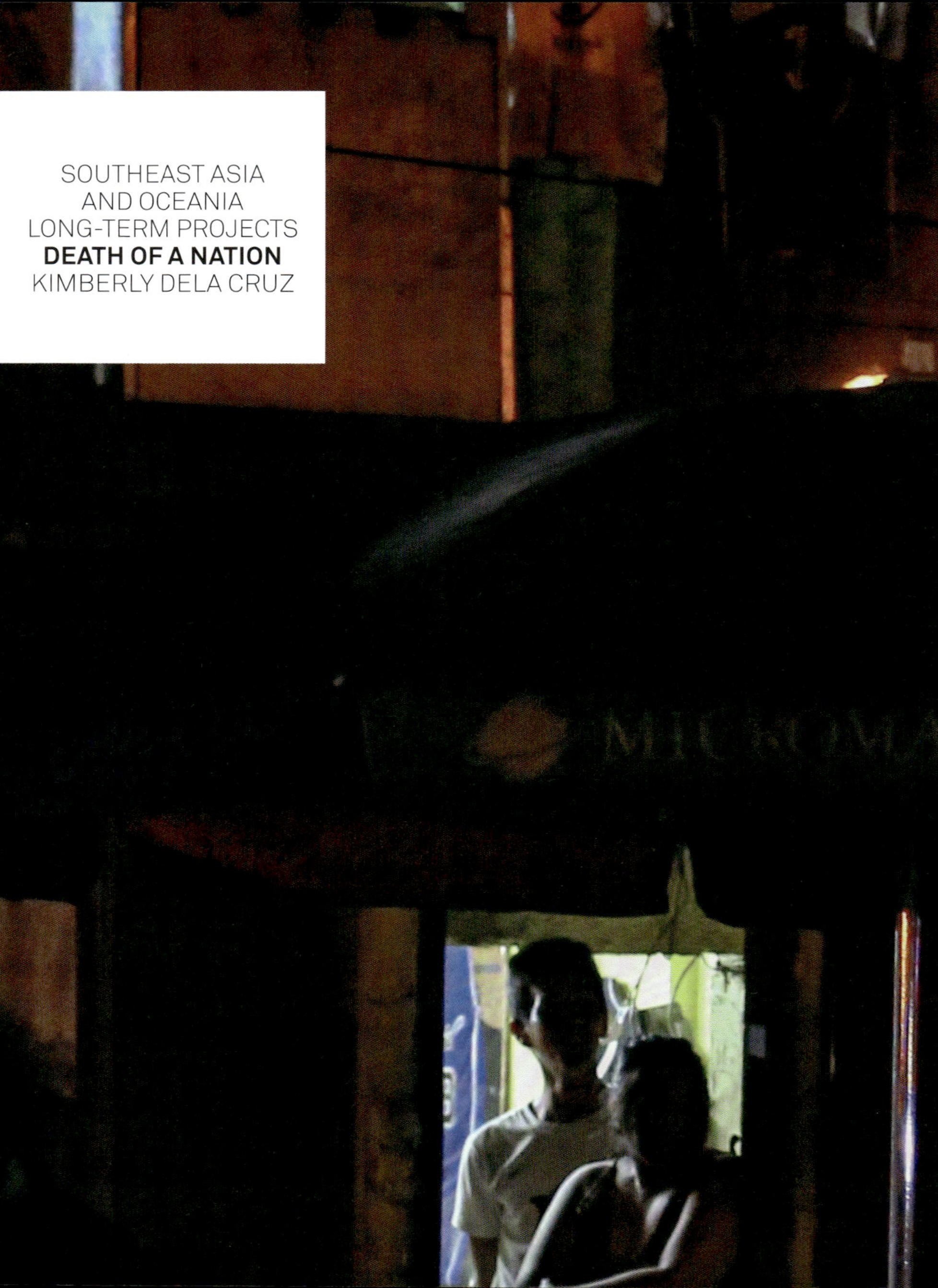

SOUTHEAST ASIA
AND OCEANIA
LONG-TERM PROJECTS
**DEATH OF A NATION**
KIMBERLY DELA CRUZ

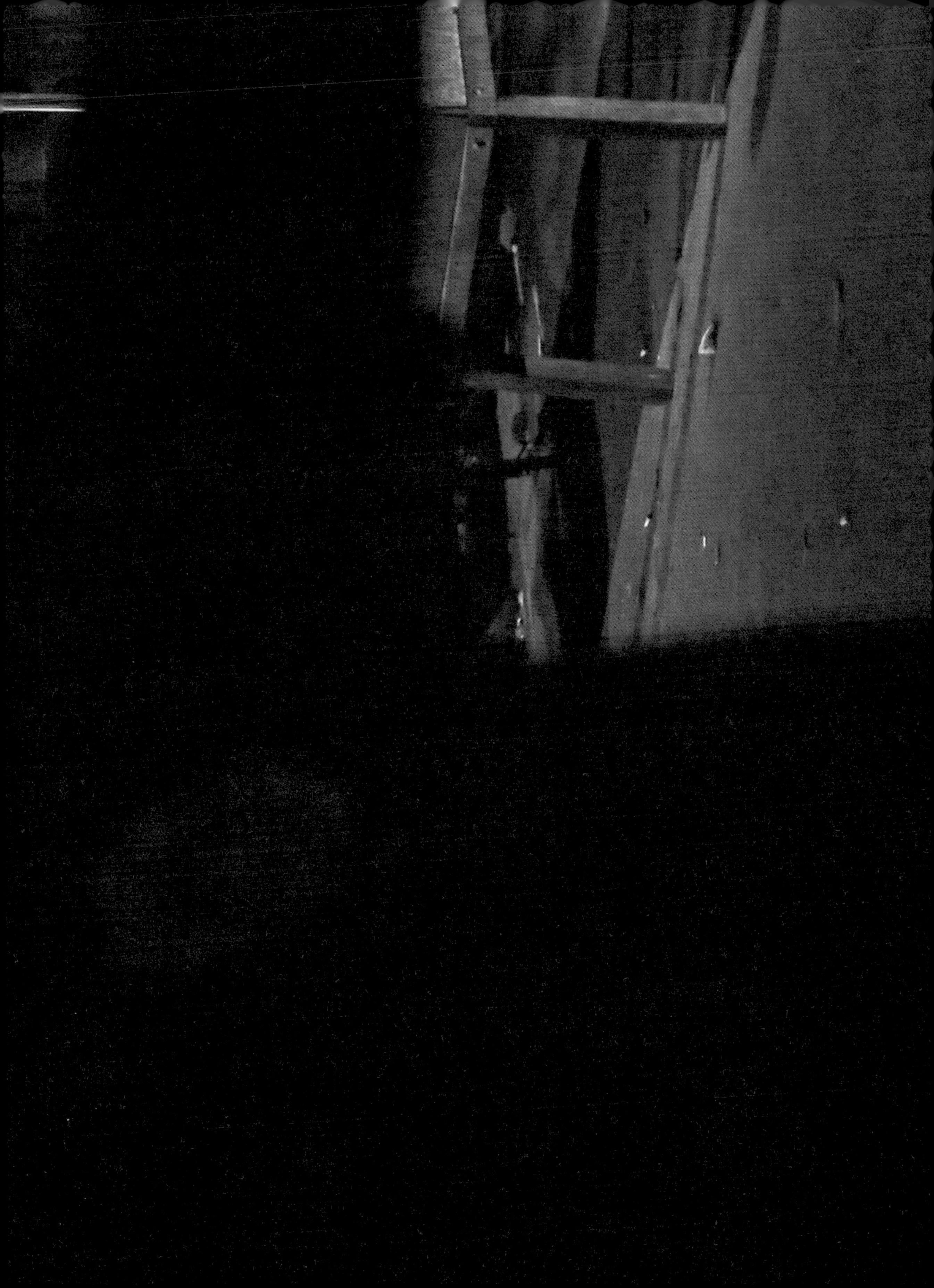

# Death of a Nation

Soon after taking office in June 2016, Philippine president Rodrigo Duterte began a concerted "war on drugs", repeatedly ordering attacks against suspects. A surge of extrajudicial killings followed, perpetrated not only by police but also by masked vigilantes and other civilians. Amnesty International reports that executions mostly target low-income communities. The Philippine National Police admits to more than 6,000 such deaths to date; local human rights organizations put the figure at 30,000. The photographer has been documenting the war on drugs since its outset, and the jury commended her ability to capture the continued impact on families involved.

Kimberly dela Cruz's personal project received support from the W. Eugene Smith Memorial Fund in 2021.

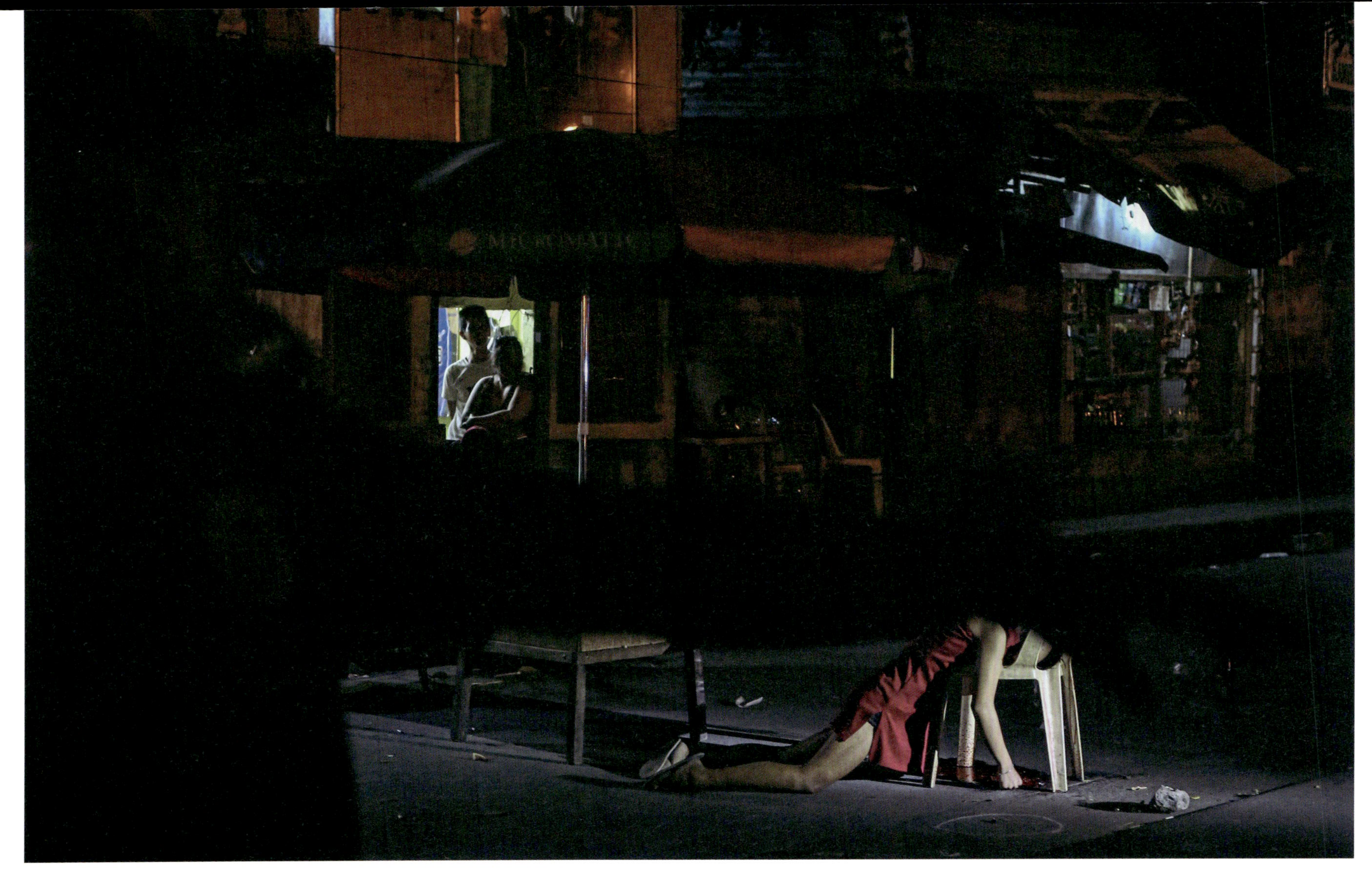

The body of Kristita Padual lies at the crime scene, after unidentified murderers on motorcycles killed her and Ernesto Mortiz while they were having dinner beside the road, in Quezon City, on 4 March 2017.

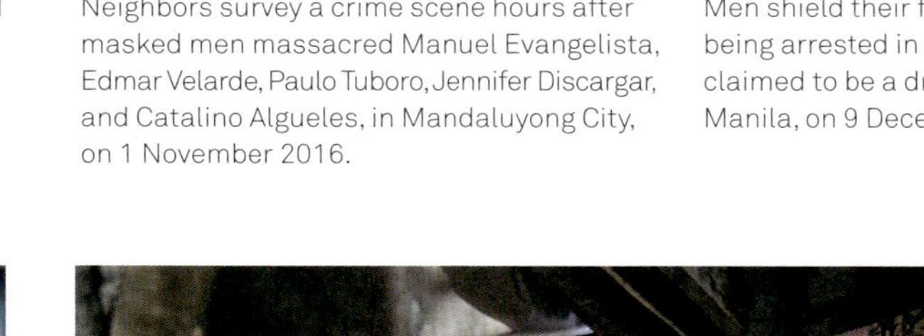

Jazmine Durana (15) cradles her month-old daughter Hazel, on 2 February 2017, at the wake of her partner John "Toto" Dela Cruz (16), who was shot by men wearing black masks a few days earlier.

AJ (16) mourns at the scene where unidentified assailants have shot his neighbor Antonio Perez outside his home in Pasay City, on 4 January 2017.

Neighbors survey a crime scene hours after masked men massacred Manuel Evangelista, Edmar Velarde, Paulo Tuboro, Jennifer Discargar, and Catalino Algueles, in Mandaluyong City, on 1 November 2016.

Men shield their faces from the media after being arrested in a food factory that police claimed to be a drug den, in Pandacan, Manila, on 9 December 2016.

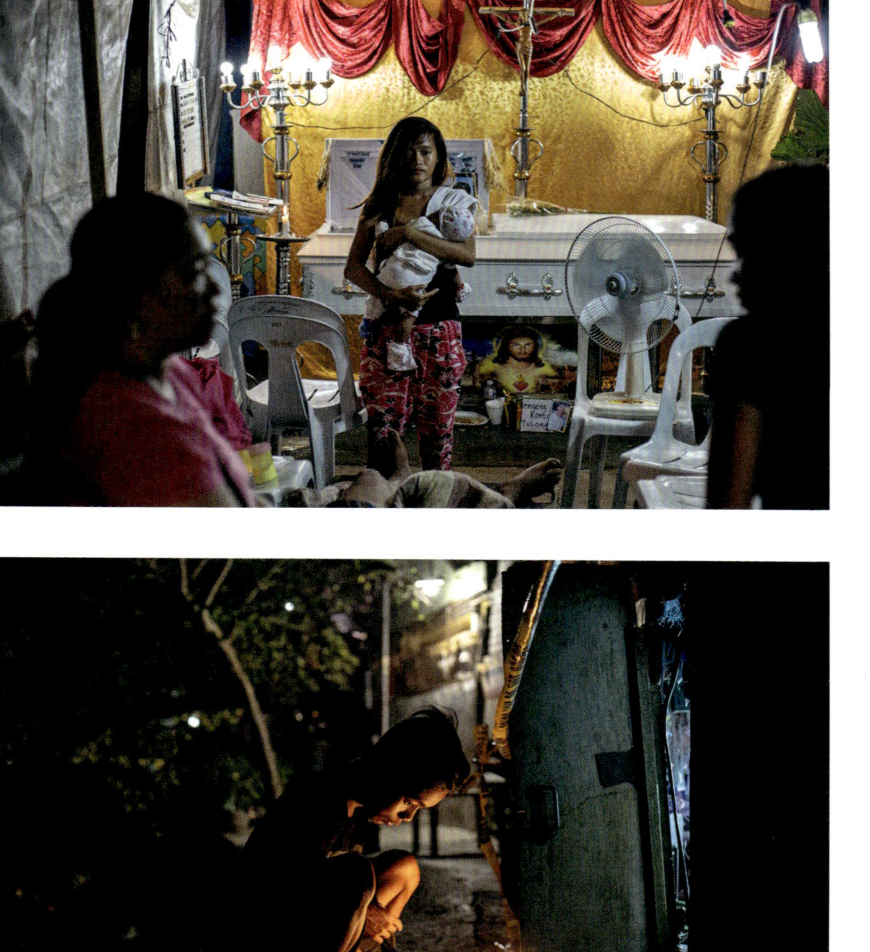

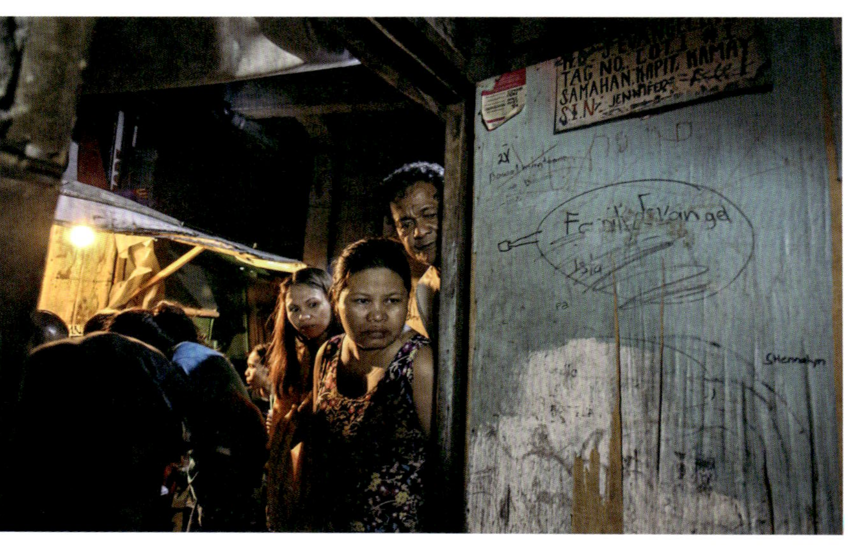

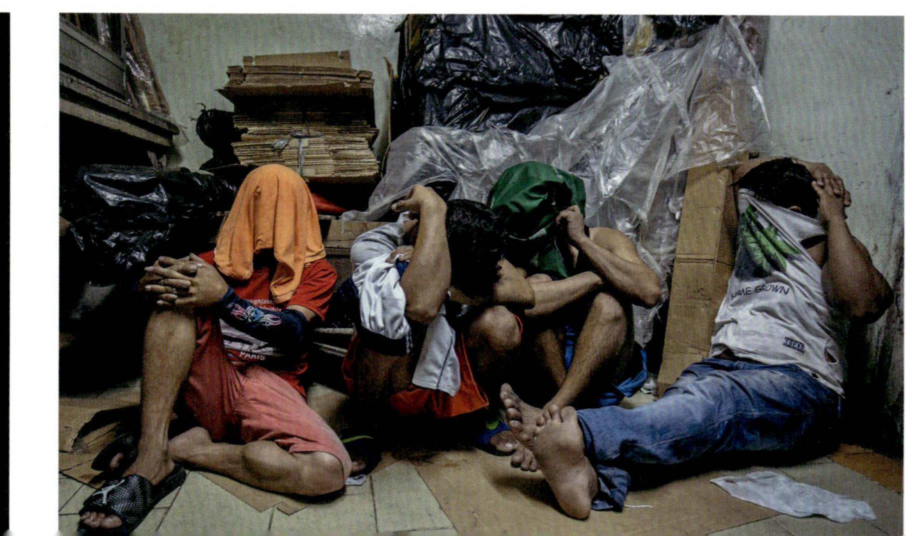

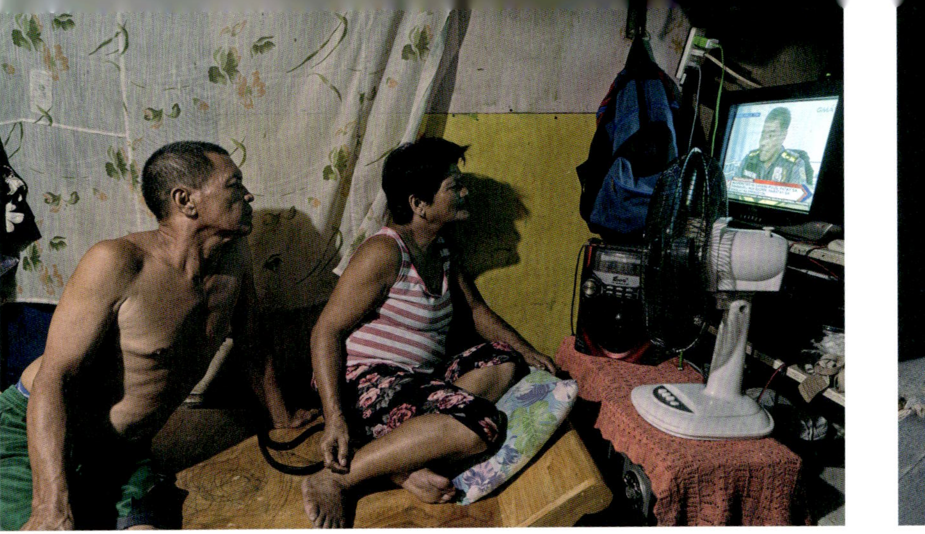

Nestor and Alma Hilbano watch the evening news, in Quezon City, on 8 September 2019. Exactly three years earlier, their son Richard was killed during a police operation.

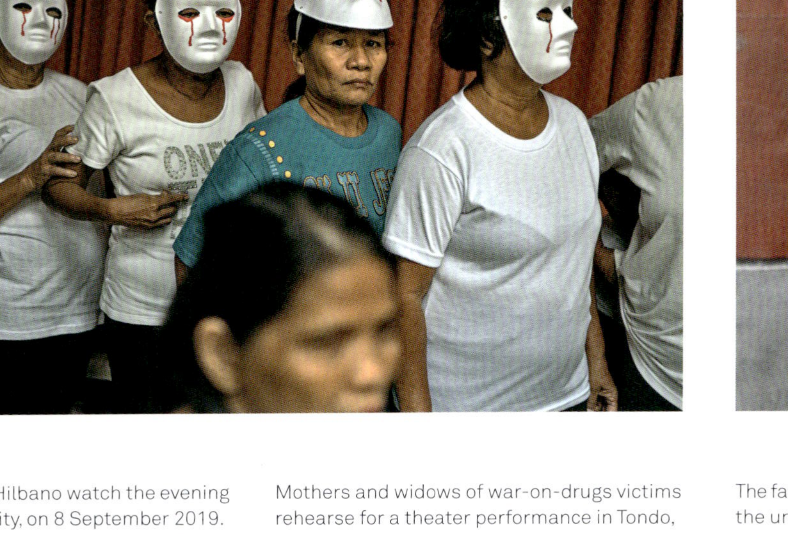

Mothers and widows of war-on-drugs victims rehearse for a theater performance in Tondo, Manila, on 22 November 2019.

The family of Rovelyn and Richard Cham receive the urns containing their ashes, in Tayuman, Manila, on 21 February 2022. Unknown gunmen killed the couple at home in 2016.

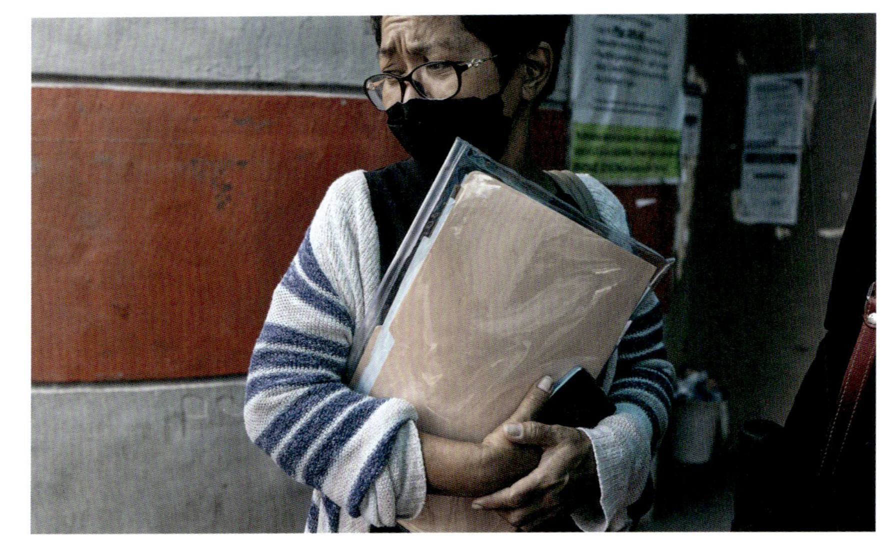

Mary Anne Domingo stands outside a Caloocan courthouse after giving testimony on 14 February 2022. She brought a case against the police after her husband and son were killed in a raid in 2016. The trial commenced in 2021.

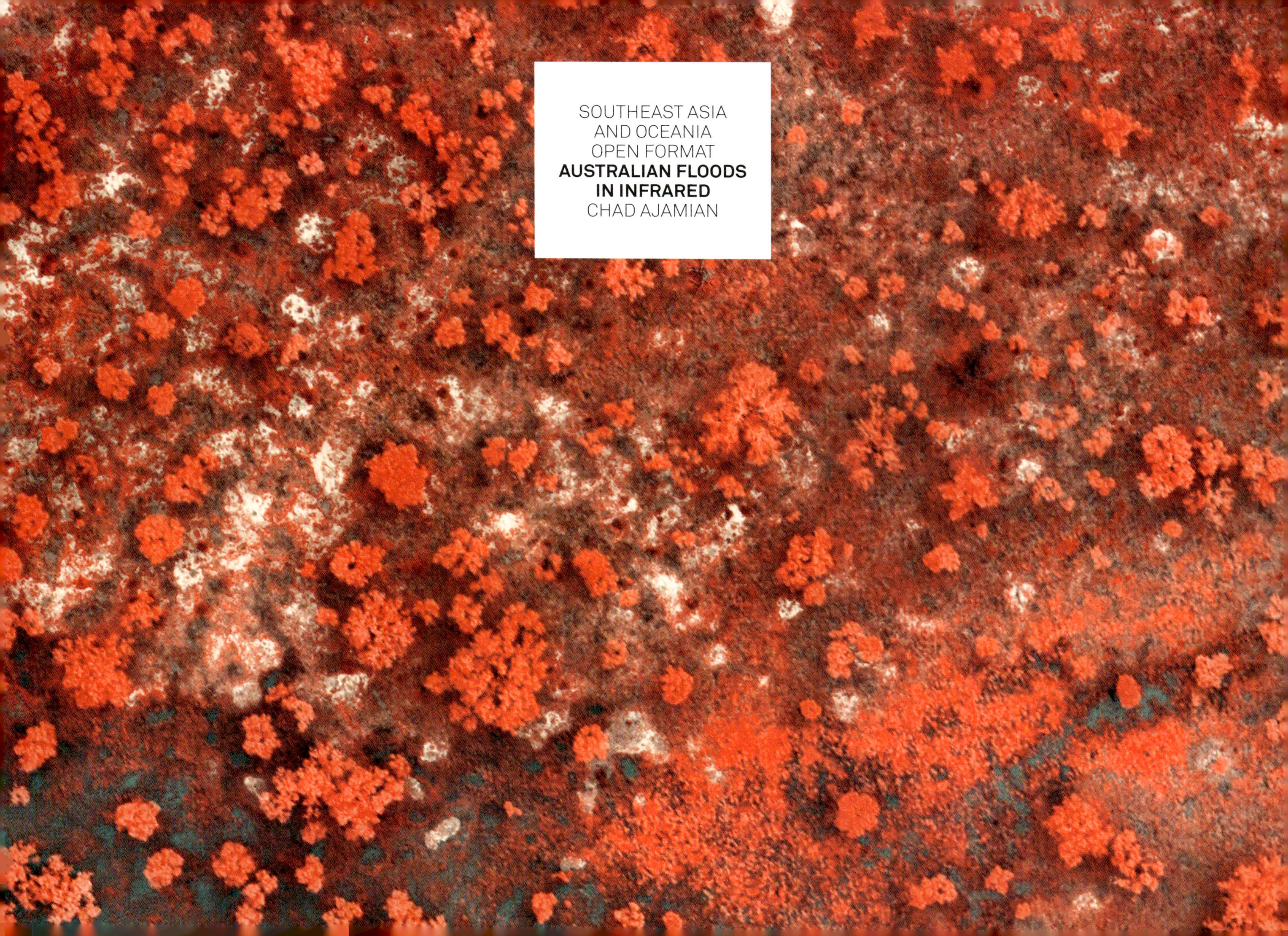
SOUTHEAST ASIA
AND OCEANIA
OPEN FORMAT
**AUSTRALIAN FLOODS**
**IN INFRARED**
CHAD AJAMIAN

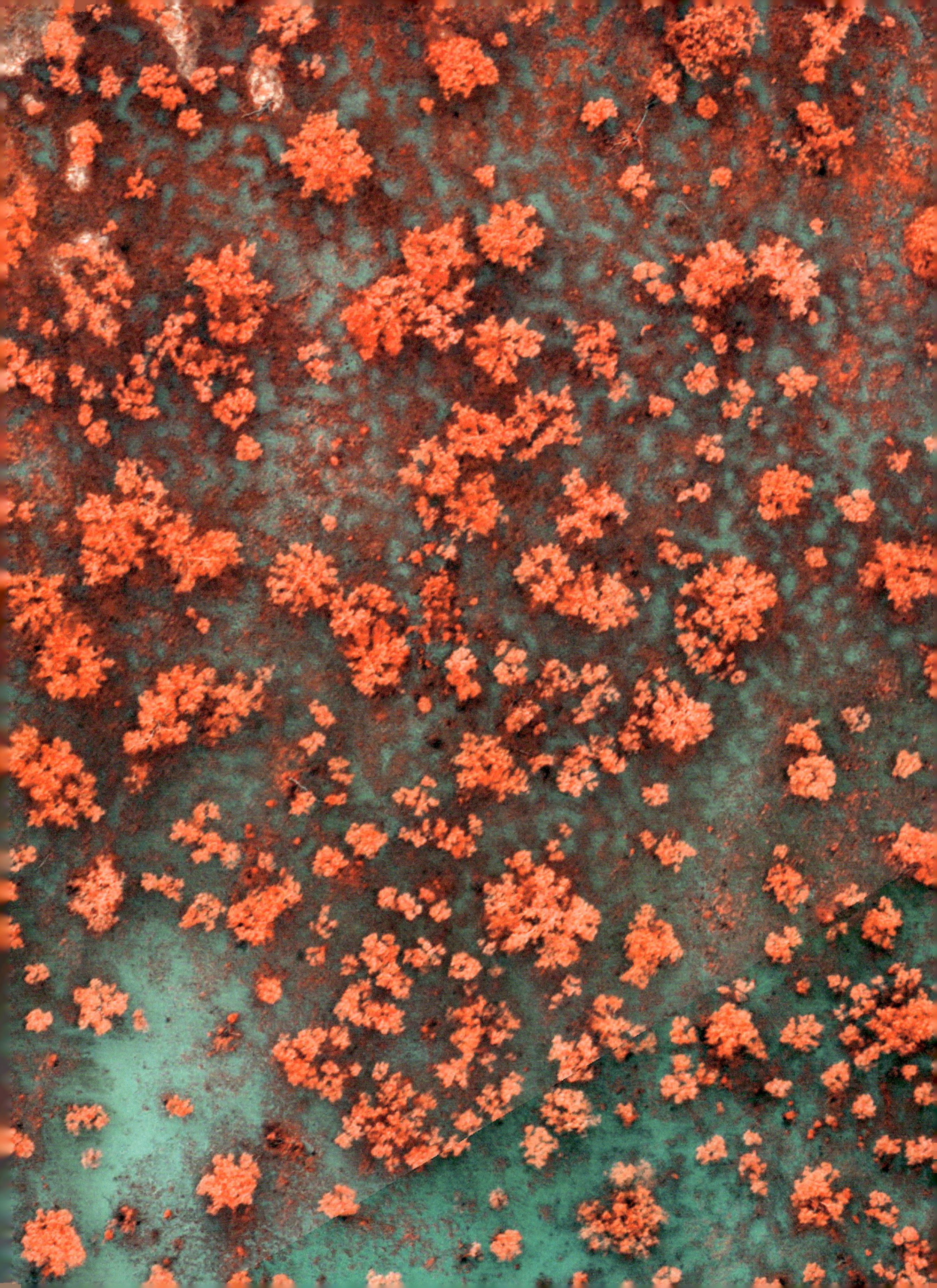

# Australian Floods in Infrared

This series offers a unique perspective on the recent floods that have devastated areas in New South Wales, Australia. Aerial infrared imaging renders vegetation in pinks and reds, contrasting sharply against blues and cyans, which represent water. These images make newly flooded areas easily discernible to post-disaster emergency responders, assisting with response and recovery. The photos in this series were taken during the round of devastating floods in New South Wales, Australia, which forced the evacuation of 18,000 people in March 2021. The increased intensity and frequency of flooding in the region is likely an outcome of the global climate crisis. The project contains adaptations from raw data in NSW Flood Imagery Viewer by DCS Spatial Services, State of New South Wales, licensed under CC BY 4.

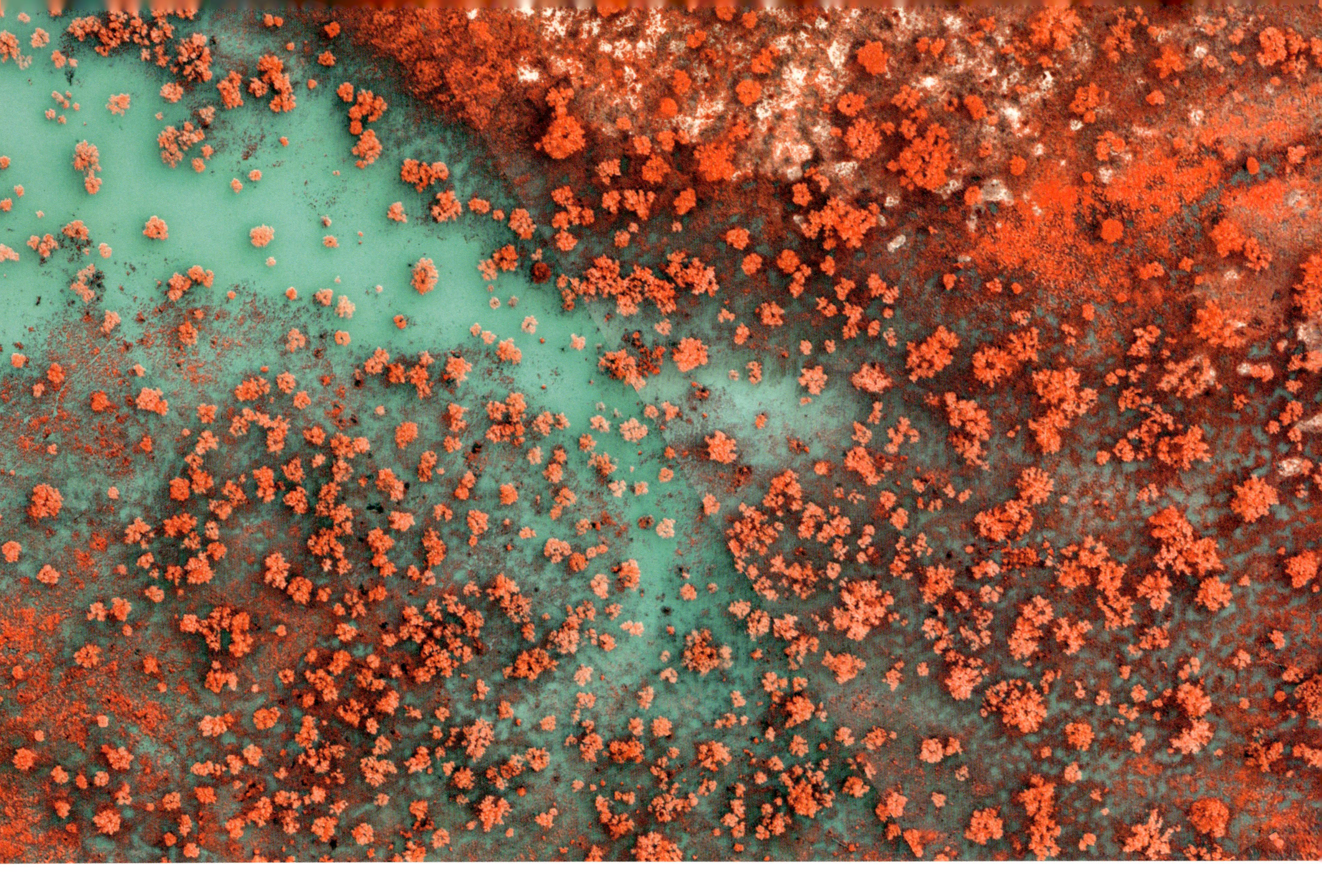

A flooded forest in Mungindi, New South Wales, on 19 April 2021. This area forms a natural basin, which can further isolate remote communities for weeks at a time, requiring emergency air supplies of food and medicine. Flooding in the region has been particularly devastating for residents due to border and road closures.

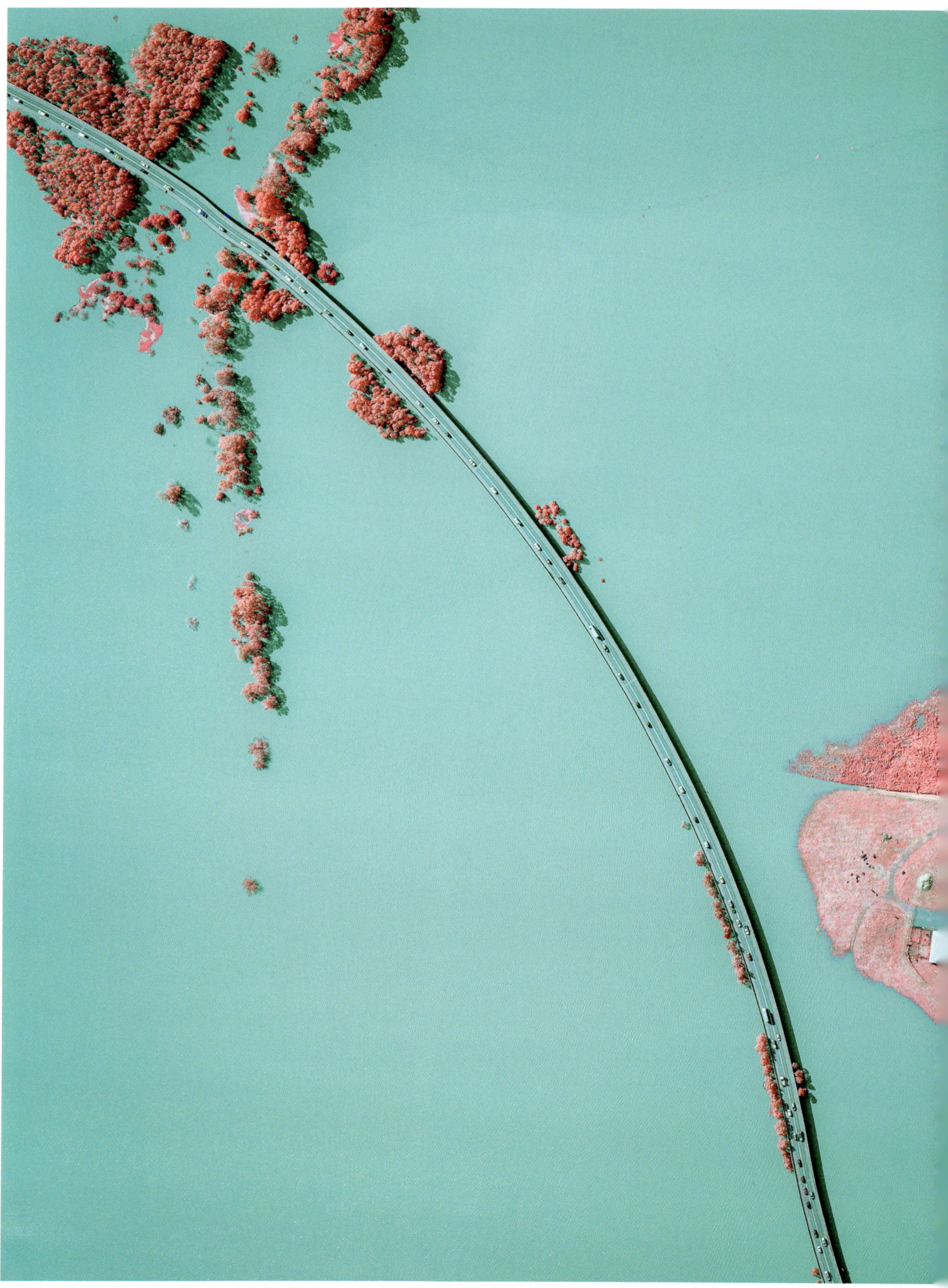

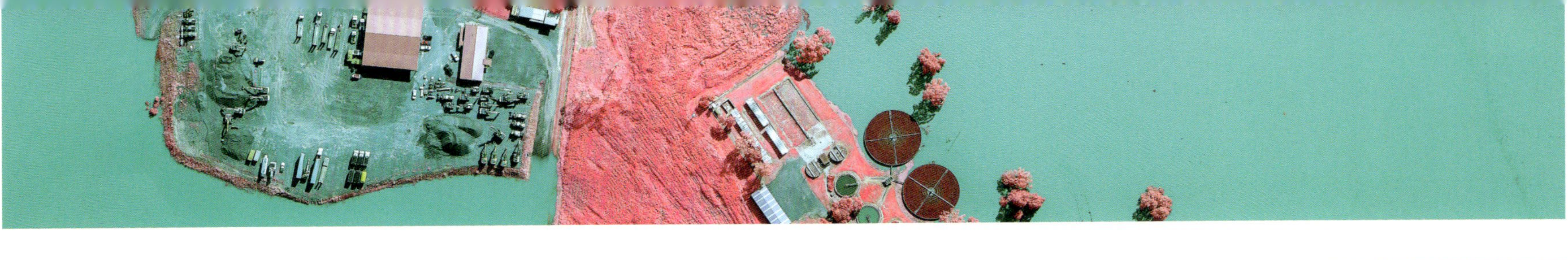

Flooding along the Hawkesbury River, a major waterway that encircles the Sydney metropolitan region, on 31 March 2022. The flood level reached an average of more than 13 meters and was the catchment's wettest 9-day period since records began.

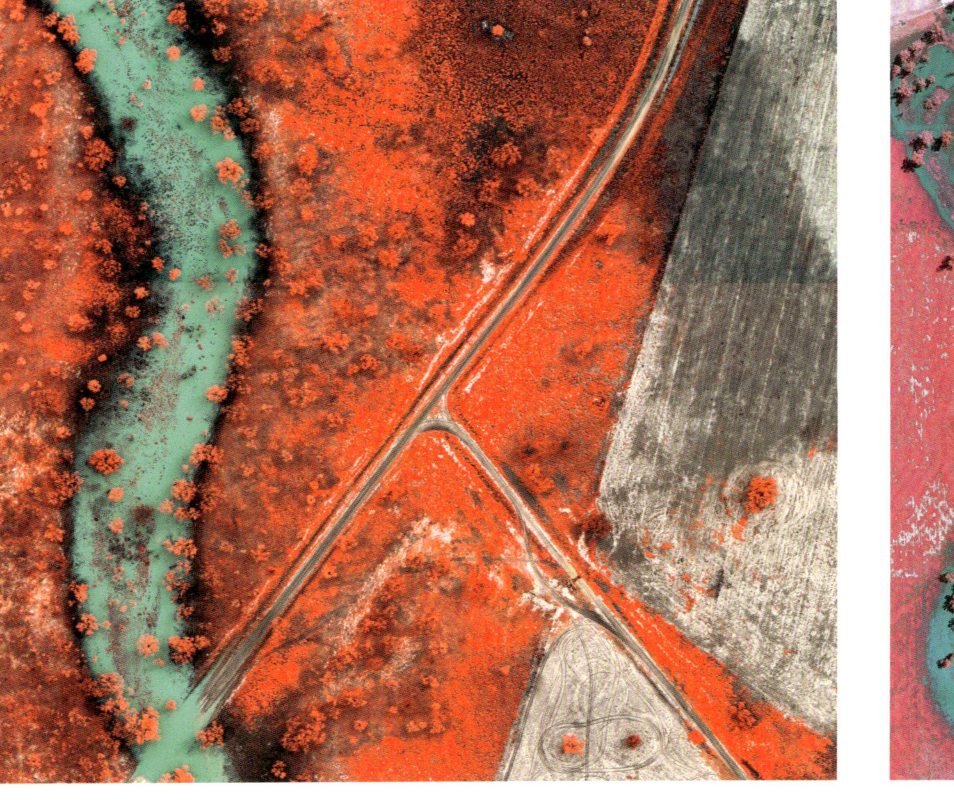

Image of a junction in Mogil Mogil, New South Wales, 19 April 2021. Emergency response agencies utilize infrared aerial imagery to determine the extent of damage and can also determine safe ingress routes for response teams.

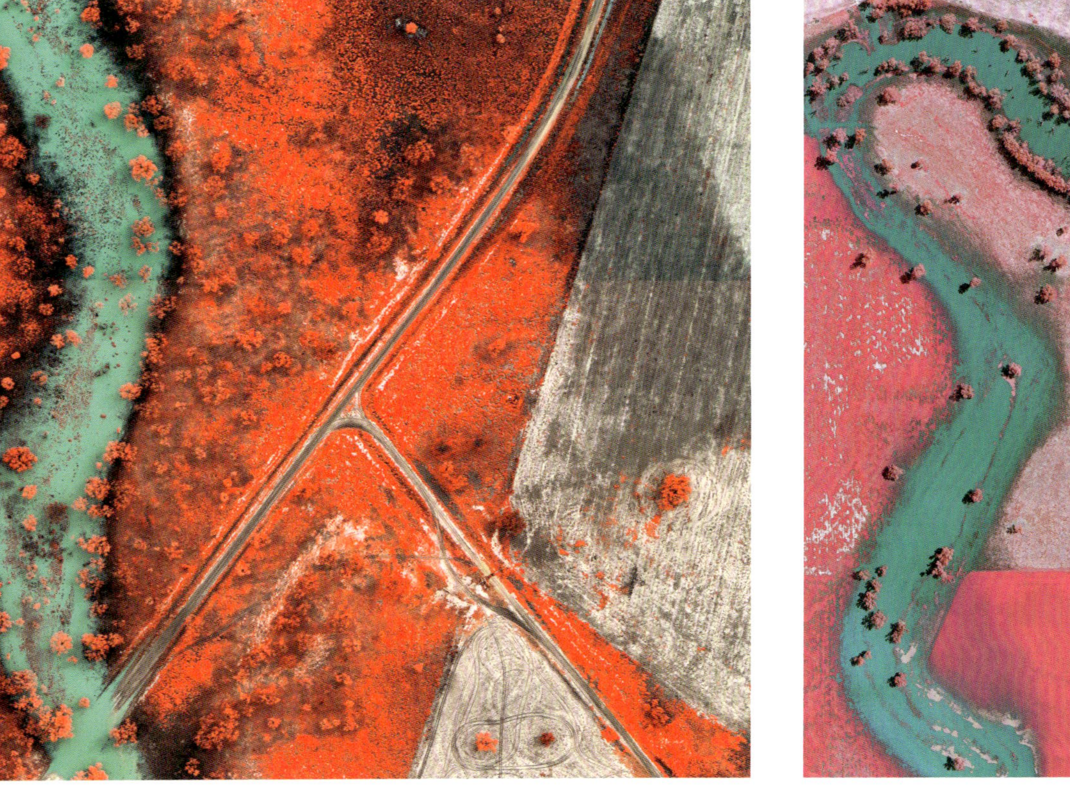

A view of the Lachlan River in the town of Forbes, New South Wales, after a flood inundated the town, blocking roads and access routes and damaging crop yields of local farms. 21 November 2021.

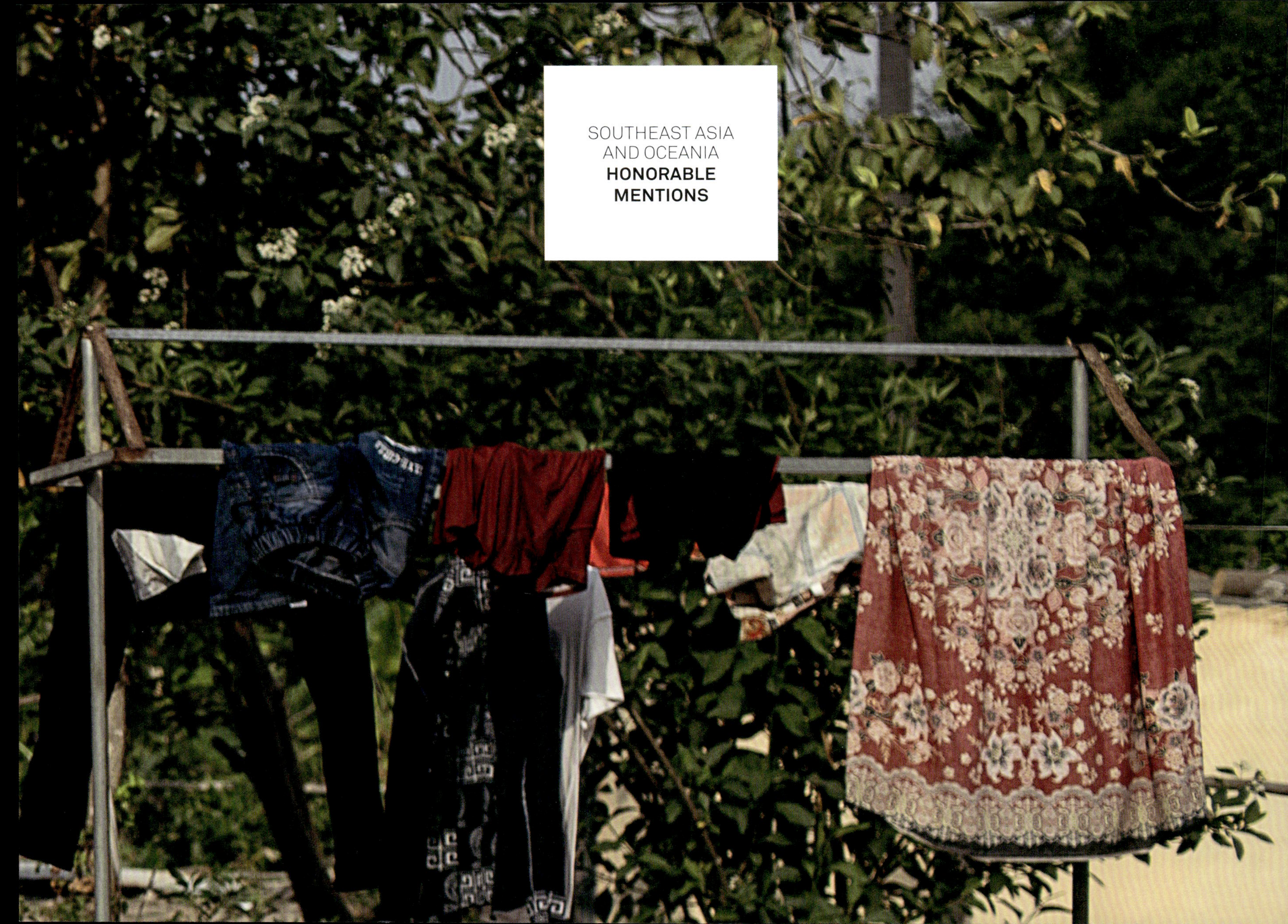

SOUTHEAST ASIA
AND OCEANIA
**HONORABLE
MENTIONS**

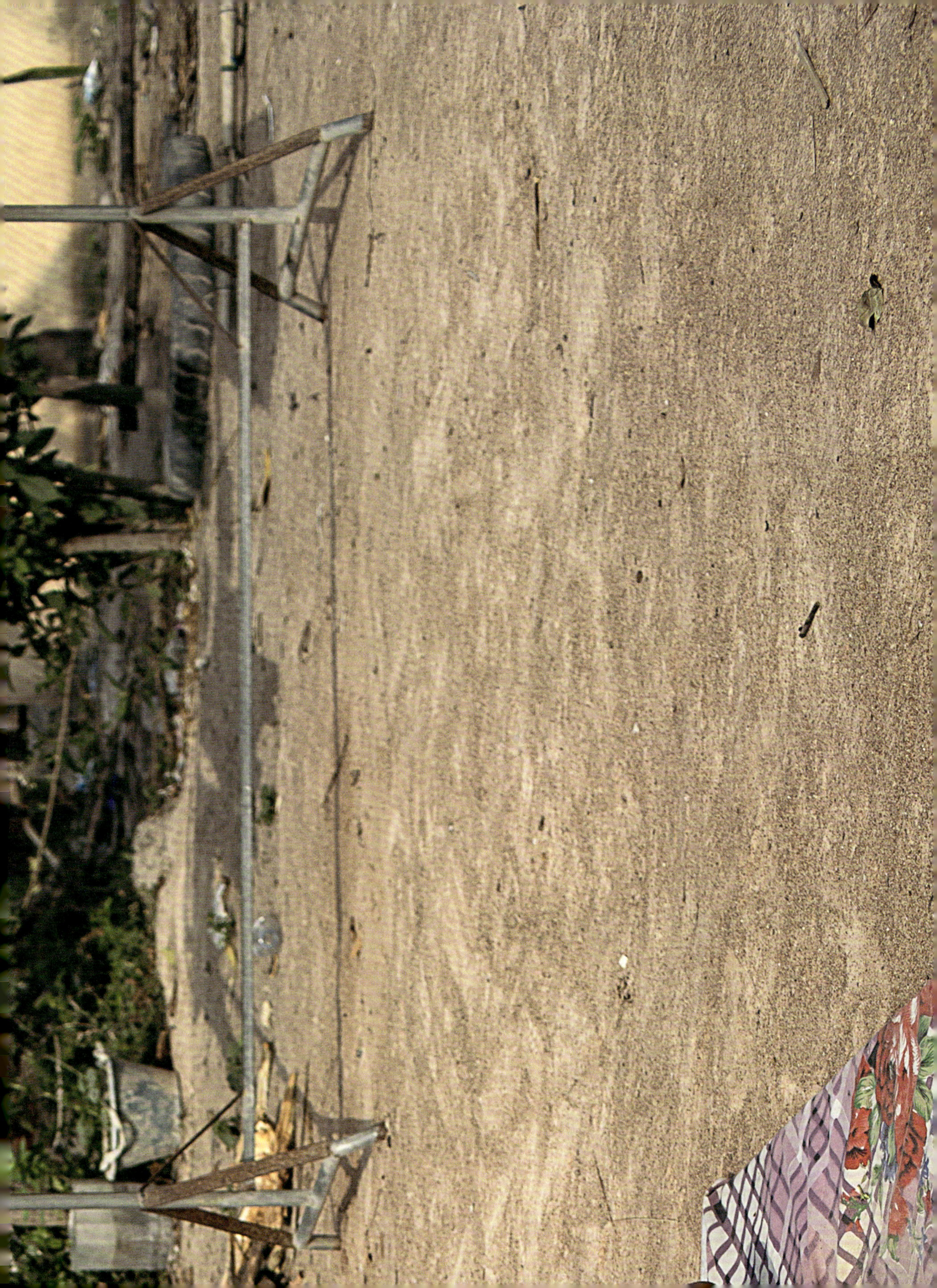

# Part of me

–

Surrogacy – the act of carrying and birthing a baby for another person or couple – was accepted practice in Cambodia until 2016. At that time, the government began to arrest surrogate mothers, charging them under the country's human trafficking laws. In 2018, 32 women were arrested and imprisoned after a raid in Phnom Penh. Nearly all gave birth in confinement and, after sentencing by the Cambodian Supreme Court, were obliged to raise the babies or face prison terms. Many of the women sought surrogacy arrangements with Chinese agencies in order to help their families escape impoverishment and, in some instances, indebtedness from microfinance loans.

Nadia Shira Cohen
United States, 1977

–

Nadia Shira Cohen is a photojournalist whose work focuses on human rights, reproductive rights, environmental issues, revolution, and migration. She is a contributor to *The New York Times* and *National Geographic*, among other international publications. She photographed these images on assignment for *The New York Times*.

–

Instagram: @nadiashiracohen

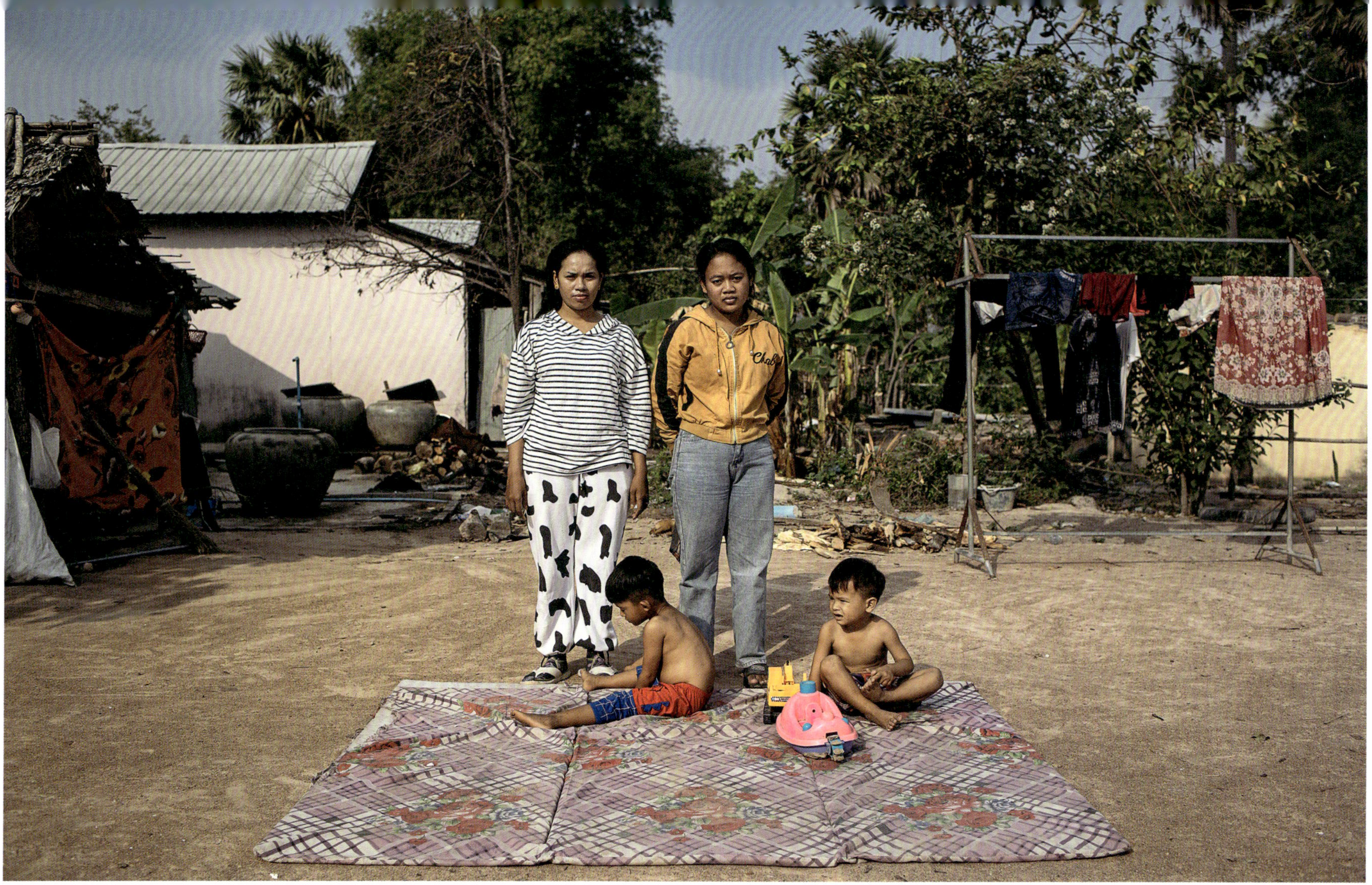

Surrogate mothers Vin Win (right) and Ry Ly (left) were arrested during a raid to fight trafficking in 2018. They live near one another and their children from surrogacy, Korng (3, left) and Phavit (4, right), often play together. Vin Win is separated from her husband who resents the situation. Kampong Speu, Cambodia, 27 January, 2022.

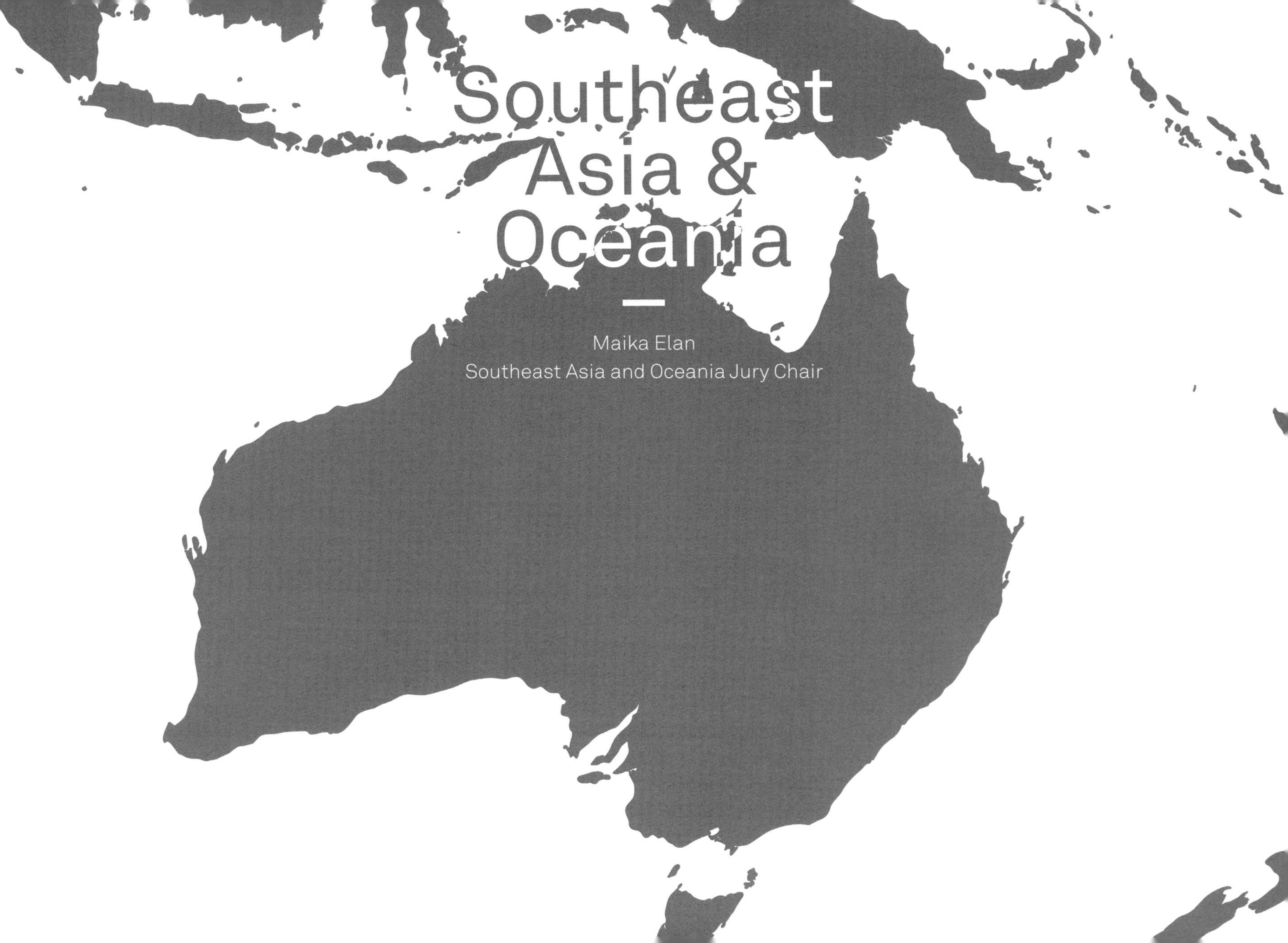

# Southeast Asia & Oceania

—

Maika Elan
Southeast Asia and Oceania Jury Chair

As members of the Southeast Asia and Oceania jury, we had the honor of reviewing an extensive range of submissions which captured the diversity and complexity of our region. Throughout our review process, we aimed to identify images and stories that best reflected the nuances and intricacies of the stories being told.

One of the most pressing issues to catch our attention was the ongoing civil war in Myanmar, which is responsible for the loss of numerous lives and the displacement of many more, with the situation continuing to deteriorate. A further crucial concern was the drug war in the Philippines, where extrajudicial killings and human rights violations are widespread. Photographs highlighted the human rights violations, and raised important questions about justice and accountability.

Climate change and environmental issues were also prominent among the submissions, particularly in Indonesia and Australia. The images and stories reminded us of the urgent need to protect our planet as a global community, and to preserve the natural habitats and wildlife that make our region so unique.

In addition to these themes, we also saw deeply moving stories of personal struggles, resilience, and identity. These included the lives of transgender people, individuals who embrace polyamorous lifestyles, people with mental health issues, and those navigating the complexities of surrogacy. Even more straightforward narratives, such as about the changing relationships between humans and dogs in Indonesia, or the challenges of motherhood, were also encountered. These stories humanized and personalized broader issues and brought attention to marginalized voices.

At the heart of our selection process was the desire to highlight stories that not only raised awareness of important issues but also provided solutions or a call to action. We sought strong and brave stories that, in the context of our countries, may have been difficult to execute or discuss openly. Our group also discussed the connection and expansion that a story can bring, not only between the characters and the photographer, but also with the audience and among ourselves. We considered what is unique to our region and what could be representative of our region outside of it.

Ultimately, we look forward to seeing how these images will continue to spark conversation and inspire action in the years to come.

# Jury

–

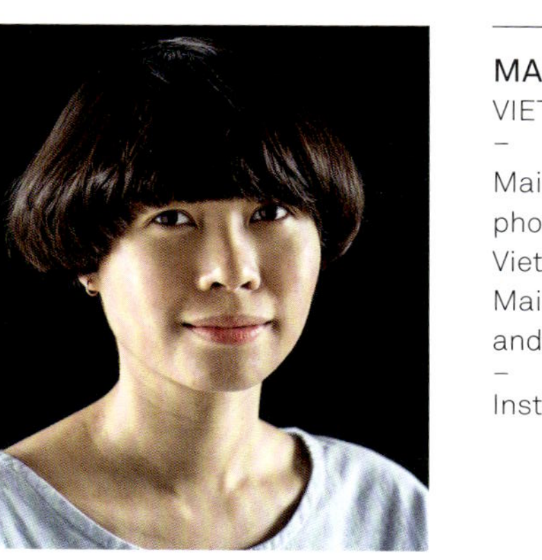

TERRY BARENTSEN

**MAIKA ELAN** / CHAIR
VIETNAM
–
Maika Elan is an award-winning freelance photographer based in Ho Chi Minh City, Vietnam. After studying sociology in Hanoi, Maika started to take pictures of her daily and private life in 2008.
–
Instagram: @maikaelan

ROSSA PANGGABEAN

**EVI MARIANI**
INDONESIA
–
Evi Mariani is a co-founder and executive director of Project Multatuli, a public service journalism initiative in Indonesia that publishes stories of marginalized communities to address news deserts and information inequality..
–
Instagram: @evimariani

# Winners

–

## SINGLES

**MAUK KHAM WAH**
MYANMAR, 1995
–
Mauk Kham Wah is a photographer, filmmaker and activist from Myanmar. His most recent work follows young Karenni fighters who joined the resistance movement following the 2021 military coup in Myanmar.
–

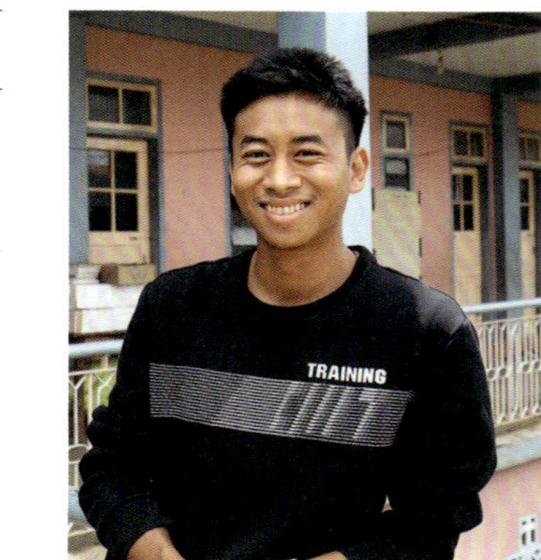


ROSALIN HTWE

## STORIES

**HANNAH REYES MORALES**
PHILIPPINES, 1990
–
Hannah Reyes Morales is a photographer and photojournalist who focuses on bringing historical memory and current events home, by looking at how they shape daily life. She is a co-founder of Emerging Islands and a National Geographic Explorer.
–
Instagram: @hannahreyesmorales

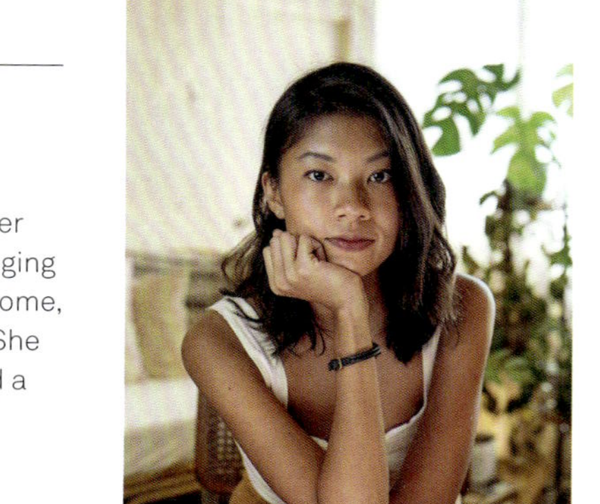

OBERT AMAGSILA

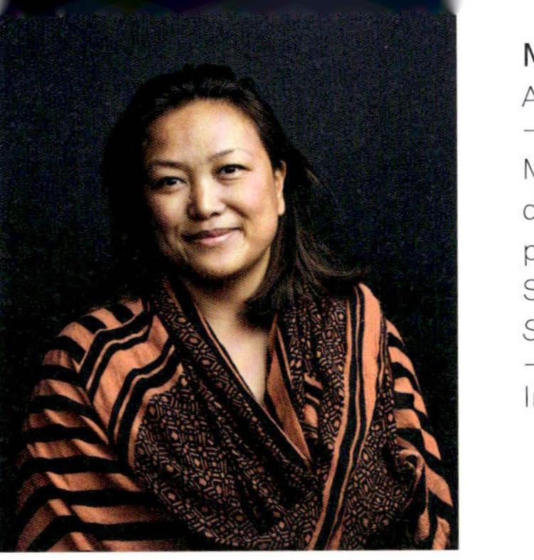

JAMES BRICKWOOD

## MAGS KING

AUSTRALIA

–

Mags King is a photo editor, curator, creative director, and mentor for numerous high-profile photographic awards and festivals. She is the managing photo editor at the *Sydney Morning Herald* in Australia.

–

Instagram: @mags__king

## VEEJAY VILLAFRANCA

PHILIPPINES

–

Veejay Villafranca is an independent photographer and visual culture lecturer based in Manila, Philippines. He covers topics such as the evolving Filipino cultural landscape, the effects of displacement on local communities, and gang activity.

–

Instagram: @vjvillafranca

JOELLE VILLAFRANCA

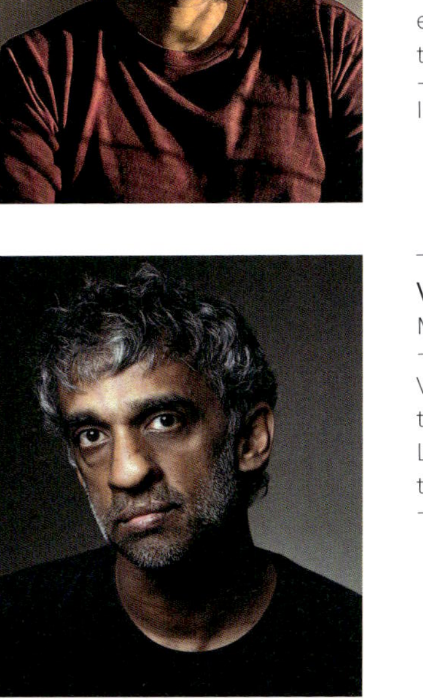

ADELINE CHUA

## VIGNES BALASINGAM

MALAYSIA

–

Vignes Balasingam is a photographer, curator, and picture-book editor based in Kuala Lumpur, Malaysia. He is the founder-director of the Obscura Festival of Photography.

–

# LONG-TERM PROJECTS

## KIMBERLY DELA CRUZ

PHILIPPINES, 1990

–

Kimberly dela Cruz is an independent photographer and journalist based in the Philippines. Her work has appeared in various publications and exhibitions across the globe. She is represented by VII under the VII Mentor Program.

–

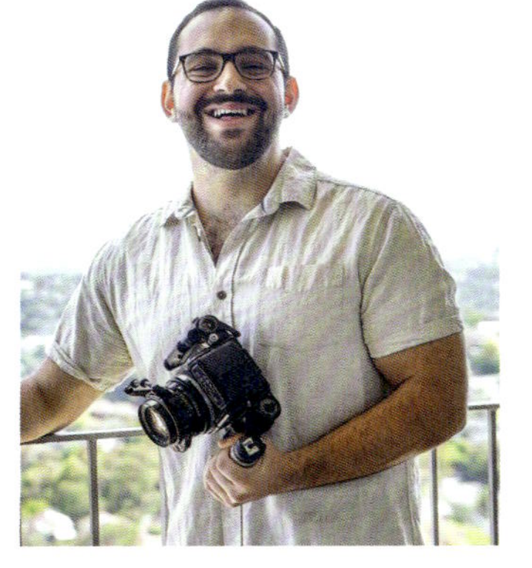

# OPEN FORMAT

## CHAD AJAMIAN

AUSTRALIA, 1996

–

Chad Ajamian is a geographic information scientist, photographer, and researcher, specializing in natural perils and infrared photography.

–

Instagram: @cajamian

CHAD AJAMIAN

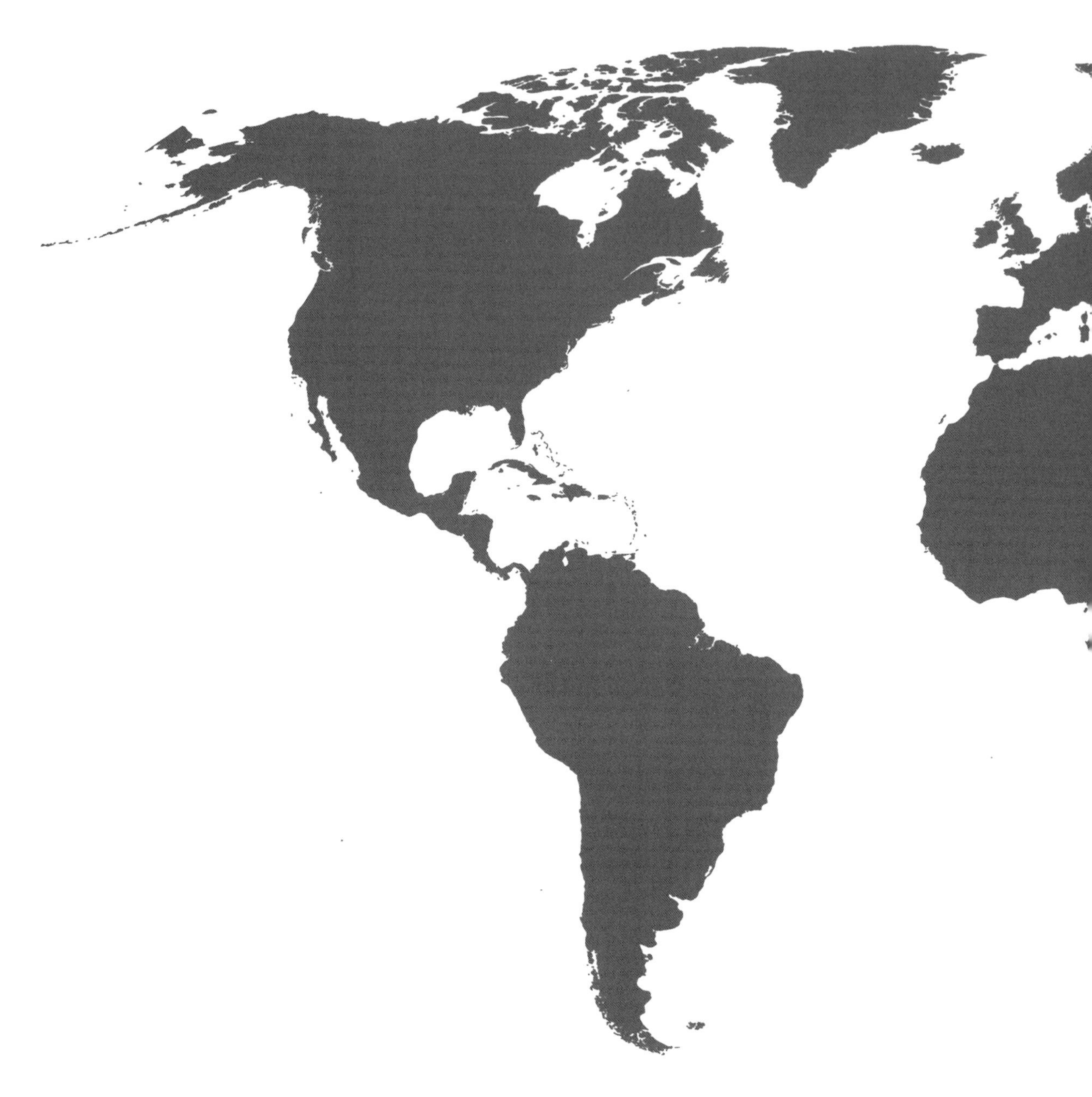

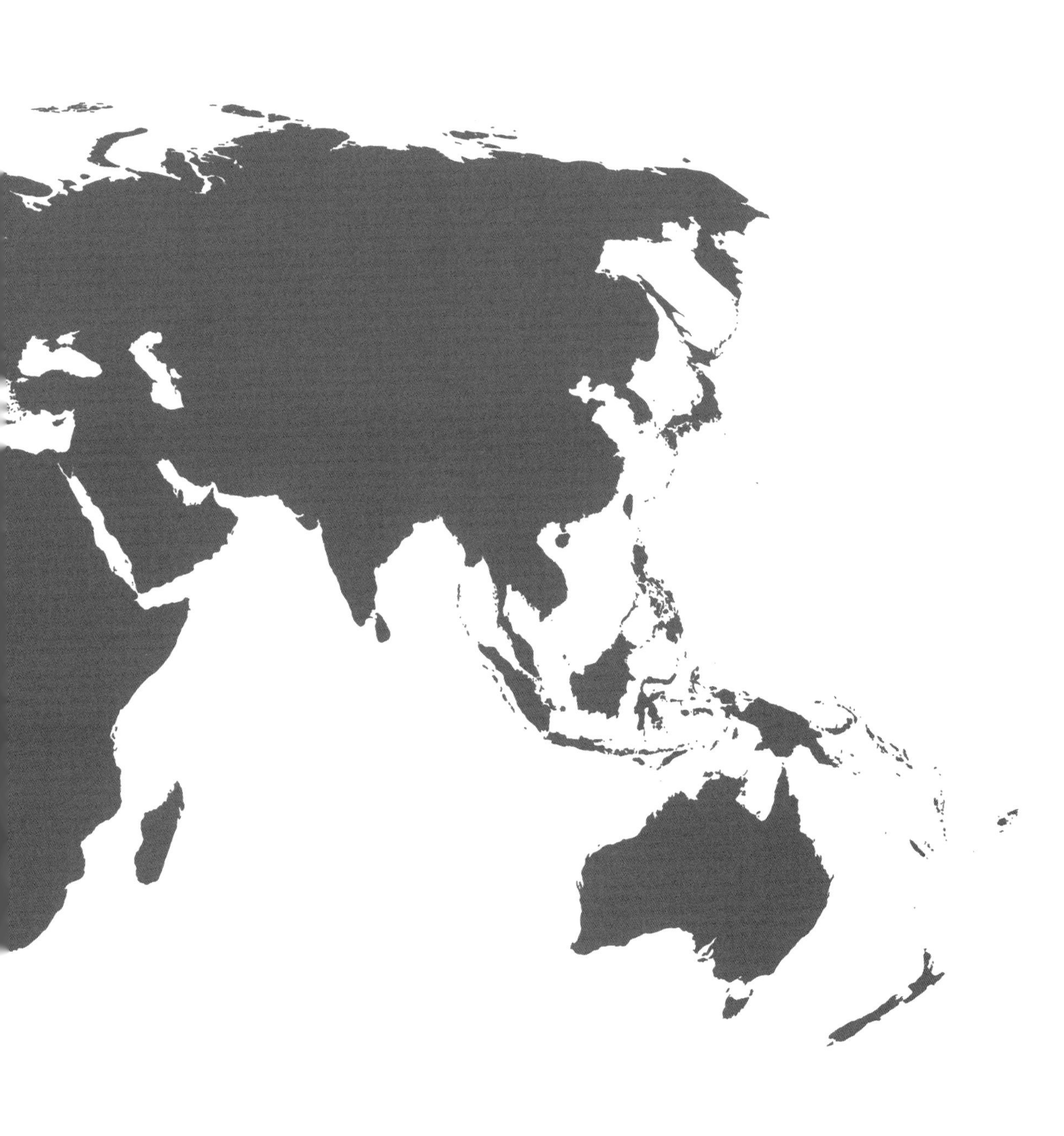

# Glo
# Win

—

Photo of
the Year

—

—

Story
of the Year

—

# bal
# ners

–

Long-Term
Project Award

–

–

Open Format
Award

–

Photo of the Year

## Mariupol Maternity Hospital Airstrike

Evgeniy Maloletka

Iryna Kalinina (32), an injured pregnant woman, is carried from a maternity hospital that was damaged during a Russian airstrike in Mariupol, Ukraine, on 9 March 2022. Her baby, named Miron (after the word for peace) was stillborn, and half an hour later Iryna died as well. An OSCE report concluded the hospital was deliberately targeted by Russia, resulting in three deaths and some 17 injuries.

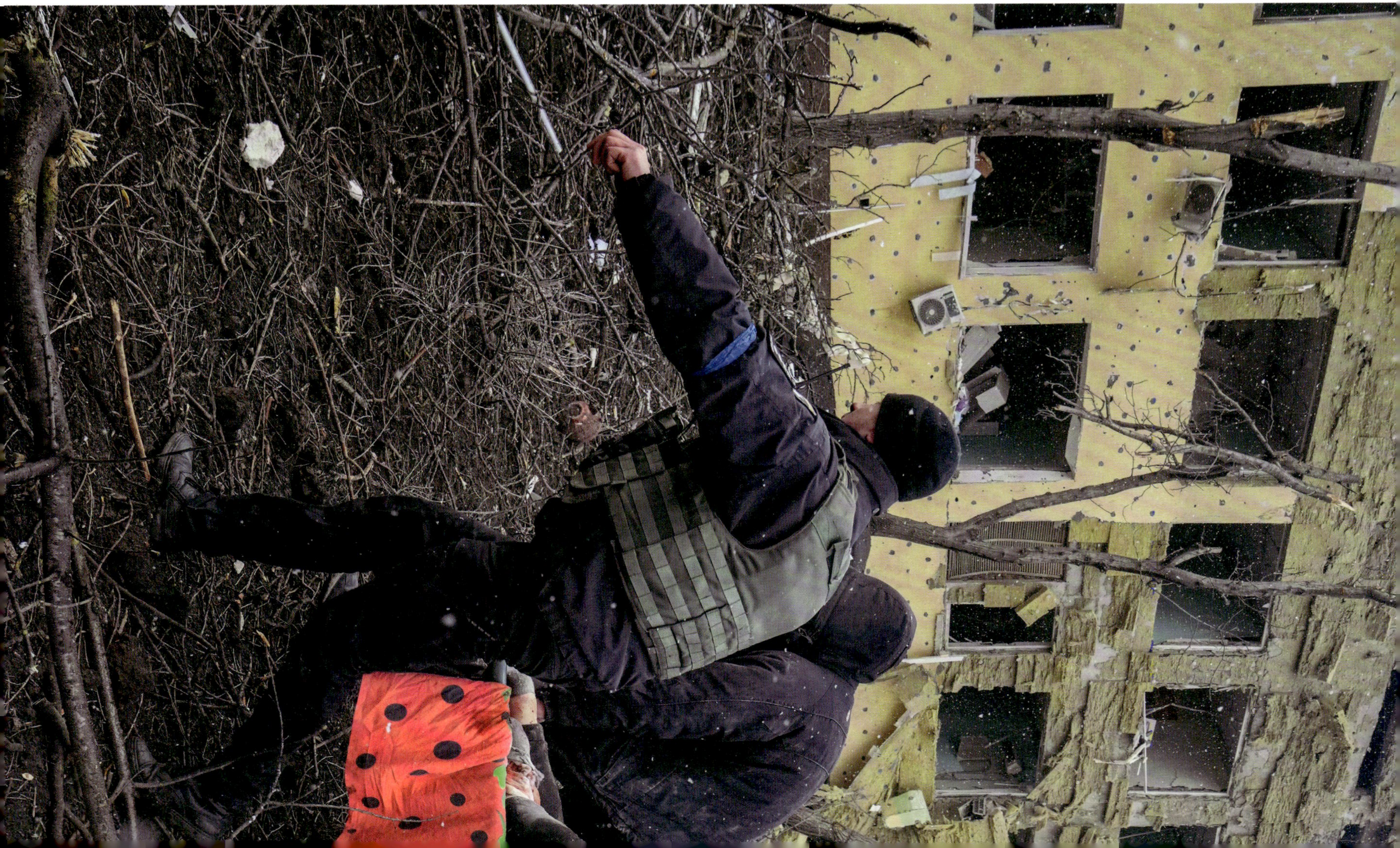

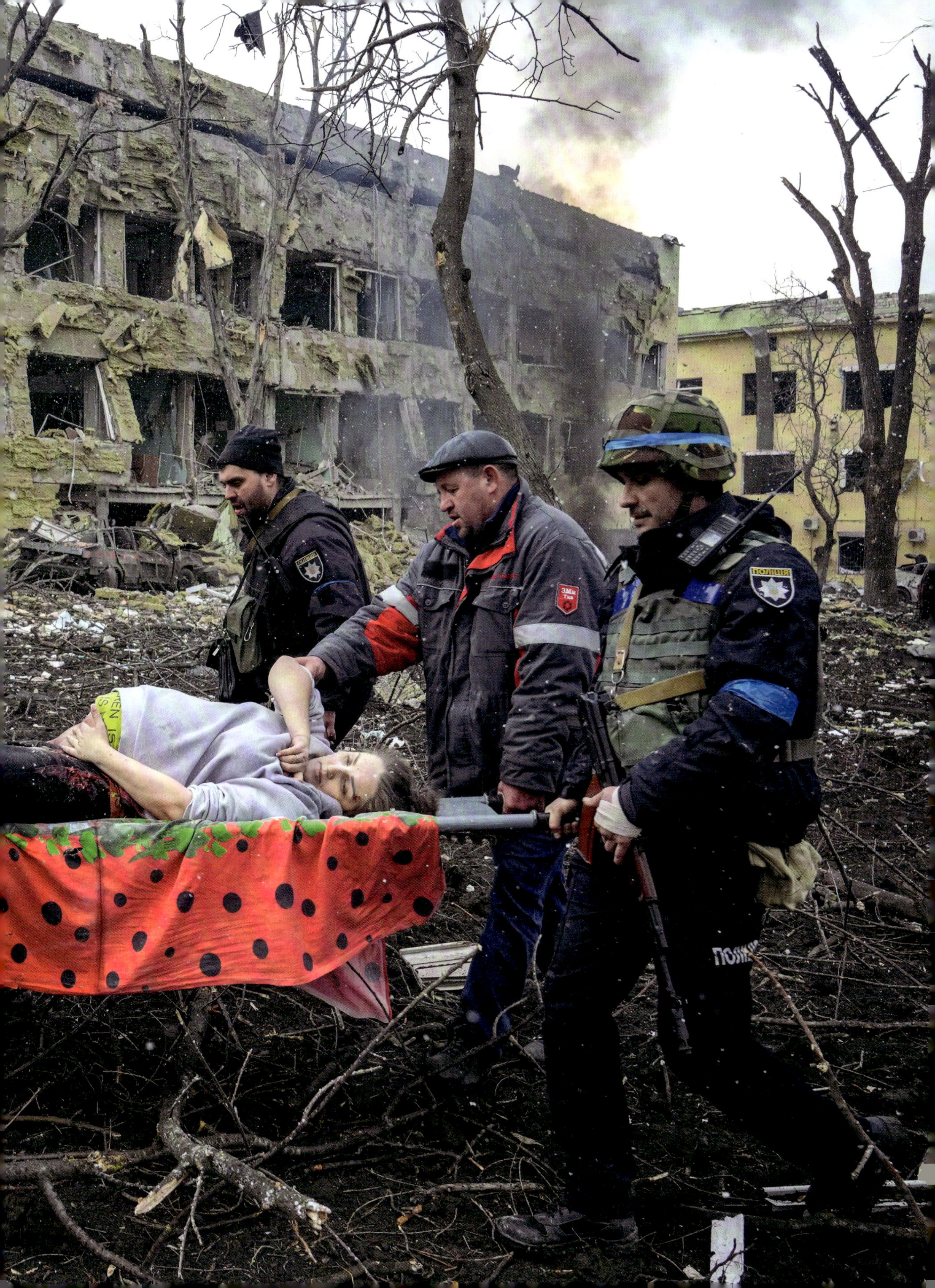
ПОЛІЦІЯ

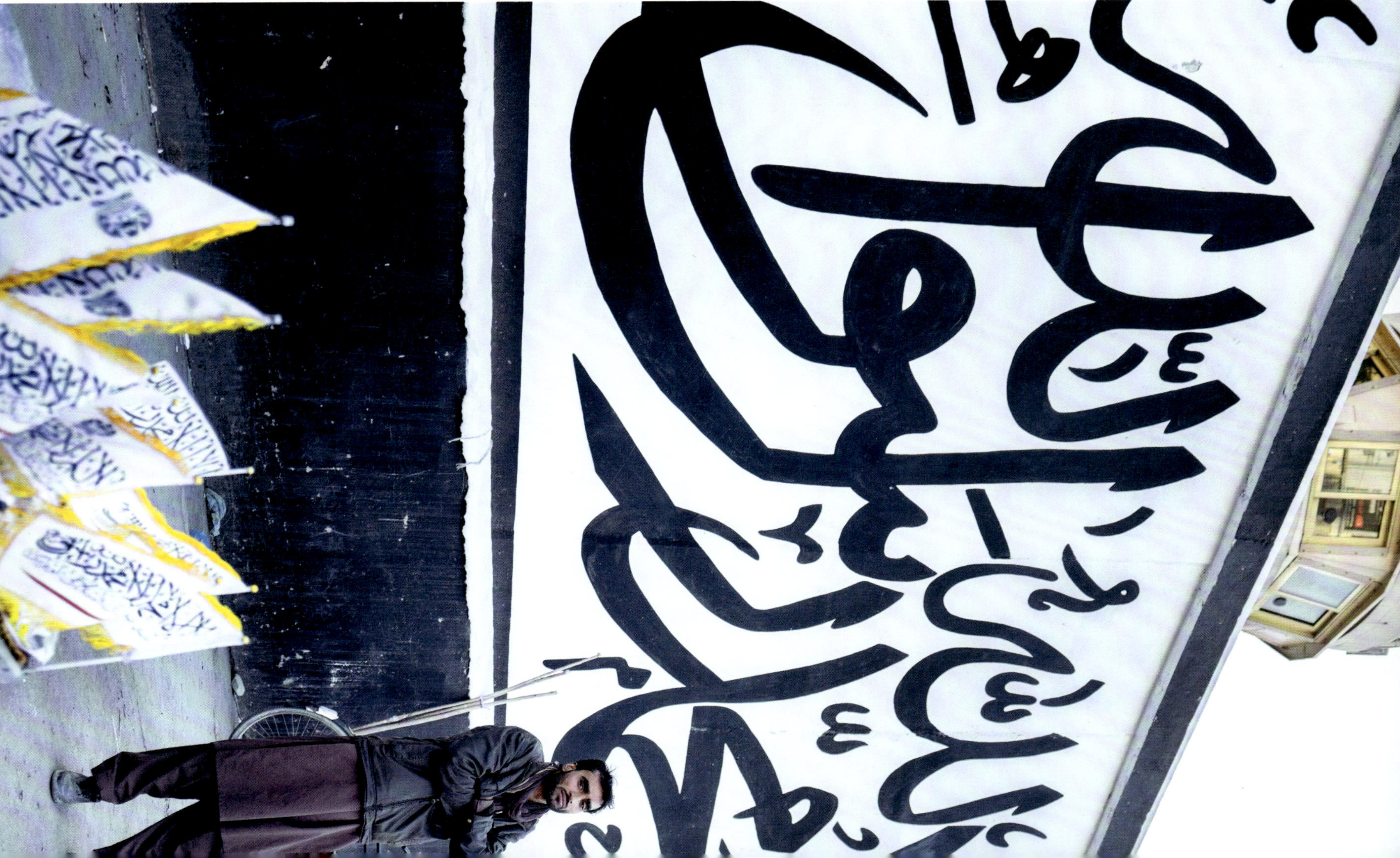


A Taliban propaganda mural covers the wall of the former US Embassy in Kabul, Afghanistan, on 13 January 2022. In front of the wall, street vendors sell Taliban flags, posters and other merchandise.

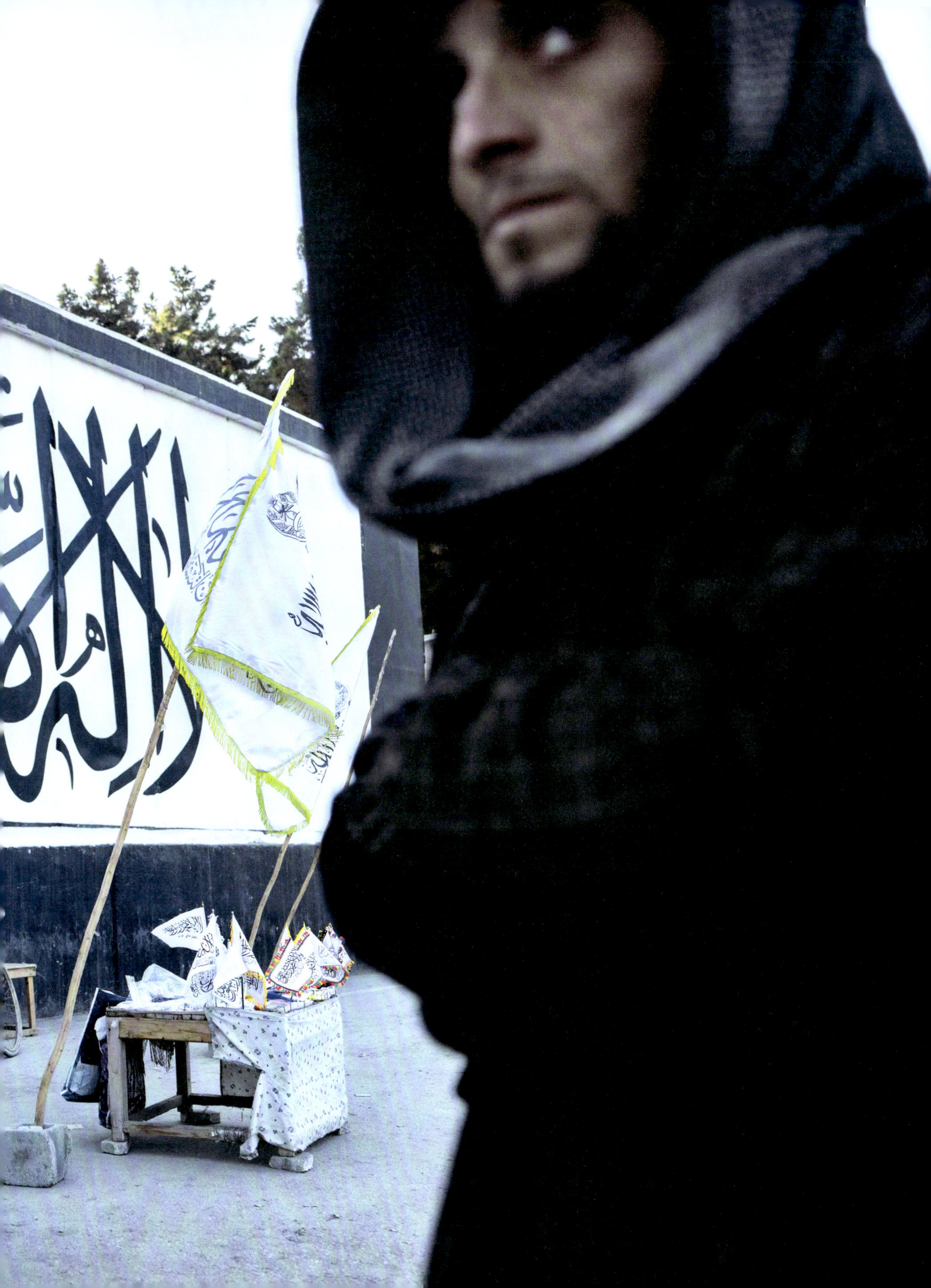

Long-Term Project Award

Battered Waters

Anush Babajanyan

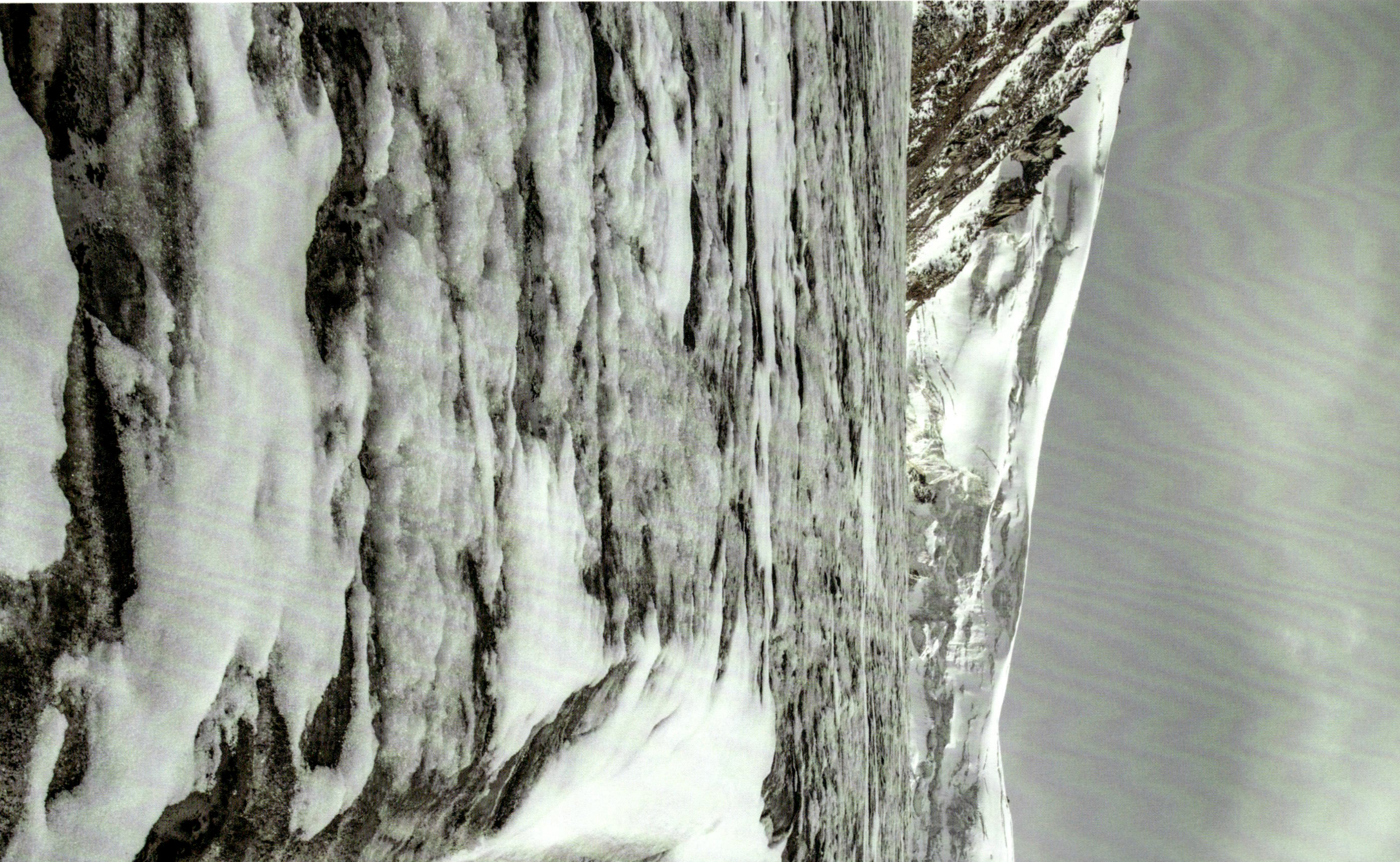

The Tuyuksu Glacier in Kazakhstan, in the mountains bordering Kyrgyzstan, has retreated over a kilometer in the last 60 years, affecting water supply to the region below. Pictured on 29 August 2019.

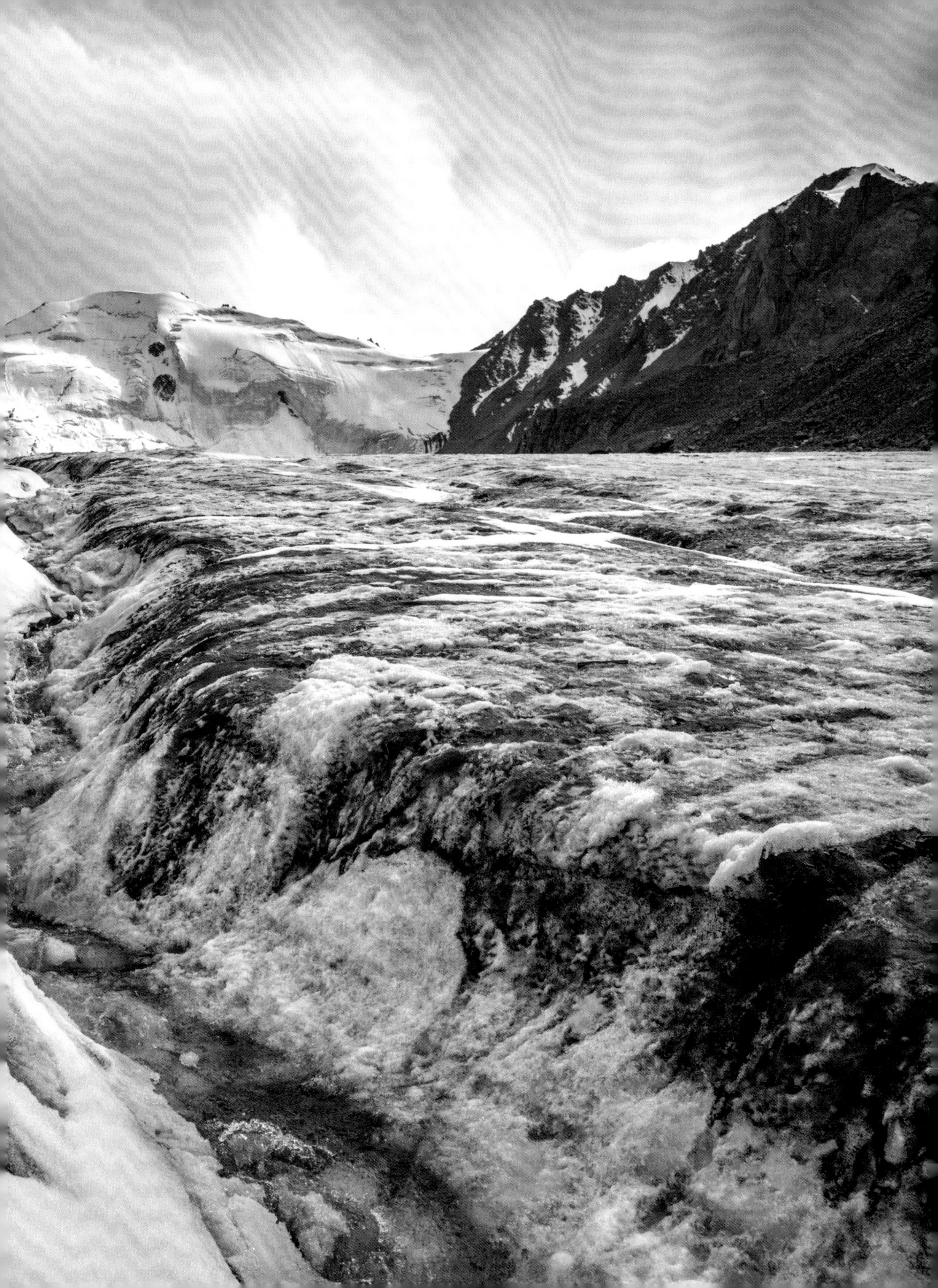

Open Format Award

## Here, The Doors Don't Know Me

Mohamed Mahdy

Utilizing found imagery and the artist's own photography, this project presents an elegy to a communal way of life on the cusp of disappearing.

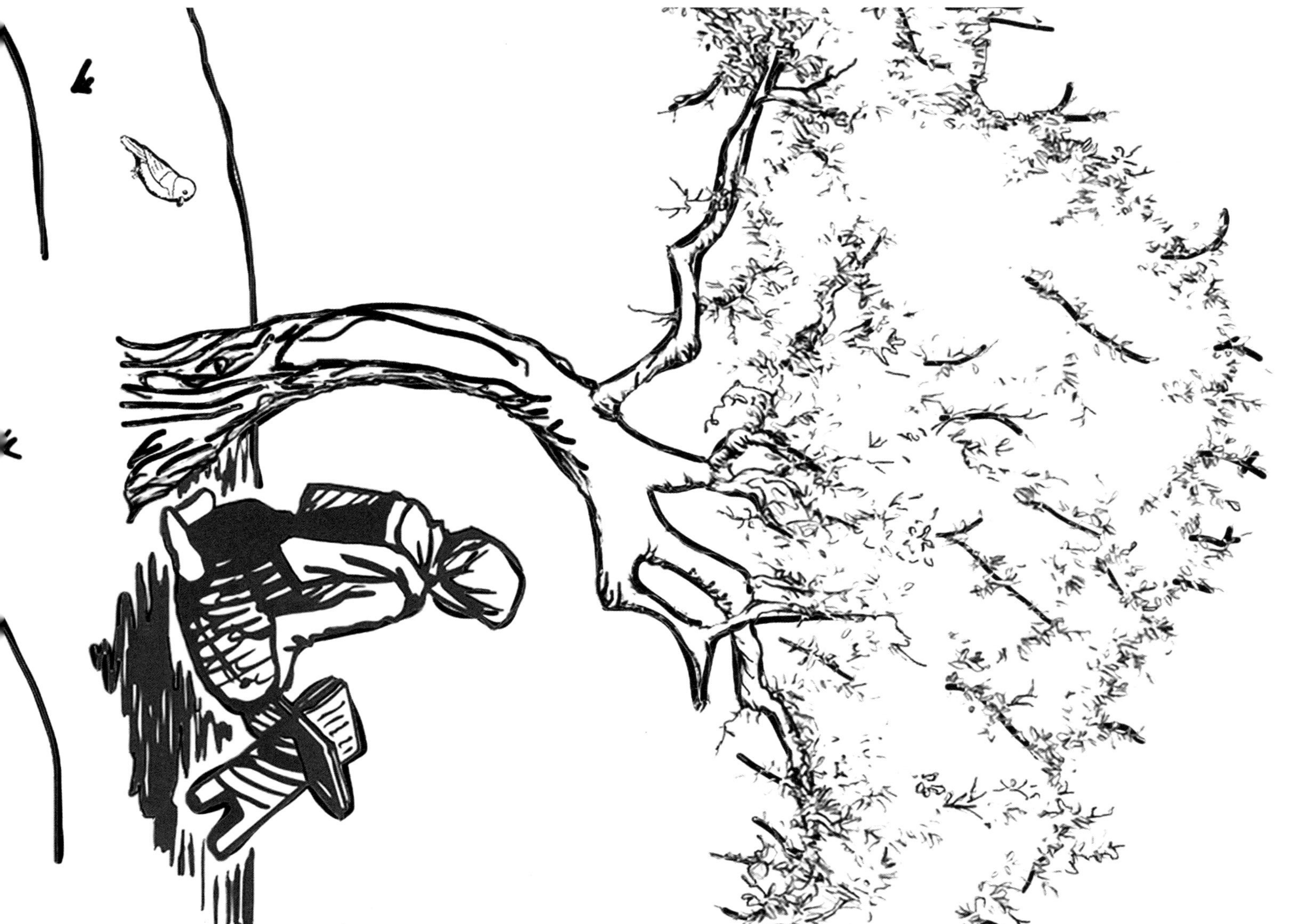

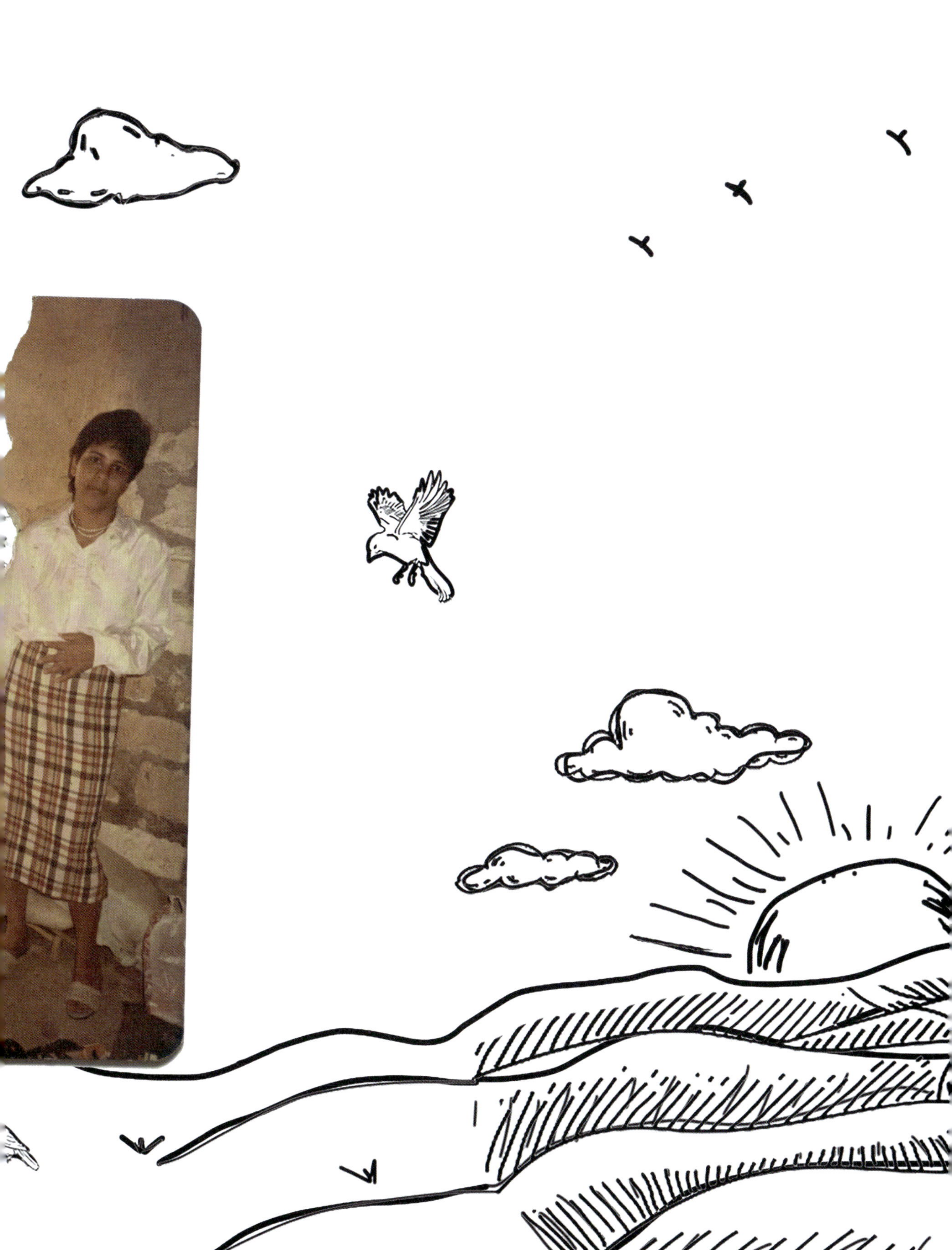

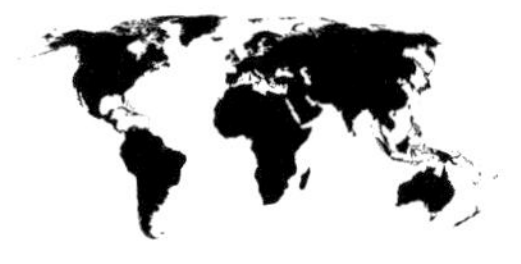

# Global Jury

Brent Lewis
Global Jury Chair

In the second year of World Press Photo's regional format, the true power of the new strategy has become apparent. In 2022 we saw powerful stories ranging from the conflict in Ukraine, and Afghanistan's first year under Taliban rule, to oil spillage in Peru and the loss of women's rights from the US to Iran. Yet we were also able to see stories of alpaca-farmers in South America, and a series of portraits of hip-hop artists that raise the question of social injustices committed against the genre's creators. All these stories were able to coexist in a collection of the most important stories from all corners of the globe.

That said, the jury did have to make the space to include many highly significant stories, especially when a great number occurred in one region. For this reason, we decided as a jury to include a second Honorable Mention in Asia, instead of awarding one in the North and Central America region. The jury felt the two stories represented were too important and visually striking not to bring awareness to, especially on a continent as diverse as Asia.

The new format also aims to award at least one local photographer and a woman or non-binary photographer in each of the regions, as well as in the global awards. However, we are still subject to what photos are submitted and to the current state of the industry as a whole. Although we were able to award a local photographer in Europe, we were unable to award a woman or non-binary photographer in the region. That was not a decision we came to lightly, but one that ensured that the best photos were chosen, and that the contest maintained its integrity in recognizing only the highest quality of work from the year.

The process by which the World Press Photo of the Year was chosen also departed from the rules this year. While the rules state that the Photo of the Year must come from one of the singles chosen in the six regions, the jury unanimously agreed that the most important and powerful image came from a story – the winning story from Europe. We could not bring ourselves to remove the story as a winner, just for the sake of awarding the single photo. This was yet another move that ensured that we awarded the best and most important photos to represent 2022.

A further critical issue that faced the jury was over-processing and toning in photos. Although World Press Photo holds forensic checks on all photos that make it into the penultimate round, the jury took a decision to look critically at photos that seemed to be toned beyond what a human eye would naturally see. Such photos were not awarded, so as not to perpetuate a level of toning that has increased in the industry over the years.

Everything considered, our four global winners represent the best photos and stories from the most important and urgent stories of 2022. They also help to continue the tradition of what it is possible to do with photography, and how photography helps us to see the universality of the human condition.

The Open Format winner *Here, The Doors Don't Know Me* does just that. The story of forced migration and loss of identity is one we are increasingly seeing across the globe, but what took this story to the next level was an amazing website which allows readers to understand the story beyond the stills, and even allows some interactive communication with people in the story. That gives the reader an opportunity to open up a line of connection with the people who have exposed their lives to make the project possible.

The Long-Term Project winner, *Battered Waters*, was a well-researched and well-photographed understanding of how four countries in Central Asia are using water, but also what is at risk as the resource becomes scarce. This work rose not only because of its ability to tell the story while maintaining a human focus, but also for its universal appeal: issues around water recurred throughout the contest.

*The Price of Peace in Afghanistan*, winner of the award for Stories, provided the jury with an insight into the lives of Afghan people over the last year, as the Taliban has reclaimed control of the country. The photos and the edit were concise, with each providing an understanding of the issues facing the people of Afghanistan as they struggle to secure their basic needs. The jury felt that this story also served as a warning note for the current conflict in Ukraine, the subject of the winning single photo.

The haunting image from the siege of Mariupol was unanimously chosen as the winner of the World Press Photo of the Year. With the vote being decided on the first anniversary of the beginning of the war in Ukraine, the jury mentioned the power of the image and the story behind it, as well as the atrocities it shows. The death of both the pregnant woman and her child summarized so much of the war, as well as the possible intent of Russia. As one juror put it: "It's like they are trying to kill the future of Ukraine".

The photographs that we have chosen to represent 2022 are indicative of this moment in time, and will serve as historical documents of what the year was like for future generations to look back on and hopefully learn from. World Press Photo has, throughout my career, served as a guiding force for what is possible with photography, and it has been my greatest honor and privilege to serve as global jury chair, and hopefully to pass that guidance on to a new generation.

# Global Winners

—

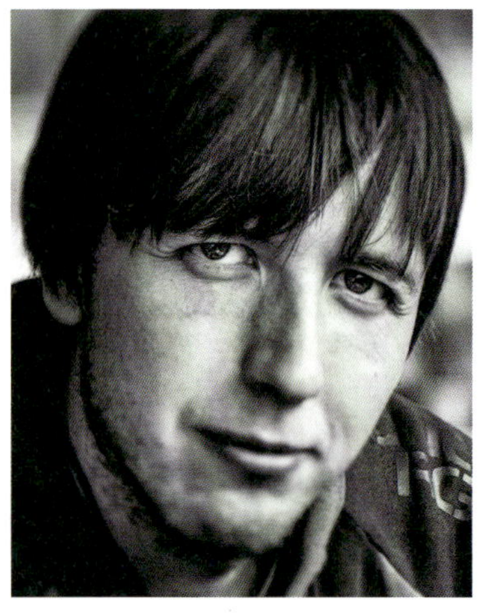

EVGENIY MALOLETKA
PHOTO OF THE YEAR

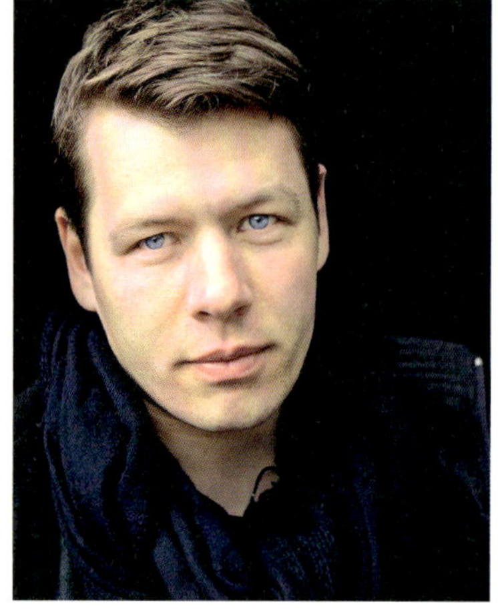

MADS NISSEN
STORY OF THE YEAR

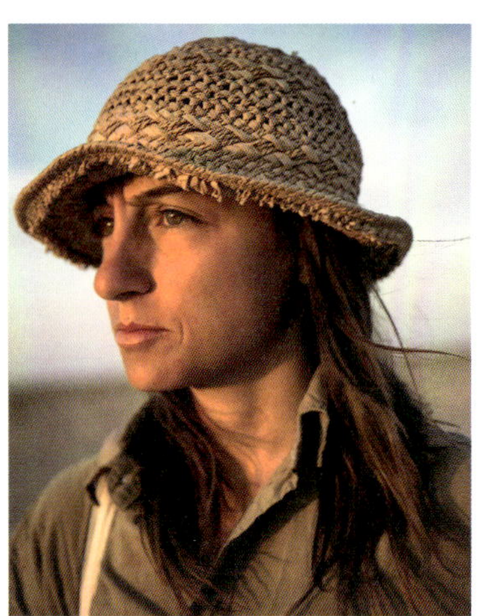

ANUSH BABAJANYAN
LONG-TERM PROJECT AWARD

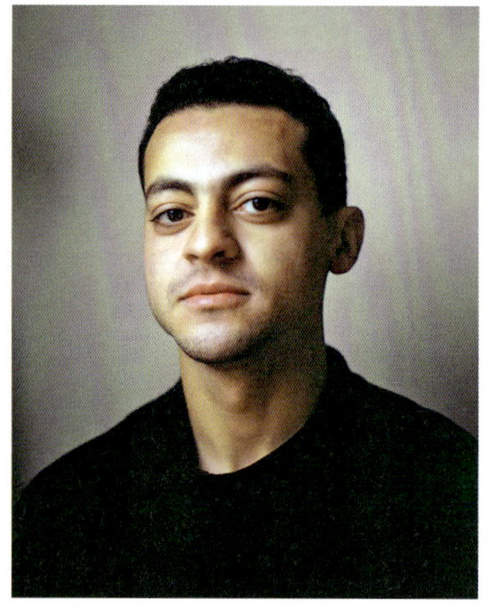

MOHAMED MAHDY
OPEN FORMAT AWARD

# Global Jury

—

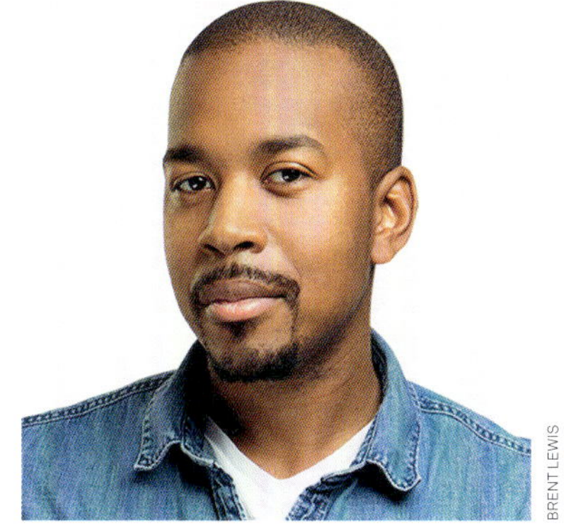
BRENT LEWIS

BRENT LEWIS / CHAIR
UNITED STATES

Brent Lewis is a photo editor for *The New York Times*, curating photos on the home page and covering breaking news around the world. He is also the co-founder of Diversify.Photo.

–

Twitter: @blewisphoto

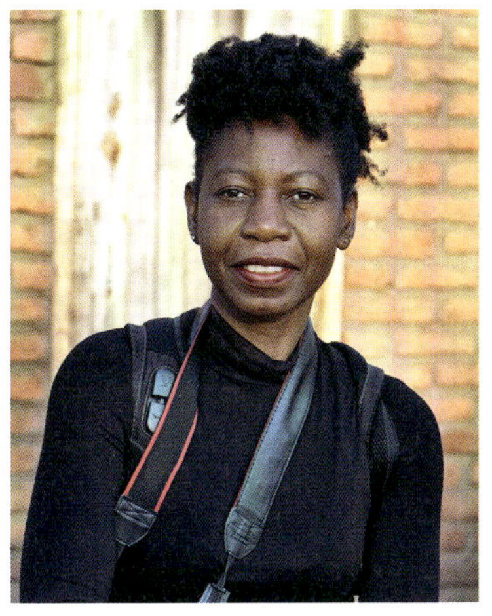

ANGELA JIMU
CHAIR / AFRICA

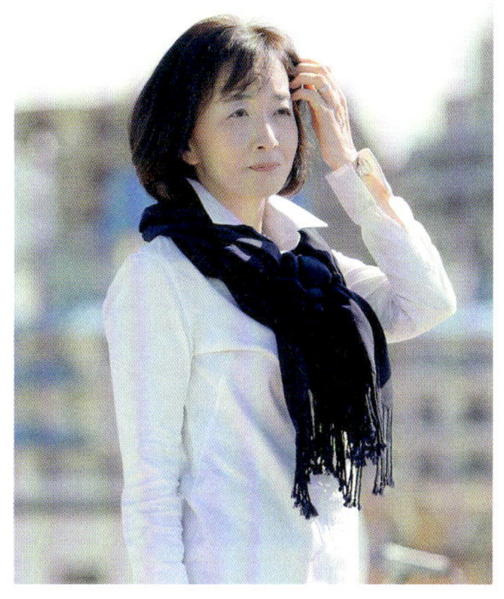

HIDEKO KATAOKA
CHAIR / ASIA

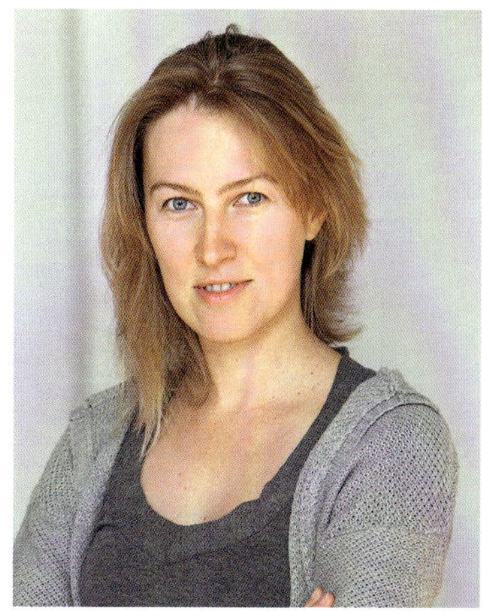

KATERYNA RADCHENKO
CHAIR / EUROPE

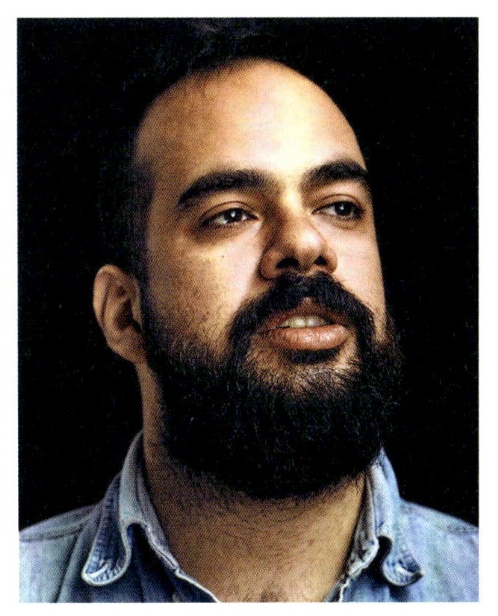

TOMÁS AYUSO
CHAIR / NORTH AND CENTRAL AMERICA

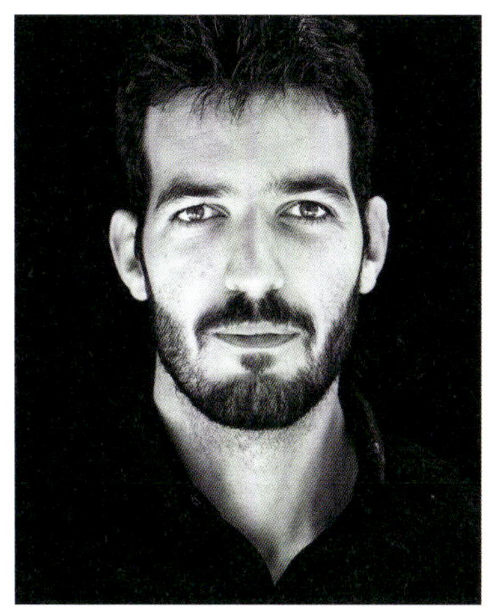

FELIPE DANA
CHAIR / SOUTH AMERICA

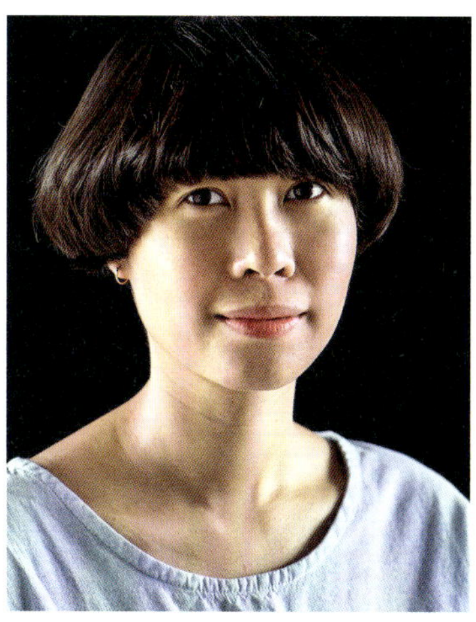

MAIKA ELAN
CHAIR / SOUTHEAST ASIA AND OCEANIA

# Africa

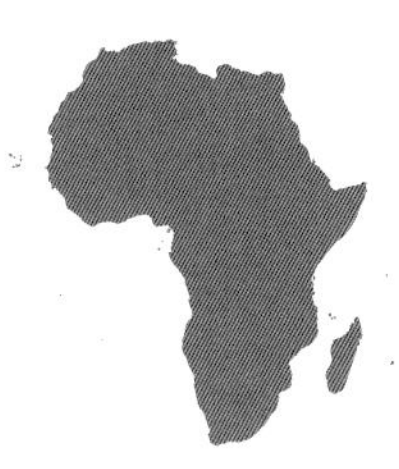

Algeria
Angola
Benin
Botswana
Burkina Faso
Burundi
Cabo Verde
Cameroon
Central African Republic
Chad
Congo
Côte d'Ivoire
Djibouti
DR Congo
Egypt
Equatorial Guinea
Eritrea
Eswatini
Ethiopia
Gabon
Gambia
Ghana
Guinea
Guinea-Bissau
Kenya
Lesotho
Liberia
Libya
Madagascar
Malawi
Mali
Mauritania
Mauritius
Morocco
Mozambique
Namibia
Niger
Nigeria
Rwanda
São Tomé & Principe
Senegal
Seychelles
Sierra Leone
Somalia
South Africa
South Sudan
Sudan
Tanzania
Togo
Tunisia
Uganda
Zambia
Zimbabwe

# Asia

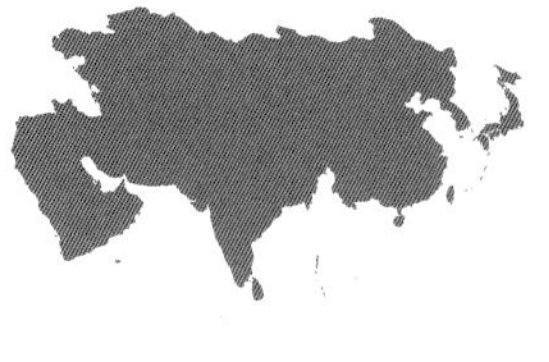

Afghanistan
Armenia
Azerbaijan
Bahrain
Bangladesh
Bhutan
China
Cyprus
Georgia
India
Iran
Iraq
Israel
Japan
Jordan
Kazakhstan
Kuwait
Kyrgyzstan
Lebanon
Maldives
Mongolia
Nepal
North Korea
Oman
Pakistan
Qatar
Saudi Arabia
South Korea
Sri Lanka
State of Palestine
Syria
Tajikistan
Turkey
Turkmenistan
United Arab Emirates
Uzbekistan
Yemen

# Europe

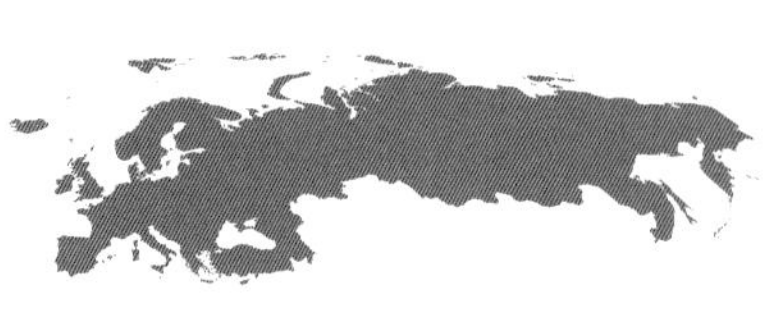

Albania
Andorra
Austria
Belarus
Belgium
Bosnia and Herzegovina
Bulgaria
Croatia
Czech Republic
Denmark
Estonia
Finland
France
Germany
Greece
Hungary
Iceland
Ireland
Italy
Latvia
Liechtenstein
Lithuania
Luxembourg
Malta
Moldova
Monaco
Montenegro
Netherlands
North Macedonia
Norway
Poland
Portugal
Romania
Russia
San Marino
Serbia
Slovakia
Slovenia
Spain
Sweden
Switzerland
Ukraine
United Kingdom
Vatican City State

## North and Central America

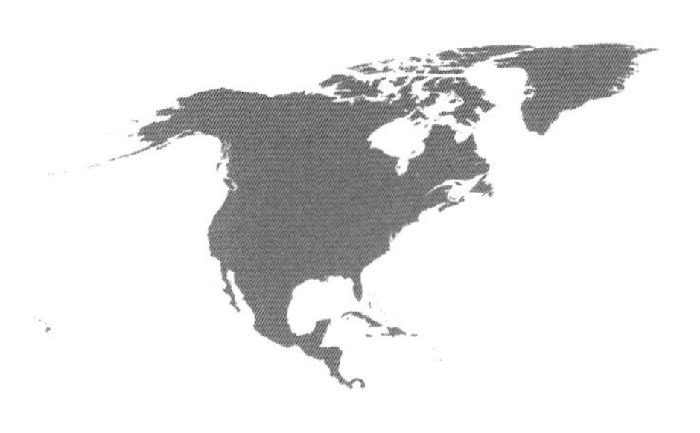

Antigua and Barbuda
Bahamas
Barbados
Belize
Canada
Costa Rica
Cuba
Dominica
Dominican Republic
El Salvador
Grenada
Guatemala
Haiti
Honduras
Jamaica
Mexico
Nicaragua
Panama
Saint Kitts & Nevis
Saint Lucia
Saint Vincent & the Grenadines
Trinidad and Tobago
United States of America

## South America

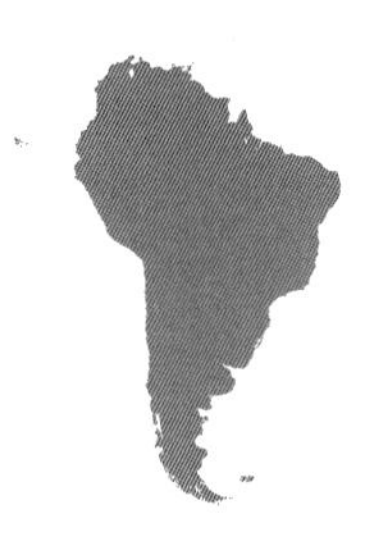

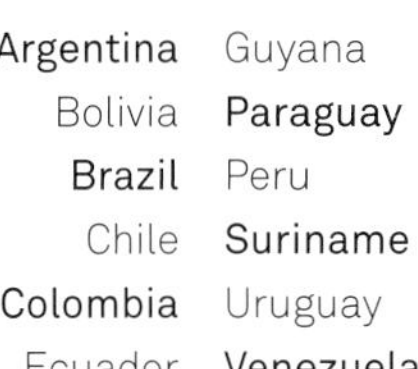

Argentina
Bolivia
Brazil
Chile
Colombia
Ecuador
Guyana
Paraguay
Peru
Suriname
Uruguay
Venezuela

## Southeast Asia and Oceania

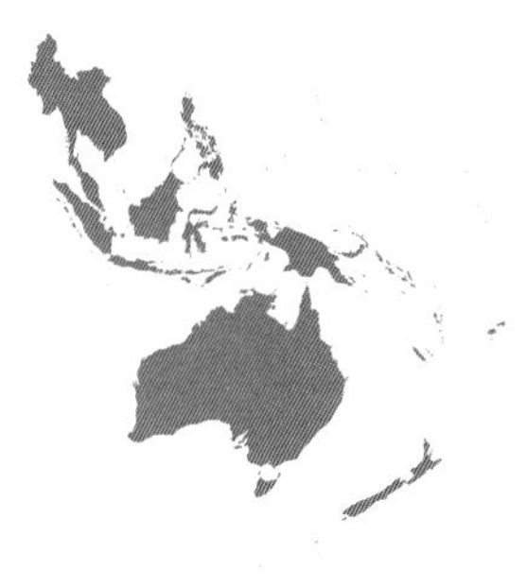

Australia
Brunei
Cambodia
Fiji
Indonesia
Kiribati
Laos
Malaysia
Marshall Islands
Micronesia
Myanmar
Nauru
New Zealand
Palau
Papua New Guinea
Philippines
Samoa
Singapore
Solomon Islands
Thailand
Timor-Leste
Tonga
Tuvalu
Vanuatu
Vietnam

**Editor-in-Chief**
Joumana El Zein Khoury

**Editors**
Rodney Bolt
Julia Kozakiewicz

**Assistant Editors**
Andrew Davies
Amanda Maddox
Daisy Corbin O'Grady
Mercedes Almagro Ocaña
George Zhu

**Production Coordinator**
Julia Kozakiewicz

**Project management**
Richard Viktor Hagemann
Juliane Steinbrecher

**Text Coordinator**
Mercedes Almagro Ocaña

**Image Coordinator**
Julia Kozakiewicz

**Research Coordinator**
Catharine Isabelle Haitzmann

**Research**
Kuljit Dhami
Nadine Joinville
Mark Sheridan
Naomi Purswani
Ryan P. R. Pears
Yatou Sallah

**Advisor**
Brent Lewis

**Design**
–SYB–
syb-photobooks.com

**Proofreading**
Iris Maher

**Typesetting**
–SYB–

**Reproductions**
Marc Gijzen

**Production**
Thomas Lemaître

**Published by**
Hatje Cantz Verlag GmbH
Mommsenstraße 27
10629 Berlin / Germany
www.hatjecantz.com
A Ganske Publishing Group Company

**Printing and binding**
Westermann Druck Zwickau GmbH

**Cover**
Ahmad Halabisaz, *Untitled*, 2022



978-3-7757-5433-0

Printed in Germany

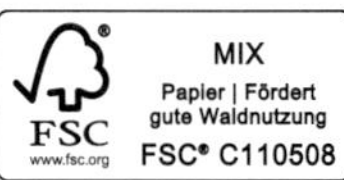


**World Press Photo Foundation**
World Press Photo, founded in 1955, is an independent, non-profit organization based in Amsterdam, the Netherlands.

#WPPh2023



**Global Partner**
Dutch Postcode Lottery
PwC

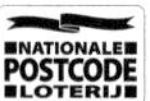

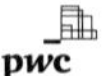


**Partners**
Chocolonely Foundation
Profotonet
Rutgers & Posch

**Supporters**
The World Press Photo Foundation appreciates the support of all its partners, funders, and individual donors.

**Official Suppliers**
EPAM
Eyes on Media & Eyes on PhotoArt
VCK Logistics

The World Press Photo Foundation holds "The Netherlands Fundraising Regulator (CBF) Recognition for Charitable Organizations", meeting industry standards for professional, trustworthy, and transparent practices.